*Studies in Economic Reform and Social Justice*

# CRITICS OF HENRY GEORGE
# *AN APPRAISAL OF THEIR*
# *STRICTURES ON* PROGRESS
# AND POVERTY

*Edited by*
Robert V. Andelson
Second Edition, Revised and Enlarged
Published in two volumes

**Blackwell**
Publishing

**The Series**
**Studies in Economic Reform and Social Justice**

Laurence S. Moss, Series Editor

Robert V. Andelson, ed.
*Land-Value Taxation Around the World*

*Critics of Henry George, 2nd edition,* volume 1 (2003)

*Critics of Henry George, 2nd edition,* volume 2 (2004)

J. A. Giacalone and C. W. Cobb, eds.
*The Path to Justice: Following in the
Footsteps of Henry George*

Christopher K. Ryan
*Harry Gunnison Brown
An Orthodox Economist and His Contributions*

*Studies in Economic Reform and Social Justice*

# CRITICS OF HENRY GEORGE
# *AN APPRAISAL OF THEIR*
# *STRICTURES ON* PROGRESS
# AND POVERTY

*Edited by*

**Robert V. Andelson**

Second Edition
Revised and Enlarged

**Volume 2**

**Blackwell**
Publishing

350 Main Street, Malden, MA 02148-5020, USA
9600 Garsington Road, Oxford OX4 2DQ, UK
550 Swanston Street, Carlton, Victoria 3053, Australia

First published 2003 by Blackwell Publishing Ltd.

Library of Congress Cataloging-in-Publication Data

Critics of Henry George : an appraisal of their strictures on progress and poverty / edited by Robert V. Andelson. – 2nd ed., rev. and enlarged.
    p. cm. – (Studies in economic reform and social justice)
    Includes bibliographical references and index.
    ISBN 1-4051-1830-X (casebound) – 1-4051-1829-6 (pbk.)
    1. George, Henry, 1839-1897.  2. Economists–United States.
3. Single tax.  4. Land value taxation.  5. Economics–History.
I. Andelson, Robert V., 1931–  II. Series.
HB119.G4C75 2003
330′.092–dc22

2003065818

A catalogue record for this title is available from the Library of Congress.

Set in 10 on 13pt Garamond Light
by SNP Best-set Typesetter Ltd., Hong Kong
Printed and bound in the United States
by the Sheridan Press

For further information on
Blackwell Publishing, visit our website:
http://www.blackwellpublishing.com

To the memory of
**Violetta G. Graham**,
known professionally as V. G. Peterson
(1902–1989),
wise counselor, untiring mentor,
and cherished friend,
this book is fondly dedicated

Robert V. Andelson at his retirement party from the Auburn University on May 21, 1992. Courtesy of Bonny Johnson Andelson

# Contents

# Preface and Acknowledgments
## to the Second Edition

The first edition of this book was published in 1979, to coincide with the centenary of *Progress and Poverty*. It filled an obvious gap, and met with a gratifying reception. A quarter of a century has passed, and it is now out of print.

Rather than simply issue a reprint edition, the decision was made to expand and revise the work:

1. Because of the importance of John Bates Clark in spearheading the movement to collapse land into capital in economic theory, I decided that an entire chapter should be devoted to him, instead of his being covered, as in the first edition, in a combined chapter also devoted to Simon Nelson Patten. The new chapter is the work of Kris Feder, whose doctoral research focused on the land-capital issue.

2. The material on Patten was rewritten by its author, Charles Collier, to form a separate chapter of its own.

3. Mason Gaffney has contributed a chapter that addresses a well-placed pragmatic objection by Edwin Cannan.

4. The first edition did not contain a separate chapter on Frank Knight, because his critique of George consisted mainly of one relatively brief article; instead, he was covered in a chapter devoted mainly to Murray Rothbard. However, the influence of that article has been such that I came to believe that a chapter on Knight would be justified.* Happily, Nicolaus Tideman (who earned his Ph.D. at Knight's department at Chicago, although after the latter's retirement) and Florenz Plassmann agreed to write it.

---

*A celebrated literary and talk-show figure who styles himself a "closet Georgist" once told me why he is not more active and open in espousing the philosophy: It seems that, upon his asking Henry Hazlitt what he thought of Georgism, Hazlitt had responded with severe disapproval, citing negative arguments from Knight. The celebrity in question (who is not ordinarily known for diffidence) was afraid that he might prove inadequate if called upon to counter these arguments in a public forum.

5. In the first edition, Spencer Heath was also treated briefly in the chapter devoted primarily to Rothbard. Fred Foldvary, whose publications have been largely focused on the proprietary community concept of which Heath was a seminal exponent, has contributed a separate chapter on him.

6. Because he devoted more space to criticizing George than did any other academic economist since Clark, Rothbard, I came to realize, warranted a free-standing chapter of his own, However, I did not wish to impose the tedious burden of disentangling him from Knight and Heath upon the venerable author of the combined chapter, C. Lowell Harriss. Fortunately, I was able to prevail upon Harold Kyriazi, who had already come to grips with Rothbard's criticisms in his admirable little book, *Libertarian Party at Sea on Land*, to undertake it.

7. F. A. Hayek's objection to the Single Tax is expressed in a mere paragraph, yet it is subtle and original, and the prestige of his name makes it important. I became aware of this during the question period after a lecture I delivered in Zürich in 1993, and addressed it in an article that the *American Journal of Economics and Sociology* has kindly permitted me to reprint in this book. It may be viewed as a sort of *mea culpa* on my part, inasmuch as my treatment of Hayek's objection, in the concluding chapter of the first edition, was inaccurate, having been based upon a common but superficial reading of it.

8. Except for a few scattered references, one looks in vain for explicit mention of George and his ideas in the copious writings of Garrett Hardin. Yet his much-reprinted essay, "The Tragedy of the Commons," is widely interpreted as directed against Georgism. In "Commons Without Tragedy," title chapter of a book I edited in 1971, I demonstrate that Hardin has been misconstrued in this respect—a judgment with which Hardin himself agrees. It has been abridged for inclusion in the present edition.

9. Like Rothbard, the charismatic Robert LeFevre was a potent influence in the development of the libertarian movement. Damon Gross, himself a libertarian, examines his critique of Georgism.

10. Finally, Mary M. Cleveland looks at the treatment of George by Mark Blaug, a respected historian of economic thought whose most

important work on the subject did not appear until after the publication of the first edition.

Needless to say, my concluding chapter has been revised to reflect some of the new material, as well as changes that have taken place over the past quarter century. It incorporates some passages from my Editor's Introduction to the third edition of *Land-Value Taxation Around the World* (the maiden volume in this series), which appeared in 2000.

This new edition, like the first, is not an anthology but rather the joint effort of a team assembled, assigned, cajoled, and coordinated by myself. Except for the passages just mentioned and four essays of my own that initially appeared elsewhere, all the chapters were expressly written either for this volume or for its predecessor.

My technological inadequacies would have proved insurmountable had it not been for the computer assistance of my kind friends, Alan Blackwood, Beverley Childress, Rod Jordan, and Tom Petee. I thank them for their generous contribution of time and knowledge. I also thank Steve Yates, without whose intelligent help the manuscript would not have met the publisher's deadline, and Laurence S. Moss, the series editor, who was understanding and supportive throughout. Pat Aller's extraordinary work in preparing the Index cannot be overpraised.

I wish to acknowledge a special debt to the late Louis Wasserman: It was the chapter on the Single Tax in his book, *Modern Political Philosophies and What They Mean* (first published in 1941), that introduced me, when a seventh-grader, to the thought of George. How appropriate that his final publication should be "The Essential Henry George," a key chapter in both editions of the present work!

R. V. Andelson
September, 2003

# Acknowledgments to the First Edition

The decision to undertake the labors of which this book is the fruition would never have been made had it not been for the encouragement of my friend, colleague, and department head, Professor Delos B. McKown, who was unfailingly supportive at each step of its development.

Funds that made its publication possible were generously provided by the Robert Schalkenbach Foundation of New York, and Basic Economic Education, Inc., of San Diego. Mr. P. I. Prentice, president of Schalkenbach, and Miss V. G. Peterson, its longtime executive secretary until her recent retirement, deserve special mention in this regard, as does Mr. Everett J. Seeley, chairman of the board of B.E.E.

Auburn University released me from my classroom obligations so that I could devote the spring quarter of 1977 solely to the project, and made available a grant for secretarial and research assistance. Dr. Taylor D. Littleton, vice-president for academic affairs, and Dr. Chester C. Carroll, vice-president for research, were particularly helpful in facilitating these favors.

The authors all took time from busy and demanding schedules to prepare their chapters, contributing their efforts gratuitously, patiently suffering my sometimes importunate demands, and graciously acquiescing in revisions that they may privately have considered brash.

Professors Alexander R. Posniak and José A. Madrigal of the Auburn department of foreign languages kindly donated many hours of assistance with translation, and the staff of Ralph Brown Draughon Library at the university was helpful beyond the call of duty. I wish to note in particular the extraordinary efforts of Mrs. Frances Honour and Mr. David N. King, both of whom have since moved on to new locations and pursuits.

The preparation of the typescript was primarily the work of Mrs. Anne C. Clark, whose dedication and efficiency cannot be overpraised. Mrs. Hildegaard Wolverton also gave able and conscientious service to this task when her departmental responsibilities permitted.

I have had the benefit of valuable comments (and, in several cases, other courtesies) from the following persons who read portions of the manuscript: Messrs. Victor H. Blundell and Richard Grinham of the Economic and Social Science Research Association (London); Mr. Weld S. Carter, executive secretary of the Committee on Taxation, Resources and Economic Development; Mr. Robert Clancy, president of the Henry George Institute, and acting president of the International Union for Land Value Taxation and Free Trade; Professors Robert B. Ekelund, Jr., Richard Higgins, Stephen O. Morrell, and Richard Saba of the Economics Department at Auburn; Professor James E. Green of the Economics Department at the University of Georgia; Mr. Gordon Hoover of Los Angeles; Professor Carl McGuire of the Economics Department at the University of Colorado; Professor Raj Mohan of the Sociology Department at Auburn, editor of the *International Journal of Contemporary Sociology*; Miss Peterson of Schalkenbach, whom I have already mentioned in another connection; Mr. Harry Pollard, president of the Henry George School of Los Angeles; Mr. William O. Ranky of Chicago; Miss Frances Soriero of Schalkenbach; and Professor Bruce Yandle of the Economics Department at Clemson University. Some of my literary contributors, notably Professors Gaffney, Hébert, and Schwartzman, also provided useful advice or other help. Of course, culpability for the defects of the volume rests ultimately with me.

Mr. Julien Yoseloff, president of Associated University Presses, Inc., extended himself in many ways to be accommodating.

Finally, these acknowledgments would be sadly incomplete if they omitted reference to my lady, who accepted the husbandry neglect that was an inevitable aspect of my more than four years of intense involvement with this volume. Were it possible to report honestly that she did so uncomplainingly, I should have reason to be apprehensive.

R. V. A.
July 1978

I wish to thank the following for having given permission to quote from published works:

*The American Journal of Economics and Sociology,* for permission to quote chapter 24, originally titled "Msgr. John A. Ryan's Critique of

Henry George," published in vol. 33, no. 3 (July 1974):273–86; and section I of chapter 19, adapted from my article "Where Society's Claim Stops: An Evaluation of Seligman's Ethical Critique of Henry George," published in vol. 27, no. 1 (January 1968):41–53.

Harvard University Press, for permission to quote from Thomas Nixon Carver, *Essays in Social Justice*, 1915.

Macmillan Administration (Basingstoke) Ltd. and The Free Press, a division of Macmillan Publishing Co., Inc., for permission to quote from Alfred Marshall, *The Early Economic Writings of Alfred Marshall, 1867–1890*, edited end introduced by J. K. Whitaker, 1975.

Oxford University Press, for permission to quote from Joseph Schumpeter, *History of Economic Analysis*, edited by Elizabeth Boody Schumpeter, 1954.

Random House, Inc., and Alfred A. Knopf, Inc., for permission to quote from *Essays in Economic Theory*, edited by Rexford G. Tugwell, 1924.

# PART IV

# Critics in the Twentieth Century and Beyond

# 21
# A Cannan Hits the Mark

By MASON GAFFNEY

Edwin Cannan (1861–1935) is best known for his 1904 edition of *The Wealth of Nations*, which became a standard. His next best-known work is a *History of Theories of Production and Distribution*, 1893. His book most relevant here is *History of Local Rates in England*, 1896. He was a professor at the London School of Economics, 1907–26, although a large inherited fortune let him live and rub elbows at Oxford, which he seemed to prefer. His later work was less noteworthy. He criticized both Marshall and J. M. Keynes, but without much impact.

## Cannan's Law

In 1907 Cannan fired off a round at local rating of site values.[1] It hit home. First he recited the logic of what today we call the "tragedy of the commons" (it was common coin long before Garrett Hardin). Then he pointed out that a city taxing only site values to provide free public services would attract too many people and too much capital.[2] A city is an "open economy," free to immigration of everything but land, something like an open range or fishery. Even if all cities tax only site values, cities with more rents per head may support public services at higher levels, and so attract immigrants. This distorts locational decisions, attracting people to jobs of lesser productivity where they may gain from better public services. This is "Cannan's Law."

There are three bad results from Cannan's Law. One is an uneconomical distribution of population, as cities with more rentable lands attract more of mobile labor and capital than they should. That is not to deny that people are attracted to New York for good economic reasons. Rather, it is that distributing economic rent freely to all

American Journal of Economics and Sociology, Vol. 63, No. 2 (April, 2004).
© 2004 American Journal of Economics and Sociology, Inc.

comers attracts people above and beyond the good economic reasons. Thus, people move to New York to earn high wages, well and good; but in addition they may receive a high quality college education from CCNY, the "poor man's Harvard," paid from local property taxes. In the glory days of the Mesabi iron range, children of immigrant Finnish miners there in Hibbing, Minnesota, enjoyed some of the best schooling in the country, paid from local property taxes on iron ore. In Alaska and Alberta, workers receive high wages to overcome the harsh climate, remote locations, and other dis-amenities. That is economically sound, but in addition they get a cash dividend each year from the overflowing oil revenues. All that tends to draw more people, like flies swarming to fresh pie, than the wages warrant.

A second bad result is what economists call "dissipation of economic rent." To make it simple, consider a rich but crowded fishery where another fishing boat added to the crowd will not raise the total catch at all, but simply take fish from other crews who were already there. Interlopers will keep entering until the average boat and crew just make costs, leaving no net rent for anyone. This has long been standard economic lore. As Cannan writes, if a locality uses its rents to benefit all its "inhabitants," people will flock to the richest places until there is no further gain to immigrants because they have wiped out all the rent.[3]

A third bad result of Cannan's Law is to lower the incentive of local governments to provide public services that are open to all comers. It fosters local institutions and attitudes that are harshly hostile to newcomers and outsiders, especially to the poor, young, homeless, hungry, and vagrant. As Woody Guthrie, the Okie bard, sang of California, "Believe it or not, you won't find it so hot, if you ain't got that do-re-mi." That was in 1935, the year Cannan died; it remains true, only more so.

Cannan goes on to say that if we are to tax site values, the tax should be national. It is not clear how sincere he is—his style is carping, condescending, elitist, and unsympathetic. Still, his logic implies it, and he does say it, however grudgingly.[4] On this point the great Alfred Marshall agreed, in a positive spirit (positive, that is, for Marshall, a famously "two-handed" economist).[5]

## Why Heed Cannan?

It would be easy to dismiss Cannan, a careless writer. One could pick at his many flaws, but it would be tedious and petty. He lacked much standing in the profession, except as a hanger-on. He is best known for editing *The Wealth of Nations*, the work of another man's genius. Marshall credits Cannan as one of many who have helped him on "special points,"[6] yet Cannan misquotes and misrenders Marshall so badly one doubts if he ever finished reading Marshall's *Principles*, with its emphasis on the distinctive qualities of land, and its virtues as a tax base.[7]

Yet it would be wrong to dismiss Cannan without heeding the crash of his siege-gun, for he aimed it well. His point is that if we are to think globally we must also act globally, or at least nationally, not just locally. Those who follow the behest to "Think globally, act locally" trap themselves in an anomaly, dooming them to the fate of Sisyphus. No locality has much incentive to share its land, unilaterally, with the rest of the world's mobile people.

Alfred Marshall seconds Cannan's point, although he notes that the "well-to-do" tend to move to the suburbs, leaving the "working classes" in central cities.[8] He rather misses Cannan's point that the "London Dukes" who owned (and still own) the best of central London are the target of land taxers. At this point Marshall minimizes the problem—his world tends to be the best of all possible ones.

## The Balkanized Tax Base

Differences among city tax bases are actually, however, extreme. Parlier, a desperate little farm town in Fresno County, has just $10,000 of assessed value per head. Here are some assessed values per head from different California cities in the County of Los Angeles: Lynwood, $21,500; Beverly Hills, $294,000 (thirteen times Lynwood); City of Industry, $5,533,000 (257 times Lynwood, and 553 times Parlier).[9] Destitute Slab City (unincorp.) in Riverside County has no land values at all. (It is an abandoned military base between a bombing range and the fragrant southern end of the eutrophied Salton Sea, with rotting algae and dying fish.) One would not expect much support in the City of Industry for a proposal to share land as common property with the transients who park in Slab City, which has no public services except a species of public schooling (paid by the county), nor would we expect the transients to stay in or return to Slab City if they could park on the streets of Beverly Hills, camp in its parks, attend its schools, and beg or "work for food" on Rodeo Drive.

This is why some critics have called the property tax "regressive." Balkanization of the property tax gives some plausibility to the otherwise bizarre claim that switching to a sales tax is less regressive than sticking with a property tax. Within each city the property tax is progressive, but when your data meld cities like poor little Parlier and Lynwood with Beverly Hills you sometimes find poor people paying more of their income in property taxes than rich people, and getting less for it.

Then there are resource tax enclaves. Hydrocarbons and hardrock minerals are unevenly distributed, geographically. McLure tells us that the Siberian *oblast* of Tyumen, with 2 percent of Russia's people, yields 65 percent of Russia's oil.[10] There are similar regional disparities worldwide.

Rich farm counties are not, generally, resource tax enclaves (except by comparison with poor farm counties). The "rural" counties today with high values per head are resort counties, like Vilas and Walworth in Wisconsin, with their prized lake frontages; or "exurban" counties like Napa in California, or Berkshire in Massachusetts. In California, you might think that fruitful farming counties like Tulare have a lot more taxable real estate value per head than urban ones. Such is a durable belief, but it is wrong. Tulare County reports assessed values per head of $38,100. The whole state averages $60,000 per head. Suburban Marin County weighs in with $95,400; urban Los Angeles County has $59,000; Orange County has $74,000.[11]

You might also think that Tulare, being rural, has a higher fraction of land value in its mix, but again, not so, going by state-equalized assessed valuations. The Land Share of Real Estate Value (LSREV) in Tulare County is 28 percent, compared to a statewide mean of 40 percent, and 47 percent in Orange County. Grazing and mining counties like Inyo have high values of LSREV, but they are a small share of the farm economy. Counties with intensive working farms, like those of the San Joaquin Valley, have low values of LSREV.[12]

Switching just the *local* property tax to land ex buildings will do little to correct such disparities. It will therefore make little progress toward overall distributive justice, and the wide support that would evoke. There is, in fact, a natural cap on local property tax rates imposed by local particularism. The City Council of Beverly Hills will not raise land taxes in Beverly Hills to help voters in Parlier and Lynwood move to Beverly Hills and share the rents.

### Local Particularism Caps the Property Tax Rate

Everything above points to there being a low ceiling on Georgist taxation applied locally. Henry George recognized that the power elite of landowner/employers use Malthus's doctrine to oppose raising wages—it would just spawn an invasion of new brats into the work-force, they said, bringing wage rates back down to bare subsistence. To make his points, George had to refute Malthus. George's view mostly prevailed, with exceptions, until fairly recent times. Neo-classical economists even hijacked it, with a reverse spin, to trivial-ize land values. Whatever we may think of Malthus today, there is no doubt that the fear of population increments from outside the taxing polity now plays the role that George ascribed to Malthusian-ism, and plays it with devastating effect.

Meantime, while academicians bandied words, many applied politi-cians saw Cannan's Law clearly, and used it to further their ends. The authors of the U.S. Constitution, all landowners and mostly large ones, arranged for that document to block direct federal property and land taxes, unless the taxes be proportioned to state populations—a crippling provision. They allowed property taxes at state and local levels—even encouraged them by blocking interstate tariffs, then the most common alternative form of revenue. They also guaranteed free interstate migration. Thus they assured that local particularism would cap land tax rates, while local fiscal preemption would obstruct federal use of property taxes. *The Federalist Papers* suggest that was a conscious objective.[13] Possibly Madison and Hamilton were forced into this position to win the support of the majority of landowner-delegates, but it was they who left their fingerprints on *The Federalist Papers.*[14]

Austen Chamberlain, an English politician who (with his half-brother Neville) battled against proposed national land taxation from 1920–38, formulated the Tory strategy thus:

> It is certain that if we do nothing the Radical Party will sooner or later establish their national tax, and once established in that form any Radical Chancellor . . . will find it an easy task to give a turn of the screw. . . . On the other hand if this source of revenue . . . is once given to municipalities, the Treasury will never be able to put its finger in the pie again, . . .[15]

Parliament followed his lead, and thus set the stage for repealing Snowden's national land tax (it was enacted in 1931, but died aborning). Poor Neville Chamberlain was to be the goat of such penury when he had to let Hitler humiliate him, but meantime English landlords were spared paying taxes for any national purpose.

Upton Sinclair's 1934 run for Governor of California on the radical EPIC platform, with strong Georgist elements, was winning until the enemy found the formula of anti-Okie-ism.[16] Jackson Ralston mounted single-tax initiatives in the same decade, and lost to the same tactic. He based his campaign on "Home Rule" for cities.[17] Critics noted that each single-tax city would attract more than its share of hungry dust-bourl refugees, and destitute Californians as well. Desperate conservatives in Washington, besieged by radicals of the Huey Long-Father Coughlin-Dr. Townsend stripe, could observe like Chamberlain that local particularisms would cap local property taxes, while local fiscal possessiveness would block any national tax on property.

### Evanescent Local Successes and Their Failings

There have been many temporary and partial political successes, applying Georgist ideas locally, in spite of Cannan's Law. These are something like correcting bad vision using eye exercises instead of glasses. There are enough minor successes, after heroic efforts, to lead us on, but only to frustration. Local action alone cannot achieve the main goal. Here are a few such stories.

Some successes entail barriers to immigration. Alaska early on set out to limit its social dividend to citizens with five years' prior residence in Alaska. It immediately lost out to the ghost of Madison. In *Zobel v. Williams* (1982),[18] the U.S. Supreme Court called this provision a barrier to interstate migration, and struck it down. Alaska's annual oil dividend survived, but were it not for *Zobel* might be much higher than today. Meantime, Alaskan landowners pay low property taxes. There goes much of the dividend, and Anchorage is the most sprawled city in North America.

Significantly, exclusionary zoning has NOT been ruled a barrier to interstate migration. Neither have state and city commuter taxes that tax the income of people who live in one state and work in another. It may depend on whose ox is being gored.

Ethnic political machines tap into local rents while restricting the benefits to a closed circle that is hard to enter. Their role in urban American history is well known. So are their shortcomings, which need no belaboring here. Note, though, that many machine politicians—Al Smith is the poster boy—have been friendlier to Georgist reforms than have patrician "good government" reformers.

Theocracies with a religious test for entry are noteworthy. Two obvious cases are Congregationalist New England of the seventeenth century, and Mormon Utah of the nineteenth century. Each was marked by egalitarian sharing of rents among the faithful. Neither was able or wanted to expand its example to encompass other faiths, however, except via conversion.

California has quite a history of taxing land for public benefits. But what public? California cannot exclude U.S. citizens directly, but does so indirectly by winking at the widespread use of illegal alien labor for stoop and sweatshop work. These aliens repel eastern U.S. immigrants, while the aliens, mostly nonvoting, are excluded from most public benefits.

Another set of successes came from selling voters on the gains from growth and immigration. Henry George was apparently elected Mayor of New York City in 1886 (although counted out). He had Irish support, but was not selling an ethnic machine—Tammany and the Irish Catholic hierarchy turned against him. He preached on the benefits of growth. Immigrants would not dilute rents as much as they augmented them, said George. It is a central point he underscores in his major work, *Progress and Poverty*.

Edward Polak (1915), a George supporter in the Bronx Borough, repeated George's argument in supporting the proposed exemption of buildings in New York City—an exemption that was implemented, 1922–32, with a strong boost from Governor Al Smith.[19] Now, however, there is a visible loss of belief in economies of scale of population—except in dying towns whose people feel their loss keenly, too late.

George also brought out a countervailing point that Cannan, in his exclusive concern with protecting high central rents from invasion, overlooked. Taxes on the use and improvement of marginal lands sterilize them, said George, "and tend to drive population and wealth from them to the great cities." Godfrey Dunkley argues convincingly that that is what VAT did, when South Africa adopted it for the very purpose of making marginalized blacks pay taxes.[20] That is not the last word on the subject either, but shows there is more to it than Cannan began to disclose. As George maintained, aborting rent on marginal land, not just rent sharing on superior land, distorts locational decisions.

Chambers of commerce and real estate boards have generally followed the same tack as George, touting the gains of growth. In the single-tax era in western Canada, that crested ca. 1919, organized real estate people were a major force promoting the exemption of buildings.[21] They often support land tax increases: some of them even opposed Proposition 13 in California. They recognize the role of infrastructure in promoting economic development, and the benefits of untaxing buildings. Chambers of commerce, however, now put much more emphasis on attracting capital than labor. Changes in fiscal federalism, discussed below, have reshaped their incentives and attitudes.

Public universities have been a screening device attracting an especially desired form of immigrant. Local support for education is, however, lopsided, overbalanced for graduate and technical education.

In sum, local growth orientation has become too weak, partial, and spasmodic to overcome the restrictive force of local particularism, which today dominates policy almost everywhere. The resulting exclusionary policies, when practiced by all or most localities, drive landless proles from pillar to post until they become so desperate they will serve landowner-employers for very little. It is not enough to "think globally": we must act globally. "Some for the Glories of This World, and some/ sigh for the Prophet's Paradise to come; . . .". Now, it seems, to win some glories of this world we must do more than just sigh for the Prophet's Paradise, we must work for it.

### Acting "Globally"

One way to act globally (or at least nationally) is through a national land tax, or some reasonable facsimile thereof, coupled with a national citizens' dividend. The Income Tax Act of 1894 did include land income in the tax base, thanks to the persistence of a handful of single-tax congressmen—yes, really, there once were such men, six of them at that time. The U.S. Supreme Court struck it down because property income was in the base,[22] but President Taft (of all people), Congress, and the voters came back with the sixteenth Amendment, adopted in 1913, that did include land income in the tax base. When Congress, led by single taxers Warren Worth Bailey (of Johnstown, Pa.) and Henry George, Jr. (of Brooklyn), first implemented the amendment it virtually exempted wages and salaries by exempting incomes below a high cutoff point.[23] The brunt of federal taxation fell on property income, much of it land income, and it was enough to finance World War I.

Since then the income tax has evolved, step by step, into its present anti-labor form, with most property income exempt *de facto*, and high rates on earned income.[24] It is obviously constitutional to reverse that trend, because we have been there before. It would also be desirable, but here we will focus on the cognate matter of "fiscal federalism."

To enable basic tax reform at the local level we must deal with local particularism. To do that, in turn, we must deal with "fiscal federalism." How are central governments to distribute funds from their so-called surplus: to people (as a social dividend), or to local governments representing landowners? When we wake up to smell this coffee, we will find that a lot of economists have gotten up first. Many of these economists deal with land rent, defined as Ricardo would.[25]

The reason it is so hard to sell growth policies—like land-value taxation—at the local level today is that fiscal federalism, as practiced today, is perverse. Central governments, imbued with the anti-personnel spirit of Austen Chamberlain, tax people as people, while handing out subventions to landowners as such, and to local governments as such. The landowners can get the subventions without having people, so who needs people? That's our problem in a nutshell. Persons as such become fiscal pollutants, from the local view. After the T-Men have plucked their feathers, working persons are less able to pay local taxes; while federal grants relieve local landowners from needing population to share public costs.[26]

Perverse fiscal federalism is DEsocialization of rent—creating new private rents using public monies wrung from workers. This is inherent in grants for capital spending, e.g., for sewerage; and tax exemption of muni bonds. These grants and exemptions are given to municipalities as such. That is only a step away from returning dollars to landowners as such, because municipalities are defined as areas of land, a group of local landowners.[27] Desocialization is inherent in farm subsidies, e.g., payments to fallow land, using tax money from workers. It is inherent in preferential assessment of farmland, e.g., California's Williamson Act, where the state pays localities for their lost tax revenues from underutilizing lands. It is inherent in the use of property-tax exemptions to subsidize many underutilizations of land and hobbies of the rich, like redundant airports for private jets, cemeteries, golf courses, campuses, church parking lots, conservation easements, timber, etc. Some of these may foster socially defensible uses, but note it is the lands, not the personnel, that are tax-exempted.

Canada's classic Carter Commission Report[28] led the right way, but Canada's actual equalization program leads the wrong way.[29] Equalization grants from Ottawa to the provinces are lower to provinces whose taxable capacity per head is higher, and of course vice versa, according to a detailed formula. So far, so good, but the devil is in the definition of "taxable capacity." Canada specifically excludes land value from measures of taxable capacity.[30] Buildings are included as part of the potential tax base; a hardworking productive population is included; a thriving commerce is included; but land value is quietly excluded. Thus a province wherein vast and valuable lands are under-used is considered a charity case, eligible for alms from Ottawa; while another province that makes productive use of meager lands has to pay more taxes, but gets less relief. That helps explain why Ontario and Quebec, despite their great urban and locational advantages, still rank below the provincial average in measured taxable capacity.[31] It is not the capacity that is lacking, but the measurement of it. The tilt is patent; it could hardly be an accident. If any one of the many brilliant economists, politicians, and bureaucrats who prate or publish on equalization payments, horizontal fiscal federalism, and Canada's Representative Tax System (RTS) has even peeped on this point, I am not aware of it. Their consciousness has fallen below the threshold of perception, and needs desperately to rise.

Within provinces there are equalization programs, too. British Columbia offsets the magnetism of Vancouver by subsidizing less magnetic cities from general revenues, and by cross-subsidizing rail and utility services to distant outposts in the boonies, but it is local governments or private landowners, not people as such, that get the benefits. It is the same in every American state. The exception is public education, which is therefore the target of the most spirited attacks by privatizers (like smug George Will) who dominate the op-ed pages today.

The modern "Public Choice" school has grown terribly chic in the economics profession. It focuses on fear of "the tyranny of the majority," given votes. The basic concept is unrealistic and prejudicial, in view of the observable fact that the minority of landowners, armed with discretionary wealth, sway the majority of voters to support policies that favor landowners over the underlying population. The Public Choice school leads us to fear and fend off an imaginary problem, blinding us to the real one that is quite the reverse. Veblen explained voter behavior better by analyzing the mindset of voters as a cultural throwback to an age of marauding Viking bands organized around mindless fealty to some alpha male, whom the betas and omegas were bound loyally to support and serve at any cost to themselves. A progressive society must learn to place more value on the "instinct of workmanship," and express its unity in more egalitarian ways.

### Reversing Perverse Policies

Public spending should feature "Citizen Dividends." These are social dividends limited to citizens, thus discouraging free or illegal immigration that would dilute the dividends and erode their voter support. (The degree, pace, and conditions of legal immigration is an issue to treat separately.) Dividends take many forms other than outright per head cash grants. The G. I. Bill was a splendid example. Social Security payments are another. School equalization payments based on average daily attendance (a.d.a.) are another. A state or province cannot easily restrict benefits to its old-time citizens, as *Zobel* showed—but a nation can.

At the same time, there should be no more capital grants to localities for public works. When cities pay for their own public works they must attract population to justify the capital outlays and service the debt.

Federal taxation should bear heavier on land income, and lighter on wage and salary income, as in 1916. It was constitutional then; it still is. The combination of a citizens' dividend and income-tax reform would drastically rebalance local incentives. Cities would compete to attract median people rather than, as now, to repel them. This would not cause swamping of cities with people because it is a zero-sum game in a closed system. Competition would simply raise wage rates and lower living costs.[32]

Congress should repeal the tax exemption of state and local bonds, a massive ongoing subsidy to local landowners. This repeal will be challenged as an invasion of state sovereignty, but recall that Congress had no trouble in 1939 repealing the tax exemption of state and local employees. Would the courts find bonds to be more sacred than payrolls? To find out, we only need a simple act of Congress that would quickly be adjudicated.

The federal government should review local zoning, and other exclusionary policies, as barriers to interstate migration.

There is a federal interest in better tax assessment of land, to keep buyers of used buildings from overallocating their tax "basis" to depreciable buildings, thus arranging falsely to depreciate land, and erode federal revenues. Something like a national board of equalization is called for. The U.S. Census of Governments, with the pioneering work of Allen Manvel and political support from Illinois senator and economics professor Paul Douglas, established the precedent. While we're at it, let us outlaw the sequential depreciation of the same building by successive owners, an obvious outrage.

The result of such measures would be to restore the concepts of dignity of labor, and the key role of income-creating investing (as opposed to acquiring existing wealth and rent seeking).

### Colin Clark's National Land Tax

For nations where a national land tax is politically thinkable, Colin Clark[33] has proposed a simple technique to spike Cannan's big guns. Says Clark, "land values per head of population should first be ascertained; then the state would impose a land tax which exempted altogether those local authority areas where per-head land values were low, and which rose in a progressive scale for those with higher land values per head. Each local authority would then also impose its own tax, . . ."

Alfred Marshall, disguising his boldness under a mousy writing style, proposed an even stronger supplement to the land tax. He would make the tax base the capital value of land, rather than the annual cash value, to tap "the part of the real annual value of land which does not appear in a money form. . . ." Repeating himself for emphasis, he says that taxing capital value will "bring under taxation some real income, which has escaped taxation merely because it does not appear above the surface in a money form." That is, Marshall wants the national tax to fall on *imputed* land income, an enormous annual flow of value that now totally escapes income taxation.

And what is the value of land under old buildings? Marshall writes no nonsense about seeking the depreciated value of the old building first. Land value is the opportunity cost of the site itself: what land would bring "if cleared of buildings and sold in a free market."[34] Imagine how that set of policies, from this prissy pillar of property and propriety, would radicalize national taxation in any modern state. Beneath the cautious façade, Marshall reinforced some Georgist ideas.

Yet there is more. Marshall applauds Lloyd George's "Social Welfare" Budget of 1909, the one that humbled the House of Lords, because the proposed land tax will "check the appropriation of what is really public property by private persons."[35] Did Henry George ever say it plainer, or more provocatively "in-your-face"? No wonder Edwin Cannan shied away from mastering Marshall's *Principles*. No wonder George Stigler had to go back to a disorderly altercation at Oxford, and alleged comments that Marshall never published, shiftily to define the great Marshall as an anti-Georgist.[36] Can we, in our federal system, come up with something comparable to the ideas of Clark and Marshall? It is a matter of thinking creatively, with the right attitude.

## Notes

1. Edwin Cannan, "The Proposed Relief of Buildings from Local Rates," *The Economic Journal* 17 (1907): 36–46; Edwin Cannan, *The History of Local Rates in England* (London: P. S. King & Son, orig. 1896, 2nd ed., much enlarged, 1912).

2. (1907), pp. 43–44; (1896), p. 185.

3. (1896), pp. 181–82.

4. (1896), p. 185; (1907), p. 45.

5. Alfred Marshall, *Principles of Economics* (New York: The Macmillan Company, orig. 1890; 8th ed., 1920; 7th printing, 1959, 1948 [sic]), p. 798. More emphatic is Marshall's letter to *The Times* (London, *The London Times*, 16 Nov. 1909).

6. (1920), p. xvii.

7. (1920), pp. 169, 422, 433, 441–44, 450, 796–98, 801–04, *et passim*. There is an insightful discussion in Robert F. Hébert, "Marshall: A Professional Economist Guards the Purity of His Discipline," in chapter 4 of the present book. See also various excellent writings on Marshall by J. K. Whitaker.

8. Marshall (1920), p. 797.

9. Data from *Annual Reports*, California State Board of Equalization.

10. Charles McLure, Jr., "The Taxation of Natural Resources and the Future of the Russian Federation," a paper given at the annual meeting of the Committee on Taxation, Resources, and Economic Development (TRED), to be published in Christine Wallich (ed.), *Whither Russia: Fiscal Decentralization in the Russian Federation* (Washington, The World Bank, 1992), p. 1.

11. California Board of Equalization, *loc. cit.*

12. *Ibid.*

13. Louis Hacker, *Triumph of American Capitalism* (New York: Columbia University Press, 1947), p. 187; Charles Beard, *An Economic Interpretation of the Constitution* (New York: The Macmillan Co., 1935), pp. 156–58, 169; James Madison, *The Federalist* #10; A. Hamilton, *The Federalist #12*; John Fiske, *The Critical Period of American History* (Cambridge: The Riverside Press, 1888), p. 70.

14. Either ironically or significantly, it was Hamilton who instigated the first use of a federal property tax, in 1798, when he virtually ran Adams's cabinet and wanted money to prepare for a war he desired with France. Later, the second use came under President Madison, to fight Britain.

15. Cit. Roy Douglas, *Land, People, and Politics.* (London: Allison and Busby, 1976), p. 150.

16. Upton Sinclair, *I, Candidate for Governor: And How I Got Licked.* (Pasadena: Published by the author, 1934; Rpt. Berkeley and Los Angeles, University of California Press, 1994).

17. James Echols, "Jackson Ralston and the California Single Tax Campaign, 1933–38" (M. A. Thesis, Department of History, Fresno State College, 1967), p. 57. Home Rule was in the tradition of Joseph Fels, whose generous financial backing helped him shape single-tax politics from 1900–16, and lead the movement down the road proverbially paved with good intentions.

See also Jackson H. Ralston, "Adventures in the Life of a Washington Lawyer" (ms in the Ralston Papers, Bancroft Library, University of California, Berkeley, n.d.).

18. *Zobel v. Williams* (102 U.S. 2309, 1982).

19. Edward Polak, "Reduction of Tax on Buildings in the City of New York," *AAAPSS* 58 (1915), pp. 183–88. On the New York City experience, see Mason Gaffney, "The Regeneration of New York City after 1920," (ms available from author, 2001).

20. Godfrey Dunkley, *That All May Live* (Cape Town: published by the author, 1990).

21. Robert Murray Haig, *The Exemption of Improvements from Taxation in Canada and the United States* (New York: The Committee on Taxation, 1915).

22. *Pollock v. Farmers' Loan and Trust Co.* (157 U.S. 429, 1894); rehearing (158 U.S. 601, 1895).

23. W. Elliot Brownlee, "Wilson and Financing the Modern State: the Revenue Act of 1916," *Proceedings of the Am. Philosophical Society* 129 (2) (1985): 173–210.

24. Mason Gaffney, "Tax Treatment of Land Income," *Economic Analysis and the Efficiency of Government,* Hearings, U.S. Congress, Joint Economic Committee, Subcommittee on Efficiency in Government, Part 2 (Washington, D.C.: U.S. Government Printing Office, 1970), pp. 405–15.

Updated and expanded in Mason Gaffney, "Land Value Gains and the Capital Gains Tax" (unpublished ms, available from the writer, 1991), pp. 1–74.

25. Anthony Scott (ed.), *Natural Resource Revenues: A Test of Federalism* (Vancouver: University of British Columbia Press, 1975), with chapters by 19 leading Canadian economists.

Charles E. McLure, Jr., and Peter Mieszkowski (eds.), *Fiscal Federalism and the Taxation of Natural Resources* (Lexington, Mass.: Lexington Books,

1983), with chapters by 12 prominent American and Canadian economists and lawyers, and comments by several more. Both volumes cite dozens of other works.

Charles E. McLure, Jr., "Fiscal Federalism and the Taxation of Economic Rents," in George Break (ed.), *State and Local Finance* (Madison: University of Wisconsin Press, 1984).

26. Mason Gaffney, "Changes in Land Policy: How Fundamental are They?" *Real Estate Issues* (Fall, 1976): 72–85.

Mason Gaffney, "Changes in Land Policy," *Western Journal of Agricultural Economics* (June, 1977): 71–81.

27. To underscore the point, there are some municipalities that contain only one or two landowners. Foster City in the San Francisco Bay area, the City of Irvine and the Irvine Water District in Orange County, the Castaic Lake Water District serving Newhall lands in Los Angeles and Ventura counties, and the city of Avalon on Catalina Island are examples. Professor Merrill Goodall has published extensively on such cases.

28. *Carter Report* (Ottawa: Royal Commission on Taxation, 1966).

29. Mason Gaffney, "Revenue Sharing," *Good Government*, 867 (December, 1986): 19–24.

30. Douglas H. Clark, "Canadian Experience with the Representative Tax System," *Intergovernmental Perspective* (Winter/Spring 1986): 22–29; (Washington: Advisory Commission on Intergovernmental Relations), at p. 27, Table 2.

31. Robert B. Lucke, "Rich States—Poor States: Inequalities in our Federal System," *Intergovernmental Perspective* (Spring, 1982): 22–28; (Washington: Advisory Commission on Intergovernmental Relations), at pp. 26–27.

32. Mason Gaffney, "Tax Reform to Release Land," in Marion Clawson (ed.), *Modernizing Urban Land Policy.* (Baltimore: Johns Hopkins University Press, 1973), pp. 115–52. Republished, *Compact Cities: a Neglected Way of Conserving Energy*, Congressman Henry Reuss presiding, Joint Hearings, Committee on Banking, Finance and Urban Affairs; and Committee on Interstate and Foreign commerce, U.S. House of Representatives, 96th Congress 1st Sess. (Washington: USGPO, 1980), pp. 246–82. Republished, Kenneth Wenzer (ed.), *Land-Value Taxation* (Armonk, New York: M. E. Sharpe, 1999), pp. 58–99.

33. Colin Clark, "Land Taxation: Lessons from International Experience," in Peter Hall (ed.), *Land Values* (London: Sweet and Maxwell, Ltd., 1956), p. 144.

34. Marshall, op. cit., p. 441.

35. Marshall, letter to *The Times* (London: *The London Times*, 16 Nov. 1909).

36. George Stigler, "Three Lectures on *Progress and Poverty*," *Journal of Law and Economics* 12 (1969): 181–26.

# 22

# Davenport: "Single Taxer of
# the Looser Observance"

## By Aaron B. Fuller

Herbert Joseph Davenport (1861–1931) was a prominent, early twentieth-century American economist whose contributions to economic analysis include a sophisticated opportunity-cost theory and a series of lucid presentations of marginal utility theory.[1] Something of an iconoclast, he criticized many of his fellow economists and befriended his former teacher Thorstein Veblen at a time when most economists had lost interest in Veblen's theatrical personality and sweeping denunciations of economic principles.[2] In addition to these accomplishments, Davenport is cited by George R. Geiger in his important book *The Philosophy of Henry George*, as a major critic of George's theory of capital. Geiger argues that the "classical" distinction between land and capital was "a crucial one for George's economic system," and that "Professor Davenport was perhaps the most characteristic critic of this type of distinction."[3] But following these forthright assertions about George's system and Davenport's criticism of it, Geiger equivocates and severely qualifies his initial declaration that Davenport was "perhaps the most characteristic critic." His qualification is that Davenport's criticism is mentioned "not because his interpretation of economics—one which repudiates the classical attempts to make the science primarily a logical or ethical discipline and which instead stresses a strictly 'cost' approach—is felt to be necessarily representative of modern economic theory, but simply because of his decisive treatment of this particular [*capital theory*] problem."[4] Geiger has introduced a contradiction with his "most characteristic critic" description followed by his denial that Davenport's ideas are necessarily representative of modern economic theory, and this contradiction is present throughout Geiger's discussion of Davenport's views. Geiger offers no explicit clues as to why he decided to circumscribe the relevance of Davenport's views, but it is clear that

American Journal of Economics and Sociology, Vol. 63, No. 2 (April, 2004).
© 2004 American Journal of Economics and Sociology, Inc.

by his equivocation he severs those views from any role that they might have played as representative of how then contemporary economic theorists viewed George's ideas.[5] As we shall see in the ensuing discussion of Davenport's criticisms, Geiger's equivocation was as unnecessary as his basic point is incorrect; that is, Davenport's views on capital theory were very representative of contemporary economic theory, particularly as it was presented by Irving Fisher, and Davenport's capital theory was not a criticism of George's.

Geiger's view that Davenport was a critic of George's theoretical soundness is not absolute, because in a footnote he recognizes that Davenport favored a policy of land-rent taxation, and he correctly paraphrases Davenport's suggestion that "economists have been wrong in looking upon the single tax as a fad or hobby offering no practical discussion possibilities."[6] Even stronger recognition of Davenport's positive view of George's theoretical soundness is offered by Geiger's quotation in the same footnote of Davenport's explicit statement that "the economists have never seriously attacked the theoretical validity of the single tax program." In another footnote, Geiger cites Davenport's inclusion of himself (in the concluding paragraph of his *American Economic Review* essay, "Theoretical Issues in the Single Tax") among the "single taxers of the looser observance."[7] However, Geiger never reconciles Davenport's clear defense of the theoretical legitimacy of land-rent taxation, cited in these footnotes, with Geiger's own textual claim that Davenport is a major negative critic of George's theoretical structure. This contradiction between the main theme of Geiger's textual discussion of Davenport and the substance of the footnotes provides further evidence of Geiger's equivocal treatment of Davenport as a critic of George's theoretical soundness.

In addition to assessing the implications of Davenport's alleged criticisms of George's capital theory, we shall also examine Davenport's criticisms of land-rent taxation proposals. Davenport expressed much sympathy with the basic principle of taxing land rents, declaring that "the truth is with the single-taxers in principle but not in method."[8] The "method" to which he particularly objected was the taxation of rents already accrued at the moment of the adoption of a land-rent tax program. He argued that those economic decision makers who enjoyed the gains from past increases in economic rents should not be deprived of those fortuitous increases.

Finally, it is necessary to examine two fundamental elements of the economic ideas of George and Davenport, opportunity cost and economic methodology, in order to see that there are compelling similarities between their ideas, leading to the implication that, to the extent that Davenport was a sound economist, George was also.

Geiger's discussion of Davenport is the sole basis in the literature for the claim that Davenport was a negative critic of George' theory. Geiger was simply wrong, and a suitable explanation for his error cannot be reconstructed from the textual evidence. We may hypothesize several speculations: that Geiger, a philosopher and not an economist, simply misread what Davenport and George wrote; that Geiger did not intend to introduce equivocations and contradictions, and they were simply missed in the editorial process; and that Geiger had an ax to hone, and Davenport's ideas provided a convenient rough edge against which he could sharpen his own preconceived ideas. These and other speculations must remain unresolved because it is not the present concern to engage in a historiographical reconstruction of Geiger's motives. In fact, the issue of whether Geiger's error is the result of deliberate intent or whether it was purely accidental is irrelevant to assessment of the contents of Davenport's ideas as they relate to Henry George. But Geiger's error (that Davenport was a negative critic of George's theoretical soundness) is relevant in a broader context, the issue of whether Henry George was a competent economist. Since Geiger's book (in the main an able and valuable study) is basically a defense of George's thought, the implications of this error tend to vitiate the work's essential thrust, and, were he aware of them, could not fail to have been distressful to its author.

Geiger's initial identification of Davenport as a theoretical critic of George establishes a perspective in which George's conceptual foundations are viewed as being in conflict with the ideas of prominent economists. Geiger states that George's distinction between land and capital "has been severely attacked by more recent economic critics," and then he goes on to identify Davenport as the "most characteristic" of these severe critics.[9] Geiger's presentation is symptomatic of a major presupposition that underlies much of the literature that

presents George's ideas—the preconceived, untested notion that
George's ideas stand on one side of the issues he addresses and that
the ideas of respected economists stand on the opposite side. Geiger
to the contrary, Davenport was not a critic of George's economics.
Davenport's and George's concepts of capital are different but compatible because they addressed different analytical needs, Davenport's
the capital budgeting (optimal investment decision) problem and
George's the theory of production and distribution. Extending beyond
Geiger's presentation, Davenport did object to the retroactive taxation of accrued land rents, but this is an objection grounded in
normative differences about what "ought" to be, not in positive
differences based on theory about what "is." There is no basis here
for arguing that Davenport was a negative critic of George's economics, because different policy prescriptions based on different
value judgments are perfectly consistent with simultaneous agreements about the objective analytical facts. Finally, in two major conceptual areas (opportunity cost and methodology), Davenport and
George were in agreement, and this provides a far more substantial
basis for arguing that Davenport and George shared similar analytical conceptions than Geiger's error does for arguing that Davenport
and George were conceptually opposed. Geiger's error is unimportant in and of itself, but when related to the larger issue of whether
George's ideas are outside the framework of accepted economic
analysis, it deserves to be exposed. Such an exposure cannot prove
that George was a good economist, but it can prevent false proof
from being tendered that he was not.

### Capital Values and Capital Goods

It is in chapter 3, "George's Economic Solution," that Geiger presents
what he interprets as the differences between Davenport and George:
Davenport "broadly" defines capital as "all durable and objective
sources of valuable private income," while George "narrowly" defines
capital as "wealth used in the production of more wealth." In Geiger's
view these definitions are radically different, with Davenport's
representing "the continual shift away from the classical separation
between land and capital . . . which is becoming more and more a

characteristic element of present-day theory," and with George's representing the traditional classical position stated in the works of Adam Smith, David Ricardo, and John Stuart Mill. In order to assess Geiger's interpretation of the conflict between these concepts of capital, we must simultaneously address several related issues. First, is Geiger correct that these concepts of capital conflict? Second, what does George's definition mean in terms of his analytical approach? Third, what does Davenport's definition mean in terms of his analytical approach?

Geiger is incorrect that Davenport's view of capital is a criticism of or is in conflict with George's view of capital. Geiger fails to recognize that Davenport's concept of capital is intended for a different analytical purpose from George's, and that different definitions of capital are appropriate to different analytical contexts. Davenport's concern with capital is in terms of what is currently called the capital budgeting problem, or alternatively, the problem of optimal investment decisions.[10] This modern capital budgeting theory relies heavily on Irving Fisher's seminal analyses of capital theory, where consumption is viewed as the final aim of economic activity.[11] Davenport was well aware of Fisher's work, and he footnotes his discussion of the theory of capital and interest in *Value and Distribution* (1908) with the comment that "Professor Irving Fisher's admirable treatise upon *The Rate of Interest* appears as the present work is passing through the press." The footnote then continues over six pages of close type, taking up nearly all of the pages with a careful exposition of the basic elements of Fisher's capital and interest theories. Based on the Fisherian view, the balancing of consumption opportunities over time becomes the central economic allocation problem and it is broadly conceived as encompassing all rational economic choice.[12] The time element is a critical feature of this balancing process because it means that rational economic decision-making revolves around choices to consume income now or to abstain from consumption now and to wait to consume income in the future. Capital is then defined as current income that is not consumed but is "invested" to provide for consumption in the future, or in Hirshleifer's elegant phrasing, "capital is the present embodiment of future-dated consumption goods."[13] This view of capital emphasizes what economists call "capital value," and it is this capital value, the present market value of future income streams, that solutions to the capital budgeting problem are intended to maximize over time.

Davenport's definition of capital cited by Geiger, "all durable and objective sources of valuable private income," is in fact a definition of "real capital" or "capital goods" that is consistent with the Fisherian view of capital, shared by Davenport, which identifies capital as the present embodiment of future-dated consumption goods. The durable and objective capital goods provide the sources of the income streams that are allocated over time to maximize consumption over time. The source of these income streams is irrelevant to the capital budgeting (optimal investment) decision; what is important is that these income streams exist. Geiger's emphasis on Davenport's definition of capital goods is used to demonstrate that Davenport would include land in the definition of capital goods, and Geiger is correct. But Geiger's implication is that the inclusion of land in the category of capital goods is evidence of an attack on the traditional distinction between land and capital, and this implication is incorrect. Land was included in the category of capital goods because it yields an income stream that can be allocated over time, and this allocation process is what Davenport was interested in describing and analyzing. Davenport does not deny that land has unique physical properties and that it can earn rents that are payments in excess of opportunity costs, but he does deny that these features of land are relevant to the decisions regarding the maximization of consumption opportunities over time. Maximizing consumption over time through the allocation of various income streams is not influenced by the sources of the income streams.

Geiger never realizes in his narrative that Davenport's definition of capital goods refers to sources of income, while Davenport's concept of capital refers to capital values that can be allocated over time to maximize consumption opportunities. As Davenport explains, "The value of any instrument of production is the present worth of all the future income attributed to it," and this value is the capital value to which the sources of income streams are irrelevant.[14] These income streams can come from land, machinery, buildings, inventories of goods and services, and all things that can be "traded in, or valued, or rented, or capitalized."[15] In fact, Davenport's list of durable and objective capital goods includes items that are durable and objective only in the sense that they can provide allocatable income streams over time: they are durable in the sense that they persist across alternative time periods, and they are objective in the sense that they provide allocatable income streams. Some of these less obvious capital goods besides land, buildings, machinery, and inventories are "patents, copyrights, trade-marks, business connections, reputation, good-will, privilege, government favor, franchises, royalties, rights of toll and tribute, rents, annuities, mortgage rights, personal claims; and further it includes monopolies of no matter how various kinds and degrees, so far as they may become the subject of invested cost in obtaining them, so far as they are bought and sold as steps in competitive-productive investment, or are vendible upon the market as capitalized dividend-paying properties."[16] All of these capital goods are legitimate objects of capital budgeting (optimal investment) decisions, and Davenport makes this quite clear in his description of the capital budgeting process. "Actual business computations of the expenses of production include a wide range of expenditures made out of what, in the individual reckoning, stands as the total business investment, and functions in the terminology and reckoning of the business world as business capital. . . . The manufacturing entrepreneur or the corporation manager would find it a novel and perplexing doctrine which should restrict the capital investment to the buildings, machinery and raw materials of the undertaking; the corporation really possesses nothing that is not capital."[17]

Davenport's presentation of a Fisherian view of capital is not necessarily inconsistent with George's narrower view of capital as produced means of production. In the Fisherian sense, capital is anything that yields valuable services over time, and in such a circumstance "the theory of capital becomes a theory of general economic growth."[18] *Capital* simply becomes a general term denoting consumption that is put off until a later time period, and the rate of interest is the exchange rate between present and future-dated consumption. Such an approach permits various solutions to the problems of intertemporal choice and the maximization of consumption over time, but if one is interested in a different problem, such as the problem of substitution in production and distribution, then a different concept of capital might not be inappropriate. These latter words are carefully chosen, because my argument is not that the Fisherian theory of capital is incapable of yielding answers to the issues surrounding production and distribution theory (primarily substitutability among productive resources)—in fact, this broad conception of capital can be used to provide such answers; instead, my argument is that George's conception of capital is not incapable of yielding these answers either. Thus the broad Fisherian capital concept advanced by Davenport has multiple analytical applications because it is so broad, while the narrower, produced-means-of-production concept advanced by George has fewer applications, but those to which it is relevant are just as legitimate as the Fisherian applications. There is no necessary conflict between the theories of capital advanced by Davenport and George, and Geiger's perception of conflict is mistaken.

As a final note on this capital theory issue, we should recognize that George did work through a rudimentary marginal productivity theory of production and distribution, and it is to this theory that the produced-means-of-production concept of capital is relevant. Although it is possible to develop a marginal productivity theory without the distinctions between land, labor, and capital that are present in George's analysis, it is also possible to develop such a theory with them, and this is what George did in a preliminary way. The critical requirement for a theory of marginal productivity is the recognition of the substitutability condition among resources in production, and George recognizes the necessity of substitutability at the margin.[19]

### Policy Applications

In two articles dealing with single-tax proposals, Davenport does provide some evidence that he is a "critic" of Henry George, but a critic of specific policy applications of land taxation, and not a critic of George's theoretical soundness.[20] Although George is not mentioned explicitly, Davenport objects to all single taxers who would tax both the existing accrued rents and the future increments of rent.

He advocates only the taxation of the future increments, arguing that the taxation of previously accrued rents constitutes "a program which shall impose on any casual present owner of original natural bounty the penalty for a general and institutional blunder."[21] This objection is not a quarrel with the idea of the single tax on theoretical grounds; instead, it is a normative objection based on differing ethical standards. Davenport makes this clear when he declares that the "truth is with the single-taxers in principle but not in method," and that "it may be said with approximate accuracy that the economists have never seriously attacked the theoretical validity of the single tax program."[22] Davenport's strong normative views are well summarized by his rhetorical claim that "surely wholesale confiscation of existing land values is wholesale robbery."[23] In this, Davenport's rhetoric sounds similar to George's, although the objects of their rhetoric are different. To George it was robbery to permit landowners to retain the rights to accrued rents, just as surely as it was robbery to permit them to accumulate future rental increments. George rhetorically asks, "Why should we hesitate about making short work of such a system [of land rent]? Because I was robbed yesterday, and the day before, and the day before that, is it any reason that I should suffer myself to be robbed today and tomorrow? Any reason that I should conclude that the robber has acquired a vested right to rob me?"[24]

Although this difference in normative value judgments between Davenport and George provides evidence of a legitimate context in which Davenport is a negative critic, it is hardly the sense in which Geiger views Davenport as a critic. Differences in value judgments may exist between individuals who share identical scientific analytical conceptions, and the existence of such differences cannot be accepted as evidence that the individuals differ concerning their basic theoretical approaches to issues.

### Opportunity Cost and Economic Methodology

Thus far I have rejected Geiger's claim that Davenport's advocacy of a Fisherian capital theory constituted a criticism of George's analytical soundness, and I have acknowledged that Davenport and George differed with respect to the value judgments attached to the taxation of accrued rental values. Although neither of these discussions leads to the conclusion that Davenport and George were at odds on basic economic principles, they also fail to provide any strong evidence that they shared any fundamental conceptual ground. To provide some evidence of conceptual similarities, let us briefly examine what each man had to say about two central elements of economic reasoning, the idea of opportunity cost and the methodology of economics.

Davenport is widely recognized as a major contributor to the notion of opportunity cost.[25] In fact, Davenport's contribution was quite sophisticated in that it went beyond the traditional concept of the predictive theory of opportunity cost and explored the concept of choice-influencing subjectivist cost. The traditional predictive theory views costs as quantifiable values that can be determined following the act of choice, while the choice-influencing subjectivist theory views costs as subjective constraints existing in the mind of a decision-maker prior to the act of choice and determining the direction of choice.

Davenport emphasized "entrepreneur's cost," which characterized cost as a "margin determinant" purely within the personal aspects of entrepreneurship, "a managerial fact, a subjective phenomenon, in which all the influences bearing upon the psychology of choice between different occupations or between occupation and leisure have their place."[26] Davenport's basis for the psychology of choice is "the psychological law valid for all human activity: men follow the line of least sacrifice."[27] This sounds remarkably similar to George's "fundamental law of political economy" that "men always seek to gratify their desires with the least exertion."[28] Although George's presentations of opportunity cost are clearly in the traditional mold, based on measurable values sacrificed after the act of choice, there is an element of subjective choice implied in the examples he gives to illustrate the idea. George's image of the marginal workers seems to rely on an implied subjective choice context, where these decision-makers are evaluating their opportunities before the act of choice and basing their decision on their attempts to "gratify their desires with the least exertion." As George describes the framework of opportunity cost:

It is, indeed, evident from observation, as it must be from theory, that whatever be the circumstances which produce the differences of wages in different occupations, and although they frequently vary in relation to each other producing, as between time and time, and place and place, greater or less relative differences, yet the rate of wages in one occupation is always dependent on the rate in another. . . . Thus, on the verge of each occupation, stand those to whom the inducements between one occupation and another are so nicely balanced that the slightest change is sufficient to determine their labor in one direction or another.[29]

These marginal decision-makers "on the verge of each occupation" seem to be engaging in subjective evaluations of the costs to themselves of remaining in their present occupation compared to changing to another occupation. While I am not trying to suggest that George's concept of opportunity cost included the same awareness of the distinction between choice-influenced objective costs and choice-influencing subjective costs that is explicitly developed by Davenport, it is accurate to suggest that the basic notion of choice-influenced opportunity cost is present in George's ideas along with a hint of the subjectivist element. Davenport and George are discussing the same ideas with similar conceptual language, and in this respect there is common conceptual ground upon which their ideas rest.

George's methodology emphasizes that the nature of economics is as a positive science as opposed to a normative science, and he advises that in commencing to study economics (political economy) we should consider "the nature and scope of political economy."[30] This is a similar admonition to the one offered by John Neville Keynes in his classic consideration of the character of economic methodology, *The Scope and Method of Political Economy* (1890). In Friedman's equally classic article on "The Methodology of Positive Economics," Keynes is quoted with regard to the methodology issue, where he identifies a positive science as "a body of systematized knowledge concerning what is; a normative or regulative science" as a body of systematized knowledge concerning what ought to be, and an art as "a system of rules for the attainment of a given end."[31] These characterizations are quite similar to those offered by George with respect to the methodology issue.

American Journal of Economics and Sociology

> There is found among economic writers much dispute not only as to the
> proper method of political economy, but also as to whether it should be
> spoken of as a science or as an art. There are some who have styled it a
> science, and some who have styled it an art, and some who speak of it
> as both science and art. Others again make substantially the same divi-
> sion, into abstract or theoretical or speculative political economy, on the
> one side, and concrete or normative or regulative or applied political
> economy on the other side.[32]

George leaves no doubt about his views of the proper method of
political economy.

> Into this matter, however, it is hardly worth while for us to enter at any
> length, since the reasons for considering a proper political economy as a
> science rather than an art have already been given. It is only necessary
> to observe that where systematized knowledge may be distinguished, as
> it sometimes is, into two branches, science and art, the proper distinction
> between them is that the one relates to what we call laws of nature; the
> other to the manner in which we may avail ourselves to these natural laws
> to attain desired ends.

Thus, consistent with Keynes's admonition of 1890 and Freidman's
contemporary version of it, George advises us that the methodology
of economics involves the determination of laws that describe "what
is," that is, economics is a positive science. Davenport also sought to
rid economic theory of any dependence on ethical value judgments,
and the entire character of his major works is infused with the attempt
to make economics as value-free as possible. In this, George and
Davenport are alike, and their methodological approaches are consistent with the standard approach in the economic literature as represented by Keynes and Friedman.[33]

### A Normative, Not a Theoretical Critic of George

Herbert Joseph Davenport turns out not to be a theoretical critic of
Henry George at all. Contrary to George R. Geiger's claim with respect
to their different conceptions of capital, Davenport's Fisherian capital
theory is not necessarily antagonistic to George's more traditional,
produced-means-of-production concept. The two articles in which
Davenport does disagree with George are evidence of differing normative value judgments between them, not of opposing theoretical

structures. Their thoughts on opportunity costs and economic methodology reveal fundamental similarities. Geiger's error concerning their capital theories is relatively unimportant when taken in isolation from wider implications. The danger is that if it is permitted to stand uncorrected, it could lend unwarranted support to the mistaken impression that George's contribution is somehow outside the accepted boundaries of economic theory.

## Notes

1. Davenport's major ideas are presented in *The Economics of Enterprise* (New York: Macmillan, 1913), and *Value and Distribution* (Chicago: University of Chicago, 1908).

2. Philip Charles Newman, *The Development of Economic Thought* (New York: Prentice-Hall, 1952), and Joseph Dorfman, *The Economic Mind in American Civilization, 1865–1918* (New York: Viking Press, 1949).

3. George R. Geiger, *The Philosophy of Henry George* (New York: Macmillan, 1933), pp. 99–100.

4. Ibid., pp. 100–01.

5. A purely speculative explanation might be that Geiger, a philosopher and not an economist, did not regard his own assessments of economic theory as definitive, and he was not willing to commit himself to an unequivocal declaration that Davenport was a mainstream representative of economic theory. In fact, such a commitment was fully justified by Davenport's contributions. Another speculative explanation is that Geiger wanted to use Davenport's material as a straw-man basis for his own ideas.

6. Geiger, *Philosophy of Henry George*, p. 105 n.

7. Ibid., p. 157 n.

8. Herbert J. Davenport, "The Single Tax in the English Budget," *Quarterly Journal of Economics* 24 (1910): 6.

9. Geiger, *Philosophy of Henry George*, p. 100.

10. Jack Hirshleifer, "On the Theory of the Optimal Investment Decision," *Journal of Political Economy* (August 1958).

11. Irving Fisher, *The Theory of Interest* (New York: Macmillan, 1930), and *The Rate of Interest* (New York: Macmillan, 1907).

12. George J. Stigler, *The Theory of Price*, 3rd ed. (New York: Macmillan, 1966), p. 286.

13. Jack Hirshleifer, *Investment, Interest and Capital* (Englewood Cliffs, N.J.: Prentice-Hall, 1970), pp. v–vi.

14. Davenport, *Value and Distribution*, p. 242.

15. Ibid., p. 152.

16. Ibid., pp. 152–55.

17. Ibid., p. 148.

18. Stigler, *Theory of Price*, pp. 275–86.

19. Henry George, *Progress and Poverty*, 75th anniversary ed. (New York: Robert Schalkenbach Foundation, 1954), pp. 168–72.

20. Herbert J. Davenport, "The Single Tax in the English Budget"; and "Theoretical Issues in the Single Tax," *American Economic Review* 7 (1917). Davenport especially focused his policy criticism on ad valorem land taxation, which he viewed as destructive of individual investment incentives and as contrary to his conception of ethical justice.

21. Davenport, "Theoretical Issues in the Single Tax," p. 2.

22. Davenport, "The Single Tax in the English Budget," p. 279.

23. Ibid., p. 287.

24. George, *Progress and Poverty*, p. 365.

25. Edmund Whittaker, *A History of Economic Ideas* (New York: Longmans, 1940), p. 456.

26. Davenport, *Value and Distribution*, p. 273.

27. Davenport, *The Economics of Enterprise*, pp. 59–61.

28. George, *The Science of Political Economy* (1897; reprint ed. New York: Robert Schalkenbach Foundation, 1962), p. 86.

29. George, *Progress and Poverty*, pp. 210–11.

30. George, *The Science of Political Economy*, p. xxxviii.

31. John Neville Keynes, *The Scope and Method of Political Economy* (London: Macmillan, 1890), and Milton Friedman, *Essays in Positive Economics* (Chicago: University of Chicago, 1953).

32. George, *The Science of Political Economy*, p. 101.

33. See also *Progress and Poverty*, p. 13. This is not to deny that George believed that, from an ultimate perspective, "economic law and moral law are essentially one." Ibid., p. 560.

# 23
# Carver: Reluctant Demi-Georgist

## By ROBERT V. ANDELSON

In 1954, just prior to becoming a nonagenarian, Dr. Thomas Nixon Carver, who had retired from the Harvard faculty more than two decades before, began a new career as a weekly columnist for the *Los Angeles Times*. The vigorous and trenchant pieces that appeared under the by-line of this remarkable man until his death, seven years later, at the age of ninety-six, are well remembered by the present writer, who was then pursuing doctoral studies at the University of Southern California—coincidentally, Carver's alma mater.

Iowa-born, educated at U.S.C. and Cornell, Carver was the author of eighteen books (on sociology, social philosophy, and even religion, as well as on economics), including *Essays in Social Justice*, which contains a unique chapter, "The Single Tax." In 1915, when this work appeared, he was David A. Wells Professor of Political Economy at Harvard, and had just spent two years as a high official in the U.S. Department of Agriculture. The following year he served as president of the American Economic Association.

What makes the chapter unique is that in it Carver firmly endorses a large measure of land-value taxation for reasons of his own, while at the same time attacking, sometimes scathingly, many of the arguments advanced for its adoption by Henry George and his followers. Let it never be imagined that this crusty scholar was not an independent thinker!

### Nature and Morality

Carver was a Darwinian empiricist, who had no use for what he regarded as abstract metaphysical ideas of right and justice, and who defined morality as the facilitation of human adjustment to the material universe.[1] That social group the members of which best manifest such qualities as industry, frugality, enterprise, fortitude, and mutual helpfulness will be best adapted to the inexorable and universal laws

American Journal of Economics and Sociology, Vol. 63, No. 2 (April, 2004).

that govern the material universe, will be strong, and will survive in the inevitable competition with other groups:

> Instead of saying that nature is non-moral or that science is unable to discover the moral order of the universe, we should say that nature is the final authority on morality, and that our opinions, likes and dislikes, approvals and disapprovals, must be modified to suit that final authority. ... If we once perceive that morality is merely social hygiene, and that anything is moral which works well for society in the long run, which prolongs its life and enables it to grow and flourish and hold its own in competition with other societies, and beat out all those which are organized on immoral bases, we should think no more about questioning the moral order of the universe than we do now of questioning the hygienic order. We should then say frankly that whatever the order of the universe is, that, *per se*, is the moral order, likes and dislikes, approvals and disapprovals to the contrary notwithstanding. We should then say that whatever social customs and conventions are found to fit into the order of the universe, and whatever private conduct is found to permanently strengthen the social group, that is *per se* morality.[2]

Let it be immediately noted that this formulation exhibits the so-called Is-Ought Fallacy: one cannot get an *ought* solely out of an *is*, cannot derive a value judgment merely from a factual one. But this is an issue about which logicians are by no means in agreement, and, in any event, Carver would doubtless retort that if his formulation is deductively invalid, then so much the worse for the deductive method; he prefers to rest his case at the bar of induction.

Despite his stated antipathy for metaphysical abstraction, Carver sees no conflict between his Social Darwinism and "the highest form of religious thought which the world possesses today,"[3] asserting that "the laws of natural selection are identical with the laws of divine approval; and ... the process of exterminating the unfit or the unadapted is only a manifestation of divine disapproval." Behind the material universe is the divine energy and will, which not only created it but sustains and re-creates it continuously every moment. This belief is stated only in passing in the *Essays,* and is not the dominant theme even in Carver's slim volume *The Religion Worth Having,*[4] which seems to make utility in promoting human prosperity the ultimate criterion for religious value. Yet it may help to provide the answer to what would be otherwise a mysterious element in Carver's thought— the individual's motive for embracing the work ethic. Carver some-

times speaks as if the stern code of natural selection operates unde-
viatingly upon individuals, so that industrious and provident persons
automatically prosper and survive while the idle and profligate suffer
and are doomed. But, as Job protested, in this world such inevitabil-
ity of personal desert does not obtain. Although it may be that the
Puritan virtues make the possibility of individual prosperity and survival greater, still, as Carver recognizes, many a man has been so
circumstanced as to be able to enjoy a life of luxurious indolence
with no ill effect other than perhaps an occasional attack of gout.
Apart from a theological impetus, it is difficult to understand why
such a one would be moved to abandon his parasitic existence for
the strenuous "worldly asceticism" Carver would have him embrace
in order to make a productive contribution to his nation or race. True,
Carver endorses social arrangements that would remove, to a considerable extent, opportunities for luxurious indolence. Moreover,
he does not consider human nature wholly selfish. But he places
immense stress upon the cultivation of a kind of sacrificial patriotism
that, when not informed by powerful religious sentiment, one
normally observes only in wartime or other periods of extraordinary
national emergency.

Actually, it is this insistence upon rigorous personal sacrifice for the
sake of the well-being of the group that exculpates Carver's religion
(which invokes no promise of transcendental reward) from the charge
of low prudentialism. Nevertheless, although I do not wish to stray
any farther than necessary into theological excursis, there is an objection that I feel constrained to raise. Henry George's faith in God
revived when he came to believe that the grim doctrine of Malthus
described the results of human error and perversion, and was not
ingrained in the created natural order. For George, a Malthusian order
was not just, and only a just creator could be God. Carver did not
address himself specifically to this aspect of George's thought, but
had he done so there can be little doubt that he would have taken
him to task for presumptuously making his own subjective sentiments
the standard to which God must conform. This, he would have
insisted, is to worship man and his emotional predilections, not God.
But is not Carver's approach at least equally man-centered? To define
morality (and hence justice) as whatever facilitates the group's survival and prosperity, is to at least give the impression that human

survival and prosperity are the ultimate values. And to simply equate the will of God with that to which the social body must conform if it is to survive and prosper, is to make human survival and prosperity the final criteria of goodness, not goodness, that is, God, an end to be reverenced and cherished for its own sake.

Although it may seem as if we have come rather far afield before I even commence discussion of the topic of this chapter, the foregoing review of the broad framework of Carver's thought may help to illuminate the background and therefore some of the details of his critique of George.

For Carver, the state's most essential role in promoting social justice is to encourage and protect producers, and to restrain predators—to channel human conflict into competitive production, where success depends (to a much larger extent than in other forms of conflict) upon service rather than upon destruction or deception. Property rights are nothing more than a tool for the furtherance of this end, and their validity in each case depends upon whether in the long run, their recognition fosters or obstructs it.[5]

Carver divides wealth into three categories: "earnings," "stealings," and "findings." Under the last of these he places the site value of land (land rent). Since the only valid property rights are those that rest upon long-run social utility, whether or not it would be unjust for the community to confiscate rent becomes simply a question of whether or not it would be practically desirable for it to do so. In other words, does the social appropriation of rent foster socially useful production more effectively than does the individual appropriation of rent? Against the same criterion, the applicability of which Carver takes for granted, he measures all "findings," not merely land rent—and, for that matter, every form of wealth. But the social utility of earnings and the social disutility of stealings are sufficiently obvious to render unnecessary a lengthy justification of private property rights in one and not in the other.

### Productivity of Land

Before subjecting the question of rent to the pragmatic test specified above, Carver launches into two digressions somewhat hostile to George and his followers.

First, he proceeds to demolish the single taxers' supposed contention that land is not productive. He deduces this curious conclusion from their view that a site would have no economic value were it not for the community around it, assuming that this implies that the community is the sole producer.

> In the first place, this proves too much. All that is said respecting land could be said of any other factor of production. If it were not for the community round about, neither the buildings on the land nor the labor of the lawyer, the doctor, the merchant and the manufacturer would be of any great value. In the second place, if we begin at another link in the chain and follow the same method of reasoning, we could prove that land produces everything. If it were not for the land there would be no productivity, or any community either.[6]

Actually, of course, neither George nor any of his followers ever claimed that land is unproductive. Like all economists in the classical tradition, they viewed it as one of the two primary factors of production.[7] That it is productive only when conjoined with labor and (usually) capital, Carver himself would scarcely deny. As for its value, it is perfectly true that nothing would have value without the presence of a community to provide a market for it, but since the supply of land is inelastic, this leaves the community (with its public services, its aggregate improvements, its cultural, industrial, and commercial enterprises, and, above all, its demand) the only active factor in determining what land is worth. Therefore, there is some force to the Georgist argument that land value is a social product in a way that is not true of the value of other basic goods. In the quoted passage, it may be remarked, Carver appears to conflate value and productivity, two ideas that, although often related, are conceptually distinct.

After completing the supererogatory task of proving that land is a productive agent, Carver observes that "it does not follow by any means that the landowner is a productive agent"—which is all that George or any knowledgeable Georgist ever contended. Carver, however, goes on to say that just because the landowner, as such, is not a producer, one ought not to assume that he is necessarily a parasite. He fulfills, at least to some extent, a useful function, that of conserver of exhaustible resources. Carver concedes that landowners may be receiving more in the way of rent than they deserve for this, but he feels that under an unmodified single tax the function might not be performed at all, for the nominal owner would be a virtual tenant to the public. Having no interest in the future increase or decrease of the value of his land, his inclination would be to rapidly exploit the land's productive powers to the point of exhaustion and then move on. To prevent this the state would be obliged to institute controls, involving close and detailed regulation and inspection by an army of paid officials.

> Possibly a refined form of the single tax could be devised which would tax only site value and not soil or anything else which could possibly be exhausted or destroyed. In that case the public would be the virtual owner of the site alone, and the private owner would be the real as well as the nominal owner of everything else, including the soil. He would then have the same motive as now for conserving the value of everything which might be exhausted and which therefore needs conserving, leaving to the state the virtual ownership of the site, the only thing which cannot be exhausted and therefore needs no conservation.[8]

The specter of reckless exploitation had earlier been raised by Francis Amasa Walker. In the chapter on General Walker in the present volume, Professor Cord points out that absentee farm ownership, an important contributory cause of soil depletion, would tend to disappear under land-value taxation. Further, since land would be assessed and taxed according to its optimum use as determined by the market, and optimum use for farmland reflects the application of fertilizer, it would scarcely be economically feasible, says Cord, for the farmer to fail to keep his soil enriched. As for mineral resources, their depletion could be discouraged by combining a severance tax with the land-value tax, the total not to exceed the site's economic rent.

### Pioneering and Landownership

Carver's second hostile digression invidiously compares the single taxer with the hardy, enterprising pioneer: "They who desire land know where they can get it; what the aggressive single taxer wants is not *land*, but a share in the value of the land which somebody else has. . . . Moreover, it must be said, this modern movement is promoted, not by appealing to the pioneering, colonizing spirit of a sturdy, conquering race, but too often by appealing to jealousy, covetousness, and other of the less commendable motives which actuate mankind."[9] Be this as it may, since it would eliminate speculative withholding, the Georgist proposal *would* make land more readily available to those who actually wished to use it, not just to share in its value. If Carver momentarily ignores this, his next remark could not fail to delight the most rabid partisan of George, for he comments that since urban landowners find it profitable to encourage metropolitan congestion, no sympathy need be wasted on them if the masses who flock to cities should vote to confiscate land rent. The landowners will have simply paid the penalty for gambling with economic and political forces.

Carver, however, believes that such matters should be decided, not by sentiment but by constructive statesmanship, and that, from this point of view, the issue to be considered is whether priority of occupation constitutes a sufficient ground upon which to base a legal right to land and its rent, and if so, what limitations might be reasonably placed upon that right.[10]

In clearing the way for such consideration, Carver quickly dismisses "metaphysical" doctrines of human rights in general, and of property rights in particular, instancing Locke's labor theory of ownership (upon which George relied) as an example of the latter. Its major premise asserts that a man has a right to himself; its minor premise, that when he has worked upon a thing, he has put a part of himself into it; and its conclusion, that therefore he has a right to that upon which he has worked. In Carver's judgment the minor premise is "absurd and meaningless, and that is enough to spoil the argument."[11] He asked rhetorically: "If, after he has parted with the thing he has as much of himself left as he had before, can he be said to have put a part of himself into it?"[12] To which the rejoinder might be made that he can indeed, although it may have been his *past* rather than his present self. He has lost the time and effort that he would probably have expended differently were it not for the anticipation of owning the thing. Besides, he may have impaired his health or vital powers in producing the thing, in which case he has literally diminished his present self.

Long-run utility, it will be recalled, is Carver's touchstone: "Is it useful in the long run, i.e., does it work well, to allow the first occupant of a piece of land some rights in it which we deny to those who come later and want a part of it or its value? Of two communities otherwise equally favored, one of which recognizes this right while the other does not, which is likely to become the more comfortable, prosperous, and powerful?"[13]

Since he largely equates nation-building with pioneering, with subduing and cultivating new lands, and expanding productivity, Carver holds that constructive statesmanship must address itself to the question of how pioneering is affected by the present system, on the one hand, and how it would be affected by the Georgist proposal, on the other. The desire to get the future "unearned increment" of land is doubtless one stimulus to pioneering in the sense of opening and settling new territories, but the opportunity for such activity had ceased to be very significant when Carver's book appeared, giving his concern a somewhat anachronistic flavor. Intellectual and spiritual pioneering may also take place (and a strong case can be made for the proposition that they are more likely to take place) in metropolitan areas. Carver implies that a sharing in "the enormously inflated value of land in overcrowded urban centers" would induce the landless to remain in them instead of spreading out to where land is cheaper and more abundant, evidently forgetting that such sharing would tend to reduce the inflated value by taking the profit out of speculation.

Under frontier conditions, observes Carver, the distinction, so crucial to George's position, between property in land and property in other things, seems nugatory:

> If one settler saw a tree which seemed to contain certain possibilities, and chopped it down and made it into a table, it would be in accordance with social utility that the table should be his. If another settler saw a piece of land which seemed to contain certain possibilities, and cleared it and ploughed it and reduced it to cultivation, on the same reasoning the land would be his. Each settler would have found a free gift of nature, each would have worked upon it, each would have changed its form from the raw state in which he found it to a form which would suit his purpose. The mere fact that the result of one's labor happened to be a farm, and that of the other's a table, would not have appeared at the time to be a

real difference. This aspect of the case is recommended to the consideration of those who believe that the private ownership of land is forbidden by a moral law ordained from the foundation of the world. . . .

In view of all these considerations it will be difficult for any reasonable man to lash himself into a state of moral indignation against the private ownership of land. If a pioneer settler were brought face to face with a certain type of radical single taxer who makes a moral issue of the ownership of land values, and makes free use of certain formulae, such as the equal right of all to access to God's earth, the moral indignation would not be all on the side of the single taxer.[14]

This sardonic passage (which well illustrates its author's unadorned but effective literary style) contains at least one misleading implication, for not even the "radical single taxer who makes a moral issue of the ownership of land values" really objects to private ownership of land where land is so abundant that it has no value in its raw state. The Georgist stress upon the right to private ownership of labor products justifies security of improvements. It is only where land becomes so scarce that it acquires a value independent of its improvements that the moral objection to private ownership arising from first occupancy comes into play, and this objection is focused upon private retention of that value rather than of the land itself.

Curiously, Carver then develops his argument in such a manner as to arrive at much the same place as the single taxer, although, of course, basing his conclusions upon long-run social utility, and eschewing moralistic formulae of the type that serves as target for his irony. However, it should not be overlooked that his understanding of social utility is, in its way, itself profoundly moralistic: "Justice is mercy writ large. It is benevolence with a long look ahead, a look which takes in the most distant generations of the future and places them on an exact equality with the present generations; which has as much regard for an as yet voiceless individual to be born a thousand years hence as for any individual now alive and clamoring for his rights."[15] It is in the light of this that one should consider his account of what occurs when frontier conditions cease to exist:

A real difference between the table and the land would begin to appear. In the first place, it would be found that the owners of the land held control of the original raw material for the manufacture of tables and all other produced goods. When the maker of the first table [or his descendants] wished to make a new one to replace the old one when it was worn out, he would have to pay the landowner for the privilege of cutting a tree from which to make it. In the second place, the value of the land would increase in proportion to the number of persons wishing to make use of its products either for purposes of consumption or for the purpose of producing other goods. The fortunate owners of the limited supply of land would find themselves in possession of a growing income far in excess of anything which the land might have cost them [or their ancestors], whereas the owners of the tables and other goods would find themselves always compelled to expend approximately as much in the making of them as they were worth. As time goes on this difference increases, especially in a growing city, while the value of tables continues to bear a fairly close relation to their cost of production.[16]

Since pioneer conditions no longer obtain in established communities, the problem of landownership, said Carver, really becomes largely a problem of inheritance, and the issue to be resolved is whether or not there are any modifications of the right of inheritance that may logically be expected to improve social and economic conditions, stimulate the productive energies of the population, or lead to such a distribution of wealth as would foster the virtues of hard work, frugality, and useful investment.

### A Reluctant Demi-Georgist

On these grounds, the land-value tax (which falls to a considerable extent upon inherited property) has much to commend it in Carver's eyes. He specifies three distinct advantages that would result to modern society through an increase in the taxation of land values. (1) Such an increase would discourage the holding of valuable land out of use for speculative purposes. By thus bringing land into best use, it would stimulate the demand for labor and capital, augmenting the returns for working and productive saving. (2) Taxation on active industry would be reduced in proportion as the burden is placed on the site value of land. This would invariably encourage business and industry, since people would not be penalized for production or improvements, and there would be no incentive to hold a site vacant or to put it to some use below its optimum. All this would make goods more abundant for everyone in the community. (3) It would tend to eliminate the waste of the labor power of those who live upon the unearned increment of land, devoting themselves to idle self-indulgence, to what Carver caustically refers to as "the ornamental professions," or to the dissipation of their investing talent in land speculation, which is not only sterile but actually detrimental to the creation of national wealth. Because Carver believed that, "generally speaking, the leisure class is made up of the most capable members of the community,"[17] he heavily underscored the importance of diverting its ability (as well as its material assets) into productive channels. This argument for land-value taxation, which he considered probably the most important of the three, was wholly novel; even George himself does not seem to have hit upon it—perhaps because he had a less favorable impression than did our Ivy League professor of the capabilities of the leisure class.

Because of the reasons just cited, and in spite of the reservations and objections he had raised earlier in his essay, Carver concluded that a considerable extension of land-value taxation "would work well for the nation."[18]

The reader will recall that Carver had insisted upon the distinction, so strongly emphasized by George, between land and goods produced by labor, although he held that its effects do not emerge until an area is settled, and that on no account is it in any case a moral issue. He admitted that land (in the nontechnical meaning of the term) is sometimes "made" in the sense of being reclaimed from the sea or desert, whereas there are some produced goods, such as antiques and rare works of art, that resemble land (as defined in classical economics) in that their supply cannot be increased in response to market forces. But these exceptions he regarded as of little consequence. The fact that whereas nonreproducible land is the rule and reproducible land the exception, and reproducible goods of other kinds the rule and nonreproducible ones the exceptions, may be called a difference of degree only, but it is a difference of degree so great as to constitute for scientific and practical purposes a difference of kind: "As a matter of fact, nearly all scientific differences are differences of degree. It is not denied, however, that there are many resemblances between land and other goods. There are also certain resemblances between a man and a clothes-pin, but the differences are sufficiently important to warrant our placing them in different classes."[19]

The above discussion, as well as part of that to which I previously alluded on the same topic, is reproduced in Carver's *Essays* from his *Distribution of Wealth*, published eleven years earlier. This earlier work also contains an argument against the contention that though geographic land (land surface) may not be materially increased by labor, economic land (land capital) may. His treatment of this point is quoted in the chapter on Richard T. Ely in this book.

The last chapter of Carver's *Essays*, "The Distribution of Taxation," sets forth in addition two rather standard arguments for land-value taxation as a permanent levy. The first is that a tax on land values cannot be shifted, since it neither lowers supply nor raises demand. The second is that such a tax tends to be capitalized, and, hence, if it lasts over a long enough period, becomes burdenless. "It is paid once and for all when the tax is taken out of the capitalized value of the thing taxed."[20]

Of course, neither Carver's espousal of these two arguments, his defense of the key distinction between land and other goods, nor his outright advocacy of a very sizable degree of land-value taxation makes him a single taxer—as he is by no means hesitant to point out.[21] For he also recommends a stiff tax upon inherited wealth, regardless of its source or nature, and, moreover, somewhat less emphatically, a moderately progressive income tax.[22] He further maintains that a tax that is easily shifted and thus diffuses itself throughout the community (such as a sales tax), is the most suitable means of raising temporary emergency revenues, which must be gathered without "too nice a regard for absolute justice."[23]

Yet he urges that among permanent taxes preference should be given to those that fall upon natural rather than upon produced goods, and upon increments that come to individuals through natural causes over which they have no control rather than upon incomes earned by the individuals themselves.[24] A land-value tax, be it noted, is the only tax that uniformly satisfies *both* of these criteria. Thus Carver may at least be ranged alongside the single taxers in the order of his priorities.

It would probably be correct to say that Carver's aversion to Georgism had more to do with style than with substance, with presentation than with program. In spite of his extreme distaste for reasoning that he considered "metaphysical," "sentimental," or "demagogic," in the end his sturdy intellectual honesty compelled him to acknowledge, albeit with some reluctance, the merits of essential aspects of what George proposed.

### Notes

1. Thomas Nixon Carver, *Essays in Social Justice* (Cambridge, Mass.: Harvard University Press, 1915), p. 24.
2. Ibid., p. 25.
3. Ibid., p. 26.
4. Thomas Nixon Carver, *The Religion Worth Having* (Boston: Houghton, 1912).
5. Carver, *Essays*, p. 93.
6. Ibid., pp. 283 f.
7. See Henry George, *Progress and Poverty*, 75th anniversary ed. (New York: Robert Schalkenbach Foundation, 1954), pp. 38 f.
8. Carver, *Essays*, p. 287.
9. Ibid., p. 289.
10. Ibid., p. 290.
11. Ibid., p. 291.
12. Ibid.
13. Ibid., p. 292.
14. Ibid., pp. 295 f. The first part of the extract is excerpted by Carver from his *Distribution of Wealth* (New York: Macmillan, 1904), pp. 108 f.
15. Carver, *Essays*, p. 292.
16. Ibid., pp. 295 f.
17. Ibid., p. 300.
18. Ibid., p. 303.
19. Ibid., p. 296.
20. Ibid., p. 410.
21. Ibid., p. 303.
22. Ibid., chap. 12 and p. 408.
23. Ibid., pp. 409 f., 429.
24. Ibid., p. 429.

# 24
# Ryan and His Domestication of Natural Law*

By Robert V. Andelson

Monsignor John A. Ryan (1869–1945), whom James Hastings Nichols speaks of as the chief theorist of social Catholicism in America,[1] devoted the bulk of three chapters in his great work, *Distributive Justice*, to a critique of Henry George's so-called single-tax doctrine.[2] Although Ryan, as a young man growing up amid agrarian ferment in rural Minnesota, was, if we are to give credence to Eric Goldman,[3] "electrified" by George's masterpiece, *Progress and Poverty*, his mature evaluation of George reveals no trace of this early enthusiasm.

George's system falls within the natural law tradition, and rests upon the Lockean premise that private property is ultimately justified by the right of the individual to his own person and to his labor as an extension thereof. Since land is not created by human effort but represents a fund of opportunity intended by God for the use of all, this argument for private ownership cannot apply to it. No one may justly arrogate to himself the goods of nature without fully indemnifying those who are thereby deprived of an equal chance to use them. Economic rent constitutes an exact measure of the disadvantage sustained by those who are denied the opportunity to use a given site because of its preemption by the titleholder; therefore, it should be appropriated by the community as an indemnity to it, and applied to public services that would otherwise have to be paid for largely by a levy on the income from its labor.

George characterized this as "the taking by the community for the use of the community of that value which is the creation of the community,"[4] for he contended that rent is essentially a social product—the result of the presence of population, public demand, government services, and the aggregate activity of all the individuals in a given area, not of anything the owner, as such, may do to a particular site.

*This chapter was originally published in *The America Journal of Economics and Sociology* 33, no. 3 (July 1974): 273–86 under the title, "Msgr. John A. Ryan's Critique of Henry George."

American Journal of Economics and Sociology, Vol. 63, No. 2 (April, 2004).
© 2004 American Journal of Economics and Sociology, Inc.

He advocated that a tax (or more precisely, a public fee) approaching 100 percent of the annual unimproved value of land be collected by the government, and that all other taxes be abolished.[5]

### First Occupancy as a Basis for Land Rights

Ryan begins his analysis by addressing himself to George's attack upon the idea that first occupancy establishes a valid original title to landownership.

> Priority of occupation [says George] gives exclusive and perpetual title to the surface of a globe in which, in the order of nature, countless generations succeed each other! . . . Has the first comer at a banquet the right to turn back all the chairs, and claim that none of the other guests shall partake of the food provided, except as they make terms with him? Does the first man who presents a ticket at the door of a theater, and passes in, acquire by his priority the right to shut the doors and have the performance go on for him alone? . . . And to this manifest absurdity does the recognition of the individual right to land come when carried to its ultimate that any human being, could he concentrate in himself the individual rights to the land of any country, could expel therefrom all the rest of the inhabitants; and could he thus concentrate the individual rights to the whole surface of the globe, he alone of all the teeming population of the earth would have the right to live.[6]

Ryan seeks to destroy this argument by saying that George attributes to the title created by first occupancy qualities that it does not possess and consequences for which it is not responsible. He claims that the correct interpretation of this title does not attribute to it, as George imagined, an unlimited right of ownership either extensively or intensively.

> There seems to be no good reason to think that the first occupant is justified in claiming as his own more land than he can cultivate by his own labor, or with the assistance of those who prefer to be his employees or his tenants rather than independent proprietors. . . . Though a man should have become the rightful owner of all the land in the neighborhood, he would have no moral right to exclude therefrom those persons who could not without extreme inconvenience find a living elsewhere. He would be morally bound to let them cultivate it at a fair rental.[7]

But is there any limit to the amount of land a man can cultivate with the assistance of tenants and employees, assuming a sufficient number? The King Ranch in Texas, the latifundia of Brazil, the estates of the Duchess of Alba—none of these would be proscribed under this rubric. Neither, in principle, would the ownership of an entire continent. So much for Ryan's "extensive" limitations. As for the "intensive" ones, we need only ask the question: What constitutes a "fair rental"? If determined by the market, in the case he gives (one in which one man owned all the land in the neighborhood) a fair rental would be so high as to reduce the tenants to the level of bare subsistence. Ryan would doubtless reject this criterion, and say that a fair rental should be determined primarily by the tenants' capacities and needs, and secondarily by the owner's right to a return on his investment. But here we enter into the realm of subjective valuations, which admit of no impartial formula for their quantification or reconciliation.

In any case, says Ryan, George overestimates the historical importance of first occupancy. Most abuses of private landownership have arisen, not from the appropriation of land that nobody owned, but from "the forcible and fraudulent seizure of land which had already been occupied."[8] Nothing could be more ludicrous than to imply that George was unaware of this. "Is it not all but universally true," he asked in his *Open Letter to Pope Leo XIII*, "that existing land titles . . . come . . . from force or fraud?"[9] But landowners do not ordinarily appeal to force or fraud to justify their titles! As Ryan himself tells us, "The prevailing view among the defenders of private landownership has always been that the original title is . . . first occupancy."[10] That, therefore, is the contention that George was at pains to refute.

Ryan is not satisfied with having shattered, as he supposes, George's argument against first occupancy; he goes on to try to show that the logic of George's own position itself leads to the conclusion that first occupancy creates the original title of ownership. His reasoning on this point is subtle and ingenious but also highly artificial and legalistic. Because, in George's theory, the individual producer, Ryan says, must agree to pay rent to the community before he can begin to produce, "his right to the use of natural opportunities is not 'free,' nor can his labor alone constitute a title to that part of them that he utilizes in production."[11] Consequently, labor does not create a right to the concrete product, but merely to the value that the producer adds to the raw material. His right to the raw material itself originates in the contract by which he is authorized to utilize it in return for rent paid to the community. So his right to the product does not spring from labor alone, but from labor plus compensation to the community. "Since the contract by which the prospective user agrees to pay this compensation or rent must precede his application of labor, it instead of labor is the original title [Ryan asserts]. Since the contract is made with a particular community for the use of a particular piece of land, the title that it conveys must derive ultimately from the occupation of that land by that community—or some previous community of which the present one is the legal heir."[12]

Now, as a matter of fact, it is not the temporal priority of the community to the individual that, in George's system, gives it the right to collect rent from him. If the individual were there before the community, that right would still obtain. It rests, rather, indirectly upon the title of labor. Only insofar as rent is publicly appropriated (or land nationalized, which George does not recommend) can the equal right of all men to the produce of their labor be assured, for otherwise a portion of that produce must be paid in tribute to the landowner.

Ryan notes that George argues against private landownership in the full sense of the term on the basis that it shuts out nonlandowners from access to the "reservoirs" of natural opportunity. He claims that in so doing, George has completely abandoned the principle that underlies the labor argument. "Instead of trying to show from the nature of the situation that there is a logical difference between the two kinds of ownership, he shifts his ground to a consideration of consequences. He makes the title of social utility instead of the title of labor the distinguishing and decisive consideration."[13] Actually, the passage in question does not represent an abandonment of the labor argument or its underlying principle; it is an indirect deduction *from* the labor argument. And justice, not social utility, is the ruling consideration (although George believes that whatever is just will always, in the long run, also be socially useful). The private appropriation of land and rent removes access to natural opportunity except upon such terms as the landowner may set, and therefore encroaches upon the title of labor—upon the equal right of every man to reap the harvest of his industry.

If the community had instituted the social appropriation of land values from the beginning, Ryan admits, it could have rightfully done so by virtue of priority of occupation. But "when it failed to take advantage of its opportunity to be the first occupant of these values, when it permitted the individual proprietor to appropriate them, it forfeited its own claim. Ever since, it has had no more right to already existing land values . . . than one person has to recover a gift or donation that he has unconditionally bestowed upon another."[14]

George would quarrel with this analogy, for he holds that, by virtue of its nature, land cannot be rightfully subject to ownership in fee simple. No more than private individuals has any community ever had a right to "own" land in the sense in which labor products may be owned; full ownership includes the right to alienate, and the estate of the community is inalienable. Thus no community ever had a right to grant to private parties absolute title to something created for the use and benefit of all—a concept dimly and imperfectly reflected in the principle of eminent domain.

But what of present owners who hold deeds to land innocently bought with the proceeds of honest labor on the assumption that both the land and its rent would be theirs in perpetuity? Here, according to the Georgist view, the land is comparable to a stolen watch that some unsuspecting person has purchased in good faith. Those who are deprived of their proper shares of land benefits have the same right to recover them from the existing owners that the watch owner has to recover his property from the innocent purchaser. To the objection that the laws of many countries would permit the innocent purchaser of the watch to retain it as long as enough time had elapsed to create a "title" of prescription, the Georgist would reply that the passage of time cannot turn a wrong into a right, and that furthermore the natural heritage of the race is both inalienable and too basic to human welfare to fall under the title of prescription. The argument based upon prescription was anticipated by George when he wrote: "Because I was robbed yesterday, and the day before, and the day before that, is it any reason that I should suffer myself to be robbed today and tomorrow? Any reason that I should conclude that the robber has acquired a vested right to rob me?"[15]

Ryan objects that the present private owners of land differ from the innocent purchaser of the stolen watch in that they have never been warned by society that the land might have been virtually stolen, or that the rightful claimants might some day be empowered by law to recover possession. This line of reasoning, if applied generally, would preclude any kind of legislation that might cause losses to some vested interest. Think, for example, of all the innocent investors who were never "warned by society" that strip mining or industrial pollution, the employment of child labor or the combination in restraint of trade, the indiscriminate sale of narcotics or the production of noxious foodstuffs might be prohibited by law!

### Practical Justice in Land Rights

As a general and abstract proposition, Ryan recognizes the equal right of all men to the use of nature, and he concedes that "private ownership of land can never bring about ideal justice in distribution" of natural opportunities.[16] But he claims that the institution is "not necessarily out of harmony with the demands of *practical* justice," because a community may lack the knowledge or the power to establish the ideal system. This observation is not so much faulty as irrelevant. Who would deny that practical justice is represented by whatever *situationally possible* course of action most closely approximates the ideal? As applied to the land question, all Ryan's point amounts to when analyzed is the truism that private landownership is just, as long as there is no possibility of replacing it with anything more just.

But, says Ryan, suppose that the Georgist system were instituted, and the rent of land appropriated by the community. This, he claims, would work an *injustice* on existing landowners, who, if not compensated, would be "deprived, in varying amounts, of the conditions of material well-being to which they have become accustomed, and . . . thereby subjected to varying degrees of positive inconvenience and hardship."[17] It does not seem to occur to Ryan that the same argument could be used to oppose the abolition of protective tariffs, to which he was himself committed.[18]

Actually, of course, few if any Georgists advocate the immediate appropriation of all rent, but rather the gradual implementation of the system in such a way as to militate against the likelihood of severe

individual hardship. In his entire discussion, furthermore, Ryan virtually ignores the fact that under George's system the increase of the
tax on land values would be accompanied by a corresponding
decrease in other taxes, particularly in taxes on improvements. Hence
any landowner who made efficient use of his land would actually
benefit from the reform. In the state of South Australia, three-fifths of
the landowners in a locality must approve any change from the old
taxing system to land-value taxation; the law permits reversion to the
old system if voted by a bare majority. Yet more and more localities
have been switching to land-value taxation for a long time, and (as
of this writing) not one reversion poll has been successful.[19] Similar
instances could be adduced from the experience of New Zealand and
other places to show that, inasmuch as most landowners are also land
*users*, the majority find themselves better off wherever an approach
to George's system has been made.[20]

Ryan warns that the social consequences of the confiscation of rent
would be "even more injurious than those falling upon the individuals despoiled."[21] The opposition of the landowners would threaten
social peace and order, while the popular respect for all property
rights would be greatly weakened if not destroyed, since the average
man would not grasp George's distinction between land and other
kinds of property in this connection. "Indeed," Ryan writes, "the proposal to confiscate rent is so abhorrent to the moral sense of the
average man that it could never take place except in conditions of
revolution and anarchy. If that day should ever arrive, the policy of
confiscation would not stop with land."

It is simply not true that the confiscation of rent could never take
place except in conditions of revolution and anarchy. Even when
Ryan wrote, a substantial percentage of rent was being confiscated in
Australia, New Zealand, and elsewhere under quite stable and orderly
conditions. As for the United States, there is no reason why a nation
that has come to take the federal income tax for granted could not
be educated to accept the confiscation of rent, which is, after all,
*unearned* income.

After conjuring forth the injury to which George's proposal would
presumably subject the landowner, Ryan goes on to state that,
conversely,

the persons who own no land under the present system . . . suffer no such degree of hardship when they are continued in that condition. They are kept out of something which they have never possessed, which they have never hoped to get by any such easy method, and from which they have not been accustomed to derive any benefit. . . . Evidently, their welfare and claims in the circumstances are not of the same moral importance as the welfare and claims of persons who would be called upon to suffer the loss of goods already possessed and enjoyed, and acquired with the full sanction of society.[22]

Elsewhere in his book Ryan contends that an employer has a moral obligation to pay his workmen "a living wage" (by which he means not merely a subsistence wage but one that would enable a man to support a good-sized family in modest comfort), and his various writings make it clear that he would have this obligation enforced by the state.[23] He qualifies this obligation by saying that it is not incumbent upon the employer who would be thereby driven out of business, or reduced to a standard of living little higher than that of his workmen. But no employer has a right to "indulge in anything like luxurious expenditure, so long as any of the employees fail to receive living wages."[24]

But suppose (as one may well do) that the employer had become used, with the full sanction of society, to a standard of living characterized by luxurious expenditure. And suppose (as one might well have supposed at the time the book was written) that the workmen were unaccustomed to what Ryan calls "a living wage." The relationship between employer and workman then becomes analogous to that between landowner and landless man, and in order to be consistent Ryan would be forced to say that, if obliged to pay a living wage, the employer would be deprived of conditions of material well-being to which he has become accustomed, and thus unjustly subjected to positive inconvenience and hardship, whereas, if he were not so obliged, the workers would suffer no such degree of hardship since they would merely be continued in their previous condition, and hence that the welfare and claims of the latter are not of the same moral importance as those of the former.

The decisive place the issue of compensation occupies in Ryan's thinking is suggested by the fact that while he condemns the confis-

cation of even future increments of land value as morally unjust
without compensation,[25] he indicates that if landowners were compensated "with a sum equal to the present value, or the capitalized
rent, of their land," the Georgist plan would be only *probably* inferior to the present system.[26] He maintains that "the moral sense of
mankind recognizes that it is in accordance with equity to compensate slave owners when the slaves are legally emancipated. Infinitely
stronger is the claim of the landowner to compensation."[27] The first
half of this statement is a mere assertion, and the second, debatable
for reasons that space limitations compel me to omit. But even if both
were to be accepted, Cord observes that gradual imposition of full
land-value taxation over a period of forty years is exactly equivalent
to immediate compensation without interest. If 3 percent interest
were given on the unpaid balance, then sixty-four years would be
necessary.[28]

### Rent as a Social Product

Ryan rejects the Georgist argument that rent should be appropriated
by society because it is socially produced. He remarks, to begin with,
that *all* land value is not socially produced; although no land can
have value without being brought into relation with society, neither
can it have value if it possesses no natural qualities suitable for the
satisfaction of human wants.[29] George would not, of course, have
denied this, but would have insisted that that portion of the value
attributable to natural qualities is, like the land itself, an inalienable
patrimony of the whole community, not properly subject to private
usurpation.

But Ryan would not allow to society any right even to that portion
of rent that he admits that it produces. He refuses to accept the proposition that the socially produced value of land ought to go to the
social producer rather than to the individual proprietor, except in the
case of future increments, and then only if the proprietor were indem-
nified for the loss of anticipated speculative increase reflected in his
purchase price. He points out that "men do not admit that all production of value constitutes a title of ownership. Neither the monopolist who increases value by restricting supply, nor the pacemakers

of fashion who increase value by merely increasing demand, are regarded as possessing a moral right to the value that they have 'created.' "[30] The ultimate basis of the producer's right to his produce, or to its value, is the fact that this is the only way in which he can get his just share of the earth's goods, and of the means of life and personal development. His right does not rest upon the mere fact of value production.

"Why," Ryan asks, "has the shoemaker a right to the value that he adds to the raw material in making a pair of shoes?" It is

> because men want to use his products, and because they have no right to require him to serve them without compensation. He is morally and juridically their equal, and has the same right as they to access on reasonable terms to the earth and the earth's possibilities of a livelihood. . . . To assume that he is obliged to produce socially useful things without remuneration is to assume that his life and personality and personal development are of no intrinsic importance, and that his pursuit of the essential ends of life has no meaning except in so far as may be conducive to his function as an instrument of production. . . .
>
> As a producer of land values, the community is not on the same moral ground as the shoemaker. Its productive action is indirect and extrinsic, instead of direct and intrinsic, and is merely incidental to its principal activities and purposes. . . . The activities of which land values are a resultant have already been remunerated in the price paid to the wage-earner for his labor, the physician for his services, the manufacturer and the merchant for their wares, and the municipal corporation in the form of taxes. On what ground can the community, or any part of it, set up a claim in strict justice to the increased land values?[31]

This last paragraph contains some truly astonishing assertions. The "activities of which land values are the resultant" have *not* already been remunerated, at least not in full, for a large part of what would otherwise be remuneration has had to go to landowners in the form of rent—landowners who, as such, contributed nothing positive to the production of those values. Only where rent has not yet arisen can the activities that lead to the production of future rent be said to have already been fully compensated, and physicians, manufacturers, and municipal corporations are seldom found in places where land has, as yet, acquired no value whatsoever.

Let it be granted that the community does not produce land values in the same direct and intrinsic sense in which the shoemaker produces the value that he adds to the leather. Does the landowner? The only value that the landowner, as landowner, produces is speculative value stemming from monopolistic scarcity, which Ryan specifically admits creates no moral title.[32] And the appropriation of land value by the landowner prevents both the community in its corporate capacity and its members in their individual capacities from enjoying the full benefits of the values that they do directly and intrinsically produce. It is they who are being compelled to serve the landowner without compensation, to divert to him by way of tribute a portion of their rightful recompense.

### Natural Right and Social Utility

We have seen that, according to Ryan, the community has no right either to land or to rent. The private owner, however, has a right to both. Ryan goes as far as to call it a *natural right*, but he uses the term in a sense different from that in which it is commonly understood.

He claims that it is a natural right because it is indirectly necessary for the welfare of the individual. By "indirectly necessary," he says he means necessary as a social institution rather than as something immediately connected with individual needs as such. Something is regarded as "necessary as a social institution" if, although neither an intrinsic good nor an indispensable means to the satisfaction of vital individual needs, it is capable of promoting the welfare of the average person or the majority of persons to a greater degree than any alternative.[33]

Thus, in the last analysis, Ryan, the spokesman of natural law and scathing nemesis of utilitarianism, rests his defense of private property in land upon what he considers to be its superior social utility as an institution. This judgment of superior social utility he derives, first, from certain pragmatic objections to the alternatives, socialism and Georgism, and second, from a view of private ownership in terms of its ideal potentialities.

I shall not review here Ryan's objections to socialism (objections with which I happen to concur) because they are not germane to the topic of this study. His pragmatic objections to Georgism are preceded by the acknowledgment of several important benefits to which the system would lead:

> Since no man would find it profitable to retain control of more land than he could use himself, the number of actual land users would be increased. The land speculator would disappear, together with the opportunity of making and losing fortunes by gambling on the changes in land values. Owing to the removal of taxation from the necessaries of life and from industry, consumers would get goods cheaper, and some stimulus would be given to production and employment. Those monopolies which derive their strength from land would become weaker and tend to disappear.[34]

These benefits, however, would be counterbalanced, in his opinion, by the following fancied disadvantages:

1. *Many holdings would deteriorate because of those who would exhaust the land through careless or rapacious exploitation.* This has not occurred in practice. In fact, the Georgist system creates an incentive to *increase* fertility, since the tax would not reflect the value of improvement but only of land in its virgin state, and of location. Increased fertility through more careful cultivation has been the rule in Denmark, Australia, the California irrigation districts, and wherever an approach to Georgism has been instituted.

2. *The administrative machinery would inevitably involve a vast amount of error, inequality, favoritism, and corruption, for the land tax would be on the full amount of the annual rent instead of on a fraction, as at present.* This is absurd. There is no reason why, if all the rent were taxed, there should be proportionately any more error or corruption than when a fraction of it is taxed; in fact, there should be less, since public scrutiny would be keener. Furthermore, since land cannot be hidden, chances for error, favoritism, corruption, and the like are less than with other sources of tax revenue, and under George's system only land would be taxed. Virtually all current and most past authorities concede that a single tax on land would be uniquely free of these very ills. When one imagines the reduction in corruption that would accompany the abolition of the income tax, Ryan's objection becomes doubly curious!

3. *Cultivators would not have the inducement to make improvements that arises from the hope of selling both improvements and land at a profit, owing to the increased demand for land.* It is true that

under a Georgist system improvements would not be made with an eye to speculative profits from land sales, but they would be made with the expectation of profit from the improvements themselves, and their making would be stimulated by the fact that it would not be penalized, as now, by a tax increase.

4. *The reform would lead to instability of tenure because, owing to misfortunes of various kinds (such as one or two poor crops), many landholders would be temporarily unable to pay the full amount of the rent and would lose their titles.* The tax is supposed to reflect current market value, determined by frequent reappraisal. Poor crops would reduce the value of land, and hence the tax. Granted, marginal and less efficient producers might tend to be forced out (although their being taxed the full economic rent would be mitigated by the absence of other taxes, and the lower cost of commodities), but they would have a much better chance than at present of resuming their operations elsewhere because of cheaper land prices.

When we turn to Ryan's view of the ideal potentialities of private ownership, we come to an odd paradox. We find that he is not really interested in defending landownership as it has existed historically, but only "in its essential elements, and with its capacity for modification and improvement."[35] He admits that "we should be tempted to declare that the most extreme form of Agrarian Socialism could scarcely have been more productive of individual and social injury" than private landownership as it obtained in certain empirical instances. And the model he constructs in chapter 7 for a modified and improved system has little in common with the institution as we now know it.

The chapter is entitled "Methods of Reforming Our Land System." By the time Ryan gets through reforming the system, he has moved about halfway down the Georgist road. He would prohibit the alienation of lands now publicly held, insisting that they be leased instead of sold. He would have future increases in the value of land socially appropriated (with owners compensated for positive losses of interest and principal). He would gradually transfer the taxes on improvements and personal property to land. And he would impose progressive supertaxes upon valuable mineral, timber, and waterpower holdings, and upon certain agricultural lands not cultivated by the owners. Practically speaking, in terms of the foreseeable future, today's Georgist would probably be only too glad to settle for these reforms.

It is against this semi-Georgist model, not against landownership as historically practiced, that Ryan measures and finds wanting the full-scale George proposal. He belittles the George proposal as an "untried system."[36] Yet where has his own ideal system been tried in its totality? The George proposal, as we have seen, has been given limited and partial application in many places. To the extent that it has been applied, its social utility has been amply demonstrated— even more conclusively since the time when Ryan's critique appeared. Consider, for example, the Hutchinson Report, a survey comparing the six Australian states in terms of the degree to which their local jurisdictions use this method of obtaining public revenue. Queensland, New South Wales, and Western Australia have much heavier land-value taxes and much lower improvement taxes than do South Australia, Victoria, and Tasmania. According to the report, in the period considered the first group of states had increases in land under crops, while the second group had decreases. The value of improvements as compared to land was found to be 151 percent in the first group, as against only 79 percent in the second, and was highest (198 percent) in Queensland, which collects the greatest amount (54.4 percent) of economic rent. Factory wages were higher in the first group and larger in purchasing power. Last, it was discovered that population was flowing from the second group to the first group, indicating that people in Australia found conditions better in the first group. The inflow to Queensland, the state taxing land values the most, was the greatest.[37] So even from a standpoint of social utility, the criterion according to which Ryan proclaims private landownership to be a natural right, the Georgist approach would seem empirically to be at least as capable of vindication.

## Notes

1. James Hastings Nichols, *Democracy and the Churches* (Philadelphia: Westminster Press, 1951), p. 131.

2. John A. Ryan, *Distributive Justice* (1916; rev. ed. New York: Macmillan, 1927), chapters 3, 4, and 5. Chapter 2 is reproduced, with minor omissions, in vol. 14 of the Modern Legal Philosophy Series. I refer to the single tax as "so-called" because its singleness is not its essential feature, and, strictly speaking, it is not a tax but rather a public fee.

3. Eric F. Goldman, *Rendezvous With Destiny* (New York: Vintage Books, 1956), p. 85. For a more restrained account, see Ryan's autobiography, *Social Doctrine in Action* (New York: Harper, 1941), p. 9.

4. Henry George, *Progress and Poverty*, 75th anniversary ed. (New York: Robert Schalkenbach Foundation, 1954), p. 421.

5. It should be emphasized that George did not regard his theory as a mere fiscal reform. He thought of it as a means whereby free enterprise, in which he ardently believed, could be rendered truly free by eliminating a fundamental and pervasive monopoly that interferes with the normal operation of the market and diverts a major share of wealth to those who make no positive contribution to the economic process. Rent, he taught, belongs to the community by right, and as long as it is privately appropriated, it serves as a fetter upon production and a barrier to the right of individuals to enjoy the fruits of their toil. Interest, on the other hand, he viewed as the capitalist's just return for that increase in wealth attributable to his saving and investment. If, he held, rent were taken by the public, the speculative element in land prices would disappear, and the consequent cheapness of land would place natural opportunity within the reach of all. Production would be stimulated, wages would rise, the cost of goods would be reduced, and with the extirpation of its basic cause, involuntary poverty would tend to vanish.

6. George, *Progress and Poverty*, pp. 344 f.

7. Ryan, *Distributive Justice*, pp. 25 f.

8. Ibid., p. 26.

9. Henry George, "The Condition of Labor: An Open Letter to Pope Leo XIII" (1881), *The Land Question* [and other Essays] (New York: Robert Schalkenbach Foundation, 1953), p. 36.

10. Ryan, *Distributive Justice*, p. 24.

11. Ibid., p. 28.

12. Ibid., p. 29. The same kind of legalistic hairsplitting that characterizes Ryan's approach in the argument just cited also marks his treatment of a passage in which George speaks of travelers in the desert, saying that those who had had the forethought to provide themselves with vessels of water would have a just property right in the water so carried, against which the need of their less provident fellows could establish a claim only of charity and not of justice. "But suppose others use their forethought in pushing ahead and appropriating the springs, refusing when their fellows came up to let them drink of the water save as they buy it of them. Would such forethought give any right?" The obvious intent of this passage is simply to point up the

distinction between "the forethought of carrying water where it is needed" (labor), and "the forethought of seizing springs" (first occupancy). Ryan, however, makes it the occasion for insisting that since the water in the vessels was originally abstracted from some spring, the right to it stems, initially, not from the labor of transporting it or filling the vessels with it, but from seizure of an ownerless good, quoting a paraphrase of Grotius to the effect that "since nothing can be made except out of preexisting matter, acquisition by means of labor depends, ultimately, on possession by means of occupation." It is patent that the act of appropriation is temporally antecedent to productive labor, but it is far from evident why this truism should be accorded such overriding moral significance as to constitute the definitive factor in establishing ownership. Moreover, it should be noted that he who fills vessels from a spring does not (unless the spring is about to run dry) deprive others of the opportunity to use a natural good. George, "The Condition of Labor," p. 29; Ryan, *Distributive Justice*, p. 31.

13. Ryan, *Distributive Justice*, p. 31

14. Ibid., p. 49.

15. George, *Progress and Poverty*, p. 365. In 1967 the California Supreme Court answered this rhetorical question in the affirmative when it enjoined Sacramento Assessor Dr. Irene Hickman to cease assessing real property at 100 percent of market value as provided by the state constitution. The court declared, in effect, that previous assessors had ignored that constitutional provision for so long that real estate owners had acquired a vested right to its nonenforcement! No doubt, the court is privy to some arcane answer to Herbert Spencer's famous query: "At what rate per annum do invalid claims become valid?" Herbert Spencer, *Social Statics* (original version, 1850; reprint ed. New York: Robert Schalkenbach Foundation 1954), p. 105.

16. Ryan, *Distributive Justice*, p. 35.

17. Ibid., p. 38.

18. See John A. Ryan, *Declining Liberty and Other Papers* (Freeport, N.Y.: Books for Libraries Press, 1927), p. 142.

19. Harry Gunnison Brown, Harold S. Buttenheim, et al., eds., *Land-Value Taxation Around the World* (New York: Robert Schalkenbach Foundation, 1955), p. 11. For an update, see the most recent (3rd) edition, R. V. Andelson, ed. (Malden, MA: Blackwell Publishers, 2000).

20. Ibid., pp. 13, 33.

21. Ryan, *Distributive Justice*, p. 41.

22. Ibid., p. 39.

23. See, for example, *Declining Liberty and Other Papers*, pp. 200 ff.

24. Ryan, *Distributive Justice*, p. 324.

25. Ibid., p. 103.

26. Ibid., pp. 54–56, 61, 66, 73.

27. Ibid., p. 39.

28. Steven B. Cord, *Henry George: Dreamer or Realist?* (Philadelphia: University of Pennsylvania Press, 1965), p. 65.

29. Ryan, *Distributive Justice*, p. 42.

30. Ibid., pp. 46 f.

31. Ibid., pp. 47 f.

32. Ibid., p. 45. I am willing to concede that some owners perform a useful entrepreneurial function in finding the best use for (and thus actualizing the latent value of) their sites. In this case, a portion of the rent is really wages, for it is attributable to mental labor rather than to mere ownership. But it would seem as if at least as many owners, through ignorant allocation or too prolonged withholding, prevent or inhibit optimal use, while the role of others is simply passive—responding to the entrepreneurial initiative of nonowners. The last instance demonstrates that the entrepreneurial function would continue to be performed (and not necessarily by public officials) even if all private land titles were extinguished.

33. Ibid., pp. 57–60.

34. Ibid., p. 54.

35. Ibid., p. 56.

36. Ibid.

37. A. R. Hutchinson, *Public Charges Upon Land Values* (Melbourne: Land Values Research Group, 1963).

# 25
# Alcázar's "Most Voluminous of All Assaults"

By JAMES L. BUSEY

In 1917 there appeared in Spain the most voluminous of all assaults upon the teaching of Henry George—a 383-page tome by Father Juan Alcázar Alvarez, bearing the appropriately ponderous title, *Estudio filosófico crítico del libro "Progreso y miseria," de Henry George, en sus cuestiones fundamentales y el alivio social*. It was published by Perlado, Páez y Compañia of Madrid, with the imprimatur of the bishop and ecclesiastic governor of Madrid-Alcalá.

By now it is doubtful that many people are much influenced by or would take the trouble to wade through this tedious and rambling work, but the *Estudio filosófico* is of some significance because (1) it indicates that during a period of several decades in which sustained literary discussion of George was extremely rare, there were individuals in far away Iberia who deemed him to be so potent a thinker that he deserved 383 published pages of response; (2) it draws together most of the more notable misconceptions about Georgist theory into one albeit too-lengthy book, and thus becomes a useful if dreary compendium of anti-Georgist absurdities; (3) it does point up important areas where George left himself open to unnecessary attack; and (4) it offers some insight into the curious contest that went on during the 1880s between Henry George and prelates of the Catholic Church. This chapter will be organized around these four major points.

### Perceived Significance of Henry George

Father Alcázar left no doubt that he considered Henry George's philosophy to be worthy of the most serious consideration. The *Estudio filosófico* fairly bristles with expressions indicating the importance that Alcázar attached to Georgism. The first, introductory chapter asks (p. 2):[1] "What do I believe regarding the single-tax theory, today so much in vogue? What does the inexorable tribunal of pure reason tell

American Journal of Economics and Sociology, Vol. 63, No. 2 (April, 2004).
© 2004 American Journal of Economics and Sociology, Inc.

us about the significance of this theory propounded by the eminent George?"[2]

There are several verbose and irrelevant excursions into intricate questions of philosophy and metaphysics (e.g., pp. 128–35, about the difference between the *possible* and what *ought* to be); but in general, Alcázar devotes the first of two parts (eleven chapters and 178 pages) to a drumbeat attack on what he alleges to be the proposals of Henry George. On page 66 he announces that "now we have pulverized the arguments of Henry George . . . ," and after 117 more pages of "pulverization" promises on page 183, at the beginning of the second part (eleven more chapters, 200 pages) that he will no longer attack Henry George's theories directly, but will present positive proposals for alleviation of social distress. This he succeeds in doing only in part. In chapter 3 of part 2 (pp. 198–206), the author urges that world peace be assured by creation of Supreme International Tribunal, designed to arbitrate and settle disputes among nations. Unlike the Permanent Court of International Justice, created three years after publication of the *Estudio filosófico* and now known as the International Court of Justice, Alcázar's Supreme International Tribunal would be directed by the Pope.

Chapter 4 (pp. 207–16) expresses sincere concern over the huge military expenditures incurred by governments, and stresses that if these could be reduced, thus lightening the burdens of taxation, the ravages of pauperism would be lessened. With settlement of disputes and conflicts under guidance of a papally directed international tribunal, and achievement of divinely inspired mutual human love among peoples, wars and dangers of wars would diminish and so would the terrible burdens of huge armaments, armies, and navies, and the dangers of aerial bombardment.

An improbable chapter 5 (pp. 217–36) within part 2 follows the theme that "the civil State ought to subordinate itself to the Catholic Church," a concept that antedates the Doctrine of the Two Swords, propounded by Pope Gelasius I at the end of the fifth century.[3] Pope Gelasius, in contrast to Father Alcázar, contended that the political state should be left to handle matters of a temporal nature, with the Church held responsible for spiritual affairs. It is doubtful that many

Catholics today, or even in 1917, would adhere to such a premedieval point of view as that of Father Alcázar; but this does not prevent him from contending that all the problems of the world result, not from the maldistribution of property, but from the failure of mankind to put itself under the headship of the Roman Catholic Church.

Chapter 6 (pp. 237–53), on "Liberty and Libertinism" (*libertinaje*), is in much the same vein, and points out that moral, religious guidance must be the controlling force in society; that the world will be saved from calamity only when subjected to direction by God, Jesus Christ, and the Pope.

Chapter 9 (pp. 314–31) includes a section on agricultural collective syndicates that were appearing in Spain at the time, and Father Alcázar indicates his support for these and his hope that the state will stand out of their way; and chapter 10 (pp. 332–44) expresses considerable agreement with George on the subject of free trade, though with an admixture of mutual aid, cooperation, and conceptions of universality.

Otherwise, much of part 2 of the *Estudio filosófico* lambastes Henry George and Georgism as much as does part 1. Chapters 7 and 8, "Wages" and "Rent," and sections throughout other chapters continue the attack on Henry George and all his works. The book is supposed to conclude on page 351, with the statement that the author does not doubt that if a man "so valiant as Henry George" were to follow less sterile principles, the economy would receive a gigantic protective force. But this is not all. A two-part appendix (pp. 353–83) comments in detail on the debate between Henry George and the Duke of Argyll;[4] and, apparently after having read *Protection or Free Trade* subsequent to his preparation of chapter 10 on the same-subject, Alcázar makes it clear that he agrees with Henry George somewhat, but not too much.

To Juan Alcázar Alvarez, in other words, Henry George was a dragon to be thrice slain. Later I shall have occasion to comment on the obvious fact that at one time the theories of Henry George were vastly more prestigious than they are now; and on the factors that may have contributed to the decline of public awareness of Henry George and his philosophy.

### To the Attack

Like his fictional compatriot, the knight of La Mancha, Alcázar seems to have had a penchant for tilting at windmills. The *Estudio filosófico* never comes clear as to exactly what Henry George did propose. Chapter 2 of part 1, "The Single Tax Opposed to Reason" (pp. 4–9), comes somewhere near the mark when it charges that George would unjustly make only one sector of society, the landlords, support all the rest of the population. Alcázar finds this to be a form of slavery, an unjust punishment without trial, and returns elsewhere (pp. 136–70 and *passim*) to the theme that taxation should be imposed equitably on all classes, not on just one. This iniquitous tax scheme would pick out a single class as social pariahs, a state of affairs that Father Alcázar finds to be intolerable.

Alcázar never bothered to explain why George would allegedly single out this particular economic class for taxation, and offers no explanation of the nature of unearned increment from economic rent, or its effects on the society.[5] Instead, the *Estudio filosófico* moves quickly to the implication that the single tax would fall especially on the agricultural classes and small, productive, middle-class elements, "the proprietary agricultural classes. . . ." (p. 17). Again and again Alcázar returned to the theme that to single out the "agricultural" element for this sort of treatment would be very wrong and would deny it recompense for past labors and sacrifices. According to Alcázar, it would be manifestly unjust that the "opulent classes" should live off taxation imposed on the "humble, honorable worker on the land" (p. 17), or that big industrialists, who after all only improve products secured from the land, would be so exempted from taxation at the expense of the hard-working agricultural producers (p. 28). There is no doubt that such an arrangement would be the very epitome of injustice, but of course Henry George never proposed anything of the sort. George was talking about unearned economic rent, most of which arises in heavily populated and urbanized areas. Of all the people Henry George had in mind, farmers and ranchers would be less taxed than any, simply because their unearned economic rent per acre is almost nil.[6] Whether deliberately or otherwise, Alcázar persisted throughout his book in conveying the impression that the whole Georgist proposal was directed against the agrarian sector, which is, of course, exactly opposite to the truth. It is for this reason that, in an attempt at making positive proposals for the alleviation of social distress, Alcázar wrote the later section to which I have alluded, wherein he advocated encouragement of the agrarian collectives that were appearing in Spain at the time. Alcázar called George a "communist" (pp. 119, 133, and *passim*) but turned out to be more of a communist than the individualist Henry George.

Alcázar's book is completely misleading about the single tax and its purpose. More than this, the book soon moves away from any allusion to the *impuesto único*, and contends variously and inconsistently that Henry George proposed collectivization or state ownership of the land, or simple division of it among the whole population. On the matter of collectivization (which Alcázar seemed to favor if in the form of agricultural syndicates), the author argued (p. 55) that if it is wrong for the individual to own property or use it for his own purposes, it is just as wrong for the state to do the same; that according to Georgists, "the State, not the individual, should be the master of the land" (p. 237); that Henry George would turn over the land to state functionaries, deputies, and bureaucrats, who would try to work the lands themselves or more likely put them into hands of vagabonds and political favorites (pp. 75, 76); that maybe man did not make land, as George said, but neither did society or the state, which therefore has no special right to its possession (p. 374); and that Henry George nowhere proves that collective use is better than individual use of the land (p. 125).

Apparently unaware of the inconsistency, Alcázar contended elsewhere that George advocated the equal division of the land (p. 46); and the *Estudio filosófico* argues at some length that because of differing aptitudes of individuals, such division or distribution of the land would not make everyone equal, but that some would remain poorer than others (p. 164).

Of course, George never proposed either the collectivization or the equal or any other kind of distribution of land.[7] Though the long disquisitions in *Progress and Poverty* against private property in land, including his statement that "we must make land common property,"[8] had the unfortunate effect of misleading many readers about George's ultimate proposal, what he advocated was the socialization of land values or economic rent, not of the land itself[9]—and, as I shall have occasion to point out later, there is a fundamental difference between the two.

Henry George was by no means the first to contend that the right to property arises out of one's own exertions.[10] Theorists such as Adam Smith and John Locke held to an identical view; and in an odd sort of way, even the Marxist labor theory of value and its denunciation of private collection of "surplus value" are in the same tradition.[11] Alcázar agreed that "the fundamental principle of the right of property is labor" (p. 21), and further, admitted that everyone has a "right" to land, but that this "right" can only be implemented by "labor and worthiness" and more to the same effect (part 1, chap. 8, pp. 81–109).

From that point Alcázar not only moved far away from the Georgist position, but also revealed a profound misunderstanding of the philosophy and proposals of Henry George. He persisted in supposing that land values arise out of labor performed on the land, and that it would therefore be unjust and despotic for the state to abuse "agrarian property" after its owners had acquired it by their hard work and given value to it through their strenuous efforts, while leaving "other elements free of tribute" (p. 42). It would be terribly wrong, he contended, to take land with which the owner has mixed his life, his labor, and his sweat, and divide it among other individuals (p. 44). The result of imposition of land tax would be that agricultural proprietors would cease to work, since they would be more oppressed and vexed the more they produced (pp. 26–27). He argued that the value of land is given to it by those who work it, who should therefore enjoy recompense for their labors.

Vaguely aware that Henry George might have been saying something he did not comprehend, Alcázar asked (p. 153): How can the value of land be separated from its improvements? If land is worth nothing at first, but made more valuable by improving it, then the collectivization of such land is especially wrong (p. 74). In a chapter devoted entirely to the subject of rent, which Alcázar obviously did not understand at all, he contended that the single tax would fall on work performed on the land; and stressed over and over that rent can arise only out of labor performed on the land. Thus, he argued, land is no different from capital, both of which are made valuable by labor; and wages are paid to labor after deductions for returns to capital, including rent (part 2, chap. 8 pp. 285–313). In the same chapter Alcázar thought he had caught George in an inconsistency: If land has no value until labor is performed, how is it that rent can rise steeply though the owner does no work?[12]

Of course, the labor to which George was referring was labor contributing to productivity throughout the community, not labor on a specific piece of land. What George was saying, and what Alcázar either could not or would not understand, was that the value of land results from labor on the part of the whole society, not labor on the part of the individual landowner. The point that George emphasized repeatedly, and that was the whole basis for his contention that private collection of economic rent is unjust, was precisely that land values are irrelevant to and not affected by labor performed on the land in question.[13]

Alcázar never admitted to an understanding of the concept of economic rent; nor did he conceive that there is a distinction between the income arising from unearned economic rent and that arising from labor on land, nor that Henry George was bent upon socializing unearned economic rent but not the products of labor. Even John Locke, though favoring the private ownership of land, saw clearly that this could depend only upon actual use of and labor upon it, and could not extend to unused land allowed to go to waste.[14] Alcázar assumed that all privately held land, of whatever condition, represented an admixture of "labor and sweat," and that therefore all its income should accrue only to its owner. It is conceivable that some hard-working early American frontiersman might hold to such a belief, but difficult to understand how such a contention could come out of Spain, of all places.

Alcázar understood that George based his theory on conceptions of both justice and utility, but pointed out that even if private ownership of land were incompatible with its best use, it might still be compatible with justice—which, in the view of Alcázar, was obviously the case (pp. 110 ff.); and, certainly, justice must prevail over utility. In the mind of Alcázar, however, the George proposal did not even have utility to recommend it. Because soils differ so much in their composition, the problems of assessment would be unbelievably complex (p. 137). Also, how could the state determine what part of production from the land was of material worth, arising out of the largesse of the earth, and what was the result of labor and intellectual effort, which should be rewarded? Alcázar offered the example of a mine. How could one know how much metal is contained within it? Or, as would be more likely, the tax would have to be imposed after extraction had occurred. How could the state determine what had been extracted as a consequence of intelligence and ability, and what had simply been taken because it was lying around (pp. 171–78)?

Such confusion about George's proposals boggles the reviewer's mind. Again, Alcázar was revealing his incomprehension that economic rent is something to be determined by general market value as a reflection of community demand, not by labor or extraction performed on the land. The last thing that Henry George would propose would be to assess a tax on production. Alcázar saw the *impuesto único* as some kind of severance tax to be determined by the value of crops or minerals or timber or whatever else could be extracted from the land. The gap between this idea and the idea of land value as arising out of general societal demand or need, and as occurring in large measure because of the efforts of the whole community, was too great for the *Estudio filosófico* to bridge; but this is not an unusual source of confusion about Henry George's thought, and may be central to much public misunderstanding of his proposals. The single tax was deceptively simple in appearance. People do not turn conceptual corners easily, and many have been bewildered by the same misconceptions that plagued Juan Alcázar Alvarez.

It was in this connection that Alcázar did pose a problem that could be quite real for the application of Georgist devices in many countries where conceptions of public probity are not of a high order. The *Estudio filosófico* points out that assessors and tax collectors could be bribed by landowners to adjust their fiscal impositions in proportion to subornations received (pp. 173–74). It is not surprising that such an idea would occur to a writer in the Hispanic world. As George himself readily conceded (in a letter in 1888 to William Lloyd Garrison,

II) his system is not a panacea. No more than any other social theory can it succeed apart from supportive attitudes and institutions. It is therefore scarcely surprising that its modest triumphs of implementation have occurred almost exclusively in English-speaking and Scandinavian lands, with long traditions of responsible self-government. One could not realistically be very sanguine as to its chances for successful application in such states as Haiti, Nicaragua, Bolivia, or even Honduras.

Large parts of *Estudio filosófico* are devoted to the building up and knocking down of straw men, of views that Henry George never propounded. I have delineated several of these above. Another example deserves brief mention. Alcázar sees George as predicating individual happiness on the welfare of society, not the welfare of society on individual happiness (p. 165), and then fills three pages with an attack on this point of view. Of course, Henry George never took any such position, and Alcázar nowhere cites the section of *Progress and Poverty* that is supposed to argue in its favor.

Elsewhere (pp. 303–07) Alcázar reveals his total misunderstanding of the problems Henry George describes. In *Progress and Poverty* George tells the tale of the first immigrant who comes to a vast, unclaimed land; and of how, as new settlers come into the region, the value of the first colonist's property rises, not because of any improvement in its productivity or special effort on the part of the owner, but because of the interweaving cooperation of the increasing population. Years later, according to George, the land of the first immigrant is surrounded by a great city, and its owner is made wealthy by the increasing value of his land.[15] George says, "Our settler, or whoever has succeeded to his right to the land, is now a millionaire. Like another Rip Van Winkle, he may have lain down and slept; still he is rich—not from anything he has done, but from the increase in population."[16]

To Alcázar, who comprehends nothing about the sources of economic or ground rent, this could occur only because of the suffering and hard labor undergone by the original settler on the land, and his descendants are properly entitled to the resulting rewards. He quotes George accurately enough, but adds, "the man could be sleeping today, but the fruit of so many past sufferings continues giving optimum results. And everything is due essentially to the first colonist who was the most suffering and the hardest worker" (p. 306). Everything else that George said about an increasing land value arising from the efforts and cooperation of others is entirely lost on Juan Alcázar Alvarez. In a paragraph that is often quoted by his adherents, George said:

> Place one hundred men on an island from which there is no escape, and whether you make one of these men the absolute master of the other ninety-nine, or the absolute owner of the soil of the land, will make no difference either to him or to them.
>
> In the one case, as the other, the one will be the absolute master of the ninety-nine—his power extending even to life and death, for simply to refuse them permission to live on the island would be to force them into the sea.[17]

Readers with a taste for irony will find it unintentionally gratified by Alcázar's grave reply to this. He says that to analyze such a situation, we must determine how these hundred people got onto the island. They could have arrived only (1) as a government colonization project, (2) by shipwreck, or (3) voluntarily. In the first case the government would set up rules and regulations and provide guards to prevent any one person from seizing full control. In the second, there would be no reason for the ninety-nine to submit to the claims of one individual, since they were all shipwrecked together; and in the third, they would certainly have drawn up rules and agreements before arriving. In any event, should such an island-owner somehow appear on the scene, he would be obliged by considerations of Christian mercy to provide alms and succor for the ninety-nine people without land; or, if worse came to worse, why should ninety-nine men put up with the demands of only one who is no stronger than any of them (pp. 56–63)? This, of course, is exactly what George had in mind.

Alcázar was not entirely devoid of social conscience. He admitted that many *latifundistas* do indeed use their lands quite badly or not at all, and that when the national interest requires it, they have a social responsibility to their countries (p. 320). He also declared that it would be permissible, *after* the state has utilized its own lands fully and has taken all other possible efforts to alleviate human distress, *then* to undertake measures to require that privately monopolized lands be put into more effective production (p. 325): "The order of things is this: First, put into cultivation the diffuse State-owned fields; if this is not sufficient for the satisfaction of the needy elements of society, then resort to obliging private owners to cultivate their private *latifundios*, respecting their property rights, or indemnifying them for terrains which would pass to the social State for cultivation."

Where Alcázar found, or thought he found, similarities between the Georgist philosophy and his own doctrine, he offered lavish praise to the American theorist. The Spanish priest found much to his liking in book 10, "The Law of Human Progress," and quoted at length from a section of *Progress and Poverty* that he deemed to be critical of the Darwinian theory of evolution (pp. 169–70).[17] In general, and despite his rejection or distortion of all Georgist concepts about private property in land and public collection of ground rents, Alcázar did not undertake a personal vendetta against Henry George, and for the most part referred to him civilly and even with some grudging admiration.

In the last section of this chapter I shall discuss Alcázar's social views, which were drawn from the most conservative doctrines of the Spanish Catholic Church of the time. Suffice it to say here that Alcázar rejected the whole idea of equalization of individual opportunity that was implicit in all of George's writings. It was the view of the Spanish priest that any such scheme would tear down the whole structure whereby some social categories are preeminent over those that are inferior (p. 184). It was his view, drawn straight out of medieval and even ancient Greek doctrine, that poverty and wealth, which vary from person to person, form a total and desirable equilibrium of forces (p. 193): "From which I deduce that the existence of poor and rich carries within itself the true total beauty of material society. For that reason, it is not possible to point to a remedy which would put an end to *material* poverty and wealth."

Alcázar saw no way whereby the disparities between poverty and wealth could be bridged in this world, and indeed saw little reason why they should be. The next world was another question, which I shall consider in the concluding pages of this chapter. In any event, the *Estudio filosófico* came from a part of this world and a body of thought that were about as far away from those of Henry George as one could get and still be within the sphere of Western European culture and ideas. This vast difference between the world of Father Juan Alcázar Alvarez and the world of Henry George opens avenues for disturbing contemplation regarding the possibility of acceptance of Georgist philosophy in many regions of the earth, several of which are even farther from the thinking or environment of Henry George than was the semi-medieval European, Hispanic culture of Father Alcázar.

### Chinks in the Armor

Much of the Alcázar book inveighs against the thesis that private property in land must be abolished (pp. 29–109 and *passim*).[19] Chapter 5 of part 1 (pp. 29–48) questions the Georgist argument that private ownership of land is unjust.[20] Chapter 6 (pp. 49–65) attacks George's view that private landlordism leads to the enslavement of laborers.[21] Chapter 7 (pp. 66–80) argues that it would be unfair and unjust to refuse to indemnify landowners if their land were seized from them by the state.[22] Chapter 8 (pp. 81–109) finds little empirical evidence to support the Georgist view that in earlier times land was held in common but was later obtained by force or fraud from the communities that previously enjoyed its use.[23] From Henry George's argument that private property in land has arisen out of military conquest, and the influence of a "sacerdotal class" and a "class of professional lawyers,"[24] Alcázar launches into a furious assault on the notion, invented by Alcázar himself, that Henry George would abolish or somehow eliminate soldiers, lawyers, and priests (pp. 103–04).*

These are among the most stirring passages in *Progress and Poverty*, but as worded and placed in the book they also opened George to unnecessary attack. In his many pages on the iniquities of private

---

*In book 9, chap. 4, of *Progress and Poverty* George merely expresses the belief that the adoption of his remedy would so simplify the administration of justice as to dry up the demand for lawyers, and that it would foster such a growth of independence among the masses as to discourage the maintenance of standing armies. No mention at all is made of priests.

property in land, Henry George seemed to be moving inexorably toward actual abolition of private titles to land, and some kind of general nationalization of land ownership—in other words, toward monopolization by the politically organized state of land and the resources beneath it.[25] Indeed, in one section he used the word *nationalization* where he declared that "by the time the people of any country such as England or the United States are sufficiently aroused to the injustice and disadvantages of individual ownership of land to induce them to attempt its nationalization, they will be sufficiently aroused to nationalize it in a much more direct and easy way than by purchase. They will not trouble themselves about compensating the proprietors of land."[26]

Phraseology of this sort created unnecessary difficulties for Henry George and provided a field day for critics such as Father Alcázar. Well before the days of Alcázar Alvarez, writers too numerous to cite fully here had clearly seen the potential authoritarian pitfalls that lay in the way of governmental monopolization of land or anything else.[27]

Had Henry George actually been talking about iniquities of land ownership per se, or been about to propose that private land titles should be confiscated and transferred to the state, his long and moving presentation on the subject would have been to the point and essential for the development of his final proposal. As it turned out about three-fourths of the way through *Progress and Poverty*, Henry George was agitated about the private collection of ground rent, not about private ownership of land; and he was intent, not upon confiscating land, but upon confiscating rent. After devoting seventy-four pages to the denunciation of private land ownership, proclaiming in italics that "*we must make land common property*," and talking about nationalization of the land, and rejecting the idea that landowners should be compensated for loss of their titles, Henry George finally comes to the point: "*It is not necessary to confiscate land; it is only necessary to confiscate rent.*"[28] Henry George filled the next sixty-eight pages of his book with a defense, not of confiscation of the land itself, but of confiscation of unearned economic rent arising out of ownership of the land. Owners would continue to hold title to their lands, and would enjoy the fruits of their labor and capital investment as applied to their lands; but their unearned economic rent, which is quite a different concept and arises out of the efforts of the community around them, would be taken by the state for the defrayal of public expenses.

Professor Andelson expresses the point quite well when he says that the public appropriation of ground rent would serve simply "as a mechanism whereby such ownership may be rendered ethically and practically innocuous."[29] The ownership would still be there, and the state would *not* nationalize the land. There is a vital difference between the concept of land and the concept of unearned economic rent derived via land ownership from the surrounding community. In taking so long to get around to this crucial point, Henry George did nothing to allay the concerns of later critics such as Juan Alcázar Alvarez. George's seminal proposal to confiscate rent, not land, could have been placed and justified at a much earlier point in *Progress and Poverty*, probably in his chapter, "The True Remedy,"[30] which instead included the unfortunate phrase that "we must make land common property"; and then, in presenting his arguments about the injustices of private property in land, he could have inserted enough references to the iniquities of private collection of rent, not owner-ship of land, to leave no doubt as to the position he was taking.

Alcázar himself noted this damaging inconsistency in Henry George's book, and pointed out the inherent logical conflict that lies between the Georgist claim that private property in land is unjust and not compatible with its best use, and the Georgist willingness to solve the problem by letting the state collect the rent (pp. 125–26). Here Alcázar finds a further Georgist inconsistency, in that George attrib-utes the miseries of India and China to the rapaciousness of govern-ments, and specifically condemns the exorbitant land and salt taxes imposed by England upon the poverty-stricken producers of India.[31] Alcázar then launches into the indicated attack, and asks why George would suppose that governments, possessed of the power to collect economic rent as their only source of revenue, would be any more just or magnanimous with their subjects than was the imperial English government in India (pp. 185–88). Alcázar is full of his own incon-sistencies, and, as we have seen, never comes clear as to whether George advocated distribution or state nationalization of the land, or public collection of a land tax; but Henry George himself can be held partly responsible for some confusion on these points.

### Alcázar, George, and the Catholic Church

As would be expected, Father Alcázar saw the problems of the world and their alleviation in the light of his devoutly religious point of view. To Americans today, whether Catholic or otherwise, some of his expressions on this point seem to be extraordinarily quaint and drawn from much earlier epochs of Catholic thought. At the same time, the religious doctrine that is central to Alcázar's analysis is reminiscent of and may throw some light on the checkered pattern of relationships that prevailed among Henry George, Georgism, and the Roman Catholic Church.

Alcázar contended that social problems are far too complex and heterogeneous to be solved by a simple single tax (pp. 314–15)—though of course, as we have seen, he did not consistently clarify that this was Henry George's central proposal. At the same time, a reading of *Estudio filosófico* reveals that Alcázar himself had his own simplistic moral and religious solution to the problems of the world.

Early in the Alcázar book, the reader detects where its message is likely to lead. It is not *property*, Alcázar tells us, that leads to individual enslavement, but the *abuse* of property by individuals not sufficiently guided by moral law (pp. 49–65, 351, and *passim*). "The social problem does not depend on distribution [of the land] but on good or bad men; it is licentiousness that brings human troubles in its wake" (p. 367). Are misery and decadence the consequences of maldistribution of property, or of moral depravity, the lack of moral conscience? The latter, of course (pp. 49–65). Just because of the *abuse* of property ownership, private property should not altogether be eliminated (p. 55). The only type of economy that can solve human problems is "moral economy" (p. 349). According to Alcázar, the search for material rather than spiritual solutions is a sterile quest that will have no good effects in alleviation of the social condition (p. 65).

This is by no means an unusual approach, even in contemporary times, and it is shared by religious and moral leaders of many faiths and points of view. The general phrase that covers this idea, and indeed is used as a title by a particular segment of the community of idealistic thinkers, is *moral rearmament*. It is not the purpose of this chapter to argue for or against this position, though something may be said in favor of an eclectic stand that would permit moral and material solutions to buttress each other.

But Alcázar goes much further than this, and as his argument develops it becomes more extreme. He argues, as might be expected, that under the guidance of moral law, just wages will be paid, and the concern of Henry George and other writers on this score will be without foundation (p. 254). The moral law, according to Alcázar, is to (1) love God and (2) respect the lives of the underprivileged (p. 61). People must love God, who loved the poor (pp. 194–95); and poverty may be alleviated somewhat in this world through the introduction of divine love into the affairs of men (p. 194). On a concluding page of his appendix, Alcázar unexpectedly argued that George was wrong in contending that any landowner can be the absolute master of land, since only God can be absolute master of anything (p. 370); and in reality, only the reign of Jesus Christ can solve the problems of the world (p. 189).

To this point Alcázar's argument is still not too surprising, and coincides with Geiger's finding that the typical response of certain circles in the Catholic Church was to argue for Christian loyalty and charity as the only real solutions to human suffering.[32]

According to Alcázar, social conditions may be bad; but they were much worse in ancient times, before the advent of Christianity—hence the replacement of all other faiths and beliefs by Christianity, under guidance of the teachings of Christ, offers the only means to remedy the human distresses that were the concern of Henry George (pp. 49–65). Within the framework of Christianity, however, only the Catholic faith and the Catholic Church, and complete obedience to them, can resolve the multifold problems of mankind (pp. 217–36, and *passim*).

Early in his book, Alcázar proclaimed (pp. 45–46): "The only means that there are to put an end to these fears that someone may obtain not only exclusive right to 160 or 640 acres, but to a whole section, a whole state or to a whole continent, is to proclaim loud and clear [*predicar*] the Christian, Catholic, and Roman religion."

However, one can only accomplish so much in this material world. In the end we should not worry so much about what is mine and what is thine, for God will ultimately take care of everything—not Henry George, even though he thinks himself to be some kind of God and to have the solution to everything (pp. 79–80).

We move, then, to the inevitable but still startling conclusion: In this world there will always be problems. The remedy is not in this world, but in the one to follow (p. 349); it is in the next life, not this one, where the solutions will be found (p. 193): "In this material world, constantly variable in its phenomena, it is impossible to find stable good fortune; in the other, spiritual, varied but not variable, there does indeed exist that which we long for so much and dream of obtaining in this one."

As the old revolutionaries used to sing it, "You'll get your pie in the sky when you die!"

This was, of course, the most reactionary type of doctrine possible, and was by no means shared by all Catholics or even by all high Catholic prelates, during either the time of Alcázar or that of Henry George. However, an undercurrent of opposition to Henry George did appear in the highest councils of the Church, and it is likely that the expressions of Father Alcázar, who wrote under authorization by the bishop and ecclesiastic governor of Madrid-Alcalá, may have reflected a fear in some circles that George's proposals constituted a threat to the promises of the Church for ultimate salvation from despair.

As is well known to persons conversant with the Henry George years, one of his staunchest and most effective supporters in New York City, especially among the large Irish population, was Father Edward McGlynn.[33] Because of his support for Henry George, Father McGlynn was excommunicated in 1887, but in an unusual reversal of its act, the Holy See removed the excommunication in 1892 and restored Father McGlynn to his priestly functions.[34] The papal act of excommunication was much influenced by the pressures brought to bear by Archbishop Michael Corrigan of New York, whose views seem not to have differed very much from those of Father Alcázar.[35] However, there is much evidence that Catholic opposition to George went quite beyond the circles of Archbishop Corrigan and the temporary influence he could bring to bear. Other high prelates of the Church spoke out strongly against Henry George, and though not actually putting *Progress and Poverty* on the Index (which would have forbidden all Catholics to read it), the Holy Office did rule it to be "worthy of condemnation," which meant that any bishop could rule it to be prohibited reading for any Catholics within his jurisdiction.[36]

George saw this attitude as a "perverted Christianity to soothe the conscience of the rich and to frown down discontent on the part of the poor," and more to the same effect,[37] and in this instance he was, of course, attacking exactly the kind of Christianity that at a later date Juan Alcázar Alvarez was to vigorously espouse. George may have been more than half right when he perceived *Rerum Novarum*, Pope Leo XIII's encyclical "On the Condition of Labor," to be more directed against his views than against those of Marx or other assorted collectivists.[38]

But, as is true of many doctrines and institutions, Catholicism has not been on only one side of the Georgist question. Of course, there was Father McGlynn. There were other priests, such as Father Thomas Dawson, who gave George their full support,[39] and no doubt there were others who less conspicuously but no less strongly sympathized with his message. George received very warm support among the Catholic clergy of Ireland, including especially Thomas Nulty, Bishop of Meath;[40] and, of course, the reversal of Father McGlynn's excommunication was the work of many influential elements within the Church—including Archbishop Francesco Satolli, papal nuncio or ablegate who had just come to the United States as a direct representative of the Pope, and who carried on an impartial or even sympathetic investigation, as well as the theologians of Catholic University who helped prepare the favorable and decisive report that led to the reversal.[41]

In conclusion on this point, it is relevant to quote one of the strongest statements of support for Henry George to come from a religious source of high prestige and authority:

After the Gospel, this is the book that I love and admire the most. It does not surprise me to learn that, after the Bible, it is the most widely published book in all the world. I think I do not offend God when I say that *Progress and Poverty* plays in the material realm the same role that the Gospel unfolds in the spiritual world.

It is a profound book, of intense philosophical, moral and political radiance. It has simplicity and grandeur.

No religion has been able to condemn it, because it is supported by the most profound and noble sentiment that God has placed in the heart of man: The sentiment of justice.

And since this book, in the last analysis, preaches nothing but the application of justice to the economic activity of mankind, I think I can present it with this single phrase:

Here we have the Gospel of Abundance!

The source? Dom Carlos Duarte Costa, Bishop of Rio de Janeiro, Roman Catholic Church of Brazil![42]

Catholic reaction to Henry George, it can be said, was quite mixed and by no means of one point of view. Had Bishop Carlos Duarte Costa of Rio de Janeiro, Brazil, instead of Father Juan Alcázar Alvarez of Spain, written the *Estudio* (or in Portuguese, *Estudo*) *filosófico*, the book would have turned out very differently from the way it did under authorship of the conservative Spanish priest.

The *Estudio filosófico* tells us something about the reaction of an important segment of the Catholic Church to *Progress and Poverty*, and may throw some light on the reasons for that reaction. Though the criticisms by Father Alcázar were often extreme, distorted, and unwarranted, they do remind us that in his haste to get his book into print, Henry George committed some errors of expression and organization that he could have corrected in a second edition—but instead of preparing a revised edition of *Progress and Poverty*, George went on to write other books.[43] At least this writer, who is sympathetic to the views of Henry George, would wish that he and his followers had concentrated more fully on the truly unique contribution of *Progress and Poverty*. No other works of Henry George were so original or so potentially radical as this one.

Because the Alcázar volume launches the attack against Henry George from every possible quarter, fair and unfair, accurate and hopelessly misleading, it enables the reader to see Henry George in the light of his most implacable critics. We all tend to be too uncritical of our heroes, and this can be a valuable exercise in itself.

One would wish that Alcázar's book had been written with less turgid, repetitious verbosity. But Henry George himself, though he wrote in a more moving and appealing style, was not given to undue brevity. Certainly one gets the impression from Alcázar that Henry George was not a theorist to be trifled with. From *Estudio filosófico* and from other clerical reactions to Henry George, we may deduce that influential elements within the great Catholic Church saw in Henry George a real challenger of its doctrinal and institutional hegemony over a large part of the Christian world.

One derives some satisfaction from knowing that Henry George was so important. One would be more gratified if his followers were more effective in translating his ideas into political reality. According to Henry George: "The truth that I have tried to make clear will not find easy acceptance. If that could be, it would have been accepted long ago. If that could be, it would never have been obscured. But it will find friends—those who will toil for it; suffer for it; if need be, die for it. This is the power of Truth."[44]

It is well to have friends who will toil for a worthy idea. It is even better that such friends have some awareness of the need for political organization and action.

In 1917, date of publication of the *Estudio filosófico*, Marxists seized power in Russia and soon after transformed it into the Union of Soviet Socialist Republics. One cannot but reflect that the success of Marxists in attracting the support of millions of followers, and in threatening the rest of the world with ultimate subjugation, results as much from their political strength as from any logic or reason in their philosophy. Marxism operates from a bastion of political power. Georgism does not.

In 1917, it would appear, Georgism seemed as likely as Marxism to sweep the world. That it did not, and that the fears of Juan Alcázar Alvarez did not materialize, may be attributed in large measure to that singular inattention to political action that has characterized Georgism almost since its inception.

Political Georgism was of short duration. In the view of Charles Albro Barker, it died when Tom Johnson left office as mayor of

Cleveland in 1909.[45] Even Henry George himself, though he ran twice for mayor of New York, tended to reject political involvement and to prefer less boisterous speaking and writing activities. It was appropriate that Henry M. Hyndman, who had been both friend and socialist opponent of Henry George, said shortly after George's death: "He has died in a chivalrous attempt to accomplish the impossible without even organizing his forces for the struggle."[46] Georgists have only rarely organized their forces for the struggle. Juan Alcázar Alvarez need not have worried.

### Notes

1. Pages in *Estudio filosófico* will be cited parenthetically in the text, by number.
2. I am responsible for all translations from the Alcázar book. This summary probably represents the closest it has ever come to being rendered into English.
3. George H. Sabine, *A History of Political Theory*, 3rd ed. (New York: Holt, Rinehart and Winston, 1961), pp. 194–96.
4. George Raymond Geiger, *The Philosophy of Henry George* (New York: The Macmillan Company, 1933), p. 69; Charles Albro Barker, *Henry George* (New York: Oxford University Press, 1955), pp. 196, 314, 331, 408–09, 529; Edward J. Rose, *Henry George* (New York: Twayne Publishers, Inc., 1968), pp. 82, 107, 108, 109–13.
5. Henry George, *Progress and Poverty*, 75th anniversary ed. (New York: Robert Schalkenbach Foundation, 1954), pp. 165–72, 218–24, 230–96, 333–57, and *passim*.
6. Ibid., pp. 438, 449–52. See also James R. Brown, *The Farmer and the Single Tax*, 4th ed. (New York: Manhattan Single Tax Club, n.d.).
7. In *Progress and Poverty*, pp. 321–27, Henry George specifically and categorically rejected the notion that land should be divided or distributed among the population.
8. Ibid., pp. 328–57, esp. p. 328, and *passim*.
9. Ibid., pp. 405–72, esp. 405–07.
10. Ibid., p. 334.
11. Geiger, *Philosophy of Henry George*, pp. 197–99; John Locke, *An Essay Concerning the True Original, Extent and End of Civil Government* (1690; in *Social Contract*, intro. Sir Ernest Barker, New York and London: Oxford University Press, 1948), pp. 17–20; Adam Smith, *Wealth of Nations* (1776; New York: Random House [The Modern Library], 1937), pp. 121–22; Karl Marx, *Capital* (London: Swan Sonnenschein & Co., 1889), p. 6.
12. George, *Progress and Poverty*, pp. 165–68.

13. E.g., ibid., pp. 165–72, 333–46, and *passim.*

14. Locke, *Essay on Civil Government*, pp. 20–30.

15. George, *Progress and Poverty*, pp. 235–42.

16. Ibid., p. 241.

17. Ibid., p. 347.

18. Ibid., p. 476.

19. Ibid., pp. 328–30, wherein George proclaimed, in italics, "*We must make land common property*" (p. 328).

20. Ibid., pp. 333–46.

21. Ibid., pp. 347–57.

22. Ibid., pp. 358–67.

23. Ibid., pp. 368–84.

24. Ibid., p. 372

25. Ibid., pp. 328–402, and *passim*

26. Ibid., pp. 362–63.

27. E.g., and for example only, Max Hirsch, *Democracy vs. Socialism*, 4th ed. (New York: Robert Schalkenbach Foundation, 1966), pp. 263–336 and *passim*; or see the magnificent discussion of this fatal contradiction inherent in all socialist and collectivist theory, in Theodore D. Woolsey, *Political Science, or the State* (New York: Charles Scribner's Sons, 1877), 1: 314–23, or, Henry George himself, *Progress and Poverty*, pp. 319–21.

28. George, *Progress and Poverty*, p. 405.

29. Robert V. Andelson, "Where Society's Claim Stops: An Evaluation of Seligman's Ethical Critique of Henry George," *The American Journal of Economics and Sociology* 27 (January 1968): 41–53.

30. George, *Progress and Poverty*, pp. 328–30.

31. Ibid., p. 118.

32. Geiger, *Philosophy of Henry George*, p. 361.

33. This is a long and detailed story that cannot be recounted here, but is available in other sources. See Barker, *Henry George*, pp. 457, 463, 513–14, 619, 621, and *passim*; Geiger, *Philosophy of Henry George*, pp. 69–70, 338–39, 343–60, 363, 368–72; Rose, *Henry George*, pp. 125–32; Mason Gaffney, *Henry George, Dr. Edward McGlynn, and Pope Leo XIII* (New York: Robert Schalkenbach Foundation, 2000).

34. Geiger, *Philosophy of Henry George*, pp. 353–56.

35. Barker, *Henry George*, pp. 126, 472, 476, 575; Geiger, *Philosophy of Henry George*, pp. 347–48, 353, 363; Rose, pp. 127–29.

36. Barker, *Henry George*, pp. 489–90; for further substantiating evidence of this anti-Georgist Catholic attitude, see pp. 477, 486–91; and in Geiger, *Philosophy of Henry George*, the entire chap. 6, "Henry George and Religion," pp. 336–80.

37. Geiger, *Philosophy of Henry George*, pp. 339–42.

38. Barker, *Henry George*, pp. 571–73.

39. Ibid., pp. 121, 366, 574.

40. Ibid., pp. 350–52.

41. Ibid., pp. 576, 588; Geiger, *Philosophy of Henry George*, pp. 354–56.

42. Henry George, *Progresso e pobreza*, trans. Americo Werneck Junior, 2d ed. (Rio de Janeiro: Gráfica Editora Aurora Ltda., 1946), flyleaf. My translation from the Portuguese.

43. I.e., *The Condition of Labor*, 1881; *The Land Question*, 1881; *Social Problems*, 1883; *Protection or Free Trade*, 1886; *A Perplexed Philosopher*, 1892; *The Science of Political Economy*, publ. posthumously, 1898.

44. George, *Progress and Poverty*, p. 555.

45. Barker, *Henry George*, p. 633.

46. Rose, *Henry George*, p. 153.

# 26
## Ely: A Liberal Economist
## Defends Landlordism

*By* STEVEN B. CORD and ROBERT V. ANDELSON

Richard T. Ely was a member of that small yet growing group of advanced economists who, even during Henry George's lifetime, advocated a substantially greater role for government in the economy. After earning his baccalaureate degree at Columbia, he pursued graduate study for three years in Germany, receiving the doctorate from Heidelberg in 1879. Following a little more than a decade on the faculty of Johns Hopkins, he became director of the School of Social Science, History and Economics at the University of Wisconsin where, in 1920, he founded the Institute for Research in Land Economics and Public Utilities. Later he moved this organization to Northwestern University and ultimately to New York, changing its name, after the first move, to the Institute for Economic Research.

Under his direction, the Institute, which was privately funded and that at one time had a staff of twenty-five or thirty, conducted graduate courses, produced a considerable amount of economic literature including a quarterly journal, and engaged in adult education through an arrangement with the United YMCA Schools. One of the founders of the American Economic Association, Ely was author of more than twenty-five books, and co-author or editor of many others. His potency was by no means confined to scholarly efforts; not least of his accomplishments was that of fathering two children after his second marriage at the age of seventy-seven. He had wide influence as a teacher and advisor clear into the 1930s. Msgr. John A. Ryan, the subject of a chapter in the present volume, was among his many protégés, and Woodrow Wilson, Frederick Jackson Turner, and John R. Commons studied under him. His circle of personal friends included such luminaries as Theodore Roosevelt, Robert M. LaFollette, Oliver Wendell Holmes, Jr., and Cardinal Gibbons, not to mention numerous leaders in academe, on the one hand, and the world of commerce and industry, on the other. Raised in a strict Presbyterian home,

American Journal of Economics and Sociology, Vol. 63, No. 2 (April, 2004).
© 2004 American Journal of Economics and Sociology, Inc.

he retained a strong lifelong Christian involvement, and lectured frequently to diverse denominational gatherings, and also to meetings of the Chautauqua Society, which was religious in its origins and overall atmosphere.

While at Wisconsin, Ely was the subject of a sensational trial before the Board of Regents, stemming from charges of socialism by the state superintendent of education. The assault upon him turned into a fiasco, and, as part of their statement of exoneration, the regents issued a famous declaration upholding academic freedom, which was inscribed on a tablet in Bascom Hall. Before he left for Northwestern, they conferred upon him an L.L.D. and other honors.

Despite his rejection of laissez faire, Ely did not regard himself as a socialist. He held that only certain areas of business are inherently monopolistic,[1] and he did not, by and large, consider land ownership to be among them. Psychological reasons for his generally sympathetic attitude toward land ownership may perhaps be revealed by his autobiographical remark that "a strong attachment to the land is characteristic of nearly all the Elys and of most New England families. . . . We, in Connecticut, loved the land we owned and would not let it go."[2] While he nowhere essayed a thoroughgoing critique of Henry George's writings, he did devote some adverse paragraphs to the single tax, and doubtless displayed his antipathy toward it orally in such a way as to inculcate his students, most of whom came to occupy positions that enabled them to further disseminate his unfavorable opinions.

In spite of his antipathy to the single tax, Ely, to his credit, was capable of generous sentiments concerning George's broader contribution:

> Perhaps the greatest service of all which Mr. George has rendered is to be found in the discussions of right and wrong in economic affairs and institutions which he has provoked. There have always been plenty to advocate the economic rights of the individual, and it is very fortunate that now, at least, a few leaders of thought are urging us to look at rights from the standpoint of the public as well as the individual. . . . The question is frequently asked: "Are property rights safe?" I have no fear about the property rights of the individual, but I have much fear that the property of the public will be stolen in the future as it has too frequently in the past. Henry George and others like him are helping to protect the

property of the public, and for this the millions whose rights are too often overlooked ought to be grateful.[3]

### Jorgensen's Response to Ely's Earlier Criticisms of George

Ely's most extensive criticisms of the single tax are contained in his *Outlines of Land Economics* and his *Outlines of Economics*. The first of these, which was originally published in three volumes in mimeographed form in 1922, was written to set forth fundamental principles upon which the more specialized monographs of the Institute would be grounded. In 1928, 1931, and again in 1940, its subject matter was revised and rearranged with the co-authorship of George S. Wehrwein, and brought out in a single volume, *Land Economics*. The foreword to the 1964 reprint of this work by the University of Wisconsin Press opens with the statement: "In the history of land economics, the Ely-Wehrwein volume is probably the single most influential book."[4]

In 1925 Ely, his Institute, and his *Outlines of Land Economics* were the targets of a 205-page attack by a Georgist, Emil O. Jorgensen, the vitriolic tone of which is typified by its cumbersome but pugnacious title. *False Education in Our Colleges and Universities: An Exposé of Prof. Richard T. Ely and His "Institute for Research in Land Economics and Public Utilities"* was published in Chicago by the Manufacturers and Merchants Federal Tax League, of which Jorgensen was information director. It accuses Ely of bias, hypocrisy, and mendacity, and strongly implies that the policies of his Institute were tailored to accommodate the landed interests prominent among its donors.[5] While this implication may seem uncharitable, it is perhaps worthy of remark that as soon as Ely moved his Institute away from the University of Wisconsin, the regents of that school resolved "that no gifts, donations, nor subsidies shall in future be accepted by or in behalf of the University of Wisconsin from any incorporated educational endowments or organizations of like character"[6]—as if the Institute's dependence upon vested interests had threatened the integrity of its erstwhile host.

Whether or not Jorgensen was justified in impugning Ely's motives, he could scarcely have chosen a better way to vitiate the

effectiveness of his offensive. One finds it difficult to escape the conclusion that, were it not for Ely's prestige, many of his postures would
be dismissed as perverse by most economists, regardless of their estimate of George, and that these postures fairly invited Jorgensen's
intemperate response. Had Jorgensen been content to concentrate his
fire on these without resorting to personal invective, his book might
have been more successful in accomplishing its purpose. However,
in his attempted refutation of the thirty-two chief fallacies that he pur-
ports to find in the *Outlines of Land Economics* and, to a lesser extent,
in other works by Ely, Jorgensen does manage to score some telling
points. Space does not here permit a review of his treatment of all
thirty-two "fallacies," so the present authors will occupy themselves
only with the thirteen most pertinent objections. Of those with which
we shall not deal, some are trivial; others cast aspersion upon Ely's
intellectual honesty; others merely assert dogmatically propositions
contrary to those of Ely; while still others reflect what appear to be
misreadings or distorted interpretations of the passages in question.
Our method will be to state each "fallacy" in Jorgensen's words, to
present a citation from Ely substantiating that he actually held the
position ascribed to him, and, finally, to summarize in each case
Jorgensen's rejoinder, with sometimes a comment of our own. The
"fallacies" are numbered here as they originally appeared.

"3—*That Land CANNOT be Monopolized, While Capital and the
Products of Industry CAN be Monopolized*": "Of all the factors of production land is the most difficult to monopolize. . . . In land ownership there is usually the freest and fullest competition, so that the
returns yielded by land are reduced to a lower level than the returns
to fluid capital. Land requires more care and gives smaller returns in
proportion to what is put into it in the way of capital and enterprise,
than standard investments of other kinds. . . . It is a curious thing that
people speak of land as a monopoly when it, of all things is the least
monopolizable."[7]

Jorgensen's rejoinder: "Land cannot be duplicated, but capital can
be duplicated indefinitely," and, indeed, "must be constantly duplicated to keep it from returning to . . . the dust of the earth. Competition, therefore, cannot affect land in the same manner and in the
same degree that it affects capital. . . ." "Land has no cost of produc-

tion, capital has. And whereas in civilized society land always starts at zero and *appreciates* in value, capital—minor disturbances apart—always starts at its cost of production and *depreciates* in value."[8]

"6—*That Invention, Discovery and Material Progress Have the Effect of REDUCING Land Values Instead of RAISING Them*": "Progress brings economy in the use of land, making the same area go farther toward satisfying the need for land. With a stationary population, if society progresses, a land supply, though constant in area, increases relatively through improvements in the utilization of agricultural land and through improvements in transport in the case of urban land. As a result land will fall in value."[9]

Jorgensen's rejoinder: The reverse of the above is true because human wants are insatiable. Improvements elevate the standard of consumption. This constantly increases the demand for land (even when population is stationary) and hence land values. To support his argument, Jorgensen quotes from various authorities, including Adam Smith and Thorold Rogers.[10] Later, he administers the coup de grâce by quoting another passage from the same volume (p. 111) in which Ely, asserting that a progressive society that increases in prosperity "inevitably adds to the selling price of the land,"[11] takes a stand directly opposite to that under discussion.

"7—*That the Rent of Land Has Not RISEN During the Last Hundred Years, But Has Remained STATIONARY*": "Henry George and others hold that the rent of land absorbs the increase in wealth. The history of the world in the last hundred years, however, shows wealth increasing and the rent of land remaining fairly stationary. In the period from 1850 to 1910 the rent of land never amounted to as much as ten percent of the annual wealth of the United States, while in England the rent of land has decreased."[12]

Jorgensen's rejoinder: Contrary to Ely's contention, rent has been steadily rising over the last hundred years, even in England. For example, farm rent that 200 years ago stood at zero, now absorbs from 20 to 60 percent of the farmer's annual income. Urban residential site rent, next to nothing in the days of Benjamin Franklin, now takes from 12 to 40 percent of the earnings of the people who live on the sites. Royalties for coal-bearing sites are as much as 26 percent of the price the coal sells for at the mouth of the mine, oil royalties, from 12 to 20 percent of the price of oil at the well. "In short, we know that the rent of land, which, in the seventeenth century absorbed nothing from the wealth produced by capital and labor, now absorbs twenty, thirty, forty and sometimes sixty percent of that wealth, instead of less than ten per cent as claimed by Prof. Ely."* Dr. Sun Yat-sen is quoted (New York *Independent* 13 June 1912) as saying that the value of land in Shanghai had increased ten thou-sandfold (100,000 percent!) during the past century.[13]

"8—*That Unearned Increment is Not to Be Found in Land RENT, But Is to Be Found in WAGES and INTEREST*": "Unearned increments . . . are due to two great causes; namely, monopoly and conjecture. In the case of land ownership the first is eliminated, whereas in many other parts of the economic field both operate."[14]

Jorgensen's rejoinder: Jorgensen offers the standard Georgist reply, pointing out that wages and interest are, by definition, earned, while rent, not being the product of individual effort, cannot be earned by individuals. He quotes John Stuart Mill's observation (*Principles of Political Economy*, bk. 5, chap. 2, sec. 5) that landlords "grow richer as it were, in their sleep, without working, risking or economising."[15] We would add that Ely simply calls speculative profits (which cer-tainly apply to land) "rent of conjecture" instead of monopoly rent, ignoring the fact that without some element of monopoly, conjecture would seldom yield rent, which results from the combination of a monopoly of location and/or subsoil assets with population increase and improvements in the area. He says (p. 55) that this speculative profit should be called "conjectural surplus" or "rent of conjecture" rather than the unearned increment of land, yet on the next page (p. 56) he explicitly classes it as an unearned increment.

"10—*That the Amount of Good Land Held Out of Use Is Not LARGE, But Very SMALL*": "The idea that good land is held out of use in large areas is a fiction."[16]

Jorgensen's rejoinder: The table of vacant land in thirteen U.S. cities,

---

*If it be objected that, by going back to the seventeenth century or to the days of Franklin, Jorgensen does not really speak to Ely's point that rent has not risen over *the last hundred years*, the truly immense appreciation in land values over the past three decades certainly supports his general position.

compiled by a staff member of Ely's Institute, and upon which he bases the above statement, actually does not support it, for it shows Spokane to be 63.5 percent, St. Paul to be 51.9 percent, Chicago to be 31 percent, St. Louis to be 29.8 percent, San Francisco to be 26.7 percent, and so on, unimproved. "But the situation is emphatically worse than the table indicates. For one thing, its accuracy in several places is rather doubtful—Chicago, for instance, having, according to the assessment officials, approximately 55 percent of its land vacant instead of 31 percent." Furthermore, even if the table were correct, it would be misleading because of the vast amount of land that is classified by public officials as improved, but that is so underdeveloped as to be practically vacant—where the "improvement" (which may be nothing but a billboard) bears no relation to the value of the site. Ely seeks to substantiate his claim only with respect to urban land, but Jorgensen documents the existence of immense tracts of desirable coal, mineral, waterpower, timber, and agricultural land that were either undeveloped or underdeveloped, citing figures from the Forestry Department, the 1914 federal report on *The Lumber Industry*, and Gifford Pinchot.[17]

"11—*That Speculation in Vacant Land Is an ASSET to a Community Instead of a LIABILITY*": "It should be apparent that the owner of vacant land supplies these conditions (available land for gardens, lawns and open air spaces) at a rather low cost. . . . Did we not have the public revenues yielded by vacant land privately owned while undergoing the ripening process, the tax rate would have to be raised. . . . He (the owner of vacant land) has made an investment: he has performed economically desirable functions, he has taken great risks, he has paid significant sums in taxes and assessments. Very uncertain and often inadequate are the gains that finally come to him."[18]

Jorgensen's rejoinder: The vacant lots in question do not in the main consist of gardens, lawns, and so forth, as Ely implies, but largely of weed-patches, mud puddles, and dumping places for junk and garbage. Their price is too high for those who would like to beautify them. This high price forces congestion on the land that is improved, *reducing* the availability of fresh air and sunlight. As for taxes, "if it were not for the chronic undertaxation of vacant land everywhere there would be no resultant overtaxation of improved land." Land ventures, it is true, do not always turn out profitably. But Ely thinks that speculators are entitled to a profit for making such investments and taking such risks. "Figs! The bandit who purchases a revolver and waits all night for his victim to come by is not always successful either. He, too, has made an 'investment,' has 'worked hard' and has 'taken great risks' and if the vacant land monopolist whose object is to hold up the land user is fairly entitled to a profit, so is the bandit." But the chief loss that the withholding of land imposes on the community is: (1) in the greatly increased cost that it lays on government, first, by making it more expensive to obtain land for public improvements, and second, by compelling states and municipalities to build and keep in repair an enormous amount of unnecessary improvements because of "suburban sprawl"; and (2) in the immense obstacles that it puts in the way of the legitimate production and distribution of wealth, because land available for use is not compactly situated.[19] These two points, it may be parenthetically remarked, were never put more dramatically than by Winston Churchill in 1909, on the stump in Lancashire. What he said there on the topic was published as the fourth chapter of his book, *The People's Rights*,[20] and is heartily commended to the attention of the reader.

"13—*That Most Land is Owned by POOR People, and Not by RICH People*": "Few of the men of great wealth whose names are familiar to us have made their money in land. . . . Land is the poor man's investment and should be such."[21]

Jorgensen's rejoinder: Jorgensen presents a table showing that 10 percent of the U.S. population owns 90 percent of the total land values, 40 percent owns 10 percent of the total land values, and 50 percent owns no land values whatsoever. He then points out that the names of very few wealthy persons are "familiar" to the public at large, since they are chiefly nonproducers and therefore have no pecuniary reason to advertise their names. In any case, he says, it is not true that few of the famous multimillionaires made their money in land, and he backs this assertion with various citations, including the following from John R. Commons (*The Distribution of Wealth* [New York: Macmillan, 1893], p. 253): "If the size of fortunes is taken into account, it will be found that perhaps 95% of the total values represented by these millionaire fortunes is due to those investments classed as land values and natural monopolies, and to competitive industries aided by such monopolies."[22]

"15—*That the Separation of Land and Improvements is NOT PRAC-TICABLE, But IMPRACTICABLE*': "Among the many reasons why we should not tax separately the value of the land and the value of improvements is the difficulty of separating the two values."[23]

Jorgensen's rejoinder: Jorgensen denies that such a difficulty exists, instancing the successful application of the Somers System in Cleveland and Columbus, Ohio; Springfield and Joliet, Illinois; Des Moines and Dubuque, Iowa; Phoenix, Tucson, and Prescott, Arizona; Houston, Beaumont, Waco, Galveston, San Antonio, and Corpus Christi, Texas; Denver, Colorado; Augusta, Georgia; and Redlands, California; and elsewhere; as well as the separation of land from improvement values in Australia, New Zealand, South Africa, Canada, Denmark, and Hungary, together with New York City and the California Irrigation Districts. In further support of his position he cites the authoritative *Principles of Real Estate Appraising* by John A. Zangerle, and *The Taxation of Land Values* by Louis F. Post, a Georgist who served as assistant secretary of labor under Woodrow Wilson.[24]

"22—*That Consumption Taxes Will Not HURT the Poor People, But Will HIT the Rich People*': "The 'masses' have a surplus that can be taxed. . . . On every hand can be seen an enormous surplus of income over needs of subsistence. The expenditures of the public for prize fights, 'movies,' ice cream, candy, tobacco, chewing gum, perfumery and beverages of all kinds run into the hundreds of millions, yes, even billions of dollars every year. . . . Taxes on consumption and various indirect forms of taxation must be employed to a larger extent."[25] "Now, we have a great many people of large means who own tax-exempt securities and the aggregate of these securities runs into many billions of dollars. We can reach these people, and that without violation of faith, by indirect taxes."[26]

Jorgensen's rejoinder: If there really is a margin that allows the workers to indulge in "movies" and ice cream, and if they earned it by rendering useful services, it properly belongs to them, and should not be sucked away from them in order to "enable the owners of our natural opportunities to put in their pockets a still larger amount of ground rent which they do not earn."[27] As for indirect taxes being a means of reaching the rich: "There is no way in which indirect taxes can be placed upon the food, clothing and luxuries of the people that will not strike the poor, in proportion to their means, infinitely harder than they will strike the rich—not if they are intended to raise any substantial amount of revenue." For to raise much revenue, they must be levied upon such articles as are in wide and common use, and the millionaire does not consume a significantly larger quantity of these than does the day laborer.[28]

"23—*That to Take the Socially-Created Rent of Land is CONFISCA-TION, But to Take the Earnings of Capital and Labor is NOT Confis-cation*": "Many are disturbed because property in land yields income. Our attention is frequently called to a corner lot in a city, from which the owner derives, let us say, $30,000 a year. Taxes and all improvements are paid by the owner of the building erected on the lot. The owner of the lot may live in idleness, and it is said that he makes no return to society for what he receives. . . . Unless we are prepared to go over to Socialism and abandon private ownership of productive property, we must expect to find men receiving an income from property, and using this income sometimes wisely and sometimes ill. . . . The solution of our land problems is not at all to be sought in confiscation of land values."[29]

Jorgensen's rejoinder: To the above, Jorgensen juxtaposes Ely's passage on consumption taxes for the masses, quoted under the last heading. The obvious conclusion to be drawn from comparing the two passages is that Ely maintains that it is the landowner's own business what he does with his income, but that if workers spend money on such nonessentials as ice cream and "movies," they should be penalized by indirect taxation. It could, of course, be objected that such taxes would apply to landowners as well, but Jorgensen contends that the landowner's income, being a social product, is something that "justly belongs to the whole community," whereas the wages of labor and the interest on capital are returns for human effort expended and useful services rendered, and therefore rightfully belong to those who have earned them. "Hence, if any portion of these funds of wages and interest be appropriated by taxation, it is—

so long as government has its own source of revenue—nothing less than robbery, robbery under the forms of law."[30]

"24—*That the Singletax Means, Not INDIVIDUALISM, But SOCIAL-ISM and COMMUNISM*": "According to the single tax theory all land is a gift of nature to society; consequently all the returns from utilizing land belong to society, not to any individual owner."[31]

Jorgensen's rejoinder: Jorgensen correctly asserts that "the single-tax theory *does* hold that 'all land is a gift of nature to society,' but it *does not* hold that 'all the returns from utilizing land belong to society, not to any individual owner.' The singletax holds just the opposite of this; namely, that 'all the returns from utilizing land' belong to individuals and not to society."[32] Upon analysis, Ely's statement would indeed appear, as Jorgensen complains, to place the single tax "in the same class with socialism and communism." Whether this was, as he charges, Ely's design, is less clear. Yet Ely's treatment of George in his *Recent American Socialism* lends a degree of credence to the charge, for in that work George is presented as a harbinger and abettor of socialism (which to some extent he unintentionally was), with scarcely a hint that he was also a firm believer in the rights of capital and in free market competition.[33]

### Later Criticisms by Ely

Ely's *Outlines of Economics* went into six editions over a period lasting from 1893 to 1937. Most of these had various co-authors, and the views expressed in them were not always uniform, but Ely, as senior author, was ultimately responsible for the content of each edition. While all the editions tended to be unsympathetic to the single tax, the fullest discussion of it is contained in the two last ones, and it is therefore to these that we shall primarily refer.

"On what ground of justice or ethics," asked Ely, "shall the landowner be singled out for taxation?"[34] Why should the rich merchant or stockholder go tax free while the landowner, who may be either rich or poor, is taxed to the point of confiscation? Ely maintained that the only just basis for taxation is ability to pay, and so was a strong exponent of the progressive income tax (although, as we have seen, he also favored taxes on consumption).

Ely's objections to the single tax were practical as well as moral. Allusion has already been made to his belief that the tax would be difficult if not impossible to implement, because of the problem of trying to separate the value of land from the value of improvements on or to it. Unlike General Walker, who advanced the same objection, Ely concerned himself with urban as well as with rural land, and asked how we could separate from the bare land value the value of such capital improvements as grading, landscaping, drainage, and the installation of sewers, streets, and utilities.[35] Curiously, this flatly contradicts his stand in earlier editions, where he raised the problem with respect to agricultural land only, and acknowledged that "it is easy in cities to separate economic rent from rent for improvements, and it is done a thousand times a day."[36] The final (sixth) edition, published in 1937, and co-authored by Ralph Hess, does not take a definite position one way or the other on this issue.

Ely was one of the first to broach the charge of inelasticity, which was to appear again and again in the writings of opponents of the single tax. He felt that the amount of land rent in a community did not necessarily equal the amount of revenue required for public purposes. At times the land-value tax might yield more than the government needed, but at other times it might yield less. In periods of emergency, such as depression or natural disaster, the land-rent fund would tend to diminish just when more public revenue was called for.[37]

To this indictment the single taxers replied that the land-value tax would collect so much revenue that all possible governmental needs would be satisfied. Although, on both moral and economic grounds, George advocated collecting all but a small fraction of the land rent, some of his more moderate followers (notably, Thomas Shearman and Charles B. Fillebrown) pointed out that any of it not needed for legitimate public expenditures would not have to be collected. All of the single taxers argued that the government should live off its own rightful income just as any individual or corporation is expected to do, and should therefore limit its expenditures according to the capacity of the socially produced land-rent fund. They reasoned that a government expenditure should create an equivalent amount of land value because it presumably increases the desirability of living in the area served by the government; this increased desirability is reflected in location value, that is, land rent. Hence, if a government expenditure did not increase land rent by an amount at least equivalent to the expenditure itself, it should be condemned as wasteful and ill-advised.

Although it is widely conceded that in George's time land rent would have met the cost of government at all levels, and although after three decades of geometrically increasing land values, the most informed estimate is that U.S. annual land rent is now probably double U.S. corporate after-tax profits,[38] many would question whether even this would yield a sum sufficient to support today's gigantic public budgets. As for the single taxers' "rightful income" argument, while it might hold true in a utopia where all men are rational and no one infringes upon the just claims of his fellows, its applicability to our present nonutopian world seems rather dubious. In a utopia, huge outlays for defense and police would not be necessary. But today the size of such outlays is determined by urgent practical need rather than by the amount of land values they might generate. On the other hand, Georgists would be quick to point out that the effect of land-value taxation with respect to employment, housing, and numerous other domestic problems might well be such as to eliminate or at least drastically reduce the requirement for public spending in these and related areas.

Furthermore, it should be realized that the inelasticity criticism applies only to the single tax, not to a land-value tax imposed as one tax among others. Somewhat unaccountably, Ely, in most of his writings, refused, as did many other professional economists, to consider the land-value tax as anything else than a single tax.[39] Yet there is no real reason why the land-value tax, if insufficient for justifiable government expenditures, could not, consistent with George's premises, be supplemented by other levies based on the concept of payment for benefits received.[40] And even most contemporary economists (who reject the benefit theory) recognize the peculiar advantages of land-value taxation as one source of public revenue.

Ely's argument that it is practically impossible to separate urban improvement values from bare land values was not borne out by the experience of many municipalities that even in his day were assessing land and improvements separately. This may be why the argument does not appear in the final edition of his book. Assessors were and are doing what he claimed was impossible. To the examples instanced by Jorgensen, we may add Kiao-chau during its period as a German protectorate prior to World War I, Jamaica, Hawaii, and the Pennsylvania cities of Pittsburgh, Scranton, Allentown, and Harrisburg. Only the costs of grading, drainage, and other types of site development that "merge with the land" present a genuine difficulty, but solutions do exist. One good method is to permit tax deductions, spread over a number of years, for the increase in land values resulting from these site-development expenses.

What about Ely's contention that ability to pay (as an application of the more general social utility theory) is the most just criterion for a tax? Like other "liberal" economists who reflected the influence of study in Bismarck's Germany, he was contemptuous of the idea that people should be obliged to pay only for specific benefits received from the community, holding that the individual has no rights apart from society, and that the privilege of being part of society is a general benefit for which he should be made to pay whatever he is able.[41] To George, an uncompromising Jeffersonian individualist whose social philosophy was squarely grounded on the doctrine of natural rights, this approach was, of course, anathema. He maintained that all true taxation was morally wrong, and that the so-called single tax was not really a tax at all. It was merely the public appropriation of a publicly produced phenomenon, land rent, for public purposes.[42]

But when he used the word *tax* in the broader and more conventional sense (as he often did as a concession to common parlance), George maintained that it was better to tax a special privilege like the exclusive use and disposition of a site (a portion of that earth that God created for the habitation and sustenance of all His children) than an ability such as business acumen or inventiveness. Why fine a man by taxing his ability when by using it he cannot help but benefit society? A contemporary proponent of land-value taxation might add that we should adopt it because it fulfills better than any alternative the canons of taxation generally accepted ever since the days of Adam Smith. While no Georgist would ever advocate "soaking the rich" as a matter of principle, if for some reason this were still deemed necessary or desirable by the elected representatives of the public, other taxes could be added for the purpose.[43]

The sixth (last) edition of the *Outlines of Economics* contains a criticism that we have not yet considered, which also appears in germinal form in the fifth edition and is similar to arguments earlier advanced by Carl C. Plehn, John Bates Clark, and Frank Fetter:[44]

> Henry George's social philosophy was based . . . on the fundamental distinction he drew between land and capital. . . . But modern economic thought has come to recognize that land, like capital, is an agent of production which owes its usefulness to human toil. Land, in the economic sense, can be said to exist only in so far as it is brought into use by man, and, in this sense, the supply of land, like the supply of capital is susceptible of increase in response to demand.[45]

But decades before Ely gave it currency, this point had been forcefully addressed by Thomas Nixon Carver, who stoutly upheld the distinction between land and capital in the following words:

> Now land capital [economic land as distinguished from mere geographic land] cannot possibly mean anything else than land *value*, since it is used in a way which excludes improvements placed on the land such as buildings and fences. But to argue that though land surface may not be increased land value may, is to beg the whole question. One might as well say that during the supposed coal famine of the winter of 1902–1903, it was not coal in the economic sense, but only in the material sense, which was scarce; that though there were few coal-tons there was much coal-value; and that therefore there was as much coal, in the economic sense, as ever: but that would be a travesty on the science of economics.[46]

Carver went on to point out that although there are certain ways (such as improved transportation facilities) by which the scarcity of land can be alleviated when the pressure becomes great enough to furnish inducement, they cannot do so sufficiently to prevent land from "rising to enormous values in thickly populated centres"—which is manifestly the case with capital only temporarily when at all.

George Raymond Geiger, expanding upon remarks by Harry Gunnison Brown, subjects Ely's argument to yet another line of contravention, with which it seems appropriate to bring this chapter to a close:

We are told, by Ely *et al*, that the utilization of land is possible only through labor, since the use of land demands accessibility, and that therefore in this sense land is *produced*. "How utterly irrelevant is all this to the real problem about land rent! If landowners alone paid the entire cost of 'creating means of access' to their land, such as bulding all the railroads, roads, bridges, and wharves required, maintaining them, and replacing them when worn out or obsolete; if the various owners paid, each in proportion to the increased land value received by them; and if the total capitalized land value did not exceed the reproduction cost, minus depreciation and obsolescence, of these 'means of access,' then Ely's discussion would have relevancy to the problem of private enjoyment of land rent." We are told that bridges and dams and irrigation projects are irreproducible, and that therefore to distinguish between land and capital is old-fashioned! In other words, we are indirectly informed, by an argument like this, that depreciation of *all* capital can be neglected. Or perhaps we are supposed to believe that land *site* depreciates just as much as manufactured articles. (That *fertility* does decline is obvious, but what "land economist" is prepared to argue that the depreciation of farm land *in general* is commensurate with that of buildings and improvements?) This is the type of argument that is used to overthrow the classical contention that land space is set by natural forces, that man can *in no significant way* amend that work of nature or extend it, and that man can and does produce and reproduce goods—wealth and capital. Is it any wonder that some of us become very impatient with our emancipated economic theorist?[47]

## Notes

1. Richard T. Ely, *Ground Under Our Feet* (New York: Macmillan, 1938), p. 268.
2. Ibid., p. 4.
3. Richard T. Ely, "The Single Tax," *Christian Advocate*, 25 December 1890, p. 856. Cited in Arthur N. Young, *The Single Tax Movement in the United States* (Princeton, N.J.: Princeton University Press, 1916), p. 318.
4. Richard T. Ely and George S. Wehrwein, *Land Economics* (1940; reprint ed. Madison, Wis.: University of Wisconsin Press, 1964), p. v.
5. According to Ely himself, contributors included the Carnegie Corporation of New York, the Laura Spellman Rockefeller Memorial Foundation, railways, public utility companies, land companies, lumber companies, etc. "An Open Letter," *Institute News*, October 1924.
6. Resolution of the Board of Regents, August 1925.
7. Richard T. Ely, assisted by Mary L. Shine and George S. Wehrwein, *Outlines of Land Economics* (Ann Arbor, Mich.: Edwards Bros., 1922), 2: 52, 53, 73.

8. Emil O. Jorgensen, *False Education in Our Colleges and Universities: An Exposé of Prof. Richard T. Ely and His "Institute for Research in Land Economics and Public Utilities"* (Chicago: Manufacturers and Merchants Federal Tax League, 1925), pp. 38 f., 40.

9. Ely et al., *Outlines of Land Economics*, 2: 58. See also Richard T. Ely and Edward W. Morehouse, *Elements of Land Economics* (New York: Macmillan, 1924), p. 262.

10. Jorgensen, *False Education*, pp. 43–50.

11. Ibid., p. 72.

12. Ely et al., *Outlines of Land Economics*, 2: 74.

13. Jorgensen, *False Education*, pp. 51 f.

14. Ely et al., *Outlines of Land Economics*, 2: 56.

15. Jorgensen, *False Education*, p. 53.

16. Ely et al., *Outlines of Land Economics*, 3: 98.

17. Jorgensen, *False Education*, pp. 61 f.

18. Ely et al., *Outlines of Land Economics*, 3: 105 f.

19. Jorgensen, *False Education*, pp. 64 f.

20. Winston Spencer Churchill, *The People's Rights* (1909; reprint ed. New York: Taplinger Publishing Company, 1971).

21. Ely et al., *Outlines of Land Economics*, 3: 98.

22. Jorgensen, *False Education*, pp. 75–78.

23. Ely et al., *Outlines of Land Economics*, 3: 115.

24. Jorgensen, *False Education*, pp. 85–87.

25. Ely et al., *Outlines of Land Economics*, 3: 93.

26. Richard T. Ely, *Taxation of Farm Lands* (St. Paul: Webb Publishing Company, 1924), p. 25.

27. Jorgensen, *False Education*, p. 107.

28. Ibid., pp. 109 f.

29. Ely et al., *Outlines of Land Economics*, 3: 102 f., 105.

30. Jorgensen, *False Education*, p. 113.

31. Ely and Morehouse, *Elements of Land Economics*, p. 323.

32. Jorgensen, *False Education*, p. 117.

33. Richard T. Ely, *Recent American Socialism* (Baltimore, Md.: Johns Hopkins University Press, 1884), part 2.

34. Richard T. Ely, Thomas S. Adams, Max O. Lorenz, and Allyn A. Young, *Outlines of Economics*, 5th rev. ed. (New York: Macmillan, 1930), p. 462.

35. Ibid., pp. 444, 460.

36. Richard T. Ely, *Outlines of Economics* (1893; reprint ed. New York: Macmillan, 1905), p. 366.

37. Ely et al., *Outlines of Economics*, 5th rev. ed., p. 460.

38. Mason Gaffney, "Adequacy of Land as a Tax Base," in *The Assessment of Land Value*, ed. Daniel M. Holland (Madison: University of Wisconsin Press, 1970).

39. An exception would be *Land Economics*, co-authored by George S. Wehrwein, in which taxation as a land-use control is sharply distinguished from the single tax. See p. 477.

40. This is implied by Ely and Wehrwein, ibid.

41. See, for example, Richard T. Ely, *Property and Contract in their Relations to the Distribution of Wealth* (1914; reprint ed. Port Washington, N.Y.: Kennikat Press, 1971), 2: 504. For a discussion of this position as advocated by E. R. A. Seligman, see the chapter on Seligman in the present work.

42. Henry George, *Progress and Poverty*, 75th anniversary ed. (New York: Robert Schalkenbach Foundation, 1954), p. 421.

43. The income tax is not so much of a "soak the rich" tax as many people think. There are many loopholes in the income tax law, and rich men can employ able accountants and lawyers to find them. Most large incomes are derived from capital gains, only 40 percent of which are subject to taxation for individuals and 25 percent for corporations. Income splitting among family members, a loose interpretation of business expenses, income from tax-exempt government bonds, profit-sharing trusts, stock options, etc., are legal means of tax avoidance. In addition, it is well known that tax evasion is wide-spread at the high and medium income levels, whereas salaried employees must pay their full share and more of the tax load.

In 1955, 84 percent of the income tax revenue was derived from the 20 percent basic rate that all taxpayers paid on taxable income, and only 16 percent of the revenue was derived from the progressive rate (which ranged from 22 to 91 percent). How much more progressive (i.e., based on income) is the income tax when compared with a national sales tax?

Census figures indicate that in 1955 the highest income-tenth received 29 percent of the national personal income before federal income taxes and 27 percent after. The highest income-fifth received 45 percent before and 43 percent after. (See Gabriel Kolko, *Wealth and Power in America* [New York: Praeger, 1966], p. 34.) The disparity has become even greater since then.

Since the more valuable land is owned almost entirely by rich people, a land-value tax would fall much more on them than upon the poor. In the light of the above statistics, it is certain that the land-value tax would be more progressive than the income tax!

44. Plehn's criticism was presented in a paper read before the Massachusetts Single Tax League, 8 December 1902; Clark's argument is found in his *Distribution of Wealth* (1900), and Fetter's in "The Relations Between Rent and Interest," *Publications of the American Economic Association*, 3d ser., 5, no. 1, pt. 1.

45. Richard T. Ely and Ralph H. Hess, *Outlines of Economics*, 6th ed. (New York: Macmillan, 1937), p. 465.

46. Thomas Nixon Carver, *The Distribution of Wealth* (New York: Macmillan, 1904), p. 113 f.

47. George Raymond Geiger, *The Theory of the Land Question* (New York: Macmillan, 1936), pp. 76 f. The interior quotation is from Harry Gunnison Brown, *The Economic Basis of Tax Reform* (Columbia, Mo.: Lucas Bros., 1932), p. 115 n.

# 27
# Knight: Nemesis from the Chicago School

By Nicolaus Tideman and Florenz Plassmann

Frank Hyneman Knight (1885–1972) was one of the most influential economists of the twentieth century. He received his Ph.D. in economics from Cornell in 1916, under the guidance of Allyn A. Young. He taught at the University of Iowa, Cornell, and the University of Chicago, where he was Martin D. Hull Distinguished Service Professor and one of the founders of the "Chicago School" of economics. Among his students were such famous economists as James Buchanan, Milton Friedman, and George Stigler. During the 1930s, he was one of the editors of the *Journal of Political Economy*, and he became the president of the American Economic Association in 1950. In 1957, he was awarded the Francis Walker medal, which is awarded every five years to the "living American economist who has made the greatest contribution to economics."

Knight was a man of forceful disposition, with opinions strongly held, bluntly expressed, and tenaciously retained. One of these opinions was hostility to Georgism. This hostility, however, did not extend to personal relationships—as witnessed by his gratuitous offer to nominate a Georgist, Harry Gunnison Brown, to the presidency of the American Economic Association.

Knight's most famous contribution to economics, developed in his 1921 book *Risk, Uncertainty and Profit*,[1] concerns the difference between "risk" and "uncertainty." As he defined these terms, "risk" is concerned with known probabilities and can be dealt with through pooling and insurance, while "uncertainty" is concerned with unknown probabilities and is the source of true economic profit.[2]

Besides being a widely respected economist, Knight was also a social philosopher who strongly believed in individual freedom and opposed all forms of social engineering. In a famous 1924 article,[3] he responded to Arthur Pigou's claim that road congestion justifies taxes on roads users. Knight argued that such congestion is a result of the

American Journal of Economics and Sociology, Vol. 63, No. 2 (April, 2004).
© 2004 American Journal of Economics and Sociology, Inc.

absence of property rights in roads. The assignment of property rights, Knight asserted, would induce owners of congested roads to demand tolls from travelers, yielding the same efficient allocation of road space as taxation. This insight laid the foundation for James Buchanan's and Ronald Coase's famous analyses of property rights.

Knight did not believe that unregulated markets had the ethical merit that some economists have claimed. In a 1923 article on the "Ethics of Competition,"[4] he agreed that competitive markets allocate resources efficiently and that they reward every market participant according to the value of his marginal contribution to output. However, he argued, not only are real markets unlikely to meet the assumptions that are necessary for competition to yield the theoretically predicted outcome, but it is also impossible to conclude that any ethical implications are embedded in the theory of competition.[5] The only justification of competition is that "it is effective to get things done; but any candid answer to the question, 'what things,' compels the admission that they leave much to be desired."[6]

While rejecting an ethical defense of markets, Knight still defended laissez-faire because he considered it impossible to preserve individual freedom when governments have great power. In a public lecture at the University of Chicago in 1944, he said:

> Extensive positive action as a unit by a large group, defined by residence in a contiguous area, means delegation of power to a limited number of officials, politicians and bureaucrats. If this is done on an extensive scale, as it is done by planners and "neo-liberals," the agent cannot be held responsible for the use of power, even to a technical majority of those for whom he acts. Such grants of power tend to become irrevocable and the power itself tends to grow beyond assignable bounds.[7]

This distrust of extensive government power may have been at the root of Knight's negative position on the single tax. It is possible that Knight regarded George's call for government action to rectify the ethical problem posed by the private appropriation of rent as just another utopian call for social planning. On at least one occasion, he characterized the single tax as "socialist" confiscation.[8] But Knight's main argument against the single tax was his claim that there is no conceptual difference between rent and interest, and that "pure land value" simply does not exist. A tax on land value, he believed, would lead to the same inefficiencies as a tax on capital.

### Knight's View of Land as a Factor of Production

To understand Knight's argument, we must establish what he meant by "pure land value." This is not an easy task because of Knight's elliptical writing style. However, a reasonable inference can be developed from Knight's view of factors of production, which differed notably from the view of classical economists.

Classical economists divided the factors of production into land, labor, and capital. "Land" was defined as everything that had not been produced by human effort. Human beings were classified as "labor." "Capital" was defined as everything that had been produced by human effort, except human beings. This division implies that the supply of land is fixed (or "inelastic"), while the supplies of human labor and capital are variable (or "elastic"). Labor supply can be increased either by producing offspring or by working more or harder, and the supply of capital can be increased by investment.

Knight found such a division useless. He argued that, while it might be possible to divide hypothetical productive factors according to their conditions of supply, such an exercise would be irrelevant for the productive factors that actually exist.[9] All factors of production should logically be classified as "capital," because the supply of every factor can be regarded as the result of past investment.[10] Labor supply, for example, can be regarded as the outcome of an investment choice in either additional training or additional children. Similarly, Knight argued, land is produced by investment in exploration and development:

> Capital goods in fact differ widely in the length of time required to adjust supply to changes in demand. If there are any agencies not subject to reproduction through investment at all, they conform to the classical description of land. It is the writer's view that such agents are practically negligible and that in the long run land is like any other capital good. Investment in exploration and development work competes with investment in other fields and is similar in all essential respects to other production costs. The distinction between goods relatively flexible and those

relatively inflexible in supply and the recognition of a special category of income (Marshall's "quasi-rent") for the latter is possibly expedient. With uncertainty absent such a distinction is, of course, irrelevant.[11]

From Knight's perspective, the classical notion that land is not produced "reflects a false conception of production."[12] He wrote:

> Production was defined as production of wealth. But in fact, primary production consists in the rendering of services. Wealth is an agency by which services are rendered, not a product in the primary sense. . . . Wealth axiomatically is produced either to replace some item which is used up in rendering its service or to add to the total stock of service rendering agencies. . . . The use of the new wealth increment . . . constitutes production of services simultaneously rendered; and the same services cannot be produced twice.[13]

In other words, Knight believed that the idea that land was not produced confused the concepts of stocks and flows. Economic production, he maintained, refers not to physical creation (as of the earth, a stock), but rather to the transformation (a flow) of inputs into outputs. Although the earth was obviously not created through human effort, Knight assumed that it would not render any services until human activity (production) had transformed it into useful (economic) land.

How does one produce land? From Knight's point of view, the production of land ("opportunities") consisted of the appropriation of an undeveloped resource as well as the transformation of the undeveloped resource into a productive factor. He wrote:

> [I]n real life, the original "appropriation" of such opportunities by private owners involves investment in exploration, in detailed investigation and appraisal by trial and error of the findings, in development work of many kinds necessary to secure and market a product—besides the cost of buying off or killing or driving off previous claimants.[14]

For example, the transformation of soil located below sea level into useful land requires the decision that such transformation is economically feasible ("investment in exploration, in detailed investigation and appraisal by trial and error of the findings" [call this "Cost category 1"]), the effort to ensure exclusive access to the area ("the cost of buying off or killing or driving off previous claimants" ["Cost category 2"]), as well as the actual transformation ("development work of many kinds necessary to secure and market a product" ["Cost category 3"]).

If the transformation of undeveloped resources into land yields something valuable, then the "production" of land will become attractive as soon as the land's value equals the value of the funds that must be used in its production. It is not necessary that the transformation of resources into land lead to positive costs in all three categories. Even if there are no exploration and development costs, somebody will find it worthwhile to spend funds (Cost category 2) to ensure that he receives exclusive access to the resource if such exclusive access is valuable. Competition would induce developers as a group to spend an amount equal to the value of the land in the attempt to secure exclusive access to the undeveloped resources.[15] Knight would consider this struggle to secure exclusive access to be an example of the production of land.[16]

If markets are competitive, then production does not create new value but simply transforms inputs into outputs of equal value. It follows that the value of land is equal to the value of the funds that have been spent in its production. Thus Knight concluded that "[p]ure land value in the sense assumed by the advocates of the single tax does not exist,"[17] and this conclusion provided the foundation of his rejection of the single tax:

> [T]his dogma of unconditional fixity of supply was made the basis for the single-tax propaganda. We cannot discuss this position at length, but must take space to remark quite briefly that it is utterly fallacious. It should be self-evident that when the discovery, appropriation, and development of new natural resources is an open, competitive game, there is unlikely to be any difference between the returns from resources put to this use and those put to any other. Moreover, any disparity which exists is either a result of chance and as likely to be in the favor of one field as the other, or else is due to some difference in psychological appeal between the fields; i.e., goes to offset some other difference in their net advantages. Viewing as a whole the historic process by which land is made available for productive employment, it must be said to be "produced"; i.e., to have its utility conferred upon it in a way quite on a par with that which holds for any other exchangeable good.[18]

If one were to accept Knight's conception of land, then his critique of the single tax might be acceptable.[19] But Knight's treatment of all factors of production as capital ignores a difference between the ways original property rights in capital and land are established. This difference leads to inefficiency if original property rights in land are established through competition, and it motivates the separation of land and capital into different factors.

The usefulness of Knight's conception of land depends on the claim that the three cost categories of land production are equivalent to the three costs categories of capital production. If one accepts Knight's view that land development counts as part of land, then Categories 1 (investigation) and 3 (transformation) apply to the production of land and capital in the same way. Costs in Category 2 (securing exclusive access), however, require a more detailed analysis. Category 2 costs may arise in two different circumstances: they arise first in the context of the original establishment of property rights, and second in the context of the transfer of already established property rights. Costs related to the transfer of already established property rights may arise for any transferable good, and therefore for capital as well as for land. But the costs of establishing original property rights in land and capital differ in most societies.

How does one establish original property rights in factors of production? Many societies recognize a difference between the original establishment of property rights in labor and in capital. Frank Knight referred to this recognition when he wrote:

> From the standpoint of causality, the productive capacity in one's person is generally the result, more or less, of activity on his own part, which has, more or less, the character of investment, and, in addition, every human being is originally "created" by the use of "resources" belonging to other persons . . .
>   But all this does not mean that the human being as a source of economic services can be treated in theory as wealth or capital, or additions to human productive capacity treated as product, or the act of making them as production, as in the case of material wealth. There is a fundamental difference, in the form of a somewhat paradoxical limitation to the individual's ownership of himself. The principle of inalienable rights, recognized in all free societies, means not merely that one cannot sell himself outright, but that one cannot so much as give a valid lien on his services or make an enforceable contract to deliver them for any considerable time

in the future. In other words, he cannot capitalize his earning capacity. Having no economic value to anyone but himself, he has in effect none at all.[20]

Although it would be possible to develop economic theories that are based on an individual's ability to capitalize his own earning capacity, the predictions of such theories would have little relevance to actual societies that recognize inalienable rights. Thus it seems necessary for economic analyses to acknowledge the existence of social conventions.[21]

In many societies, original ownership in produced things is established through legal ownership of the factor services that produced the things. If one does not want to evoke theories of natural rights, then one might defend such a convention on the basis of accepted notions of fairness or efficiency. Again, it seems necessary that economic theory take such conventions into account because the accepted rule of establishing ownership in produced things directly affects the implications that one can draw from a theory of investment.[22]

In Frank Knight's framework, the effort that is used to secure exclusive access to nonproduced resources is part of the production of land. In societies in which produced things belong to their producers, Knight's conception of land thus provides an explanation of the establishment of original property rights in land. His conception of land seems appropriate because the value of the effort to secure exclusive access is a true cost for the person who appropriates the resource. However, funds that are used to acquire property rights are wasted from a social point of view because their only purpose is to ensure that one person rather than another obtains exclusive access. It would be possible to achieve the same outcome by simply granting one person exclusive access to the resource. Combining land and capital into a single category obscures this fact, and makes it difficult to notice that the original acquisition of property rights can entail social inefficiency.

Instead of assuming that land and capital are indistinguishable, it is more appropriate to maintain the classical separation of factors of production into land, labor, and capital. But now the classical separation acquires a new meaning, because factors are defined in terms of ways of establishing original property rights. Human beings, who own themselves and whose ownership is inalienable, are classified as "labor." Things that are not human beings but came into existence through human effort and are therefore owned by their producers are classified as "capital." Everything else is classified as "land." According to this definition, land is the same as an unimproved natural resource, and the value of a plot of land is the highest amount someone would be willing to pay to obtain exclusive access to it (Cost category 2) if it were unimproved.[23] Land investigation and development (Cost categories 1 and 3) produce capital but do not affect the value of the land itself.[24]

Unlike Knight's conception of land, the new (or old) conception does not suggest an immediate solution to the problem of establishing original ownership. However, it emphasizes that any effort that is made to establish original ownership in land represents a waste of resources from a social point of view. A community is free to adopt any convention for the establishment of ownership in land. The single tax is an example of a convention that leads to social efficiency. It requires that the community be permitted to impose a tax on land that is privately owned. Thus the community would charge the developers of new resources a fee (or impose a tax) equal to the maximum amount anybody else would be willing to pay for exclusive access to the resource. In competitive equilibrium, nobody will receive any special profit from the resource, but the community will have the proceeds of the fee.[25]

It is interesting to note that Frank Knight was among the first economists who addressed the social benefits of private property rights. In his discussion of Arthur Pigou's analysis of social costs,[26] Knight argued that, in the absence of owners who control access to their property, users of land have an incentive to disregard the congestion costs that they might impose on others. The result is an inefficiently intensive use of the land. If land is privately owned, then owners have an incentive to charge a fee that limits land use to the socially optimal level.

It seems to be only a small step to extend this notion to the acquisition of land itself. However, Frank Knight declined to make this extension. In a footnote to the paragraph in which he explained the benefit of private ownership of land (or "opportunities"), he wrote:

> The relation between "investment" and "opportunity" is an interesting question, by no means so simple as it is commonly assumed to be. In the writer's view there is little basis for the common distinction in this regard between "natural resources" and labour or capital. The qualities of real significance for economic theory are the conditions of supply and the degree of fluidity or its opposite, specialization to a particular use. In a critical examination neither attribute forms a basis for erecting natural agents into a separate class.[27]

We can only speculate as to why Knight did not apply his analysis of property rights to the acquisition of land. It is possible that he did not consider this to be a "small step." When Pigou claimed that road congestion justifies taxation of roads users, Knight showed that the establishment of property rights restores market efficiency and removes the need for government intervention for the "social good." The single tax, on the other hand, requires government intervention to resolve a market failure. Even though in both cases the problem results from missing property rights, the remedies that restore overall efficiency are the exact opposites of each other. Knight did not believe that it would be possible to maintain individual freedom in the presence of a powerful government, and he might have thought that the danger of assigning additional power to the government would outweigh the potential benefit of the single tax.

An alternative explanation for Frank Knight's failure to apply his analysis of property rights to the acquisition of land is that his conception of land may have prevented him from recognizing that Category 2 costs have different efficiency implications for natural resources and for capital. He repeatedly emphasized that the "production" of land yields the same return as other investments, and his main argument against the single tax seems to have been that, because the production of land does not yield a profit if markets are competitive, there is no unearned increment to which the single tax could be applied.[28] It is at least possible that he did not realize that the single tax is not levied on any profit that may be made from developing the land, but rather on the value that is dissipated by costs in Category 2.

### Knight's View of the Ethics of Private Ownership in Factors of Production

The discussion of Knight's conception of land and his rejection of the single tax emphasized the positive argument for adopting a tax (interpreted as a user fee) on the use of natural resources: such a tax improves upon the market outcome by restoring social efficiency. But Henry George's main motivation for proposing a *single* tax on land was derived from a normative argument: land belongs to everybody in society, and private appropriation of rent is therefore morally wrong. Humans belong to themselves and capital belongs to the person who produces it, which implies that public appropriation of portions of wages and interest through taxation is morally wrong as well. What was Frank Knight's view on the ethics of private ownership of land, labor, and capital?

Throughout his life, Frank Knight very eloquently defended the position that economic theory and ethics belong to separate realms,[29] and he was suspicious of economists who advocated government action for ethical reasons. Whenever he addressed claims that individuals are not entitled to the returns of productive agents in their possession, he attempted to show that there is no fundamental difference between the returns of different productive agents. If no such difference exists, he argued, then it is illogical to single out the returns to a particular agent—one can only claim that individuals are either entitled to the returns of all agents or to no returns at all.

Knight explained his position most forcefully in his analysis of socialism:[30]

> The ethical questions as to whether an individual deserves to receive and enjoy the income produced by any productive capacity in his possession may be divided into two parts. The first has to do with the source of the economic power in question, or how the individual comes into possession of it, and the second with the manner or conditions of its use. In both cases—property in the narrow sense and personal capacities—possession originates in a similar list of facts and processes. These include,

in both cases, first, inheritance, and second, the working of social-cultural and legal processes over which the individual has no control. Beyond this causally given basis or nucleus, productive power is created in the individual by a process of investment—in education and training in the inclusive sense—which is neither economically nor ethically different in any respect from the investment which gives rise to any other productive agency. All these factors are affected to a large if not overwhelming extent by all sorts of imponderables and contingencies which may be lumped under the head of "luck."

There is no visible reason why anyone is more or less entitled to the earnings of inherited personal capacities than to those of inherited property in any other form; and similarly as to capacity resulting from impersonal social processes and accidents, which affect both classes of capacity indifferently. And in so far as the creation of either form of capacity is due to motivated human activity on the part of the individual concerned or his parents, or to anyone else, the motives may in either case be ethical or unethical in any possible sense or degree. And finally, the use of productive capacity of either type may similarly be more or less intelligently motivated in accord with ends or ideals which are ethical or unethical in any degree and in any meaning.[31]

Knight's position follows from his understanding that all productive agents ought to be defined as capital, because all are the result of some activity (the transformation of inputs into outputs, called "production") in the past. But past activity alone is not sufficient to answer ethical questions regarding the right to the returns of productive factors. For example, one might argue that Knight's argument:

> productive power is created in the individual by a process of investment—in education and training in the inclusive sense—which is neither economically nor ethically different in any respect from the investment which gives rise to any other productive agency

is inconsistent with respect to a person's socially accepted rights to his labor earnings. To the extent that personal capacities result from the activities of a person's parents, it would be consistent to assign the income that results from such "investment" to the parents rather than to the child. Instead, society has decided to assign such income to the child, which may be regarded as the result of "the working of social-cultural and legal processes over which the individual has no control." However, such a catchall phrase does not answer ethical questions at all because any assignment of rights can be "explained" or "defended" by the "working of social-cultural and legal processes." Instead, it is important to be aware of the implications and origins of such processes, and to understand how they form the ethical framework that a society has adopted. Even if Knight had made a convincing argument that there is no fundamental mechanical difference between the returns of different productive agents, the example suggests that such an argument may not be not very helpful to answer ethical questions of entitlement. It may be best to follow Knight's own suggestion and not to mix economic and ethical arguments.

### Two Occasions to Ridicule Henry George's Philosophy and to Object to the Single Tax

Frank Knight argued against the soundness of the economic foundations of the single tax in several of his academic articles, and he criticized Henry George's ideas directly in two of his writings: a 1933 review of George Geiger's, *The Philosophy of Henry George*,[32] and a 1953 article titled, "The Fallacies in the Single Tax."[33]

The review of Geiger has the form of a diatribe against George and does not contain much of an argument.[34] Knight briefly repeated his earlier criticism that an investment in land can be expected to yield the same return as any other investment, but he did not add a reference to his theory of production; he probably thought that he had made his point already in 1921.

Frank Knight's most detailed account of his view of the single tax appears in the 1953 article. In addition to his earlier argument that the idea of the single tax is fallacious because investment in exploration and land development does not yield higher returns than investment in other activities, Knight raised eight other objections against the single tax. Two of his objections question the practical feasibility of implementing a tax on land, while the remaining objections are directed against the theoretical and ethical motivations of the single tax.

*Objections Regarding the Practical Feasibility of the Single Tax*

Knight's first objection is concerned with what he saw as an unsolvable practical problem:

If "society" means all mankind, treated equally, we must assume an all-wise, all-powerful, and completely benevolent world government. But such "practical" difficulties are a small matter to a reformer "hipped" on a panacea for the world's ills.[35]

and:

I have mentioned the practical question of *what* "society" would have the right to take the land value from private holders. The only answer that is at least defensible in terms of natural-rights premises is "mankind," "the world." And that is what the single-tax propagandists say. Since this is clearly and absurdly impossible, one can only guess at their actual meaning. If a superhuman agency were to confiscate any type of wealth and distribute it equally among all living human beings, it would be immediately dissipated and lost, with the demoralization of organized society everywhere. This fact is enough to destroy all reasoning from abstract rights and to make any sensible person realize that practical problems have to be solved in terms of expediency, the requirements for civilized living, and some hope for progress.[36]

Knight is right that acceptance of the idea that rent belongs equally to all persons implies that all humanity must be accorded equal rights to land. But this does not require world government. It is sufficient to have a world-wide shared understanding that any nation that claims exclusive access to more than its share of the gifts of nature has an obligation to pay into a fund that compensates the nations that thereby have less than their shares.[37]

Knight's second objection is also practical rather than theoretical:

[I]t is a detail hardly worth noting that rent is not actually "paid" in the case of a man farming (or otherwise using) his own land, but it would be "there" just the same. More important, the amount paid or "imputed" in any case would be only an approximation to the theoretically correct figure. And for the same reasons, if it were to be appropriated by the government, some official, some "bureaucrat" with power, would have to appraise it—subject to error, prejudice and acute disagreement. Moreover, the levy would evidently have to be the estimated real value of the land for use in the most economical way. To collect such rent, the government would in practice have to compel the owner actually to use the land in the best way, hence to prescribe its use in some detail. Thus we already see that the advantage of taxation over socialization of management has practically disappeared.[38]

Once again, Knight is half right. The rent of land is observed as a market price only when an owner leases unimproved land, which is rare. A system of public collection of rent requires an assessment system, and assessments can be expected to be less than perfect. But the goal of assessment need not be to determine "the estimated real value of the land for use in the most economical way." If there is a difference between the value of a parcel in the use to which the person who values it most highly would put it and the value when used by the person who values it second most highly, then it is reasonable to base the tax on the second value. This is the "cost" of using the parcel in its most highly valued use. Thus a suitable target for the assessed rental value of each parcel is the value of the parcel to the person who values it second most highly.

The question of how an assessor might identify such a value is a complex question. It would not be possible to use sale prices, as occurs under current property taxes, because sale prices would tend toward zero and would be determined primarily by expected assessment errors as the share of rent taken in taxation approached 100 percent. But there are other devices. An assessor could purchase title to a cross-section of parcels with improvements of minimal value, demolish the improvements and auction the parcels, under a rule that the auction price would be the tax for the first year, and taxes in future years would be determined by similar auctions of nearby parcels. Prior to such auctions, an assessor could invite land specialists to participate in a contest to offer formulas that would predict the winning bids of such auctions as a function of location and other land characteristics. An assessor could contract with persons interested in land development to provide land with specified characteristics for development, if it became available. The prices in such option contracts would provide estimates of the rental value of parcels. Thus there are ways to assess the rental value of land when the government is seeking to collect the opportunity cost of using land. None of these ways requires the government to supervise the use of land. Knight's suggestion that such supervision would be required is without foundation.

*Objections Against the Theoretical Foundations of the Single Tax*

In his next two paragraphs, Knight takes up what he sees as the crucial error in land-value taxation:

> For the crucial error in the theory, however, we have to look further. The way anyone becomes a landlord and comes into possession of the "surplus" or the "unearned increment" of the sale value which is its capitalized worth, is to buy it from a previous owner. He will, of course, have to pay a price which includes any expected future increase in the capitalized yield. Land has "always," practically speaking, been private property, freely exchanged against other wealth—including human beings when these could be owned. Possession through inheritance also involves no distinction and need not be considered. (In fact, other advantages besides property are inherited, and raise the same ethical problem.) Thus the value alleged to be socially created is always paid for before it is received—as far as the parties most interested are able to predict its arising.
>
> Following this sequence back through time, we come to the conditions of original exploration and settlement. The allegation that our pioneers got the land for nothing, robbing future generations of their rightful heritage, should not have to be met with argument. The whole doctrine was invented by city men living in comfort, not by men in contact with the facts as owners or renters. How many preachers of single-tax doctrine would care to live their lives and bring up their families under the conditions of the frontier, fight off the savages and other enemies, and occasionally be massacred, suffer the hardships, overcome the difficulties or succumb to them, do without the amenities of civilization, including medical attention for their families—for what the average pioneer got out of it? The question answers itself. Their heirs, near or remote, often got unearned wealth, but again that is not a sequel peculiar to land. Consequently, if society were later to confiscate land value, allowing retention only of "improvements" or their value, it would ignore the costs in bitter sacrifice and would arbitrarily discriminate between one set of property owners and another set, where there is no difference to justify this action.[39]

George's supporters can agree that the owners of title to land have generally paid for those titles. They can agree that the Europeans who first seized land from the Indians suffered great hardships. The point of disagreement is with Knight's claim that "if society were to later confiscate the land value, . . . it would . . . arbitrarily discriminate between one set of property owners and another set, where there is no difference to justify the action."

If the owner of the only taxicab company in a town were to endure hardship and sacrifice persuading the town council to pass a law prohibiting any new firms from entering the taxicab business in the town, one would expect the owner's hardship and sacrifice to be reflected in a higher value of his business. Still, neither the owner nor anyone who bought his business would have a reasonable complaint if a subsequent town council were to repeal the restrictive law. People should be free to enter the taxicab business if they wish. Anyone should be able to understand this. If a town council is so misguided that it restricts individual freedom to enter the taxicab business, no one can reasonably claim that subsequent councils have an obligation not to correct the earlier council's error. George's supporters see titles to land in a similar light.

George's supporters assert that all persons have equal rights to the gifts of nature. If there is land that has no value to anyone else (marginal land), then for as long as the land remains marginal, anyone may freely use as much as he or she wishes. If land that had previously been marginal comes to have scarcity value, anyone who wishes to continue to use the land incurs at that time an obligation to take account of the rights of others. Even if previous users endured hardship and sacrifice in establishing their use, they do not obtain special rights.

It may be objected that value is created by those who explore previously unexplored land and identify uses for it that would not otherwise be known. This value is compensated by a system that grants titles to first users and is not compensated when first users have no special rights. There are three replies. First, giving ownership rights to first users overcompensates them, leading to the inefficiency of a land rush. As Knight had pointed out, if it was possible to establish ownership in a natural resource by a specified unproductive sacrifice, someone could be expected to make that sacrifice as soon as it yielded a positive expected profit. Thus the value of natural opportunities tends to be dissipated by a rule granting ownership to first users. Second, justice does not necessarily yield efficiency. Correspondingly, a demonstration that a particular institution is inefficient does not prove that it is unjust. Finally, even if justice does not require that all creation of value be compensated, a community can choose to compensate discovers of new knowledge if it wishes. However, a community that wished to compensate explorers of new land efficiently would not want to compensate them with titles in perpetuity. That would be excessive because it would ignore the likelihood that eventually someone else would make the discovery if the actual discoverer did not. Efficient compensation for discovery would reward the discoverer with the increase in value from the fact that the discovery was made sooner than it otherwise would have been. Thus a society that taxes the rent of land and does not tax the income from capital does not "arbitrarily discriminate between one set of property owners and another set, where there is no difference to justify the action." The difference between the two sets of property owners that justifies the action is that the owners of capital have created or purchased the value of the capital, while the "owners" of land have undertaken to exclude others or purchased a right to exclude others from what ought to be everyone's common heritage. Even if original users created some value by discovering uses earlier than they otherwise would have been discovered, the time when such uses would have been discovered by someone else is almost certainly long past in almost all cases, and the discoverer did not have a claim in justice to be compensated in any case.

On the remaining one and a half pages of the article, Knight raises six additional arguments against the single tax. First, he claims that taxation of rent is an example of confiscation that would lower people's incentive to accumulate property:

> Of course there is a large element of luck in all exploration and development activities. Some did make very high returns on their outlay; others lost their all, and often health or life itself besides. If society proposes to confiscate the gains of the winners it must compensate the losers—or not only work arbitrary injustice but set a precedent that would warn anyone against undertaking risky ventures. This would at once force establishment of outright socialism or put a stop to all forward-looking activity.[40]

The arbitrary injustice component of this argument has already been addressed. As to setting a precedent, that depends on how the action is justified. If a society were to say, "Because you have made a very

high return on your outlay, we will confiscate your gain," then this
could indeed be expected to discourage people from undertaking
risky ventures. However, if a society says, "You may keep all of the
gains that you have accrued through your labor and through your
investments in capital, however high those gains may be. But we will
require you to compensate the rest of us for any exclusive access that
you seek to maintain to a disproportionately large share of natural
opportunities," then the only risky ventures that one would reasonably expect to discourage would be those directed at appropriating
natural opportunities.

Second, Knight argues that most land is not indestructible, and
therefore needs to be maintained:

> The value of agricultural land is accounted for largely by qualities that are
> not "indestructible," but have to be maintained at a cost to keep the land
> productive. Its original and indestructible qualities hardly enter into its
> value, after a short period of use, in which the fertility is "mined out";
> during that time it is like depletable mineral deposits, which present
> special problems in the field of profit, but have nothing to do with the
> land value of the Single Taxers.[41]

Knight is right that some parts of land value can be "mined" away.
Whether this occurs in an ordinary mine or in an agricultural field, it
highlights an issue to which George's supporters need to attend. If
land is taxed without regard to this fact, there will be an incentive
for owners of land to mine away such advantages inefficiently rapidly,
to save on future taxes. To counter the inefficiency and injustice of
having people save on taxes by mining their land, a land tax needs
to be combined with a severance tax, levied at a rate that charges
landowners the present value of the future taxes saved by mining.
Then there is no net incentive for inefficiently rapid or slow depletion of depletable opportunities provided by nature.

Third, Knight suggests that land speculation has an important economic purpose:

> Men do not hold land "speculatively" for an expected increase in value.
> This is a social service, tending to put ownership in the hands of those
> who know best how to handle the land so that the value will increase.
> And the familiar psychology of gambling makes speculation in general a
> losing business to the whole body of those who engage in it. They obvi-

ously do not need to keep it idle to get the increase, and do not, if there is a clear opening for remunerative use.[42]

Knight returns later to the theme of land speculation:

A favorite, supposedly very practical argument is that a tax on land value will force idle land into use. It will not—unless unused land is taxed more than what is used, in relation to its potential value; and it does not so operate where the expedient has been tried. If land having value for use is not used by an owner it is because of uncertainty as to how it should be used, and waiting for the situation to clear up or develop. An owner naturally does not wish to make a heavy investment in fitting a plot for a use which does not promise amortization before some situation may require a different plan.[43]

Knight's meaning in the first two sentences of the first quotation is not clear. Is he saying that land speculation never occurs? That is so clearly untrue that one looks for another meaning in Knight's words. One expects a Chicago economist like Knight to acknowledge that holders of land will treat land in whatever ways they expect will earn them the greatest profits. What he might mean is that land is generally held by people who do not see themselves as land speculators, and the buying and selling of land that might look like speculation is necessary to put land in the hands of those who can use it most valuably. George's supporters agree that a free market in land titles is valuable and tends to put land in the hands of those who can use it best. But that does not mean that land speculation never occurs.[44]

The third sentence suggests that Knight would not defend land speculation. But that is not the issue. The question at issue is, is there land speculation, and how does land taxation affect land speculation?

The final sentence of the first quotation is qualified by the last two sentences of the second quotation. Sometimes landowners do need to keep land idle to profit from the increase in its value, as Knight explains in the second quotation. When the intensity with which land can profitably be used is rising rapidly, it can be worthwhile to leave land unused or used unintensively, to avoid the loss of future opportunities and the cost of premature disposal of the improvements associated with the less intensive use. Whether it is in fact consistent with maximization of the present value of the returns to land to keep it presently unused or used unintensively depends on future circumstances, and people have differing beliefs about these.

The person to whom a parcel of land is most valuable is often the person who has the most extreme belief about how rapidly its productivity will rise, in ways that others do not perceive.[45] If such persons are perpetually optimistic about the rise in land value that is about to occur, then it can be subjectively rational to postpone building improvements on land, year after year. The holding of land by such a person is land speculation, and such speculation occurs, even if, as Knight says, "the familiar psychology of gambling makes speculation in general a losing business to the whole body of those who engage in it." Land becomes concentrated in the hands of those who see the greatest value in refraining from using it, creating an artificial scarcity of land.

Land taxation reduces the profit from land speculation. If the rent of land were taxed away completely, land titles would have a selling price of zero and there could be no profit in land speculation. Holding land would be attractive only to those who wanted to use land. Any increase in land taxation reduces the profit from land speculation, thereby reducing the amount of land speculation and the consequent artificial scarcity of land.

Fourth, Knight takes note of the argument that the claim of landowners to compensation for the social appropriation of rent is parallel to the claim of slave owners to compensation for the freeing of slaves:

> But there are specific "arguments" for the social appropriation of ground rent which it may be interesting to consider briefly. The case is often represented as parallel to that of slavery. Since slavery was always "wrong," no one could ever get a just title to slave property, hence summary liberation was just. This is invalid on both counts, economically and ethically. On the one hand, slave-owning and the capture and marketing of slaves were carried on under competition. It is improbable that the individuals concerned ever made appreciably more out of the business than they could have had by using their labor and capital in ways that have continued to be treated as legitimate. And ethically, the society, which established and sanctioned slavery, was "to blame." By rights it should have borne—i.e., distributed—the loss to individuals when it changed its mind and condemned and abolished the institution.[46]

Knight's argument that slave owners received only ordinary returns on their investments in slaves is irrelevant to the ethical question. It is equivalent to his earlier argument that landowners earned only ordinary returns. The reason that it is appropriate to require both slave owners and landowners to bear the costs of not having foreseen the moral progress of their societies is that this gives them an incentive to apply their capacity for moral foresight to their investment decisions. If a person is fully insured against the possibility that society will realize that an activity that has been considered legitimate will one day be seen to be not legitimate, then that person has no economic incentive to seek to understand and anticipate the moral progress of society. The failure to understand that it is not possible for one human being to own another or that all persons have equal rights to the gifts of nature is a "moral accident." While spreading, as advocated by Knight, is one way of dealing with accident costs, we usually find it worthwhile to identify individuals who could have prevented accidents and assign the costs of accidents to them. If it were possible, one would want to assign substantial portions of the costs of slave owning or landowning to the persons who were most instrumental in devising those institutions. But those individuals are long dead, and it may not be possible to identify individuals living today who have assets deriving from those actions. Therefore we are left with identifying individuals alive at the time when institutions are changing, who could have helped to reduce the costs of slavery or landownership. From this perspective, the slave owners or the landowners are logical candidates. They could have perceived the moral difficulties with slave owning or landowning and changed their behavior. Each such action by an individual would tend to increase the differential return to the morally wanting activity. And the greater the differential return grew, the more likely it would be that others would perceive the moral problem with the activity. Assigning the costs of such moral accidents to the owners of the assets that have come to be understood to be illegitimate has the additional advantage, in the theory of assigning accident costs, that it saves on administrative costs.[47]

Fifth, Knight argues that it is impossible to give all persons equal rights to land:

So, with respect to land, it is said that every human being has an absolute right to access to the earth, by which he must live. But everyone actually has this right, subject to competitive conditions, i.e., that he must pay for it what it is worth (which is less than it has cost). The alternative would be that he get the permission from some political agent of the government. And the simplest economic analysis shows that if the government wants to use its resources most productively, it would have to charge the users of land precisely the rent which tends to be fixed by market competition among private owners. Any attempt to give every person an unconditional right to the soil would establish anarchy, the war of all against all—and is of course not approximated by a confiscation and distribution of "rent" or its employment for "social ends."[48]

Knight's statement, "The alternative would be that he get the permission from some political agent of the government," is off-target. The existing system of land titles involves getting permission from the government, in that to own land you must have a land title issued by the government. George's supporters endorse the continuation of that system. In terms of legal theory, George's supporters propose that the rights of all to the soil be protected by a liability rule, while the right of holders of title would be protected by a property rule, subject to liability payments.[49] That is, there would be a continuation of the rights of the individual holders of title to land to use land as they saw fit (subject to liability payments in the form of taxes). The rights of all to the soil would be recognized as rights of those who have less than their shares of exclusive access to land, to receive compensation from those who have more than their shares. If everyone who has more than his or her share of land is required to compensate those who have less than their share, the selling price of land titles becomes approximately zero, so anyone who wants title to additional land can get it at a nominal price, subject to payment of taxes.

The question of whether the rent of land should be distributed or employed for social ends is a complex question. Three sources of land rent can be distinguished: nature, public services, and private activities on surrounding land. The component of land rent that comes from nature is the part to which all persons have equal rights. Still, if the citizens of a particular community wish to pool their income from this source and use it for public purposes, they do not infringe on the rights of anyone outside their community. The component of rent that comes from the provision of public services is the natural source of financing for public services. If people have similar tastes, public services produce benefits in limited areas, and labor and capital are mobile, then public services will increase rent by an amount equal to the value that the service provides.[50] The component of rent that comes from private activities on surrounding land is most efficiently employed in rewarding those activities, but communities have no obligation to use it for that purpose if they do not wish to do so.

Sixth, Knight objects to the idea that there is anything that might be called land monopoly:

> It is true again that many economists have called land a monopoly, and held that a monopolist charges all that the buyer can be forced to pay. But such ideas are nonsense, by whomsoever expressed.[51]

To respond to this argument, one must address the question of how the meanings of words are established. From its Greek origin, a monopoly is a market in which there is only one seller, and to monopolize is to arrange to be the only seller in a market. These meaning of monopoly and monopolize goes back at least to the 1500s.[52] But from early on, these words have had figurative meanings as well. "Monopoly" came to mean an arrangement of arbitrary and excessive prices. Thus in 1601 one finds, "Setting also price before hand of that which they sell, and of that which they will buy, and so committing open Monopoly."[53] Adam Smith wrote,

> The rent of the land, therefore, considered as the price paid for the use of the land, is naturally a monopoly price. It is not at all proportioned to what the landlord may have laid out upon the improvement of the land, or to what he can afford to take; but to what the farmer can afford to give.[54]

Smith used "monopoly price" in an established sense of a price not related to cost of production. "Monopolize" acquired the figurative meaning of "to obtain exclusive possession or control of, to get or keep entirely to oneself."[55] Thus in 1659 one finds, "Nor shall mute Fish, the Sea Monopolize."[56] When we speak of someone monopolizing a discussion, we mean that the person is appropriating for himself more than his rightful share of speaking time, leaving others with inadequate shares. Thus a person who expresses concern about land monopoly is not asserting that there is a single seller of land services. Such a person is saying that some persons are appropriating for themselves more than their rightful shares of exclusive access to land, leaving others with inadequate shares.

It might be objected that in economics at least, "monopoly" has the technical meaning of a market with a single seller, and economists should refrain from using "monopoly" in other senses. However, the quote from Adam Smith above makes it clear that this was not the understanding of the person whom many regard as the founder of economics. The technical meaning of "monopoly" probably came to the fore in economics with the publication of Alfred Marshall's *Principles of Economics* in 1890. Thus it might be reasonable to say that an economist who used the word "monopoly" at the time Knight was writing or since, in any sense other than its technical sense, would be unreasonably courting misunderstanding. But this is not a valid criticism of Henry George's use of the term "land monopoly," because the technical meaning of the term had not eclipsed the figurative meaning at the time that George was writing.

### Concluding Remarks

How should one assess Frank Knight's objections against the single tax? His objection against the practical feasibility of the taxation of land value certainly requires attention. But economists have suggested solutions to many of the practical problems of taxing land value. Although it needs to be tested whether these solutions are feasible in practice, it would be premature at this point to reject land-value taxation purely on practical grounds. Imagine a proposal to introduce a sales tax or a capital gains tax if no such taxes had ever been levied. The amount of information that needs to be gathered to implement such taxes would seem (and is) enormous, and the possibilities to evade these taxes would seem (and are) high enough to require highly intrusive enforcement activities. In addition, such taxes lead to an inefficient allocation of resources by distorting people's incentives. In comparison, the practical difficulties of levying a nondistortive tax on visible and immobile land seem rather small. We do not find any of Frank Knight's theoretical objections against the single tax compelling. The only objection that we cannot dismiss is the possibility that the single tax may provide funds to and thereby increase the power of nonbenevolent governments. Even though Knight did not explicitly raise this objection, his writings suggest that it may have been on his mind. But this objection applies to every tax, and the possibility that governments might abuse the levied funds is one of the costs of permitting governments to correct market inefficiencies through taxation. A society must decide whether this cost outweighs the expected benefit of government action.

In concluding his article on the "Fallacies of the Single Tax," Frank Knight wrote:

> The heart of the matter is that the rental value of land, when not a payment for personal service or a return on investment, is a *profit* like any other, a speculative gain due to an unanalyzable mixture of foresight and "luck."[57]

He considered this the fundamental objection against the single tax. But the heart of the disagreement between Knight and George's supporters is that George's supporters see an important difference between the rent of land and other returns.

George's supporters use a system of categories in which an increase in return to a resource that is caused by the effort or abstinence of the owner of the resource is called a return to capital. The rent of a parcel of land is never the product of the effort or abstinence of the person with title to that land; it is produced by a combination of nature, public infrastructure, and private activities on surrounding land. If a person has exclusive access to land of greater value than others can have, he puts his fellow citizens at a disadvantage that deserves rectification, and a good society rectifies this disadvantage by public collection of rent.

### Notes

1. Frank H. Knight. *Risk, Uncertainty and Profit* (London: Lund Humphries, 1948 [originally published in 1921]).
2. Entrepreneurs who agree to engage in an uncertain project can demand compensation ("economic profit") for the possibility that their project yields an unfavorable outcome whose costs they will have to bear.

3. Frank H. Knight. "Fallacies in the Interpretation of Social Cost," *The Quarterly Journal of Economics*, 38 (1924): 582–606.

4. Frank H. Knight. "The Ethics of Competition," *The Quarterly Journal of Economics*, 37 (1923): 579–624.

5. This was in contrast to Jonn Bates Clark's assertion that market outcomes are proper because the owner of each factor receives that factor's marginal product.

6. Knight, "Ethics of Competition," p. 623.

7. Frank H. Knight. "The Planful Act: The Possibilities and Limitations of Collective Rationality," in Frank H. Knight, *Freedom and Reform* (New York and London: Harper and Brothers, 1947), p. 369.

8. Frank H. Knight, "The Fallacies in the 'Single Tax',' *The Freeman*, August 10, 1953, p. 810.

9. Knight, *Risk, Uncertainty and Profit*, p. 149.

10. Frank Knight was not the first major economist to argue that the return to all factors of production ought to be classified as interest. Irving Fisher had already done so in 1907. Irving Fisher, *The Rate of Interest* (New York: Macmillan, 1907).

11. Knight, *Risk, Uncertainty and Profit*, pp. 169–70.

12. Frank H Knight, "The Ricardian Theory of Taxation and Distribution," *Canadian Journal of Economics and Political Science*, 1 (1935): 18.

13. Ibid., pp. 4–5.

14. Knight, "Interpretation of Social Cost," p. 591.

15. Assume that the value of having exclusive access to the resource is worth $x$, that there are $y$ risk-neutral developers, and that each developer thinks that he has a probability of $1/y$ to be the one who develops the resource. In the attempt to gain exclusive access to the resource, each developer would be willing to spend his expected gain, $x/y$, and the developers as a group would spend $x$. (See Dennis C. Mueller, *Public Choice II* [Cambridge: Cambridge University Press, 1989], pp. 231–35).

16. In his discussion of David Ricardo's economic theory, Knight wrote (Knight, "The Ricardian Theory," p. 18):

[T]he notion that what are called "natural agents" are not produced (in the sense in which any material agents are produced) is false and reflects a false conception of production. In so far as . . . there was effective competition, the use of labor and property in pioneering and all exploration and development activities could not yield a return smaller or greater than that obtainable in any other use. That is, the result must be equal in value to its cost. This is true even if possession be obtained by a mere contest of fight, and not less so because such activity would not be socially necessary or useful.

17. Frank H. Knight, Review of George R. Geiger, "The Philosophy of Henry George," *Journal of Political Economy*, 41 (1933): 688.

18. Knight, *Risk, Uncertainty and Profit*, p. 160.

19. "Might be" because Knight's critique does not address the ethical motivation that is behind the proposal to impose a *single* tax on land.

20. Knight, "The Ricardian Theory," p. 17.

21. Frank Knight disagreed with this conclusion. He wrote (*Encyclopedia Britannica*, vol. IV (1946), pp. 779–801. Reprinted under the title "Capital and Interest" in *Readings in the Theory of Income Distribution*, American Economic Association (ed.), Philadelphia: The Blakiston Company, 1947, pp. 384–409):

> The distinction between human beings and property and that between personal and real property are important in law and human relations, but no fundamental economic differences correspond to them. . . . Realistic economic analysis must avoid any general classifications of productive agents and make distinctions on the basis of facts that are significant for the problem at hand. For general analysis, it would be desirable to drop also the traditional classification of income forms, and to speak of the yield and "hire" of productive agents, irrespective of kind. (ibid., p. 395).

However, if economic theory is to be used to draw any inferences about an existing economy, it is difficult to understand how distinctions that are "important in law" are not "facts that are significant for the problem at hand."

22. See, for example, the literature on the economic effects of the taxation of capital and investment.

23. This definition of land is slightly broader than the classical definition. According to this definition, produced things will be classified as land if it is impossible to find either the person who created them or his heirs, or anyone who has legitimately acquired them. For example, the wealth of victims of the Holocaust that is stored in Swiss bank vaults and whose legitimate owners or their legitimate heirs cannot be found would be classified as land.

24. Classifying factors of production according to social conventions might make it necessary to adopt a new classification system when social conventions change. For example, if a society adopts the convention that produced things do not belong to their producers, it might become appropriate to combine land and capital into a single factor. In a society that does not acknowledge any private property and considers it a citizen's duty to contribute his labor to society according to his ability, it might be appropriate to classify all factors of production as a single group. There is a certain irony in the fact that Frank Knight's suggestion to subsume all factors under the label "capital" seems to be most applicable to a purely communist society.

25. If natural resources are privately owned and the community levies a tax that is equal to the maximum amount that developers are willing to pay to obtain exclusive access to the resource for a fixed amount of time, then the market value of natural resources will be zero and the question of ownership is irrelevant from an economic point of view.

26. Knight, "Interpretation of Social Cost."

568    *American Journal of Economics and Sociology*

27. Ibid., footnote 8 on p. 591.

28. In a reply to Knight's review of George Geiger's book *The Philosophy of Henry George* (Knight, "Review"), Harry Gunnison Brown made the point that investment in land does not in general yield an extraordinary return. See Harry G. Brown, "Anticipation of an Increment and the 'Unearned Decrement' in Land Values," *The American Journal of Economics and Sociology* (1943): 343–57, reprinted in *Selected Articles by Harry Gunnison Brown: The Case for Land Value Taxation* (New York: Robert Schalkenbach Foundation, 1980).

29. In a 1922 essay (Frank Knight, "Ethics and The Economic Interpretation," *The Quarterly Journal of Economics* 36 (1922): 454–81), Knight argued for a separation of the science of economics, culture history (the explanation of motives), and ethical inquiry.

30. Frank Knight. "Socialism: The Nature of the Problem," *Ethics* 50 (1940): 253–89. See also Knight, "Capital and Interest," pp. 407–9.

31. Knight. "Socialism," pp. 277–78.

32. Knight, "Review," pp. 687–90.

33. Knight, "The Fallacies in the 'Single Tax'," pp. 809–11.

34. For example, Knight wrote (Knight, "Review," p. 688):

All this reasoning is on a mental level not above that involved in the simpler operations of arithmetic. The economic and social ideas of Henry George are as a whole at the same per-arithmetical level, the level of those held before and since his time by all who have held any at all, apart from an insignificant handful of competent economists and other negligible exceptions. Henry George's claim to be an economist (or social philosopher either) rests on the possession of linguistic powers not uncommon among frontier preachers, politicians, and journalists, and on the fact that his particular nostrum for the salvation of society appeals to a number of people, no doubt for much the same reasons that made it appeal to him, and which give many other nostrums their appeal.

35. Knight, "The Fallacies in the 'Single Tax'," p. 809

36. Ibid., pp. 810–11.

37. This idea is developed in Nicolaus Tideman, "Global Economic Justice," *Geophilos*, Autumn, 2002, 134–46, and "Creating Global Economic Justice," *Geophilos*, Spring, 2001, 88–94.

38. Knight, "The Fallacies in the Single Tax'," p. 809.

39. Ibid., pp. 809–10.

40. Ibid., p. 810.

41. Ibid., p. 811.

42. Ibid., p. 810.

43. Ibid., p. 811.

44. For an account of land speculation in the United States, see Aaron M. Sakolski, *The Great American Land Bubble; The Amazing Story of Land-Grabbing, Speculations, and Booms From Colonial Days to the Present Time* (New York and London: Harper & Brothers, 1932).

45. The name "winner's curse" has been given to the phenomenon that the highest bidder for an object will be the person who has made the most extreme upward error in estimating its value. See Paul Milgrom and Robert J. Weber, "A Theory of Auctions and Competitive Bidding," 50 *Econometrica* (1982): 1089–1122.

46. Knight, "The Fallacies in the 'Single Tax'," p. 810.

47. For a discussion of the theory of assigning accident costs, see Guido Calabresi, *The Costs of Accidents* (New Haven: Yale University Press, 1970). For a more detailed discussion of the accident-cost argument for not compensating landowners, see Nicolaus Tideman, "Property Rights and the Social Contract: The Constitutional Challenge in the U.S.A.," in Richard Noyes, ed., *Now the Synthesis: Capitalism, Socialism and the New Social Contract* (New York: Holmes and Meier 1991) pp. 47–59.

48. Knight, "The Fallacies in the 'Single Tax'," p. 810.

49. For a discussion of the relationship between entitlements protected by liability rules and entitlements protected by property rules, see Guido Calabresi and Douglas Melamed, "Property, Liability and Inalienability: One view of the Cathedral," 85 *Harvard Law Review* (1972): 1089–1128.

50. See Richard J. Arnott and Joseph E. Stiglitz, "Aggregate Land Rents, Expenditure on Public Goods, and Optimal City Size," 93 *The Quarterly Journal of Economics* (1979): 471–500. For a discussion of the consequences of relaxing the assumptions, see Nicolaus Tideman, "Integrating Rent and Demand Revelation in the Evaluation and Financing of Services," in Hiroshi Ohta and Jacques-François Thisse, eds., *Does Economic Space Matter?* (London: Macmillan, 1993), pp. 133–50.

51. Knight, "The Fallacies in the 'Single Tax'," p. 810.

52. *Oxford English Dictionary* (Oxford: Clarendon Press, 1989), Vol. IX, pp. 1026–27.

53. Ibid., p. 1027.

54. Adam Smith, *An Inquiry into the Nature and Causes of the Wealth of Nations* (Indianapolis: Liberty Fund, 1981 [originally published 1776]), p. 161 [chap. XI, par. 5].

55. *Oxford English Dictionary*, p. 1026.

56. Loc. cit.

57. Knight, "The Fallacies in the 'Single Tax'," p. 810.

# 28
# Heath: Estranged Georgist

By Fred E. Foldvary

Spencer Heath (1876–1963) pioneered the theory of proprietary governance and community. He was in his initial career an engineer, inventor, and businessman, developing propellor patents and special machinery for propeller manufacture. His factory produced some 70 percent of the propellers used by American forces during World War I. He also practiced patent law in Washington, D.C. In 1931, Heath retired from engineering research and patent law to devote himself to his avocation of horticulture and to research into the foundations of the natural and social sciences.

He was an arresting figure—tall, bald, and white-bearded in a day when beards were scarcely ever seen. The singularity of his appearance was further emphasized by a pince-nez held in place by two black cords tied at the back of his head. He spoke in beautifully constructed sentences, but in a voice so quiet that hearing him oftentimes required an effort.

### Heath the Georgist

Spencer Heath was greatly influenced by Henry George and was one of the founders of the Henry George School in New York City. In a letter, he wrote,

> I am much pleased to have your letter of June 5 thanking me for my efforts to be of service to the Henry George School. I am proud to have been, in one way or another, a supporter of the School from its first beginning and that I was able to aid and encourage the noble project of Oscar Geiger from the time it was first proposed.[1]

What attracted Heath was George's espousal of free trade: "the basic philosophy of Henry George—the philosophy of absolute freedom of exchange—must be the foundation of all the social advance or improvement that the near or distant future can achieve."[2]

With respect to rent, Heath wrote, "It must be learned that ground

American Journal of Economics and Sociology, Vol. 63, No. 2 (April, 2004).
© 2004 American Journal of Economics and Sociology, Inc.

rent is purely a social product—the payment and the measure of all the services that are social and public—and that until it is completely used, 100%, in payment of the public wages and other costs there must continue to be serious violation of the principle of free exchange and its attendant evils."[3]

But in his main work *Citadel, Market and Altar*, Heath saw the title holder of land as also being an entrepreneur who could create land values.[4] This is not inconsistent with George's thought, since in his main work *Progress and Poverty*,[5] George recognized that an owner of land was also often an owner of capital goods and also exerted labor. In the Georgist system, improvements to sites are capital goods, not land as such,[6] and so the "land value" created by a title holder is really the value of a capital good attached to land. Heath noted that "Any divergence between my views and those of Henry George respecting the Remedy has reference only to its mode of operation and its effects, and not to the remedy itself."[7]

In his theory of proprietary communities, Heath did not therefore contradict Henry George, but took his thought in a new direction. Heath's vision was a society in which collective goods are produced and provided by entrepreneurs and financed from the site rentals they generate. In his paper, "Outline of the Economic, Political, and Proprietary Departments of Society," Heath viewed his concepts as a refinement of those of George:[8]

> The proposal of Henry George to deprive the service department of society[,] that is, the political authority, of all its power of predatory taxation and thus restore the proprietary department to its function of disbursing the public revenue of rent to those public servants who collectively constitute the political department, carries with it the necessary implication that the proprietary department eventually will take on and exercise its full administrative functions over all the public services.

Heath adds, "the balance of rent not required for these purposes will be the clear earnings of the proprietors who have administered and supervised the enterprise," a proposal that would be consistent with Georgism if that rental was due to the efforts of the proprietors, but not if it is rent not generated by them.

To Georgists, the concept that the proprietors would collect all the rent and keep that not generated by them seemed like landlordism rather than Georgism. Georgists also disagreed with Heath that land-lords as such provide a social service. Frank Chodorov, for example, wrote in a letter to Heath, "the phrase 'land ownership is a protection' involves the idea that land owners render a service. The only service that they might render is to hold the land against thieves who could pick it up during the night and walk away with it . . . Because your basic concept is historically incorrect, economically and morally unsound, I cannot see any validity in your thesis."[9]

### Heath a Critic of Henry George

Faced with such rejection, Heath became a critic of Henry George. Spencer Heath's scathing review, *Progress and Poverty Reviewed and its Fallacies Exposed*, was published as a booklet by *The Freeman* in 1952, but evidently was written as early as 1945.[10] The foreword is by John Chamberlain, who also wrote the foreword to *Citadel, Market and Altar*. Heath had already formulated his objections to the theories in *Progress and Poverty* at least as early as 1939.[11] The booklet was advertised in the classified section of various periodicals, with a monetary prize offered to anyone who could refute it. The ad labeled George's theory "land communism," but Heath later regretted calling George a "land communist."[12] Rather than stimulating a debate, this review alienated most Georgists and closed off further contacts.

Heath's critique of George has been influential in the libertarian movement. Murray Rothbard, a prominent libertarian economist and movement leader, based much of his criticism of Henry George on the thought of Spencer Heath in addition to that of economist Frank Knight.[13] Contemporary libertarians still derive much of their beliefs about Georgism from Rothbard's treatment, hence second-hand from Heath.

Heath characterizes George as having a "condition of sadness tinged with anger and bordering on despair." Heath labels the work as an "emotional reaction against the institution of private property in land."[14] Thus does Heath begin by tainting George by implication as writing out of emotional feelings rather than reasoned analysis.

George indeed did not write a dry text; he was passionate about justice and liberty. But this does not by itself make his work deficient in analysis. George's rhetorical flourishes add juice and spice to the work. For the analysis, they are a fifth wheel that can be set aside in judging how well his thought is warranted in logic and evidence.

Next, Heath alleges an inconsistency in what George states is his aim. George claims his intent is to "follow truth wherever it may lead," but in the preface admits that the conclusions in *Progress and Poverty* are an elaboration of his pamphlet of 1871, *Our Land and Land Policy*,[15] mistakenly called "Our Land and Labor Policy" by Heath.[16] This confuses discovery with methodology. Of course in writing *Progress and Poverty*, George knew the policy conclusion before he jotted down the first word. He did not discover the concept of using rent for public finance in the process of writing the book. But the methodology in the book is a logical deduction of the policy, starting with basic premises and following a logical derivation, with historical evidence to back up the argument. This process is similar to constructing a proof in geometry: the author knows the conclusion before writing the proof, but in the proof, the conclusion follows from the logic and not just the say-so of the author.

George's policy proposal was to abolish all taxation except on land value or land rent. In *Progress and Poverty*, George explicitly states[17] that he does not propose to nationalize land titles; these will still be individually held, and the title holders would have full rights of possession, including the control of land use and of transfer. Heath, however, claims[18] that nationalization would be the effect, since government would take the value, the kernel, of ownership, leaving only the "worthless" shell of title.

But why are the rights of possession worthless? Tenants willingly pay rentals in exchange for having possessory rights to use a site and its improvements. The landlord takes the kernel, but evidently the shell is worth the full expense to the tenants. Indeed, in the Heathean proprietary communities, leaseholders would pay for just such rights.

In developing his three-factor theory of the production and distribution of wealth, George states that land rent is the return to the land factor, as distinct from wages to the labor factor. Heath criticizes George for ignoring "the distributive services performed by land owners."[19] Indeed, Heath *defined* "ground rent" as "the recompense for this distributive public service,"[20] and even the rent due to "the gifts of nature" is "the value received for making *social* distribution of these natural things."[21] The proposition that rent pays for the distributive service of the landowner is an old argument; it was made a hundred years earlier by the French economist Frédéric Bastiat in his book *Economic Harmonies* (1851).[22]

The rental paid by a tenant includes returns to all three factors. As George wrote,[23] "Many landholders are laborers of one sort or another. And it would be hard to find a landowner who is not also a capitalist." George also recognized that many people do not understand the distinctions: "in common thought the characters are confounded."[24]

Heath would counter that in selling land, the seller does not just transfer title, but also performs a social service, for which he is owed the total rent and land value. But these "exchange services"[25] are labor, often done by real-estate agents for a commission, typically 6 percent of the property value. Clearly the owner and his agents perform a social service when land titles are exchanged, but Heath does not confront the question of why the typical commission does not suffice as the labor payment, and why the total rent should be the morally or economically proper return for this exchange function.

Heath adds that the rent of land "is a voluntary recompense for distributive services."[26] This "voluntary" issue begs the moral question. If the title holders do have a morally proper claim to the rent, then its taxation is immoral, and the owner is entitled to all the rent. If, in contrast, the natural land rent (that element of the rental due to the natural features of land and the value apart from that created by labor and capital goods) belongs in equal shares to the members of some community, if not all humanity, then the title holder's retention of the rent is not truly voluntary, but a theft, via government, of property properly belonging to others.

The slave trade was also a voluntary transaction between a seller and buyer of slaves, but it was not voluntary to the slave, who morally was the proper owner of his own labor. Likewise, if rent is properly owned by members of a community, the transaction between seller and buyer or landlord and tenant is a trade of stolen property. Heath does not provide an analysis of the morally proper ownership of natural rent, the rent of land due to its natural qualities.

Even aside from the question of the morally proper owner of the rent, the selling or renting of land is not entirely voluntary if the legal context is involuntary. The government imposes a particular set of laws that apply to real estate. Buyers and renters must adhere to these laws. If some of the laws are unjust and are not desired by some of the persons affected, then the transactions are not voluntary just because they occur. When one buys shoes, for example, one pays a sales tax. Nobody forces one to buy those particular shoes, yet the sales tax is involuntary because the government threatens coercion against those who would execute the exchange without paying the tax. Only if there is no arbitrary cost or restriction on the purchase of shoes is it purely voluntary.

Heath[27] criticizes George for imputing to the rent of land "the anti-social character of taxation" not given in recompense for services. But George did not say that rent *per se* is an evil or that it should not be paid. In Georgist analysis, the anti-social character of rent is due to three reasons. First, as a matter of justice, the rental of a site belongs to the provider of civic goods and to the community, and therefore the retention of rental payments by the title holder (who does not provide the civic goods) is theft. Second, land speculation, when incited by public works not paid for by landowners, artificially increases the demand for land, raising the price of land and possibly shifting development to less productive fringe or marginal lands, distortions that increase the cost of living and reduce the real wages of workers. Third, landowners gain because the public works provided by government increase their rent and land value, and if the financing is from taxes on wages, this amounts to a forced redistribution of wealth from workers to landowners. The public collection of site rentals eliminates all three anti-social phenomena, as does, to some extent, the collection of the rentals by private communities. So it is not rent itself that is anti-social, but the land tenure and tax systems.

In analyzing the distribution of wealth to the owners of the factors of production, George leaves out taxation. Heath repeatedly criticizes George's "ignoring taxation,"[28] treating "taxation expressly as having no effect upon distribution,"[29] and dismissing "the wolf of taxation."[30] But George is entirely correct in leaving out taxation from the laws of distribution. The initial distribution of wealth goes to the owners of the factors. That distribution can then be subject to secondary distributions, i.e., redistributions. As George states,[31] after setting forth the initial distribution, we can then see what bearing taxation has.

The contribution of labor is paid to workers as wages; the providers of capital goods obtain rentals and returns in accord with their contribution; and the surplus left over after paying for labor and capital goods goes to rent. The rent is there whether it goes to the title holder or to the members of a community. If the rent goes to the community members, this is the initial distribution of that rent.

If government taxes wages, part of one's wage is taken away and redistributed to others. This redistribution in no way detracts from the initial distribution as wages. The taxed money or resources is still wages; it does not cease to be a wage just because it is taxed. If a thief were to steal one's wages, the funds and resources do not cease to be wages. These are wages that are transferred to the thief; the origin of the funds or resources is still labor.

Heath also disagrees that land is, as George describes it, a monopoly.[32] In the classical meaning, monopoly is not confined to an absolute monopoly of one seller. The classical economic meaning of monopoly is an industry or resource in which it is not possible or feasible for firms to enter and increase the supply. An example is taxi service where the legal provision requires a license and the number of licenses is fixed by law at a constant number. If a firm wishes to enter that industry, it cannot expand the taxi service, but must buy an existing service from one of the permit holders. The taxi firms together thus have a monopoly, and can charge a higher price than if firms were allowed to expand the supply. Land is a monopoly in that sense, since firms cannot enter the land business by increasing the supply of land, but can only transfer existing land from a title holder.

George extended Ricardo's agricultural law of rent to all land, and made it the foundation of much of his analysis. Heath provides an extensive quote of George's description of that law.[33] In the Ricardian model, labor and capital goods are treated as homogenous, all the same, while land has different grades of productivity. (In reality, of course, there is a premium for human capital that makes wages differ, but that does not detract from the basic relationship between land and rent that Ricardo and George analyze.) The least productive land in use is the "margin of production," which carries no rent. Because of competition among mobile workers, the margin determines wages for the whole economy. The "law of rent" then states that the rent of a plot of land equals its produce minus the produce at the margin or, more precisely, the produce of a plot minus the normal costs of the labor and capital that maximize the profit at that site. As the margin extends to less productive land, wages fall and rent rises.

To emphasize the nature of rent as a surplus, George notes that wages plus returns to capital goods equal the total produce minus rent.[34] Heath ridicules this "mere mathematical truism" as being "the sole support of his entire economic arch."[35] But the support is provided in the explanation Heath himself cites at length; this dismissal by Heath thus is gratuitous. George's point is that land rent is the left-over surplus output, because of the nature of land as fixed, in contrast to mobile labor and capital goods. Modern economics recognizes this surplus, but masks it from rent by calling it a "producer surplus." David Friedman[36] correctly notes in his textbook that in a highly competitive industry, this "surplus" does not go to the owners of firms but to the factors supplying the inputs.

Heath[37] claims that Henry George "could not always distinguish between a quantity and a ratio" when George wrote that an increase in wealth is accompanied by poverty. But George plainly and clearly shows he knows the difference: "I am using the word wages not in the sense of a quantity, but in the sense of proportion. When I say that wages fall as rent rises, I do not mean that the quantity of wealth obtained by laborers as wages is necessarily less, but the proportion which it bears to the whole produce is necessarily less."[38]

Heath[39] claims that George's formulation of the law of rent is conditional on rent being the difference in the produce of a plot of land relative to what the same application of labor and capital goods produces at the least productive land in use (the margin of production). Heath notes, correctly, that there will be more labor and capital goods applied in the better lands. Modern economics recognizes that mobile factors are added until the intensive marginal products, within a plot of land, equal the extensive marginal products of labor and capital goods on marginal land. Since lands of unequal quality have unequal applications of labor and capital goods, Heath claims this refutes the law of rent.

But rather than refuting the law of rent, this makes the law even stronger. The greater amount of active factors makes the output that much greater and thus increases the rent even more. The marginal product of labor, the contribution of another worker to output, diminishes with more labor, in accord with the law of diminishing returns. Workers are paid their marginal product, not their average product, which is higher. That difference goes to rent. And that rent is still a differential relative to the output at marginal land. The formulation as "the same application" means the same quality of application and is quantitatively a simplification intended to elucidate the main relation between rent and wages; making it more complete does not detract from the basic relationship. George can be faulted for not explaining this more clearly and fully, but not for falling into a fallacy.

Heath claimed[40] also that if all taxation were to fall on land rent, the government bureaucracy would prescribe tenants' occupancies, "dictating their lives." This is an absurd accusation, since a tax on land rent does not increase rent, and Georgist policy would not infringe on the rights of possession of either the owner or tenants. Indeed, since regulation is itself a tax, the single tax only on rent would also eliminate excessive regulation and the government's dictating to owners and tenants in the form of zoning laws, building codes, and other restrictions.

Heath's failure to grasp the economic effects of taxing land rent is revealed in a manuscript[41] in which he wrote:

> Taxes collected on the supposed or estimated value of *unused* land must be paid out of the production of the land that is in use. Those also must fall on land users, hence, on the earnings of labor and capital, thus reducing the demand for land and so causing more land to go *out of use* and less wealth to be produced and less rent to be paid.

Contrary to Heath, the actual effect is that in order to eliminate this drain on earnings, the site owner will put the land to its most productive use in order to generate the rental that can then pay the tax.

At the end of his piece, Heath advocated that private communities, under united proprietary governance, would provide public services resulting in "the creation of rent" that would "support this and further public services."[42] This is nothing but an application of Georgist public finance by contractual means rather than imposed government, with all the benefits that George proclaimed!

Mason Gaffney, then a graduate student in economics, responded to Heath's "review" in "Vituperation Well Answered," an article in *Land and Liberty*.[43] To Heath's claim that rent pays for the landlord's service of holding and distributing lands, Gaffney retorts that no service is rendered by mere "holding," since the land is there regardless. As to distributing land, Gaffney notes, as stated above, that this is covered by the normal commission to brokers. Gaffney also notes,[44] "A tax levied regardless of use does not impair this incentive, but rather makes it more compelling."

Regarding the monopolization of land, Gaffney[45] responds that it means "keeping something off the market." Monopolists generally can increase the price of their product by restricting the amount offered to the market, and Gaffney notes that much urban land is underused, raising the price of land generally.

Gaffney concedes that Henry George may have exaggerated the increase in rent swallowing up all the gains from enhanced productivity, but Heath missed the point that society would be better off if these gains are shared and if speculative holdings do not decrease the wage/rent ratio unnecessarily.

Gaffney avoided a detailed response to all the falsities in Heath's "vituperation," and instead asked the question, why this attack? The answer, said Gaffney, is "stranger than fiction." After condemning the concept of financing public goods from site rent, Heath, as noted above, turns around and advocates proprietary governance financed from the rent, replacing government financed from taxation. Gaffney[46] suspects that Heath feared being labeled a Georgist, but the more probable reason, judging from Heath's writing overall, is his disappointment and frustration that Georgists did not follow him into the proprietary concept.

Gaffney notes that the basic difference between Heath and George is not the concept of financing public goods from rent, but the form of the governance. Gaffney[47] claims that in Heath's vision, the governors would be a "landed élite" who would skim off the excess of rent over costs. Gaffney as well as Heath overlooked an in-between form, condominiums, residential associations, and other forms of democratic contractual governance. As for the excess rent, as Heath noted, corporations could have many shareholders, distributing the rent to many, though short of the absolute equality sought by Georgists. Without the subsidy provided by taxing labor and capital, landowners would have to pay the costs of infrastructure, protection, transportation, and other services from their rentals, bringing a proprietary world much closer to the Georgist ideal than today's world.

Spencer Heath then wrote a rejoinder[48] to Gaffney, which was submitted to *Land and Liberty* by John Chamberlain at Heath's request. This was not published. In the manuscript, Heath calls George's policy "land communism,"[49] conflating the land with its rent. One could accurately call it "rent communism," but "land communism" implies that rights of control are also in common. Moreover, the taxation of wages would have to be labeled as "wage communism" to be consistent; indeed any tax would be communist. An anti-communist should therefore logically favor a single tax on rent as a reduction of tax communism.

Heath then makes an astonishing claim that "land owners without tenants . . . have no rent to be seized" and thus taxing them would amount to complete confiscation.[50] Having read *Progress and Poverty*, Heath should have known that the economic rent is what the site would rent for to the highest bidders, regardless of who is occupying the site. This brings to mind Tolstoy's[51] observation that people do not really argue with Henry George; the critics misunderstand his theory and policy.

Heath is on sounder ground arguing against Gaffney's preference for political rather than contractual governance. He wrote that Gaffney based his argument on historical conditions such as plantations and company towns, which no longer exist. Heath notes that he and Gaffney had the common goal of freedom. This, said Heath, would be better accomplished by voluntary contractual means rather than politically imposed means.

Heath[52] also argued against the doctrinal statement of the Rev. Edward McGlynn, who supported the Georgist tax reform. There Heath stated that "land communism" draws ideological support from the belief that land rent is unearned. Heath claims it is only partial communism when wages are taxed but total communism when land rent is taxed. This is because the government would allocate access and prescribe land use. But again, this is contrary to what George proposes, since the Georgist policy would strengthen, not eliminate, private rights of possession; moreover, government does indeed prescribe rules for labor.

Heath, like so many other critics, begs the question in claiming that the "just distribution" of the rent that Georgists propose "must rest" on an "ex-propriation by the State."[53] The moral issue is the original distribution, who is the proper owner of the rent in the first place, and the charge of "redistribution" implies that this question has already been settled in favor of allodial title, where the title holder is the legitimate owner of the rights to the rent.

Heath[54] maintained that McGlynn did not differentiate between the *proprium* or *dominium*, property rights, and the *imperium*, political prerogative. This is an argument against statism rather than Georgism, since the economic and ethical elements of George's thought do not necessarily imply an imposed state. George argued that the reforms he advocated would transform government, creating a more cooperative society, an association in equality, a concept consistent with a voluntary society and with a proprietary governance whose public services are financed from site rentals.

### Heath as Pioneer Theorist of Proprietary Community[55]

While a critic of Henry George and misunderstanding George's theories, Heath himself, as noted above, drew much of his economic analysis from the thought of Henry George. In one paper,[56] Heath recognizes the Georgist concept that the value of public services is manifested as rent. Heath there saw himself as extending the concepts of Henry George, in many letters and papers citing George's preface to *Progress and Poverty*, in which George wrote that he would leave it to his readers "to carry further their applications where this is needed."[57]

Heath fully presented his theory of land and proprietary community in 1957 in his main work, *Citadel, Market, and Altar.*[58] Heath offered the hotel as an example of proprietary governance: "in all respects a public community is, in principle, the same as a hotel."[59] The hotel provides collective goods, financed from the room rentals. "And what they pay is voluntary, very different from taxation." Moreover, the payment is limited "by the competition of the market," a point also made by Spencer MacCallum.[60] Better service fetches higher rentals.

One becomes a resident of a hotel by making a voluntary contractual agreement. The agreement obligates the hotel proprietor to certain payment rates, unlike governments, which may arbitrarily change tax rates without being bound by any contractual agreements. When the proprietary concept is broadened to a larger community, the owners give "not mere occupancy alone, but positive and protective public services as well, for sake of the new rents and higher values that will accrue . . ."[61] One of Heath's principal devotees was Walter Knott, founder of Knott's Berry Farm in Garden Grove, CA, which exhibits (as do Disneyland and Walt Disney World) many features of a Heathian proprietary community.

Heath foresaw "proprietary community-service authorities, organized as local community proprietors over extensive areas, comprising many communities and establishing associative relationships among themselves in order to provide wider services on a regional, a national and eventually on an international and world-wide scale."[62]

Unlike sovereign governance, proprietary administration is subject to a market discipline. As Heath put it, "the slightest neglect of the public interest or lapse in the form of corruption or oppression would itself penalize them by decline in rents and values," a proposition elaborated on later by MacCallum.[63] This is so in contrast to coercive governments, where, as Heath recognized, ownership and management are separate.

There are economies of scale in the provision of some public goods. Industry needs "public rights of way for communications and exchange, and other common services that can be supplied only by or under a united public authority, either political or proprietary."[64] To do so, "it is only necessary that the site-owning interests, or substantial portions of it duly organized in corporate or similarly effective form, merge their separate titles and interests and take in exchange corresponding undivided interests in the whole."[65]

Some owners could hold out, "but they and their unincluded properties will naturally receive second consideration in all matters of public benefit or preferment. Unfranchised as owners, their influence and advantages all will be of second rate,"[66] many of the benefits being excludable. Heath elaborates on the concept of a unified large-area control of land:[67]

> For this purpose they will unite in a corporate or similar form on a regional basis, pooling their individual ownerships and taking corresponding undivided interests in the form of corporate shares. Thenceforth all former income will go to the Corporation as rent and to its shareholders as earnings or dividends. From this point there will be no separation of interest as between the formerly separate owners. Each will now hold his proportionate undivided interest in the entire community of property held by the corporation. His interest will not be in any particular rent or property but in the community property as a whole, that it shall provide the highest immunities and advantages to its inhabitants and thereby yield the highest combined and total rents and revenues.
>
> Thus there will be established a unitary community ownership and authority powerful and influential, having no motivation but the community welfare, automatically financed with voluntary revenues in proportion as it contributes to that welfare and in like manner penalized in degree as it fails so to do. Its general policies will be dictated by vote of its possibly very numerous owners, and they will be carried out by persons of highly specialized qualifications [engaged] for that purpose as officers and employees.

Heath noted that owners of enterprises "cannot afford to have their capital tied up" in assets not relevant to their chief operations. Businesses and professionals seldom own the premises they occupy, which require specialized administrative services.[68] Hence, specialized firms arise that own land and provide public-goods services. They not only provide for administration over the sites and various services, but also strive to "keep up the public demand" for that space, including protecting the tenants from theft and injury and keeping them comfortable.[69] The rents generated by the sites depend on the prosperity of the enterprises on the sites. As examples of specialized firms serving sites, Heath includes apartment housing, professional buildings, and shopping centers.

Thus does proprietary governance accomplish many of the objectives of Georgist governance: using rent to finance civic works, and with governance not at the arbitrary whim of a single big landowning person, but by many shareholders who seek to please the tenants because that is what maximizes the rent. Corporate proprietary governance presents an alternative to today's democracies in which landowners seek higher net rents by shifting the cost of public works to taxes on labor, capital, and enterprise rather than providing these works.

A major point of Heath's theory is that the developer creates or adds to site value. Developers today are willing to pay for land because they profit from the value added by the development. The same logic applies to single-tax enclaves. The system already requires one to pay for land, so there is no disadvantage to such enclaves relative to conventional community financing. So if such enclaves (where the leaseholder only pays land rent and not also the tax on improvements) are more efficient and attractive than conventional communities, there will be a value added that will finance additional amenities. Indeed, condominiums and residential associations today are built on purchased land, and they are developed because of the added value. In a Georgist or Heathian world, they would be that much more profitable or advantageous, since overly restrictive interventions would not hamper them.

Heath[70] clarified what he thought was the proper relationship of government agents to the proprietors: "It is the full and proper function of land servants—community political servants—to merchandise to land owners their services (labor), and also the services of their capital, in exchange for salaries and wages for their services and in exchange for either purchase price or interest, on any public capital (community capital) they supply . . . As the productivity of the economic life arose, so would rise the quality and abundance of the public services incident to the possession and use of land." This would bind government to a role of provider of services subject to market rules rather than dominating markets and persons. And contrary to conventional Georgist policy, site rentals would not finance government; rather, government would earn its keep by "merchandising" services by exchange rather than by force. This does not preclude the public servants from obtaining payment from a percentage the rents.

But ultimately Heath wanted to replace government with proprietary governance:

> To obviate the essential tyranny (coercion) of political administration the proprietary authority, *suitably organized*, must extend its jurisdiction, and thus its revenues, by itself supplying police and other community services without coercion, out of its own revenues and properties, and thus raise its own values and voluntary incomes.[71]

Heath's ultimate aim was liberty, as was George's. George saw liberty in free, untaxed trade and the equal sharing of the natural bounty. Heath envisioned free, untaxed trade, but ignored the issue of the natural bounty, and went beyond George in seeking to eradicate the political source of governmental tyranny. Heath recognized that "charters and constitutions, then as now, were really but barricades against despotic power."[72] Proprietary governance would provide contract-based governance with a bottom-up delegation of power rather than the top down structures of mass democracy, so readily captured by rent-seeking special interests.

### Ideas for Transition

Heath did not provide a specific plan for a transition toward proprietary governance and ownership. In chapter 26, "Towards the Utopian Dream," of *Citadel, Market and Altar*, he notes the increasing extent of proprietary developments, and as this tendency continued, there would be a diminution of government and taxation and an evolution toward proprietorship. "The tendency thus indicated might be supposed to lead ultimately to all private capital coming under the public proprietary administration."[73]

In his article, "Privatizing the Neighborhood," Robert Nelson[74] has proposed a specific policy for a transition to private neighborhood associations. State law would permit property owners to petition to form a neighborhood association within a proposed boundary. Approval would require an affirmative vote of both 90 percent or more of the total property value affected and 75 percent or more of the individual unit owners. The relevant governments would then authorize a transfer of services and property such as streets to the association, accompanied by tax credits in compensation for the reduction of government expenses. All property owners in the privatized neighborhood would be required to be members of the association and pay the assessments levied. Since they would already have title to the real estate, there is no financial impediment, as there would be if they had to buy the land afresh.

The present author's transition proposal, "Towards Consensual Governance," chapter 15 in *Public Goods and Private Communities*,[75] makes the membership in private communities purely voluntary. It proposes an amendment to the constitution of a country by which taxation would be shifted to user fees and ground rent. Another amendment would provide exit options from government jurisdictions to allow private communities to substitute their services and receive tax deductions. Any person or organization having title to land would be able to partially secede, to withdraw property and services from governmental jurisdiction and create its own governance. Unlike Nelson's proposal, no title holder would be forced to join an association. The government would still retain residual sovereignty, nominal jurisdiction, and could require an exit fee or on-going rental payments to compensate for property obtained and for services such as defense that the private community would benefit from. Thus, first the country would go Georgist, and then private neighborhoods could substitute their services and assessments for those provided by government. Holdouts would continue to be under government jurisdiction, and there would then be agreements for the joint provision of services such as streets that have both members and nonmembers.

Tax and service substitution is possible even if the tax system is not first Georgified. A current example is the proposal for income-tax credits for tuition paid to private schools. Members of a private community would likewise obtain tax credits for the private provision of local services such as street maintenance and garbage collection.

588 *American Journal of Economics and Sociology*

## Concluding Remarks

While Heath did not fully understand Henry George's economics and social philosophy, he should be recognized as an important pioneer of contractual governance ultimately based on a Georgian economic foundation. Heath's misunderstandings and "vituperations" should not detract from the importance of his vision and theory. The economic aims of Georgist policy can be accomplished by proprietary public finance based on site rentals.

Both the Georgist and libertarian movements would be wise to consider the private-community concepts pioneered by Spencer Heath and furthered by his grandson, Spencer MacCallum. Proprietary governance offers an important alternative to current political government and can also enhance the libertarian vision of a voluntary society.

### Notes

1. Spencer Heath, manuscript, "Pencil notes for a letter, in a notebook with materials dated 1935–1936," item #292 in Spencer H. MacCallum, ed., "Spencer Heath on Henry George and Land Administration: Correspondence & Private Notes, Published & Unpublished, from the Spencer Heath Archives," assembled for this study at Tonopah, NV: The Heather Foundation, 2002. The titles for the various manuscript items are by MacCallum.

2. Ibid.

3. Ibid.

4. Spencer Heath, *Citadel, Market and Altar* (Baltimore: Science of Society Foundation, 1957). A biographical sketch in Heath's *Progress and Poverty Reviewed* (1952; see note 10) mentions the book with a publication date of 1946, but the book as published in 1957 has no mention of an earlier edition.

5. Henry George, *Progress and Poverty* (New York: Robert Schalkenbach Foundation, 1975) (originally published in 1879), p. 452.

6. Ibid., p. 343.

7. Spencer Heath, carbon of a letter to Benjamin Burger, 9 June, 1939, item #1238 in "Spencer Heath on Henry George."

8. Spencer Heath, "Outline of the Economic, Political, and Proprietary Departments of Society," in "Politics Versus Proprietorship," manuscript, 1935, pp. 65–66.

9. Frank Chodorov, carbon of a letter from Frank Chodorov, Director, Henry George School of Social Science, New York City, to Spencer Heath, 12 August, 1940, item #1310 in "Spencer Heath on Henry George."

10. Spencer Heath, *Progress and Poverty Reviewed and its Fallacies Exposed* (New York: *The Freeman*, 1952); Spencer Heath, carbon of a letter from Spencer Heath to Raymond McNally, 4 March, 1945, item #1428 in "Spencer Heath on Henry George."

11. Spencer Heath, carbon of a letter from Spencer Heath to C. H. Kendal, *Land and Freedom*, New York, 23 August, 1939, item #1262 in "Spencer Heath on Henry George."

12. Mark Sullivan, telephone conversation, 13 July, 2002, regarding a conversation between Spencer MacCallum (Heath's grandson) and Mark Sullivan, New York City, c. 1997. MacCallum, however, in a 16 July, 2002, telephone conversation with me, said that Heath regretted being impolitic, but that Heath still believed that Georgism was "land communism" in substance.

13. C. Lowell Harriss, "Rothbard's Anarcho-Capitalist Critique," *Critics of Henry George*, Robert V. Andelson, ed. (1st ed.; London: Associated University Presses, 1979), pp. 354–70.

14. Heath, *Progress and Poverty Reviewed*, p. 5.

15. Henry George, *Our Land and Land Policy, National and State* (San Francisco: White & Hauer, 1871).

16. Heath, *Progress and Poverty Reviewed*, p. 5.

17. George, *Progress and Poverty*, p. 404.

18. Heath, *Progress and Poverty Reviewed*, p. 6.

19. Ibid., p. 8.

20. Spencer Heath, *Citadel*, p. 74.

21. Ibid., p. 178.

22. Frédéric Bastiat, *Economic Harmonies*, George B. de Huszar, ed.; W. Hayden Boyers, trans. (Princeton, NJ: D. Van Nostrand Company, 1964). Originally published 1851.

23. George, *Progress and Poverty*, p. 452.

24. Ibid., p. 452

25. Heath, *Progress and Poverty Reviewed*, p. 8.

26. Ibid., p. 9.

27. Ibid.

28. Ibid., p. 8.

29. Ibid., p. 9

30. Ibid., p. 10.

31. George, *Progress and Poverty*, p. 155.

32. Ibid., p. 412.

33. Heath, *Progress and Poverty Reviewed*, pp. 12–13.

34. George, *Progress and Poverty*, p. 171

35. Heath, *Progress and Poverty Reviewed*, p. 14.

36. David Friedman, *Hidden Order* (NY: HarperCollins, 1996).

37. Heath, *Progress and Poverty Reviewed*, p. 16.

38. George, *Progress and Poverty*, p. 216.

39. Heath, *Progress and Poverty Reviewed*, p. 17.

40. Ibid., p. 23.

41. Spencer Heath, "Pencil notes on 3X5 cards. Sometime after 1936?," item #726 in "Spencer Heath on Henry George."

42. Heath, *Progress and Poverty Reviewed*, p. 23

43. Mason Gaffney, "Vituperation Well Answered," *Land and Liberty* (December 1952): 125–27.

44. Ibid., p. 126.

45. Ibid.

46. Ibid., p. 127.

47. Ibid.

48. Spencer Heath, "Rejoinder," Manuscript, 1953.

49. Ibid., p. 1.

50. Ibid., p. 3

51. Count Leo Tolstoy, "A Great Iniquity," *The Public* (Chicago), 19 August 1905, p. 18.

52. Spencer Heath, *The Trojan Horse of "Land Reform": A Critique of Land Communism or "Single Tax" as advocated in the Doctrinal Statement prepared by the Rev. Dr. Edward McGlynn* (no date or publisher provided).

53. Ibid., p. 9.

54. Ibid., p. 8.

55. The present author earlier described Heath's proprietary-community ideas in Fred Foldvary, *Public Goods and Private Communities* (Aldershot, UK: Edward Elgar Publishing, 1994).

56. Spencer Heath, "Creative Association," in "Politics Versus Proprietorship," p. 2.

57. Henry George, *Progress and Poverty*, p. xi.

58. Heath, *Citadel*.

59. Ibid., p. 146.

60. Ibid., p. 82. See also Spencer Heath MacCallum, "The Entrepreneurial Community Concept in Light of Advancing Business Practice and Technology," Fred Foldvary and Daniel Klein, eds, *The Half-Life of Policy Rationales: How New Technology Affects Old Policy Issues* (New York: New York University Press, 2003).

61. Heath, *Citadel*, p. 146

62. Ibid., p. 96.

63. Ibid., p. 135. MacCallum, op. cit., 2003.

64. Heath, *Citadel*, p. 160.

65. Ibid., p. 135.

66. Ibid., p. 136.

67. Spencer Heath, "Marked by Spencer Heath, 'Random,'" item #122 in "Spencer Heath on Henry George."

68. Heath, *Citadel*, p. 154.

69. Ibid., p. 155.

70. Spencer Heath, "Man, Land and Community," 1939, item #137 in "Spencer Heath on Henry George."

71. Spencer Heath, "July 29, 1947," item #188 in "Spencer Heath on Henry George.

72. Spencer Heath, "The Historical Perspective," item #181 in "Spencer Heath on Henry George."

73. Heath, *Citadel*, p. 184.

74. Robert Nelson, "Privatizing the Neighborhood: A Proposal to Replace Zoning with Private Collective Property Rights to Existing Neighborhoods," in *The Voluntary City*, ed. David Beito, Peter Gordon, and Alexander Tabarrok (Ann Arbor: University of Michigan Press, 2002), pp. 307–70. It first appeared in *George Mason Law Review* 7, no. 4 (1999): 827–80.

75. See note 55.

# 29
# Hayek: "Almost Persuaded"

By Robert V. Andelson*

"It was a lay enthusiasm for Henry George which led me to economics." So wrote Friedrich August von Hayek in a letter to Peter K.
Minton in 1962.[1] Elsewhere, he explained that this enthusiasm came
about as the result of his having been "exposed to a group of single-
taxers" as a first-year law student at the University of Vienna just after
World War I.[2]

In time, however, Hayek came to reject the Georgist model because
of an objection he set forth in his magnum opus, *The Constitution of
Liberty*. This objection constitutes a superficially formidable argument
that the defenders of Georgism seem almost wholly to have neglected.
The reason for this neglect is probably threefold: First, the argument
is readily overlooked, occupying, as it does, a single paragraph in a
book of more than 500 pages. Second, it is easily confused with a
different argument—one that has been widely, and to the satisfaction
of probably all Georgists, conclusively, refuted. Third, it is expressed
following a technically inaccurate definition on Hayek's part of the
model to which his objection is directed. However, the validity of his
objection does not depend upon the accuracy of his definition, and
his argument calls for a scholarly rejoinder, not merely in view of its
author's towering prestige, but due to the fact that, once disentan-
gled from its flawed context and correctly understood, it seems at first
blush compelling on its merits.

## The Issue of Separability

Hayek's argument is important because, although presented in a
discussion having to do with practical difficulties of town planning,

*The author is pleased to express indebtedness to Dr. Gerhard Schwarz, economics
editor of the *Neue Zürcher Zeitung*, for calling his attention (during the question period
following a lecture by him at the Liberales Institut, Zürich, 12 March, 1993) to the
issue to which this chapter is addressed. The chapter first appeared as an article in the
*American Journal of Economics and Sociology*, Vol. 59, No. 1 (January, 2000).

American Journal of Economics and Sociology, Vol. 63, No. 2 (April, 2004).

it attacks the moral basis of Georgist theory. That basis is expressed
by Nicolaus Tideman, who distinguishes three different sources of
the rent of land: (1) the value attributable to nature; (2) the value
attributable to public services; and (3) the value attributable to private
activities. By "private activities," he means aggregate private improvements and other nongovernmental operations that positively impact
a neighborhood. With respect to the last of these sources, Tideman
asserts that "[t]hese increments of rent are not due to the actions of
the landholders, so landholders cannot justly complain if the increments are collected publicly."[3] While this claim may be very largely
true, since such increments usually accrue to owners who have done
little (or even nothing at all) to earn them, there are instances in which
such increments of land value on a given site are the result of
improvements by the owner of that site, either to it or to adjacent
ones he also owns. A perceptive Australian writer, Philip Day, notes
that "at least in some circumstances, some parts of increased land
value can be attributed to the quality of development constructed by
individual landholders, rather than being wholly attributable to public
planning decisions or to population growth and general community
development."[4] An obvious example would be Disney World,[5]
although in this instance, as in many others, "quality" should be
understood to embrace more than architectural superiority. One might
properly claim that it is in the Disney Corporation's capacity as developer and not as owner that the improvements have been made, and
cite numerous examples to show that the incentive to improve a site
need not depend on owning it.[6] However, this would not address the
problem that Hayek regarded as insuperable—that of separating the
increments of value created by the owner (or his predecessors in title)
from those created by natural advantages, public services, or the
private activities of others. Let us now, therefore, examine the passage
in which he made this point:

> There still exist some organized groups who contend that all these dif-
> ficulties could be solved by the adoption of the "single-tax" plan, that is,
> by transferring the ownership of all land to the community and merely
> leasing it at rents determined by the market to private developers. This
> scheme for the socialization of land is, in its logic, probably the most
> seductive and plausible of all socialist schemes. If the factual assumptions

on which it is based were correct, i.e., if it were possible to distinguish clearly between the value of "the permanent and indestructible powers of the soil," on the one hand, and, on the other, the value due to the two different kinds of improvements—that due to communal efforts and that due to the efforts of the individual owner—the argument for its adoption would be very strong. Almost all the difficulties we have mentioned, however, stem from the fact that no such distinction can be drawn with any degree of certainty.[7]

## Peripheral Considerations

The first thing to be remarked about this passage is that Hayek's definition of "the 'single-tax plan'" is really not of the single-tax plan at all, but rather of George's "second best" alternative. Socializing land and leasing it while proportionately reducing or eliminating taxes on productive effort was described by George as "perfectly feasible,"[8] and has, in fact, shown itself to be so in Hong Kong and Singapore.[9] But George's preferred approach, the single tax, would leave titles to land in private hands while socializing only its rent (whether realized or not). This error on Hayek's part is very curious in view of the decisive role played by Georgism in awakening his interest in economics, but it does not touch the hypothetical validity of his stricture since that stricture is logically applicable to both approaches.

Another puzzling thing about the passage is this: Why should socializing all or most of either land or rent while concurrently reducing to the same degree the government's levy on other property or income be characterized as "a socialist scheme" any more than the usual, converse, practice? *Any* political system funded by compulsory payment is to that extent, by definition, socialistic. Yet from a libertarian standpoint, the Georgist system has the virtue of exacting payment only from those who opt "to receive from society a peculiar and valuable benefit, and . . . [except for the occasional and usually comparatively slight surplus which is the object of the present theoretical discussion] in proportion to the benefit they receive."[10]

A third feature of the passage that requires comment is that Hayek was *not* saying that it is impossible to separate land value from improvement value, as a hasty reading might suggest. Assessors do this all the time, if not always with absolute precision, at least well enough to meet normal statutory requirements. Where they fall short, the answer is improved training, staffing, and technical equipment. Hayek was not talking about improvement value as such, but about *that portion of land value* that reflects the value of the owner's improvements. Two instances were mentioned by George himself—the value imparted to land by drainage and by terracing.[11] However, in these instances improvement value ultimately lapses into land value because over time the improvement becomes physically indistinguishable from land—a needless theoretical complication in terms of the focus of the present study. That focus is more clearly illustrated by the Disney World example, in which improvements to a given site increase the value of surrounding acreage also owned by the improver.

### An Unreasonable Standard

Having disposed of these peripheral considerations, we are now almost ready to consider whether Hayek was justified in drawing the extreme negative conclusion that he did from the alleged impossibility of clearly separating the increments of land value that reflect the landowner's improvements from those that reflect other factors. But first we must note a telling comment by Jürgen G. Backhaus, who holds that Hayek demanded an illogically high standard of separability:

> Hayek's claim, despite the forceful wording in which it is presented, is in fact vacuous. Any tax legislation has to be enforceable and actionable in a court of justice. . . . Since the degree of certainty Hayek requires for his analysis is different from the degree of certainty that actionable tax assessments require, it is sufficient to point to empirical scenarios in which a Georgian tax scheme is being implemented and where such taxes are being paid. An abundance of such empirical examples contradict Hayek's claim.[12]

This contention is supported by the testimony of such professional assessors as J. Ted Gwartney[13] (to cite just one of many), who hold that the separation can be and is being made adequately for normative legal purposes.

## A Mere Quibble

But let us set Backhaus's argument aside. Even if Hayek were correct
in supposing that it is impossible (whether absolutely or relatively)
to separate that portion of a site's value attributable to improvements
by its owner from that portion attributable to improvements by (other)
owners of surrounding or nearby properties or by the public in its
corporate capacity, one need not accept his conclusion that this constitutes a definitive refutation of the Georgist system.

Assuming that public revenue were derived entirely from land rent,
with the burden of taxation lifted proportionately from the earnings
of labor and capital, the owner of land, part of the value of which
reflected the value of improvements he made on it or on adjacent
land, would still get to keep much more of what he produced than
would be the case under any alternative public revenue system, either
existent or imaginable. This is because the owner's improvements
themselves would escape taxation altogether. Practically speaking,
therefore, it is hardly an overstatement to say that Hayek's objection
is reduced to a mere quibble.

## In What Sense Hayek's Objection is Wrong Even in Theory

Theoretically, however, the objection would appear to undercut the
system's elegance. For, if Hayek was right, we can no longer assert
literally with the late Danish parliamentarian and sometime cabinet
minister, Dr. Viggo Starke: "What I produce is mine. *All* mine! What
you produce is yours. *All* yours! But that which none of us produced,
but which we all lend value to together, belongs by right to all of us
in common."[14] The clear division between mine, thine, and ours,
which makes the Georgist paradigm so morally appealing, now looks
like rhetorical hyperbole.

And so it is, but in one sense only. There is another sense in which
the theoretical division remains quite valid.

Many years ago, when the present writer was working on his doctorate at the University of Southern California, he would occasionally
encounter on campus the striking figure of a regal-looking gentleman

whose wavy white hair and pink complexion were always set off by an elegantly-cut blue suit. Tall and erect, with luxuriant but carefully trimmed moustache and piercing blue eyes behind rimless glasses, Dr. Rufus B. von Kleinschmidt seemed every inch a university president—as, indeed, he had once been. Some years before, however, he had been elevated at USC to the chancellorship, a position insulated from contact with the faculty. Thereon hangs a tale, which may or may not be apocryphal.

The Western Association of Colleges and Universities had published the salary schedules submitted to it by the presidents of all the institutions of higher learning accredited by it, USC among them. Upon reading this report, members of the faculty began comparing notes, and soon realized that USC's salary schedule was highly inflated, bearing little relation to what they were actually being paid. When they confronted President von Kleinschmidt with this discovery, they received the following response: "But that *is* our salary schedule. I never said that we were able to meet it." Let us be charitable and leave open the question of whether this equation of the real with the ideal on von Kleinschmidt's part was an expression of Platonism or of disingenuousness.

There is a strain of qualified Platonism in Henry George's thought, but he was the least disingenuous of men. He anticipated Hayek's stricture, and addressed it head-on in an article in *The Standard,* 17 August, 1889:

> I am convinced that with public attention concentrated on one single source of public revenues, and with the public intelligence and public conscience accustomed to look on the payments required from that, not as an exaction from the individual, but as something due in justice from him by the community, we would come much closer to taking the whole of economic rent than might seem possible at present. Yet I regard it as certain that it must always be impossible to take economic rent exactly, or to take it all, without at the same time taking something more. . . . Theoretical perfection pertains to nothing human. The best we can do in practice is to approach the ideal . . .
> Is it not better that the state should, on the whole, get something less than its exact due than that individuals should be compelled to pay more than they ought to be called upon to pay? If so, we must in any case leave a margin.

This I have always seen. What that margin should be I have never attempted to formulate, and have never put it at ten percent or at any other percent. What I have always stated as our aim was that we should take the whole of economic rent "as near as might be."[15]

Perfect justice, then, is what Reinhold Niebuhr termed "an impossible possibility."[16] Our inability to attain it does not relieve us of the obligation to approach it as closely as we can. This the Georgist model does, while few of the others even try. And where, in practice, it falls short of the ideal (as, to some extent, any human effort always must), George would have it err on the side of the individual.

## Notes

1. Register of the Friedrich A. von Hayek Papers, 1906–1992, Hoover Institute Archives, Stanford University, Stanford, CA.

2. F. A. Hayek, *Hayek on Hayek: An Autobiographical Dialogue*, Stephen Kresge and Leif Wenar, eds. (Chicago: University of Chicago Press, 1994), p. 63.

3. Nicolaus Tideman, "The Economics of Efficient Taxes on Land," in Nicolaus Tideman, ed., *Land and Taxation* (London: Shepheard-Walwyn Ltd., 1994), p. 134.

4. Philip Day, *Land: The Elusive Quest for Social Justice, Taxation Reform & a Sustainable Planetary Environment* (Brisbane: Academic Press, 1995), p. 102. Day's response to this phenomenon is merely to emphasize that it is "the *existence of a community and its organised social structure*, as well as its exercise of land use planning powers which provide the developer with the opportunity to develop and to choose the quality of development which is likely to prove most profitable." (Note 3 to chapter 11, p. 109.) While this consideration may justify reducing the percentage of land value retained by the owner, it does not fully resolve the problem to which this paper is addressed, which is not so much a problem of magnitudes as it is of principle.

5. Cited by Charles Hooper in his article on Henry George in David K. Henderson, ed., *The Fortune Encyclopedia of Economics* (New York: Warner Books, 1993), pp. 789–90. Hooper sees the problem as a defect in George's proposal, but apparently not as an invalidating one.

6. In New York City, the Chrysler Building, the Empire State Building, and Rockefeller Center were all built on leased land, and the same is true of most major buildings in Hong Kong and Singapore.

7. F. A. Hayek, *The Constitution of Liberty* (Chicago: University of Chicago Press, 1960), pp. 352–53.

8. Henry George, *Progress and Poverty* (1879; New York: Robert Schalkenbach Foundation, 1962), p. 404.

9. Sock-Yong Phang, "Hong Kong and Singapore," in R. V. Andelson, ed., *Land-Value Taxation Around the World* (3rd edition; Malden, MA, and Oxford: Blackwell Publishers, 2000), chap. 20.

10. George, *Progress and Poverty*, p. 421.

11. Ibid., p. 426. Because such permanent improvements become indistinguishable from the land itself, he held that after a certain interval of time their value should "be considered as having lapsed into that of the land, and . . . taxed accordingly," which "could have no deterrent effect on such improvements, for such works are frequently undertaken upon leases for years."

12. Jürgen G. Backhaus, "Reading Henry George in 1997," a paper presented at a conference on Henry George Re-Considered, Maastricht University, the Netherlands, Oct. 28, 1997.

13. In undated correspondence and conversations with the present writer. Gwartney, chief assessor of Bridgeport, CN, was formerly assessment commissioner of British Columbia.

14. Slightly paraphrased with emphases by the present writer from "Our Daily Bread," *Proceedings of the Eighth International Conference on Land-Value Taxation and Free Trade* (London: International Union for Land-Value Taxation and Free Trade/Danish Georgist Union, 1952). The conference was held at Odense, Denmark, July 28 to August 4, 1952.

15. Reprinted in Kenneth C. Wenzer, ed., *An Anthology of Henry George's Thought* (Volume I of the Henry George Centennial Trilogy; Rochester, NY: University of Rochester Press, 1977), pp. 82, 83.

16. Reinhold Niebuhr, *An Interpretation of Christian Ethics* (New York and London: Harper & Brothers, 1935), pp. 113, 117, and 118. For an understanding of what Niebuhr meant by this term, the whole of chapter 7 should be read.

# 30
# Hardin's Putative Critique*

*By* Robert V. Andelson

Of the neo-Malthusian voices emanating from ecologist ranks, one of the most powerful and certainly the most provocative is that of Garrett Hardin (1915–2003), professor emeritus of human ecology at the University of California, Santa Barbara.

I propose to show that, despite secondary disagreements, Garrett Hardin and Henry George may, in what is most germane to the focus of these explorations, be far closer to each other than might first appear. I propose to show that what they have in common is obscured by a semantic difference—ironically, a difference in the meaning that they attach to the *word* "common."

## What George Meant by "Common Property"

When, in book VI, chapter 2, of *Progress and Poverty*, George asserted, "*We must make land common property*," he was guilty of a tactical blunder that hobbled the advance of his proposal from the start. For although he took pains later in his book to clarify this declaration, it has been used by his antagonists with deadly effect to portray him as an advocate of nationalizing land.

Actually, of course, nationalization, with its concomitant collectivization and regimentation, was not at all what George proposed. By "common property in land," he intended to signify the effectuation of common rights in land, not (except in instances involving generally-accepted public functions) its collective use. Neither did he intend to signify a common resource to be drawn on individually without concern for social consequences.

The true meaning of the phrase for George is best exhibited in book VIII, chapter 1. He first speaks there of a lot in the center of

---

*Excerpted from R. V. Andelson, "Commons Without Tragedy," in R. V. Andelson, ed., *Commons Without Tragedy* (Savage, MD, and London: Barnes & Noble Books and Shepheard-Walwyn Ltd, 1991), pp. 33–43.

American Journal of Economics and Sociology, Vol. 63, No. 2 (April, 2004).

San Francisco: "This lot is not cut up into infinitesimal pieces nor yet is it an unused waste. It is covered with fine buildings, the property of private individuals, that stand there in perfect security. The only difference between this lot and those around it, is that the rent of the one goes into the common school fund, the rent of the others into private pockets."

He then turns to the Aleutian islets of St. Peter and St. Paul, the breeding places of the fur seal, an animal so wary that the slightest fright causes it to flee its customary haunts forever.

> To prevent the utter destruction of this fishery, without which the islands are of no use to man, it is not only necessary to avoid killing the females and young cubs, but even such noises as the discharge of a pistol or the barking of a dog . . . Those who can be killed without diminution of future increase are carefully separated and gently driven inland, out of sight and hearing of the herds, where they are dispatched with clubs. To throw such a fishery as this open to whoever chose to go and kill—which would make it to the interest of each party to kill as many as they could at the time without reference to the future—would be utterly to destroy it in a few seasons, as similar fisheries in other countries have been destroyed. But it is not necessary, therefore, to make these islands private property. . . . They have been leased at a rent of $317,500 per year [partly fixed ground rent, partly payment of $2.62½ on each skin, with an annual harvest limited to 100,000 skins], probably not very much less than they could have been sold for at the time of the Alaska purchase. They have already yielded two millions and a half to the national treasury, and they are still, in unimpaired value (for under the careful management of the Alaska Fur Company the seals increase rather than diminish), the common property of the people of the United States.

Although George thus illustrates his principle by means of actual examples involving leaseholds, his prescription envisages an easier and less drastic application than that of confiscating land and letting it out to the highest bidders. Instead, he advocates that land titles be left in private hands, with rent appropriated by means of the existing tax machinery. Commensurate reductions would be made in taxes on improvements and other labor products (culminating ideally in the total abolition of such taxes), and the machinery reduced and simplified accordingly. "By leaving to landowners a percentage of rent which would probably be much less than the cost and loss involved in attempting to rent lands through State agency, and by making use of this existing machinery, we may, without jar or shock, assert the common right to land by taking rent for public uses."[1] But this is simply a practical refinement; the principle remains the same.

## The Tragedy of the Commons

In his seminal essay, "The Tragedy of the Commons,"[2] Hardin focuses on the inherent tendency of individuals, each in the pursuit of his own interests, to overgraze, denude, and use the commons as a cesspool. That which belongs to everybody in this sense is, indeed, valued and maintained by nobody. The Enclosure Movement ultimately brought an end to the commons in Europe as a basic institution, but not without exacting a baneful price in human misery that might well be termed "The Tragedy of the Enclosures."

It makes no difference, really, whether or not Hardin believes that most people are utility or profit maximizers who value their individual goods more than they do social goods. If common property is free to all without restraint, it only takes one such person, once an area's carrying capacity has been reached, to degrade the area. As with persons, so also with nations. The stocks of blue whales are so depleted that the International Whaling Commission recommends the virtual stoppage of whaling, and all but two nations have ceased whaling on the high seas altogether. But Japan and Russia continue to fish for whales aggressively, and the depletion becomes ever more acute. Soon the blue whale may be extinct. Actually, Hardin does not deny the existence of altruism either in individuals or in societies. But his "conservative policy," as he calls it, is "to regard altruism as a marginal motive."[3] To me, this policy seems only sensible. Archbishop Temple must have been thinking along similar lines when he defined the art of government as "the art of so ordering life that self-interest prompts what justice demands."[4]

When I commenced the research for the paper that evolved into this chapter, I set out, with the aid of two British colleagues, David Redfearn and Julia Bastian, to disprove Hardin's thesis. Together, we compiled an impressive list of counter-examples, showing that the historic commons, far from being an unregulated free-for-all, were mostly operated according to agreed-upon rules that ensured a fair distribution of opportunity, spread work evenly throughout the seasons, and generally tended to conserve the soil and other natural resources.[5] These rules worked effectively in England for about a thousand years. It was only after the enclosure of the open fields was well advanced that the common pastures, having been thus divorced in large measure from their traditional employment, became subject to overgrazing and other environmental abuses as the old regulatory machinery fell into abeyance.[6] Vestigial remnants of the historic commons, such as the Swiss alpine village of Törbel, survive and thrive even today.[7] As for the supposed ecologically beneficent effects of "private" as opposed to "common" ownership of land, a report in the *Financial Times* of London speaks of pollution resulting from the use of chemical fertilizers and pesticides, deterioration of habitats, erosion, loss of topsoil, acidification of rivers, desertification, unsuitable afforestation, etc.[8] But this is not a brief for "government" ownership (nationalization); there is probably no sizeable body of water in the world more polluted than is the Aral Sea, as the result of Soviet policies.

"The Tragedy of the Commons" was first published in 1968, and has been reprinted in numerous collections since that date. Among the more vigorous efforts to rebut it is an article by John Reader, which appeared two decades later. "The true commons," Reader properly insists, "was, by definition, an area of mutual benefit and responsibility, managed by those using it in a manner that acknowledged that environmental resources are not unlimited. Access to the commons was restricted by entitlement; use was regulated to ensure that no individual could pursue his own interest to the detriment of others. Far from bringing ruin to all, the true commons functioned to keep its exploitation within sustainable limits, thus providing every commoner with a dependable food supply in the short term, and maintaining the viability of available resources for generations to come."[9] A more careful analysis of Hardin's essay demonstrates that, like my own compilation of counter-examples, Reader's attack, while factual enough, is utterly beside the point: What Reader calls the "true commons" is not what Hardin meant by "the commons" in his essay. The essay presents a hypothetical illustration of a pasture open to all.

Each herdsman, seeking as a rational being to maximize his gain, will try to keep as many cattle as possible on the pasture. So long as tribal warfare, poaching, and disease keep the numbers of both man and beast below the carrying capacity of the land, the arrangement may work satisfactorily. But once that capacity is exceeded, "the inherent logic of the commons generates tragedy," since the rational herdsman, knowing that without regulation others will pursue their individual interests even if he abstains, adds animal after animal to his herd. "Each man is locked into a system that compels him to increase his herd without limit—in a world that is limited."[10] So much for the hypothetical illustration. But one looks in vain in the essay for historical references.

It is true that, in other work, Hardin alludes in passing to the ecological destructiveness of the system of English commons that was replaced as a result of the Enclosure Movement.[11] In this, he may have been historically inaccurate, but this was a mere incidental error, as in neither case was he writing to establish a historical thesis. Hardin uses the term "commons" to refer, not primarily or necessarily to any actual historical institution, but to what sociologists, following Max Weber, call an *ideal type*—a pure logical construct, in this instance, one of the four discrete politico-economic systems of environmental utilization. The "system of the commons" is the one in which the environment is utilized by the group with the proceeds going to the individual. It is, practically speaking, a synonym for anarchy.

In a piece entitled "Ethical Implications of Carrying Capacity," Hardin discusses an "excellent report" by Nicholas Wade, which ascribes the advancing desertification of the Sahel largely to (often well-intended) Western interference. Prior to this interference, the Sahelian peoples carried on a way of life that was a remarkably efficient adaptation to their environment, with migrations, routes, the length of time a herd of a given size might spend at a given well, etc., governed by rules worked out by tribal chiefs. But, according to Hardin, the "old way of treating common property in the Sahel" was not really the system of the commons but rather a kind of informal socialism.[12] It may, of course, be argued that the words "commons" and "socialism" are both used by him in idiosyncratic fashion, but an author is entitled to use words any way he chooses so long as he specifies what he is doing, and Hardin cannot in this context be accused of failing to so specify.

*"The morality of an act,"* says Hardin, *"is a function of the state of the system at the time it is performed."*[13] In the Old Testament period, "Be fruitful and multiply" might have been a sound injunction; today, it is in most cases a mandate to behave irresponsibly. For a lone frontiersman to discharge waste into a stream may harm nobody; as population reaches a certain density, such conduct becomes intolerable. "Property rights must be periodically reexamined in the light of social justice."[14] In a complex, crowded, changeable environment, statutory law cannot make adequate allowance for particular circumstances, and must therefore be augmented by administrative law. But Hardin admits that administrative law, depending as it does upon decision-making by bureaucrats, is singularly liable to corruption. To it applies with special force the age-old question: *Quis custodiet ipsos custodes?*—"Who shall watch the watchers themselves?" Hardin draws attention to this difficulty, but does not attempt an answer.

### An Implicit Endorsement

How can exploitation be adjusted to carrying capacity, allowing for particular and changing circumstances, yet avoiding the corruption and caprice of bureaucratic regulators? Inasmuch as we live in an imperfect world inhabited by imperfect beings, a perfect solution to this dilemma does not exist. Yet the program of Henry George, since it calls for a process that is virtually self-regulating, comes as close to being foolproof as anything conceivable. To leave the land in private hands, while appropriating through taxation the greater part of its annual rental value as determined by the market, would assure, not maximum, but optimum, exploitation.

In an illustration concerning the lumber industry, Hardin correctly remarks that "high taxes on land that is many years away from being timbered encourage cut-and-run."[15] But they wouldn't have this effect if combined with heavy severance taxes, which encourage conservation while reducing the land's market value. Thus the tax on annual rental value could be set at a high percentage yet still be low enough to induce retention of title, together with noninjurious harvesting schedules and techniques. Although the taxation of land rent is, of course, the method characteristically emphasized by Georgism, a severance tax is simply a different technical application of the same philosophy, adapted to different circumstances but equally amenable to determination by the market.

I make no pretense of familiarity with the whole of Hardin's copious literary output, but the adverse reference to which I just alluded is the only one I have encountered that speaks explicitly of land taxation, although he makes a slighting reference to Henry George in a discussion of the Malthusian question.[16] Conversely, in *Stalking the Wild Taboo*, one finds a glancing but favourable mention of the graduated income tax.[17] Yet he proposes internalizing pollution costs (and simultaneously discouraging pollution) through taxation[18]—a proposal very much in keeping with the Georgist accent on using the tax mechanism to protect common rights in the environment within an overall framework of private enterprise. And in a book he edited, Jay M. Anderson suggests, quite possibly with his tacit approval, "the taxation of industry at a rate proportional to used commons."[19]

But most significant, I think, is an easily overlooked passage in "The Tragedy of the Commons" in which Hardin, perhaps unwittingly, endorses by implication the essential Georgist concept:

> During the Christmas shopping season [in Leominster, Massachusetts] the parking meters downtown were covered with plastic bags that bore tags reading: "Do not open until after Christmas. Free parking courtesy of the mayor and city council." In other words, facing the prospect of an increased demand for already scarce space, the city fathers reinstituted the system of the commons.[20]

By calling this a "retrogressive act," Hardin demonstrates his belief that the meters ought to have been left in operation. Now, parking meters exemplify (in specialized form) the public appropriation of land rent; they constitute payment for the privilege of temporarily monopolizing a site—compensation to the members of the community whose opportunity to use the site is extinguished for a given time by the monopoly. The payment, to be sure, is typically only partial. Compensation reflecting the full market value of the temporary monopoly would be at levels comparable to fees charged by commercial parking lots in the vicinity of the meters.

But more than compensation is involved here. If parking meter fees, instead of being used to pay for community services or even for their own collection cost, were buried in the ground, their collection would still be justified in order, as Hardin puts it, "to keep downtown shoppers temperate in their use of parking space"[21]—i.e., as a means of rendering monopoly temporary and innocuous. So, also, the public appropriation of land rent in its more comprehensive application, by removing any incentive to hoard and speculate in land, would be warranted in terms of social justice and well-being, even if its yield were cast into the sea. For in rectifying distribution, this approach liberates production; in apportioning the wealth-pie fairly, it increases the size of the pie. Instead of being a cruel contest in which the cards are stacked against most players because of gross disparities in bargaining power, the market becomes in practice what capitalist theory alleges it to be—a profoundly cooperative process of voluntary exchange. And all this is accomplished without stressing the environment. Cities, more compact, return to human scale as artificial pressures for expansion outward and upward are removed. The availability of land at prices no longer bloated by speculation, makes profitable agriculture possible without the wholesale use of ecologically harmful chemicals and machinery.

In addition to the "system of the commons," which amounts to anarchy, Hardin distinguishes three other discrete systems of environmental utilization: "socialism," "private philanthropy," and "private enterprise."[22] He tends in general to favor the last, since under it the individual decision-maker and society usually both lose when the carrying capacity of the environment is overloaded, and thus decisions are more apt to be "operationally responsible." Yet he concedes that this is not invariably the case, and is no apologist for absolute private ownership of land.[23] Not only does he grant that an owner, seeking rationally to maximize his gains, may under certain conditions behave in an ecologically *irresponsible* fashion[24] (a conclusion set forth in greater detail respectively by Daniel Fife and Colin W. Clark[25]) but he holds that the Enclosure Acts, even though ecologically desirable, were unjust.[26] "We must admit," he asserts moreover, "that our legal system of private property plus inheritance is unjust—but we put up with it because we are not convinced, at the moment, that anyone has invented a better system."[27]

Well, someone surnamed George did "invent" a better system—one that eminently satisfies all of Hardin's criteria, one that secures the advantages of both commons and enclosures with none of the disadvantages of either. For, paradoxical though it may seem, the only way in which the individual may be assured what properly belongs to him is for society to take what properly belongs to it: the Jeffersonian ideal of individualism requires for its realization the socialization of rent. Were rent socialized, population stabilized, the costs of negative externalities internalized, and the returns of private effort privatized, we and our posterity would prosper, at least roughly, according to our deserts, and healing come to our abused and wounded habitat, the earth.

### Notes

1. Henry George, *Progress and Poverty* (1879; New York: Robert Schalkenbach Foundation, 1962), p. 403.

2. Garrett Hardin, "The Tragedy of the Commons," *Science*, Vol. 162 (Dec. 13, 1968): 1243–48.

3. Hardin, "An Operational Analysis of 'Responsibility'," in Garrett Hardin and John Baden, eds., *Managing the Commons* (San Francisco: W. H. Freeman and Co., 1977), p. 68.

4. William Temple, *Christianity and Social Order* (1942; London: Shepheard-Walwyn Ltd., 1976; New York: Seabury, 1977), p. 65.

5. See C. S. and C. S. Orwin, *The Open Fields* (Oxford: Clarendon, 1938), pp. 38–58; and *Laxton: Life in an Open Field Village* (Nottingham: University of Nottingham Manuscripts Department, Archive Teaching Unit No. 4), Introduction, pp. 12–17, Transcripts and Summaries of Documents, pp. 10–11.

6. W. G. Collins and L. D. Stamp, *The Common Lands of England and Wales* (London: Collins, 1963), pp. 56–60.

7. John Reader, "Human Ecology: How Land Shapes Society," *New Scientist*, No. 1629 (Sept. 8, 1988): 55.

8. Bridget Bloom, "Erosion Threatens Europe's Agricultural Land," *Financial Times* (London), July 18, 1988, Environment IV. See also Teri Randall, "Topsoil Erosion 'Silent Crisis' Threatens Farmers," *Chicago Tribune*, rpt. *Birmingham News* (Alabama), July 19, 1989. Randall quotes William Fyfe, geology professor at Western Ontario University: "At the root of the problem is a rapidly growing world population. Each year, 90 million babies join the

more than 5 billion humans already on earth, yet the total area of farmland available to feed them decreases."

9. Reader, p. 52.

10. "The Tragedy of the Commons," p. 1244.

11. Hardin, *Exploring New Ethics for Survival* (New York: Viking, 1972), p. 116.

12. Hardin, "Ethical Implications of Carrying Capacity" and "An Operational Analysis of 'Responsibility'" in Hardin and Baden, eds., *Managing the Commons*, p. 122 and p. 69.

13. "The Tragedy of the Commons," p. 1243.

14. Hardin, *Exploring New Ethics for Survival*, p. 127.

15. Ibid., p. 26.

16. Hardin, "The Feast of Malthus: The Social Contract," *Journal Archives* (Spring, 1998).

17. Hardin, *Stalking the Wild Taboo* (Los Altos, CA: William Kaufman, Inc., 1973), p. 177.

18. "The Tragedy of the Commons," p. 1245; *Exploring New Ethics for Survival*, pp. 123, 244 f.

19. Jay M. Anderson, "A Model of the Commons," in Hardin and Baden, eds., *Managing the Commons*, p. 41.

20. "The Tragedy of the Commons," p. 1245.

21. Ibid., p. 1247.

22. "An Operational Analysis of 'Responsibility'," p. 69.

23. *Exploring New Ethics for Survival*, pp. 125–27.

24. Ibid., pp. 125–26.

25. Daniel Fyfe, "Killing the Goose" and Colin W. Clark, "The Economics of Overexploitation," in Hardin and Baden, eds., *Managing the Commons*, pp. 76–95.

26. Hardin, "Denial and Disguise" in ibid., p. 46.

27. "The Tragedy of the Commons," p. 1247 s.

# 31
# Reckoning with Rothbard

By Harold Kyriazi

Murray Newton Rothbard (1926–1995), an economist by profession, was an active libertarian intellectual for almost fifty years, a voracious reader, prolific writer, charismatic speaker, irrepressible political activist, inspiration to myriad young libertarian scholars and activists, and one of the central figures in the libertarian movement.[1] Professionally, he received his Ph.D. from Columbia in 1956, held a teaching appointment at New York Polytechnic Institute–Brooklyn from 1966 through 1986, was the S. J. Hall distinguished professor of economics at the University of Nevada–Las Vegas from 1985 until the time of his death in early 1995, and served as academic vice-president of the Ludwig von Mises Institute at Auburn University, Alabama, from 1982 also until his death.

A seminal event in his intellectual life occurred in 1949, when he encountered Ludwig von Mises and his monumental work, *Human Action*. Rothbard attended all of von Mises's seminars at New York University, eventually becoming his intellectual successor[2] and popularizing Austrian economics in the United States. Most relevant to the task at hand, however, is that Rothbard was also the most voluminous critic of Henry George's single tax in the latter half of the twentieth century.[3]

## Rothbard and Georgism

Georgists will be interested to know that Rothbard was a long-time friend and informal student of the prominent Georgist and individualist, Frank Chodorov, from whose book service he ordered George's *The Science of Political Economy*, and whose monthly *Analysis* broadsheet he read and admired.[4] As a result, Rothbard was thoroughly appreciative and complimentary of many of George's economic

American Journal of Economics and Sociology, Vol. 63, No. 2 (April, 2004).
© 2004 American Journal of Economics and Sociology, Inc.

analyses, occasionally quoting them at length.[5] It seems reasonable to ascribe his interest in the single tax to Chodorov and, indirectly, Albert Jay Nock, whose writings Rothbard also devoured, greatly admired, and recommended to others.[6] One cannot accuse Rothbard of not having given the land question much thought, for he not only wrote about it at length, but indicated that he puzzled over some perceived Georgist inanities.[7]

All of which makes it a bit mysterious how he could have blundered so embarrassingly in his many published critical analyses of single-tax theory.[8] My first writings about Rothbard's views on the land question consisted of a straightforward critique of his most obvious errors, without any attempt at explanation.[9] But now a fuller survey of his writings has made an in-depth explanation possible. In addition, his posthumously published works contain more polished arguments and avoid his earlier, obvious errors. This essay will therefore eschew facile criticism, and instead address Rothbard's strongest points and mature, integrated position, highlighting his errors and differences with George, as well as George's own main error.

### *Rothbard's Anarcho-Capitalist World View*

Rothbard viewed all taxation as theft, and all forms of government, being funded by taxation, as coercive. He was convinced that government could do no net good, and was an unnecessary intrusion of force into the marketplace, which could provide for all human needs, including defense and law enforcement.[10] Regarding land, he believed that 1) justice consists of the first user of a parcel being its first owner, with the parcel subsequently being treated as purely private property, 2) speculation is beneficial, 3) parcels would never be withheld from use unless such use was unwarranted economically, and 4) owners and speculators earn everything they make, benefitting from "unearned increments" no more than anyone else in society. Consequently, he viewed the single tax not as ground rent collection, but as a tax like any other, and thus both harmful and unnecessary.

## Main Disagreements

### *Where George Erred*

First of all must be mentioned the only departure from justice in George's version of the single tax, because it contributed to Rothbard's faulty understanding. It has to do with who creates land value. In *Libertarian Party at Sea on Land*, I delineated four types of factors that contribute to the utility of any particular parcel of land: nature-created, and three man-made types: government-created externalities, privately created externalities, and privately created internalities.[11] "Externalities" is a term that refers to effects on neighboring land (such as the benefit to a high-rise apartment building owner in having a subway stop nearby, or the benefit in increased foot traffic to a restaurant owner in having a large department store next door), whereas "internalities" refers to values that inhere in that particular parcel (e.g., a building that sits on it). Currently most, and under Rothbard's supposed ideal system all, of the value of these factors goes to the individual land parcel owner. Under George, only the individual landowner-created internalities would belong to that landowner, and governmentally and privately created externalities would belong equally to everyone.[12] In this author's view, to the extent that the value of privately created utility can be determined, it should go to its creators—the moral principle being that the one who creates should be the one who owns. Likewise, government at all levels should be paid out of the value it creates,[13] and the remainder—nature's gift component—should go to everyone equally. This will subsequently be referred to as the "ground rent collection and distribution system."[14]

Rothbard expressed a similar concern about the expropriation of creators, when he wrote: "It is difficult to see why a newborn Pakistani baby should have a quotal share of ownership of a piece of Iowa land that someone has just transformed into a wheatfield. . . . It is difficult to see the morality of depriving him [the first user and transformer of land]* of ownership in favor of people who have never

---

*All bracketed comments throughout the essay are those of the author.

gotten within a thousand miles of the land, and who may not even know of the existence of the property over which they are supposed to have a claim."[15] Even though he here conflates nature-created and individually created internalities, there is some validity in his objection—they deserve to share in only the nature-created component of land value, and since land in Pakistan likely has natural utility similar to that of Iowa farmland (though perhaps a denser population), their main complaint lies with the legislators and landlords of Pakistan, not with the Iowa farmer.

This failure to distinguish the various factors giving utility to land has also permeated the thinking of most Georgists, who err in making general statements to the effect that "population creates land value." Such statements equate those who increase land value by making it more useful with those who add to its value merely by bidding on it, in effect conflating production and demand. But there is, in fact, no comparison between the act of, say, creating adjacent land value by putting in a subway stop, and increasing its value by bidding on it. That portion of the population consisting of (productive) people with money to spend, along with the fact that land is monopolized,* together create the demand and scarcity value, but certainly not the

---

*Note to Reader: Three caveats. The word "landlord" herein is used in the sense employed by Henry George, of applying only to the nonworking aspect of the term, the "land title holder" aspect; some owners of land are solely landlords, while others are users, planners, and developers as well. Second, the word "land" is used sometimes in its economic sense, of applying to all natural resources. Lastly, the word "monopoly" is used in reference to land ownership, because 1) land is no longer being made and has all been appropriated, 2) people, being land animals, must rent or buy from *someone*, and do not have the freedom to exist without paying tribute for the privilege, and 3) when, for example, one has a factory and wants to expand it, those who own the surrounding land have an *absolute* monopoly over the specific land one needs. Thus, "land monopoly" has both collective/global aspects and individual/local aspects, and is best thought of as an informal cartel, as pointed out by Ian Lambert in an unpublished manuscript (see endnote 46). Rothbard himself used the phrase, but only in regard to what might better be termed "inappropriate appropriation" (p. 69, *The Ethics of Liberty*, 1982): "We may call both of these aggressions [feudalism and land-engrossing] 'land monopoly'—not in the sense that some one person or group owns all the land in society, but in the sense that arbitrary privileges to land ownership are asserted in both cases . . . Land monopoly is far more widespread in the modern world than most people—especially most Americans—believe."

utility, which is a product of individual human labor and thus properly belongs to specific individual creators.

Because of such Georgist imprecision, Rothbard was not totally off-base in quoting nineteenth-century individualist anarchist Benjamin Tucker as follows: "There is justice as well as bluntness in Benjamin Tucker's criticism: '"What gives value to land?" asks Rev. Hugh O. Pentecost [a Georgist]. And he answers: "The presence of population—the community. Then rent, or the value of land, morally belongs to the community." What gives value to Mr. Pentecost's preaching? The presence of population—the community. Then Mr. Pentecost's salary, or the value of his preaching, morally belongs to the community.' Tucker, *Instead of a Book*, p. 357."[16] By this line of reasoning, consumers would "own" everything by virtue of their need (demand)—a very communistic notion indeed, and one that can play no part in correct Georgist thinking, as George himself was quite clear that justice "is that which gives wealth to him who makes it."[17]

In George's time, the comparative data and computational techniques needed to perform accurate and large-scale calculations of who created what portion of land value were largely absent, and thus George's erring on the side of the bulk of humanity (i.e., the entire working class), rather than specific, highly "land value productive" individuals, is reasonable and forgiveable. Rothbard's erring completely on the side of landlords* is less forgiveable, though we shall see that he did have superficially plausible justifications for his views.

Owing to the above, we will not here be dealing strictly with Rothbard's disagreements with George, but with his disagreements with the views of the present author and others, such as economists Fred Foldvary and Nicolaus Tideman, who consider themselves to be "geo-libertarians"[18] (and who are both authors of chapters in this volume).

Lest Georgists think this slight deviation from George to be heretical, it must be pointed out that it is, at least, not a new heresy. It was first touched upon in 1917 by Georgist economist Harry Gunnison Brown, in an essay on the ethics of land-value taxation.[19] More recently, the issue has been directly addressed by Tideman[20] and the late, Nobel Prize-winning economist William Vickrey,[21] who have both

*See note on page 614.

referred to payment to private entities, out of collected land rents, for values they have created, as "the internalization of externalities." A very thorough and competent treatment has also been rendered by "geo-economist" Kris Feder.[22]

All of Rothbard's major disagreements with George and geo-libertarians boil down to three failures of understanding on his part:

1) he never understood the favorable spatial externalities attaching to land use (though, interestingly, pre-eminent Austrian economist and Nobel Prize winner, Friedrich Hayek, was quite aware of them[23]).

2) he did not think the various contributions to land value could be separately calculated (Hayek also failed here,[24] unfortunately).

3) he did not appreciate the enormous similarity between local governments and private corporations that own and manage an area of space (such as hotels, shopping malls, industrial parks, amusement parks, condominium associations, etc.), nor, conversely, the enormous similarity between present-day coercive governments and the ultra-powerful private landlords[25] that would occupy his anarcho-capitalist utopia. (Hayek remarked about the former similarity—see the end of endnote 23.)

But rather than talk about what Rothbard failed to understand or to address, it will be more fruitful to discuss four basic economic questions he *did* address, which define the essence of the Rothbardian/anarcho-capitalist Georgist/geo-libertarian disagreement.

1. Are landlords, in their capacity as land title holders, doing any useful work, or are they instead engaged in robbery for a living? (George said they do not perform any useful function, Rothbard said they do.)

2. Is the dynamic of land ownership, under Rothbard's Rule (first user is first owner, with land being treated exactly like man-made goods thereafter), characterized by positive feedback, thus creating a "vicious cycle" and a greater concentration of land ownership, no feedback, thus tending to leave the distribution

of land ownership undisturbed, or negative feedback, thus leading to more widespread ownership of land? (George said positive feedback, Rothbard negative.)

3. Can land value be separated from the value of improvements, and can the various components of land value be separately determined? (George and geo-libertarians say yes, respectively, and Rothbard says no.)

4. Would there still be a market for land if the full rent is collected and distributed to its rightful owners, even if the calculation, collection, and distribution are performed by government (municipal or otherwise)? (George said yes, Rothbard no.)

### *The Rothbardian "Locke-out"*

It will be seen that these disagreements over economic questions animate an even more basic, ethical disagreement regarding land ownership, that is, whether or not land can ever properly be considered purely private property. Rothbard felt the facts warranted a total abandonment of John Locke's proviso that absolute individual ownership of land was justified by the "mixing of one's labor with land" only so long as "enough and as good" land remained freely available to others,[26] whereas George, by contrast, felt the proviso to be an indispensable ingredient of land justice. Rothbard, in fact, possessed the humor and chutzpah to aver that Locke was inconsistently Lockean! Writing of British political theorist Thomas Hodgskin (1787–1869), Rothbard said: "In his brilliant and logical work, *The Natural and Artificial Right of Property Contrasted* (1832), Hodgskin presented a radicalized Lockean view of property rights. An ardent defense of the right of private property, including a homesteading defense of private property in land, Hodgskin corrected Locke's various slippages from a consistent 'Lockean' position."[27] This, despite the fact that Locke stated his proviso seven times in the span of eleven paragraphs (27–37)[28] in his *Second Treatise of Government*, which would seem to make it part of the very definition of Lockean, inseparable from his "mixing of one's labor" justification of land ownership.

Tideman, reaffirming Locke's proviso, took exception to Rothbard's view as follows: "The homesteading libertarian view makes no sense in terms of justice. 'I get it all because I got here first' isn't justice. Justice . . . is a regime in which persons have the greatest possible individual liberty, and all acknowledge an obligation to share equally the value of natural opportunities."[29] And George himself lambasted the view Rothbard came to hold, on the basis of its incompatibility with the right to life.[30] We shall learn Rothbard's likely response in Question Two. But for now, let us consider the questions in sequential order.

### Question One: Are Landlords, *qua* Landlords, Robbers?

In their role as land title holders, are landlords robbing for a living? In other words, is land ownership in any way a government-granted privilege—a legal power of landowners to place their hands in others' pockets—to reap where they have not sown—even if arrived at by Rothbard's standard of "first user, first owner"?

Rothbard says no, they earn everything they make: "One of the great fallacies of the Ricardian theory of rent is that it ignores the fact that landlords *do* perform a vital economic function: they allocate land to its best and most productive use. Land does not allocate itself; it must be allocated, and only those who earn a return from such service have the incentive, or the ability, to allocate various parcels of land to their most profitable, and hence most productive and economic uses."[31] But under a full ground rent collection system, owners of land with improvements would still have an incentive to get the highest price for their property, and they would thus continue serving Rothbard's desired function of "rational allocator." Unimproved land, on the other hand, would tend to have no owner. Therefore, George advocated allowing landowners to keep a small percentage of the land rent, mainly to avoid the prospect of having all unimproved land revert to the commons. He felt that his reform could be enacted more smoothly if it maintained the appearance of continued full private ownership of land,[32] and this provision would keep land buyers going to individual landowners to purchase vacant land, rather than to a government "land office." Thus, the "service" George had in mind, for which some small compensation was deserved, was primarily not one of "real estate agent" or even "government unclaimed land office clerk," but "maintainer of appearances."

Rothbard took unfair advantage of this admission in his 1957 "Reply to Georgist Criticisms," twisting George's desire to have his remedy "go with the flow" into a nonexistent admission that landowners are needed to provide a vital service: "It seems to me that Georgists give away their entire case when they graciously allow the landowners to keep 5–10 percent of their rent. This concedes that the landowner does perform *some* service, and if one concedes that he should keep some rent, where are we to draw the line? Why not let him keep 25 percent, or 50 percent, or 99 percent? Apparently, some Georgists would let the landowner keep the equivalent of a broker's commission for distributing sites. But this again puts a very narrow 'labor theory of value' on the owner's service." Rothbard here has conflated the value of real estate services with that of monopoly privilege, and attempted to taint Georgism with a Marxist fallacy. He continued: "The Rembrandt owner, for example, may hire a broker for 5–10 percent to sell or rent his paintings. Would Georgists then confiscate 90 percent of Rembrandt values?" Certainly not. But with land value, it is as if 100 Rembrandts labored to complete the painting and *continually* labor to keep the paint from dematerializing from the canvas, and Rothbard's idea of justice is to give 100 percent of the painting's value to the broker! But justice would seem to demand that 100 percent of the land value go to its rightful owners—its creators—with land buyers paying a one-time "finder's fee" to real estate agents (or landowners acting in that capacity) who alert them to the best sites for their particular use. And, the amount of that fee should be set by the market, not by fiat.

Moreover, says Rothbard, even if landowners *are* to some extent "robbers," they are not "robbing" any more than anyone else living in a cooperative, capitalist society:*

> One striking instance of this second line of attack [on the free market, using the phenomenon of external benefits as a point of criticism] is the

---

*Even for a geo-libertarian, to say that *all* landlords are robbers is an overstatement. They rob only to the extent that they own (a) more than an equal share of nature's value, and/or (b) more man-made externalities than they create.

nub of the Henry Georgist position: an attack on the "unearned increment" derived from a rise in the capital values of ground land. We have seen above that as the economy progresses, real land rents will rise with real wage rates, and the result will be increases in the real capital values of land. Growing capital structure, division of labor, and population tend to make site land relatively more scarce and hence cause the increase. The argument of the Georgists is that the landowner is not morally responsible for this rise, which comes about from events external to his landholding; yet he reaps the benefit. The landowner is therefore a free rider, and his "unearned increment" rightfully belongs to "society." Setting aside the problem of the reality of society and whether "it" can own anything,[33] we have here a moral attack on a free-rider situation.

The difficulty with this argument is that it proves far too much. For which one of us would earn anything like our present real income were it not for external benefits that we derive from the actions of others? Specifically, the great modern accumulation of capital goods is an inheritance from all the net savings of our ancestors. Without them, we would, regardless of the quality of our own moral character, be living in a primitive jungle. The inheritance of money capital from our ancestors is, of course, simply inheritance of shares in this capital structure. We are all, therefore, free riders on the past. We are also free riders on the present, because we benefit from the continuing investment of our fellow men and from their specialized skills on the market. Certainly the vast bulk of our wages, if they could be so imputed, would be due to this heritage on which we are free riders. The landowner has no more of an unearned increment than any one of us.[34]

Not so. Favorable spatial externalities certainly derive from capital structure and the specialized skills of labor. But they are much more than this, in that their utility and value have a very strong, local character—thus the word "spatial." They are not distributed widely, but accrue uniquely to particular landowners (such as the earlier-mentioned highrise apartment owner whose building is located right next to a subway stop, and whose tenants pay for that benefit), which Rothbard never acknowledges.

He continued: "Are all of us to suffer confiscation, therefore, and to be taxed for our happiness?" (No, just those of us who receive more than our share of land value.) "And who then is to receive the loot? Our dead ancestors, who were our benefactors in investing the capital?" (No, the living individuals who create utility in land should be those who receive payment for the value of that utility, while those living individuals who own capital* either paid for or inherited that capital, and deserve the full return from that investment. (See R. V. Andelson, "Interest Originating from Invested Rent," *American Journal of Economics and Sociology*, July, 1992).

### Land Buyers Pay the Wrong People

Rothbard agreed with fellow economist Frank Knight that, because anyone can, with sufficient resources, get into the business of land speculation, a) the competition wrings out any excess profit, b) there are both winners and losers in the game, and c) it is a fair game.[35] To a Georgist, this is like arguing that slavery was fair because slave owners competed in the bidding process. As discussed above, it ignores the fact that the people who create and maintain the bulk of land value are either not being paid at all for their work (in the case of private entities), or are being paid mainly by persons other than their work's beneficiaries (in the case of government workers). Government does much to create land value, by maintaining roads, sewers, street lighting, trash pickup, police and fire protection, local parks and recreational facilities, a court system, etc., all of which is reflected in land value, and almost none of which is paid by landowners per se. In commercial districts, large stores attract lots of customers, generating foot traffic (hence value) for neighboring stores, none of which is recouped. The question becomes, is a privilege any less a privilege because many people are allowed to chase it— because many people are competing to become robbers? Certainly, the amount any one robber is able to make is lessened, owing to the necessity of paying the previous robber for the privilege. But piracy is still piracy, and what does it matter to those being legally plundered how their plunderers came by their professional licence? And how is it possible to build a consensus upon a system of "justice" that has such a high degree of institutionalized theft?

---

*Like George and Rothbard (see the latter's *Man, Economy, and State*, pp. 8–9), and unlike most contemporary economists, we are here honoring the classical view that there are three distinct factors of production—land, labor, and capital—the latter of which is a derivative of the application of labor to land.

*A Thought Experiment*

Let us close the discussion of this question about the nature of land-lordism with a thought experiment that will illustrate the errors of both Rothbard and traditional Georgism. Imagine a community where everyone used equal amounts of equal quality land in the same way. Rothbard's Rule would then be just, since everyone would have equal use of the earth and would be generating equal amounts of positive spatial externalities, and thus no one would be being robbed. In this unrealistically simplified case, then, land rent collection and distribution would be unnecessary to secure equal rights. But let us introduce a second community within the same jurisdiction, and suppose the people in the first community to be industrious, while those in the second are lazy (or simply less productive). In this case, traditional Georgism, by collecting land rent jurisdiction-wide and distributing it equally, via government expenditure, would err in taking value created by the industrious and giving it to the lazy. And in this case, assuming people in both communities had equal amounts of nature-created land value, Rothbard's system would still be ethically and practically sound (assuming that no spatial externalities extend from one community to the other). But now let us make things a bit more realistic, and mix the populations, so that the positive spatial externalities of the industrious extend into the space of the lazy, and we find that institutionalized theft enters Rothbard's ideal world as well as that of traditional Georgism (though in differing ways and degrees). But, a geo-libertarian ground rent collection and distribution system would ensure that he who creates is he who owns.

### Question Two: Does Rothbard's Rule Lead to a Vicious Cycle?

If the dynamic of land ownership under Rothbard's "first user, first owner" rule is characterized by positive feedback, such as occurs in the game Monopoly,™ it must lead to greater concentration of land ownership, while negative feedback would lead to the opposite, a more dispersed ownership.* Rothbard believed that the removal of

---

*Living organisms overwhelmingly utilize negative feedback mechanisms to produce a stable internal environment, as positive feedback creates what is known as a "vicious cycle," and generally leads to catastrophic consequences.

government and its interference with a pure free market would result in the breakup of large landholdings, and a more equal distribution of land ownership:

> The major attributes of the feudal system were: the granting of huge estates to landowning warlords, the coerced binding of the peasants (serfs) to their land plots, and hence to the rule of their lords, and the further bolstering by the state of feudal status through compulsory primogeniture (the passing on of the estate to the eldest son only) and entail (prohibiting the landowner from alienating—selling, breaking up, etc.—his land). This process froze landlordship in the existing noble families, and *prevented any natural market or genealogical forces*[36] *from breaking up the vast estates.*[37] [emphasis added]

Elsewhere he quotes Ludwig von Mises making the same case: "The effects of speculation in land disappear as the users purchase the land sites, but dissolution does not take place where feudal land grants are passed on, unbroken, over the generations. As Mises states:[38]

> Nowhere and at no time has the large-scale ownership of land come into being through the working of economic forces in the market. It is the result of military and political effort. Founded by violence, it has been upheld by violence and by that alone. As soon as the latifundia are drawn into the sphere of market transactions they begin to crumble, until at last they disappear completely. . . ."[39] [And, we are to presume, all privilege and injustice in land ownership disappears with them.]

The point seems to have no current relevance, however, as "large-scale ownership" today merely takes a different form. The Ted Turners of the world may buy hundreds of thousands of acres of minimally transformed land (Ted Turner, for example, owns over a million acres in New Mexico alone[40]), and their progeny may then rent or sell tracts at greatly inflated prices, without the appearance of "latifundia." But that does not alter the monopolistic, land-aggregating, positive-feedback nature of Rothbard's supposed "free market" system of land ownership.

Indeed, George himself made the same point in 1879:[41]

> But how, in such a country as the United States, the ownership of land may be really concentrating, while census tables show rather a diminution in the average size of holdings, is readily seen. . . . The growth of population, which puts land to higher or intenser uses, tends naturally to reduce the size of holdings, by a process very marked in new countries; but with this may go on a tendency to the concentration of landowner-

ship, which, though not revealed by tables which show the average size of holdings, is just as clearly seen. Average holdings of one acre in a city may show a much greater concentration of landownership than average holdings of 640 acres in a newly settled township. I refer to this to show the fallacy in the deductions drawn from tables which are frequently paraded in the United States to show that land monopoly is an evil that will cure itself. On the contrary, it is obvious that the proportion of landowners to the whole population is constantly decreasing.*

Rothbard seemed to believe that the governing dynamics of the game of Monopoly (with the "landing on" and buying of property corresponding to his "first use"), writ large into the real world, would lead not to a select group of winners and masses of losers, but to freedom and equality for all. He thought (correctly) that monopoly comes only from the misguided use of government power, yet whatever entity evolves in his anarcho-capitalist world to enforce his "first user, first owner" doctrine *would* be enforcing an unjust system—a monopoly.

Some readers may not be convinced by the dynamics of the game Monopoly, and, unfortunately, I am not aware of any relevant formal game theory analysis. Nevertheless, it seems to be an easily determinable contention whether Rothbard's Rule produces a world dominated by positive feedback (i.e., a vicious cycle), where wealth invested in the acquisition of natural opportunity generally produces the greatest return, in which case monopoly and gross inequality of opportunity results, or by negative feedback, in which case equality

*Things have not gotten any better since George's time. Mason Gaffney reported that in Vancouver, B.C. in 1975, the top 1 percent of landowners held 62 percent of the total land value ("Changes in Land Policy: How Fundamental Are They?" *Real Estate Issues* 1(1): 72–85, Fall 1976). Charles Geisler reported that only 15 percent of the U.S. population owns land, and that within this group (which includes corporations), the top 5 percent held 75 percent of the privately held land in 1978, with the top 0.5 percent holding an amazing 40 percent. He also noted that available data suggested that "ownership concentration is increasing rather than decreasing" ("Ownership: An Overview," *Rural Sociology* 58(4): 532–46, 1993). Moreover, Gaffney reports that "the concentration of the *value* of farm real estate is growing faster than that of farm *acres*" ("Rising Inequality and Falling Property Tax Rates," chapter 10 in Gene Wunderlich, ed., *Ownership, Tenure, and Taxation of Agricultural Land*, Westview Press, 1992).

of opportunity will, eventually, prevail.* Either dynamic would be much more visible if other, competing forms of unfair privilege were eliminated, such as the monopolies of money and the broadcast media, and "protective" legislation (tariffs, restrictive regulations, and licensing).

If Rothbard's anarcho-capitalist world were to have impartial juries sitting in judgement over disputes about land rights, they would likely represent a check on the accumulation of vast landholdings. Such juries would be unlikely to evict squatters from land owned by a wealthy entity that left the land untouched, i.e., treated as an investment. This, despite some previous owner having used the land in some way, so as to satisfy Rothbard's definition of valid ownership. But if his rules were to apply universally, unchecked, it seems obvious that they would result in an oligarchy, with poverty and injustice for most, and undreamt-of wealth and privilege for a few. Thus, his "first user, first owner" doctrine seems gravely misguided and hopelessly flawed. In his defense, the masking effect of technological innovation, in neutralizing the scarcity of land by continually making all land more and more productive, has fooled him and most of the economics profession into thinking Adam Smith, David Ricardo, and Henry George to be wrong in their judgment that unlimited land ownership is a privilege that tends to produce grave inequalities and unfairness in the distribution of wealth. But this dynamic is the main engine that has driven the modern phenomenon of "sprawl," with its attendant waste of human and natural resources.[42]

*In this regard, it is significant to note that the value of land in urban areas, where favorable spatial externalities are greatest, has often greatly outpaced the general rate of inflation. For example, in San Jose, California, between 1975 and 1995 there was a 1,278 percent appreciation of land value, whereas the consumer price index over that same period increased only 183 percent (*Worth* magazine, Feb. 1997, p. 77, in "A Piece of the Action," by Clint Willis, data by John Fried and the Urban Land Institute; and U.S. Bureau of Labor Statistics). For other examples of tremendous land price inflation during a boom period, see *House and Home*, August 1960, which demonstrated how land in the Los Angeles area, which averaged $2,000 per acre in 1952, sold for $16,000 per acre in 1960, despite a consumer price index increase of only 11.7 percent over that same period.

*A Vicious Cycle Also Governs Land Speculation*

Not only does Rothbard's Rule create a "rich get richer and poor get poorer" dynamic, but a positive feedback loop also exists with respect to land speculation. Whereas speculation in man-made goods is governed by healthy, negative feedback, where increased prices lead eventually to increased supply and then lower prices, for land, a vicious cycle develops, such that increased prices lead owners to hold out for yet higher prices, thus restricting supply and fueling a speculative bubble. The price of land typically goes through boom and bust cycles whose amplitude dwarfs that of other goods. The August 1960 issue of the industry publication, *House and Home*, was devoted entirely to the subject of land, and emphasized that the long "boom" existing at that time was doing tremendous harm to the housing industry.

*A Note on the Definition of "Use"*

To conclude this discussion of the dynamic of Rothbard's "first user, first owner" rule, I wish to note that I have elsewhere criticized the ridiculous arbitrariness in Rothbard's definition of what constitutes "use" of land (from grazing a cow to merely walking on it).[43] Rothbard might admit the fact, but as we have seen, he would also argue that it does not matter—that, once thrown on the open market, everything would eventually resolve itself fairly. It was this mistaken belief that prompted him to think that a complete dismissal of Locke's proviso was warranted. Hopefully that fatal notion has now safely been laid to rest.

### Question Three: Can the Various Components of Land Value Be Separately Determined?

As mentioned earlier, for Hayek, a "no" to this question was the *only* thing militating against adoption of the Georgist remedy. Here we will examine Rothbard's similar statements to the negative. From *Power and Market*:

> One critical problem that the single tax could not meet is the difficulty of estimating ground rents. The essence of the single tax scheme is to tax

ground rent only and to leave all capital goods free from tax. But it is impossible to make this division. Georgists have dismissed this difficulty as merely a practical one; but it is a theoretical one as well. As is true of any property tax, it is impossible accurately to assess value, because the property has not been actually sold on the market during the period.[44]

This is tantamount to saying we cannot know the value of a particular tube of toothpaste until after it has been purchased from the shelf—that we cannot reasonably estimate land value by examining the actual, going prices of similar parcels lacking capital improvements, or by looking at bid prices on the particular parcel and estimating the value of the improvements, etc.

Although most assessors today lack proper training in land assessment owing to the fact that most municipalities do not tax land and improvements at different rates, assessment itself is actually a fairly exact science and is being made more exact all the time.[45] Ian Lambert has pointed out that loss adjusters in the insurance industry routinely separate land value from that of buildings on it, "since for insurance purposes it is only possible to insure against the loss of the building; one cannot (normally) lose the site."[46] In terms of estimating particular components, the value of government services can be reasonably estimated in several ways, as can the value of privately created externalities.[47] We need not here delve into the specifics, however, because even a somewhat rough division, such as George envisioned, would provide a much closer approximation to justice and maximal economic efficiency than is now present, or that would exist under Rothbard's Rule, where no attempt at all is made to account for positive spatial externalities[48] or scarcity value.

In his 1957 essay, *The Single Tax: Economic and Moral Implications*, Rothbard admitted, briefly, that urban site value *can* be determined.

> But the single taxers are also interested in *urban* land where the value of the lot is often separable, on the market, from the value of the building over it. Even so, the urban lot today is not the site as found in nature. Man had to find it, clear it, fence it, drain it, and the like, so the value of an "unimproved" lot includes the fruits of man-made improvements.

No doubt this is why an acre of vacant land in downtown Chicago, near a commuter terminal, sells for tens of millions of dollars.[49]

Sarcasm aside, any fences and previous structures have had to have
been torn down, at some expense, and so any plus value they once
had later became minus. Moreover, the drainage as well as the streets,
street lighting, police, and some degree of fire protection, etc., is now
supplied by government, and paid for by property owners and citizens in general, rather than by the benefited landowners. How is that
fair or economically sound? And, under an anarcho-capitalist, private
system, would not landowners pay for such services? How is that fundamentally different than paying the proper, market-determined
portion of land-value rent to one's local government?

Most revealing about Rothbard's treatment, however, is that the
bulk of the value of that urban plot is created neither by the individual parcel owner nor by government, but by surrounding businesses and the productive people of the city, who likewise receive
no compensation under Rothbard's system. Had he understood anything about spatial externalities, he would certainly have mentioned
their contribution in this passage, rather than the relatively feeble
internalities of "clearing, fencing, draining, and the like." He did not
grasp it for his 1957 essay, and there is no indication that he grasped
it in 1995, in his final works.

Rothbard concluded that portion of his 1957 essay by saying, "thus,
pure site value could never be found in practice, and the single tax
program could not be installed except by arbitrary authority," and
pronounced it a "fatal flaw." But how is the possibility of being off
by a few percentage points, one way or the other, a fatal flaw? In
trying to understand why he never realized his error here, one can
only conclude that he believed market forces could never be brought
effectively to bear upon the operations of local government, which
leads right into our final question.

### Question Four: Can There Be Markets for Land Under a Full Land-Value "Tax"?

In *Power and Market*, Rothbard gives his unqualified "no": "if assessment is difficult and arbitrary at any time [it is not], how very much
more chaotic would it be when the government must blindly estimate, in the absence of any rent market, the rent for every piece of

ground land! [It would not have to "blindly estimate," having a jurisdiction full of land being rented, and having competitive bids coming
in periodically, to give notice of increased value.] This would be a
hopeless and impossible task, and the resulting deviations from free-
market rents would compound the chaos, with over- and underuse,
and wrong locations."[50] By "overuse" one may assume he means that
some land might be put to more intensive use than warranted economically, i.e., a use that would be better performed elsewhere. But
that would never happen so long as land went to the highest bidder,
because in that case each use would find its ideal location. Over-
pricing of land would be avoided by municipal governments endeav-
oring to have no vacant land—that which does not rent at *any*
price is, by definition, submarginal, and has been returned to "the
commons"—and underpricing would be avoided by paying attention
to competitive bidding.

While trying to show that any government involvement in collecting ground rents would bring inefficiency and "locational chaos,"
Rothbard failed to recognize the impediments in the current system
to efficient land use, where speculators are rewarded for impeding
progress, and creators are robbed of value they create. From *A Reply
to Georgist Criticisms*: "There is no reason for speculators to abstain
from earning rents on their land unless it were too poor to earn rents;
earning rents does not prevent land values from rising."[51] This ignores
the fact that most land users will not risk putting their businesses
upon land that they do not own or for which they cannot obtain a
long-term lease, and that land speculators are rarely willing to grant
such leases, since they generally wish to reap their profits on a shorter
time scale, i.e., while they are still alive. But in Hong Kong, one of
the most economically productive areas in the world, all land has
been owned by the government since 1843,[52] but has been leased
long-term (seventy-five-year renewable leases, and even 999-year
terms) in a way that guarantees security of improvements.

This question of markets relates to whether there are essential
similarities between relatively noncoercive local governments and
private entities that manage large-scale uses of land, and between
coercive government and landlords. In other words, can local governments be made to assume all the beneficial aspects of, say, shop-

ping malls, and can private landlords assume all the harmful characteristics of The State? Ironically, in *Power and Market*,[53] Rothbard mentioned "the affinity of rent and taxation" and "the subtle gradations
linking taxation and feudal rent" that were discussed by Franz Oppenheimer in his classic, *The State*.[54] One can only conclude that, to
Rothbard, all coercion ends when people are not forced literally
at swordpoint to work a particular parcel of land ("feudalism"), even
though they may be "forced" in the sense that no other options are
available (i.e., anywhere they turn, they must pay some landlord for
the privilege of living and working on this green earth).

He does acknowledge, though, and partly concedes, a point made
by economist Charles Tiebout[55] about the similarity between local
governments and private entities that manage land:

> Tiebout . . . argues that decentralization and freedom of internal migration
> renders *local* government expenditures more or less optimal . . . since the
> residents can move in and out as they please. Certainly, it is true that the
> consumer will be better off if he can move readily out of a high-tax, and
> into a low-tax, community. But this helps the consumer only to a degree;
> it does not solve the problem of government expenditures [how to define
> proper ones], which remains otherwise the same. [Why? Competitive,
> market pressure has been brought to bear, and if all government expenses
> have to be borne by the government's share of a scientifically calculated
> land rent, only those functions that create at least as much land value as
> they cost would tend to be performed.] There are, indeed, other factors
> than government entering into a man's choice of residence, and enough
> people may be attached to a certain geographical area, for one reason or
> another, to permit a great deal of government depradation before they
> move. Furthermore, a major problem is that the world's total land area is
> fixed, and that governments have universally pre-empted all the land and
> thus universally burden consumers.[56] [Cannot and do not individual land-
> lords similarly burden consumers?]

Holding his ground and ignoring the emergence of market forces
among municipal level governments, he also chided his friend, Frank
Chodorov, for the latter's proposal of a municipal, rather than
national, form of land value "taxation," as a way of creating a government entity that could and would administer a ground rent collection system that was more responsive to individual citizen input.[57]
(Chodorov was right in this, but, unfortunately, he had not hit upon
the full geo-libertarian formula for justice in land.) Interestingly, in an

endnote about the Tiebout article, Rothbard says that Tiebout himself seemed to admit that his conclusions are completely valid only if residents are free to form their own municipality, i.e., if they have the right of secession.[58] In this regard, one may note that the right of secession is specifically advocated in Fred Foldvary's *Public Goods and Private Communities*[59] and my *Libertarian Party at Sea on Land.*

To conclude this discussion of markets in land, we may note that for the many reasons mentioned above, Rothbard never equated land-value "taxation" with payment for services rendered, and thus never realized that it is properly considered a rental payment, and not a tax, even if it is collected by a government entity. As a result he was able confidently to state: "The search for a tax 'neutral' to the market is also seen to be a hopeless chimera."[60] By contrast, Nobel Laureate William Vickrey was equally confident that a land-value "tax" *could* be made neutral to the market, and is in fact essential to its most efficient operation,[61] as were geo-economists Kris Feder[62] and Nicolaus Tideman.[63] Technically, Rothbard's statement holds true: a land-value "tax" is *not* neutral. Rather, it has a *beneficial* effect on the economy.

### Other Illustrative Writings

Here we shall examine a few additional passages from Rothbard's writings, which will allow us further to flesh out his errors on the land question.

#### *Where Rothbard Sounds Like George*

In discussing the relationship between feudal systems, slavery, and land monopoly, Rothbard went beyond George, relatively speaking,* in advocating that the proper solution to slavery was not only the immediate freeing of the slaves, with no compensation to the slave-owners (landlords in the Georgist analogy), but compensation to the slaves in the form of the lands they had worked. He wrote:

*George never advocated that current landowners compensate their tenants for past robbery (see *Progress and Poverty*, pp. 366–67).

The *bodies* of the oppressed were freed, but the property which they had worked and eminently deserved to own, remained in the hands of their former oppressors. With the economic power thus remaining in their hands, the former lords soon found themselves virtual masters once more of what were now free tenants or farm laborers. The serfs and the slaves had tasted freedom, but had been cruelly deprived of its fruits.[64]

Henry George could not have said it better himself. But one cannot help but notice that the condition of present-day itinerant farm workers is not far removed from that of freed, but landless, serfs or slaves.

Another very Georgist-sounding passage is found in *Conceived in Liberty*:

To a Europe beset by the incubus of feudalism and statism, of absolute monarchy, of state-controlled churches, of state restrictions on human labor and human enterprise; to a Europe with scarce land, which was engrossed by feudal and quasi-feudal landlords whose vast government-granted estates *drained in rents the surplus over subsistence earned by the peasantry*—to this Europe the new and vast land area appeared as potential manna from Heaven.[65] [Emphasis added.]

This is a capsule re-statement of George's "Law of Wages"[66] for the case where all land has been appropriated. Rothbard viewed the drainage from wages to rent solely as the result of the forced nature of the feudal tenants' occupancy, which permitted no competition for labor, nor purchase of land by the serfs. One wonders whether he would have called it a fair system if the serfs were free to choose their masters, but continued being denied free access to land, and where only a small fraction of the now-freed "workers," by working overtime for years, could save up enough to become like one of their "quasi-feudal" landlords. [If *all* the workers were willing and able to labor that hard under the system, rents would simply rise to keep them all at a subsistence level.]

### Where Rothbard Sounds Most Like "the Anti-George"

In his *Economic Thought Before Adam Smith*, Rothbard denigrated Smith for his call for higher taxes on land and for his view of land-lords as unproductive beneficiaries of monopoly price.[67] In *Classical*

*Economics* he discussed Ricardo as being an intensified version of the worst of Adam Smith (!), who wrongly "puts the landlord in conflict with consumers and manufacturers."[68] He also dismissed the French Physiocrats' view that the rent farmers pay to landlords constitutes the only "net product" (i.e., Marxian surplus value) of society, and does not owe to any service provided by landlords.[69]

Perhaps Rothbard's anti-Georgist inconsistencies and anti-government prejudices are most amply illustrated by the following passage from *Power and Market*:

> Problems and difficulties arise whenever the "first-user, first-owner" principle is *not* met. In almost all countries, *governments* have laid claim to ownership of new, unused land. Governments could never own original land *on the free market*. This act of appropriation by the government already sows the seeds for distortion of market allocations when the land goes into use. [Seeds that are sterile, he later avers, having only an initial, one-time effect.] Thus, suppose that the government disposes of its unused public lands by selling them at auction to the highest bidder. Since the government has no valid property claim to ownership, neither does the buyer from the government. If the buyer, as often happens, owns but does not use or settle the land, then he becomes a *land speculator* in a pejorative sense. For the true user, when he comes along, is forced either to rent or buy the land from this speculator, who does not have valid title to the area. He cannot have valid title because his title derives from the State, which also did not have valid title in the free-market sense. Therefore, *some* of the charges that the Georgists have levelled against land speculation are true, *not* because land speculation is bad *per se*, but because the speculator came to own the land, not by valid title, but via the government, which originally arrogated title to itself. So now the purchase price (or, alternatively, the rent) paid by the would-be user really does become the payment of a *tax* for permission to use the land. Governmental sale of unused land becomes similar to the old practice of *tax farming*, where an individual would pay the State for the privilege of himself collecting taxes. The price of payment, if freely fluctuating, tends to be set at the value that this privilege confers.
>
> Government sale of "its" unused land to speculators, therefore, restricts the use of new land, distorts the allocation of resources, and keeps land out of use that would be employed were it not for the "tax" penalty of paying a purchase price or rent to the speculator. Keeping land out of use raises the marginal value product and the rents of remaining land and lowers the marginal value product of labor, thereby lowering wage rates.[70]

Thus, Rothbard admits the existence of the harmful effects of land speculation on resource allocation and wages, but only when the coercive hand of government is directly involved. For later on, he adds that all privilege and injustice end with the robbery of that first user: "Once land gets into the hands of the user, he has, as it were, 'bought out' the permission tax, and, from then on, everything proceeds on a free-market basis."[71]

One is tempted here to accuse Rothbard of what he accused Georgists of doing (in the opening paragraph of *A Reply to Georgist Criticisms*), namely, using moral arguments where economic ones are warranted. For he claims land speculation is bad for the market only when performed in violation of his moral imperative, his "first-user, first-owner principle." But can we not use his argument in favor of "free market" land speculation to argue for the benefits of speculation by a nonusing first owner? Does not the latter's charging a price for land necessarily lead to its best use, i.e., would not even *first* use be made more efficient by a bidding process? And, conversely, can we not use his argument against "illegitimate" speculators to argue against *all* speculation in land?

In his defense, because no government exists in his ideal world, there would be no bribery-induced government boondoggles to forcefully drive land speculation and all its attendant harms. There would remain, however, the problem of how to internalize favorable spatial externalities in his system (the unfavorable ones have already been dealt with—see endnote 48), which would thus be inferior in economic productivity to a system that routinely administers land rent collection and distribution, as mentioned earlier (and see endnotes 20–22 and 61–63). Thus, rent-seeking behavior would continue in any Rothbardian, anarcho-capitalist world, but in an attenuated form. The game would then be one simply of anticipating progress, and buying (land) in its path, i.e., erecting barriers to improved land use.[72] Not to say that such active speculation is required for the harmful dynamic to be manifested, as such barriers exist ubiquitously in the incentive for landowners to obtain the highest price for their land, often leading them to hold land out of use for years at a time.

## Other Disputed Territory

*Time Factor of Production*

Rothbard thought a deficiency in Georgists' appreciation of the time factor of production led them erroneously to ascribe value to land that was not in current use, which, to him, meant it *had* no current income-generating potential, but only an expected *future* value. This view permitted him to believe that his system would be one of maximal economic efficiency. From *Power and Market*:

> Georgists . . . concentrate on the fact that much idle land has a *capital value*, that it sells for a price on the market, even though it earns no rents in current use. From the fact that idle land has a capital value, the Georgists apparently deduce that it must have some sort of "true" annual ground rent. This assumption is incorrect, however, and rests on one of the weakest parts of the Georgists' system: its deficient attention to the role of time. [Here, in an endnote, he exonerates George, writing as he did when "the Austrian school, with its definitive analysis of time, was barely beginning . . .". But George did explicitly recognize the importance of time in capital formation.[73]] The fact that currently idle land has a capital value means simply that the market *expects* it to earn rent in the future. [This ignores the fact that many previous potential buyers might have thought it could be well used years ago, but were instead forced to utilize sub-marginal land elsewhere, owing to the unwillingness of the owner to sell or lease long-term.] The capital value of ground land, as of anything else, is equal to and determined by the sum of expected future rents, discounted by the rate of interest. But these are not presently earned rents! Therefore, any taxation of idle land violates the Georgists' own principle of a single tax on ground rent; it goes beyond this limit to penalize land ownership further and to tax accumulated capital, which has to be drawn down in order to pay the tax.[74]

Plausible but incorrect, as indicated in the above, bracketed comments. The one critical time factor that Rothbard ironically ignored is the fact that many landowners are seeking to benefit from the future favorable spatial externalities they expect to be created by others, and will not risk losing that windfall by selling or leasing long-term to those who wish, today, to use that land.

## Conclusion

Murray Rothbard was no land economist. He carefully sniffed the Georgist literature, detected a faint aroma of socialism, felt the presence of The State, with whose stench he was already thoroughly familiar, and without bothering to root out the minor socialist aspect of traditional Georgism or to consider Chodorov's suggested decentralized implementation, threw the baby out with the bathwater. His views on the land question were intellectually consistent, but entirely flawed, and reminiscent of the complexly interwoven, delusional alternate realities dreamed up by clever paranoid-schizophrenics. He had an answer to everything, and all of his answers were wrong. His "alternate reality" was based on a failure to understand a) the positive spatial externalities attaching to land use, b) that the contributions of these to the value of individual parcels of land could be separately assessed, c) the vicious cycle nature of purely private land ownership, and d) that any system that permits all land to be privately appropriated in a fashion that excludes some, is, to the excluded, inherently coercive, depriving them of basic rights.

Rothbard wrote that great thinkers, "however great they may have been, . . . can slip into error and inconsistency, and even write gibberish on occasion."[75] As we have seen, he himself was not immune, but this should not lead us to disparage his immense contribution to the reawakening of the spirit of liberty in the latter half of the twentieth century, much as Henry George provided in the final twenty years of the previous one, and beyond.

### Notes

1. Justin Raimondo, *An Enemy of the State: The Life of Murray N. Rothbard* (Amherst, NY: Prometheus Books, 2000); and see Ralph Raico's homage to Rothbard on the occasion of his fiftieth birthday, "Murray Rothbard on His Semicentennial" in *Libertarian Review*, vol. V(2), March–April, 1976, pp. 6, 14.

2. The works that establish Rothbard as von Mises's successor are his *Man, Economy, and State*, and his two-volume *Austrian Perspective on the History of Economic Thought*. (See next note for publication details.)

3. Rothbard's earliest published writings on the subject of land were a

1957 essay for the Foundation for Economic Education, entitled "The Single Tax: Economic and Moral Implications," and "A Reply to Georgist Criticisms," which followed in the same year. Both of these essays are available on-line at http://www.mises.org, and have been published in book form: Murray N. Rothbard, *The Logic of Action I: Applications and Criticisms from the Austrian School* (London: Edward Elgar, 1997), pp. 294–310. These 1957 arguments were repeated and elaborated upon in many of his subsequent works, such as *Man, Economy, and State* (Princeton, NJ: Van Nostrand, 1962), see especially pp. 147–52; 502–14; 813–14; 888–89; *The Ethics of Liberty* (Atlantic Highlands, NJ: Humanities Press International, 1982), see chaps. 10 & 11); *For a New Liberty: The Libertarian Manifesto* (originally published by Macmillan, New York, in 1973, revised edition by Collier Books, New York, 1978), see pp. 33–37; and *Power and Market: Government and the Economy* (Kansas City: Sheed Andrews and McMeel, Inc., 1970), see pp. 122–35. Additional insights into his thinking can be gained from his two-volume work on the history of economics, as he discusses other economists who held Georgist ideas: *Economic Thought Before Adam Smith: An Austrian Perspective on the History of Economic Thought, Volume I* (Northampton, MA: Edward Elgar, 1995); and *Classical Economics: An Austrian Perspective on the History of Economic Thought, Volume II* (Northampton, MA: Edward Elgar, 1995).

4. Raimondo, *An Enemy of the State*, pp. 45–47; Murray N. Rothbard, "Frank Chodorov, R. I. P.," *Left and Right*, 3(1), winter 1967, pp. 3–8 (available on-line at http://www.mises.org). Chodorov's *Analysis* was published during the 1940s and 1950s.

5. In endnote 43, p. 283 of *Power and Market*, Rothbard wrote: "compared with the classical school, George made advances in many areas of economic theory." Also, in *Power and Market* (p. 123) he wrote: "George waxed eloquent over the harmful effect taxation has upon production and exchange," and followed this up in endnote 42 (pp. 282–83) with a long quote from George's *Progress and Poverty*.

6. See p. xiv of Walter Grinder's introduction to Nock's *Our Enemy, The State* (originally copyrighted 1935; Free Life Editions version, first published in 1973, reprinted by Fox & Wilkes, San Francisco, 1992).

7. On p. 125 of *Power and Market*, Rothbard wrote: "The present writer used to wonder about the curious Georgist preoccupation with idle, or 'withheld,' ground land as the cause of most economic ills . . .", when in his view, "idle land should, however, be recognized as beneficial." Here, he did not mean that idle land was actually doing anyone any good, but that it is an indication of the fortunate fact that land is plentiful relative to labor. He ignored the fact that idle land in a city is positively harmful in that it increases people's travel time, and that a more compact, filled-in city is inherently more efficient.

8. C. Lowell Harriss, the commentator on Rothbard in the first edition of

this book (1979), indicated that the Foundation for Economic Education, which initially published Rothbard's critique of the single tax in 1957, stopped sending it out uninvited, owing to criticisms from within its own staff about obvious errors in Rothbard's analyses (see his endnote 1).

9. See Harold Kyriazi, *Libertarian Party at Sea on Land* (New York: Robert Schalkenbach Foundation, 2000), pp. 57–62, 79–83.

10. Rothbard, *Power and Market*, pp. vi–vii. Whether such a free market provision of defense and law enforcement would or would not evolve into a government worthy of the appellation "State" is an interesting question, and one that was brilliantly addressed by Robert Nozick in *Anarchy, State, and Utopia* (Basic Books, Inc., 1974).

11. Kyriazi, *Libertarian Party at Sea on Land*, pp. 8–13.

12. George did not distinguish the sources of the externalities, lumping them together as community creations (e.g., see *Progress and Poverty*, Centenary Edition, Robert Schalkenbach Foundation, New York, 1979, pp. 420–21, or pp. 215 and 217 of *Social Problems*, Robert Schalkenbach Foundation, New York, 1981 edition), and felt that using these funds for proper government expenditures, tending as they do to benefit everyone equally, was equivalent to individual distribution: "But it is possible to divide the rent equally, or, what amounts to the same thing, to apply it to purposes of common benefit" (*The Land Question*, Robert Schalkenbach Foundation, New York, 1982 edition, p. 53).

13. In the hierarchical, decentralized system of government that I have advocated (*Libertarian Party at Sea on Land*, p. 98), state and national government would also be paid, by local government, out of land value *they* generate, and any government service-generated land values in excess over costs could be divided equally among individual citizens, and could perhaps go, in part, to the relevant government officials as a bonus for successful performance of their duties.

14. In *Libertarian Party at Sea on Land*, I adhered to the flawed but well-worn phrase "land-value tax," and used, imprecisely, the word "rebate" to refer to the distribution, to their creators, of the value of privately created externalities.

15. Rothbard, *For a New Liberty*, p. 35.

16. Rothbard, *Man, Economy and State*, pp. 944–45, endnote 151.

17. George, *Social Problems*, p. 83.

18. The "geo" in geo-libertarian has a double meaning, referring both to our affinity for the ideas of Henry George and to our concern for the earth and its proper ownership. Kris Feder, in Foldvary's *Beyond Neoclassical Economics*, gave a similar definition regarding "geo-economics." See note 22. Fred Foldvary coined the word "geo-libertarian" in an article so titled in *Land and Liberty*, May/June 1981, pp. 53–55.

19. Brown mentioned that some individually-created values—specifically

road improvements funded by special property tax assessments, and some perhaps "politically incorrect" values arising from the exclusion of "undesirables" from residential neighborhoods—deserved to be retained by their creators. *Selected Articles by Harry Gunnison Brown: The Case for Land Value Taxation*, Chap. 1, "The Ethics of Land Value Taxation" (New York: Robert Schalkenbach Foundation, 1980); originally published in the *Journal of Political Economy*, 25: 464–92 (May, 1917).

20. Nicolaus Tideman, "Integrating Land-Value Taxation with the Internalization of Spatial Externalities," *Land Economics* 66: 341–55 (1990).

21. William Vickrey, "A Modern Theory of Land-Value Taxation," chap. 2 of *Land-Value Taxation: The Equitable and Efficient Source of Public Finance*, ed. Kenneth C. Wenzer (Armonk, NY/London: M. E. Sharpe/Shepheard-Walwyn, 1999); also pp. 30–31 of Daniel M. Holland, ed., *The Assessment of Land Value* (Madison, University of Wisconsin Press, 1970). (And see present endnote 61.)

22. Kris Feder, "Geo-economics," pp. 41–60 of *Beyond Neoclassical Economics: Heterodox Approaches to Economic Theory*, Fred E. Foldvary, ed. (Cheltenham, UK/Brookfield, VT: Edward Elgar, 1996).

23. From Friedrich A. Hayek's *The Constitution of Liberty* (University of Chicago Press, 1960), chap. 22, "Housing and Town Planning," p. 341: "In many respects, the close contiguity of city life invalidates the assumptions underlying any simple division of property rights. In such conditions it is true only to a limited extent that whatever an owner does with his property will affect only him and nobody else. What economists call the 'neighborhood effects,' i.e., the effects of what one does to one's property or that of others, assume major importance. The usefulness of almost any piece of property in a city will in fact depend in part on what one's immediate neighbors do and in part on the communal services without which effective use of the land by separate owners would be nearly impossible."

"The general formulas of private property or freedom of contract do not therefore provide an immediate answer to the complex problems which city life raises. It is probable that, even if there had been no authority with coercive powers, the superior advantages of larger units would have led to the development of new legal institutions—some division of the right of control between the holders of a superior right to determine the character of a large district to be developed and the owners of inferior rights to the use of smaller units, who, within the framework determined by the former, would be free to decide on particular issues. In many respects the functions which the organized municipal corporations are learning to exercise correspond to those of such a superior owner."

See R. V. Andelson's chapter on Hayek in the present volume.

24. Interestingly, Rothbard mentioned, in *Man, Economy, and State* (endnote 48, p. 929) that "even so eminent an economist as F. A. Hayek"

believed that the (perceived) impracticality of making these distinctions was the only thing arguing against adoption of the single tax on land value. Thus, for Hayek, the only obstacle was a lack of accurate assessment. (For Hayek's statement of this, see p. 63 of *Hayek on Hayek: An Autobiographical Dialogue*, Stephen Kresge and Leif Wenar, eds., University of Chicago Press, 1994.) Rothbard also mentions another Austrian economist (von Wieser) who was similarly sympathetic toward the single tax. Thus, Rothbard's errors are not shared equally by all, or even all the leading, Austrian economists.

25. The sovereign landlords of Rothbard's anarcho-capitalist utopia would be more powerful than those existing today in several ways: 1) they would be subject to no ground rent collection at all, whereas currently about 10 percent of the value is typically taken by local government, 2) they would be subject to no environmental regulation except insofar as they threatened to adversely affect neighboring territory, 3) there would be no use of "eminent domain," and 4) they would be legally free to set any conditions whatsoever upon those who contracted to set foot upon their land.

26. Rothbard, to my knowledge, never actually mentioned Locke's proviso, except tangentially, as where he accused Locke of being "riddled with contradictions and inconsistencies" (p. 22, *The Ethics of Liberty*). Two places where it might have made sense to mention it, if only in passing, were a long paragraph on pp. 316–17 of his *Economic Thought Before Adam Smith*, where he discussed Locke's "labor theory of property," and a long endnote in the same volume (endnote 17, p. 472), where he instead emphasized the Lockean ideas he liked: "he championed the idea of private property in land to the original homesteaders"; "Locke is trying to demonstrate the unimportance of land—supposedly originally communal—as compared to the importance of human energy and production in determining the value of products or resources."

27. Rothbard, *Classical Economics*, p. 400. Of. Hodgskin, Rothbard also wrote, p. 402: "From 1846–55, Hodgskin served as an editor of the *Economist*, the journalistic champion of *laissez-faire*... There he became a friend and mentor of the young Herbert Spencer, hailing Spencer's anarchistic work, *Social Statics*, with the exception of denouncing the early Spencer's pre-Georgist land socialism on behalf of Lockean individualism." (This is a reference to the famous [among Georgists] chapter IX—"The Right to the Use of the Earth"—in the original, 1850 edition.)

28. Locke, in paragraph 33 of his *Second Treatise of Government*, hit the point with a veritable sledgehammer, stating his proviso three times in three separate sentences, to leave no doubt in anyone's mind.

29. Nicolaus Tideman, "Peace, Justice, and Economic Reform: The 1997 Henry George Lecture" [of St. Johns University], pp. 167–80, in Joseph A.

Giacalone and Clifford Cobb, eds., *The Path to Justice: Following in the Footsteps of Henry George* (Malden, MA/Oxford: Blackwell Publishers, 2001).

30. George, *Progress and Poverty*, pp. 344–45.

31. Rothbard, *Classical Economics*, p. 91.

32. George, *Progress and Poverty*, p. 405.

33. George founded rights in the individual, not "society." In fact, he criticized Herbert Spencer for speaking of "joint rights" rather than equal (individual) rights to land; see pp. 26–33 of *A Perplexed Philosopher* (originally published in 1892, reprinted by the Robert Schalkenbach Foundation, New York, 1940).

34. Rothbard, *Man, Economy and State*, pp. 888–89.

35. Frank Knight, "The Fallacies in the 'Single Tax'," *The Freeman*, 3(23):809–11 (1953).

36. Genealogical forces would not, however, lead to a change in the *concentration* of land ownership, assuming the wealthy have as many children as the less affluent. And if they tend to have fewer children, as one might surmise, even an equal distribution of parental land would still result in an enhanced concentration of land ownership.

37. Rothbard, *Conceived in Liberty*, vol. I, p. 48.

38. Ludwig von Mises, *Socialism* (New Haven: Yale University Press, 1951), p. 375.

39. Rothbard, *Power and Market*, pp. 134–35.

40. William P. Barrett, "This land is Their Land," *Worth* magazine, Feb. 1997, pp. 78–89.

41. George, *Progress and Poverty*, pp. 322–23.

42. For sixteen articles on urban decay, sprawl, and proposed remedies, see *City and Country*, Laurence S. Moss, ed. (Malden, MA/Oxford: Blackwell Publishers, 2001). Also see Thomas A. Gihring, "Incentive Property Taxation: A Potential Tool for Urban Growth Management," *Journal of the American Planning Association* 65(1): 62–79 (1999).

43. Kyriazi, *Libertarian Party at Sea on Land*, pp. 79–83.

44. Rothbard, *Power and Market*, p. 123.

45. See Holland's *The Assessment of Land Value*, or any issue of the bimonthly *Assessment Journal*, the official journal of the International Association of Assessing Officers.

46. Ian T. G. Lambert, "A Perplexed Libertarian: A Georgist Replies to Murray Rothbard's 'Power and Market'," unpublished manuscript, 14 Nov., 1991. Mr. Lambert, an attorney, resides in the Cayman Islands.

47. Regarding the value of government services, competition among municipalities for residents and the cost of provision of similar services by private land management entities can permit their accurate determination.

Regarding the value of privately created externalities, comparative data like that compiled for use by shopping mall managers, to determine the ideal mix and relative location of store types, can provide a scientific basis for such determinations.

48. Libertarians typically recognize *negative* spatial externalities as a form of "trespass," be it matter (e.g., pollution) or energy (e.g., noise), and thus as *bona fide* harms for which recompense can be claimed. But *benefits* flowing across property lines are not viewed as deserving of payment, being in the category of unsolicited gifts. But why this prejudice? If certain actions in life cannot help but "give gifts," if those gifts are not given reciprocally, if economics teaches us that more progress is made when the value of those gifts redounds to their creators, and if ethics teaches us that justice consists in creators owning their creations, why not recognize this unique aspect of land use?

49. The *Chicago Tribune* of 25 March, 1998 (sec. 3, pp. 1–2), reported that a half-acre site at Chestnut and Wabash, two blocks from a rapid transit terminal, sold for $11.2 million, while the 2 April, 1998 edition (sect. 3, pp. 1–2) reported that a 1.4-acre site at 1 North Wacker sold for an estimated $36 million. It was within two blocks of two commuter terminals and a rapid transit station.

50. Rothbard, *Power and Market*, p. 129.

51. The same thought was expressed on p. 292 of Rothbard's *Man, Economy, and State*: "We have seen in our example that land and capital goods will be used to the fullest extent practicable, since there is no return or benefit in allowing them to remain idle."

52. Hong Kong has had nearly 100 percent government ownership of land for over 150 years, and produced one of the most vibrant economies in the world, on a slab of rock. See chapter 20, "Hong Kong and Singapore," by Sock-Yong Phang, in R. V. Andelson, ed., *Land-Value Taxation Around the World* (3rd edition; Malden, MA/Oxford: Blackwell Publishers, 2000).

53. Rothbard, *Power and Market*, p. 133.

54. Franz Oppenheimer, *The State*, originally published in 1908, available from Transaction Publishers, New Brunswick, NJ, 1999.

55. Charles M. Tiebout, "Pure Theory of Local Expenditures," *Journal of Political Economy*, 64(5): 416–24 (1956).

56. Appendix B of Rothbard's *Man, Economy, and State* (pp. 885–86), entitled "'Collective Goods' and 'External Benefits': Two Arguments for Government Activity."

57. From pp. 130–31 of Rothbard's *Power and Market*: "Caught in an inescapable dilemma are a group of antistatist Georgists, who wish to statize ground rent yet abolish taxation at the same time. Frank Chodorov, a leader of this group, could offer only the lame suggestion that ground land be municipalized rather than nationalized—to avoid the prospect that all of a

nation's land might be owned by a central government monopoly. Yet the difference is one of degree, not of kind; the effects of government ownership and regional monopoly still appear, albeit in a number of small regions instead of one big region."

58. Rothbard, *Man, Economy, and State*, p. 944, endnote 147.

59. Fred Foldvary, *Public Goods and Private Communities: The Market Provision of Social Services* (Aldershot, Hants, UK/Brookfield, VT: Edward Elgar, 1994).

60. Rothbard, *Power and Market*, p. vi (Preface).

61. William Vickrey: "A tax on land, properly assessed independently of the use made of the lot, is virtually free of distortionary effects . . ." p. 17, chapter 3 of Wenzer's *Land-Value Taxation*; also, from chapter 2 of Holland's *The Assessment of Land Value*, "Defining Land Value for Taxation Purposes," pp. 25–36: "If we follow through on the desirability of internalizing externalities (maintaining the proper balance of incentives for maximum economic efficiency both for the developer of a single parcel and for the large-scale developer), we are led to the following somewhat radical proposal: not only should improvements not be taxed, but the externalities involved in the construction of these improvements should be internalized to the investor in such improvements through an appropriate subsidy or tax allowance" (pp. 30–31).

62. "Indeed, the so-called 'Henry George Theorem' in urban economics indicates that, under certain rather general conditions of mobility and competition, a tax on land rent is necessary for full efficiency." Kris Feder, p. 48 of "Geo-economics," chap. 3 of Foldvary's *Beyond Neoclassical Economics*, pp. 41–60.

63. T. Nicolaus Tideman, "Taxing Land Is Better Than Neutral: Land Taxes, Land Speculation, and the Timing of Development," chap. 9 in Wenzer's *Land-Value Taxation*, 1999.

64. Rothbard, *The Ethics of Liberty*, p. 74, in chap. 11, "Land Monopoly, Past and Present."

65. Rothbard, *Conceived in Liberty*, vol. I, chap. 2, "New World, New Land," p. 46.

66. George, *Progress and Poverty*, chap. 6, "Wages and the Law of Wages."

67. Rothbard, *Economic Thought Before Adam Smith*, p. 466, and pp. 456 and 459, respectively.

68. Rothbard, *Classical Economics*, p. 82.

69. Rothbard, *Economic Thought Before Adam Smith*, pp. 372–74.

70. Rothbard, *Power and Market*, pp. 132–33.

71. Rothbard, *Power and Market*, p. 134.

72. From *House and Home*, August 1960, p. 99: "Says B. B. Bass, president of the Mortgage Bankers Association: 'Big speculators have been gobbling up land ahead, stifling competition, and putting the squeeze on builders.' . . . Says Nat Roog, National Association of Home Builders econo-

mist: 'Today's land situation is a killer for the builder. Land costs have climbed more than all other home-building costs combined.'"

73. George, *Progress and Poverty*, pp. 183–85; *The Science of Political Economy*, pp. 368–70 (New York: Robert Schalkenbach Foundation, 1981 edition).

74. Rothbard, *Power and Market*, p. 124.

75. Rothbard, *Economic Thought Before Adam Smith*, p. 16.

# 32
# LeFevre's Challenge

## By Damon J. Gross

Robert LeFevre (1911–1986) was a leading intellectual force in the dissemination of libertarian ideas. An articulate man of great charm and elegant appearance, he possessed no formal academic credentials, having been obliged to leave college after only a few months in order to marry and support a family. He had a varied and unorthodox career—stage actor in Southern California, disk jockey and radio personality in Milwaukee, staff member of a religious cult in Los Angeles, real estate agent and later hotel owner in San Francisco, air corps officer in Europe during World War II, radio and TV newscaster in South Florida, and editorial writer for and then editor of a daily newspaper in Colorado Springs. He also served briefly as a speaker and organizer for various ephemeral right-wing groups, but by the time he moved to Colorado his orientation had become less conventionally conservative and more uncompromisingly individualist.

In 1956, LeFevre purchased a half-section of wooded acreage in the Rampart Range near Larkspur, using a small inheritance as the downpayment. On it were two barely habitable structures. With the aid of his wife, Loy, and a handful of women friends who contributed their earnings and spare-time labor in return for spartan board and lodging, he proceeded to build a rustic campus for an institution to teach libertarian principles. It was called the Freedom School, and began by offering noncredit summer courses in concentrated two-week shifts. He brought in well-known exponents of the free market to teach them, and did much of the teaching himself, while continuing for nearly a decade to hold down his newspaper job. Eventually, the program was expanded to offer courses at the campus throughout the year, as well as seminars sponsored by companies for their management-level employees at other locations. By 1968, the Freedom School had reached the point where it prepared to offer master's degrees; accordingly, it changed its name to Rampart College. At the same time, however, a decline in financial support necessitated

American Journal of Economics and Sociology, Vol. 63, No. 2 (April, 2004).

the sale of the Colorado campus, and a move by the college to Southern California, where sporadic seminars were held until its closing. By then, LeFevre had resigned as president and ceased to be involved in its affairs.[1] After the demise of Rampart College, he continued to write and lecture.

LeFevre's thirty-three page article, "A Challenge to the Georgists," was published in 1965, in the second issue of the *Rampart Journal of Individualist Thought*,[2] a short-lived scholarly periodical he had founded in connection with the Freedom School. Robert Clancy, then director of the Henry George School of Social Science in New York City, responded with "A Challenge to Libertarians" in the next issue,[3] which also contained a brief response by LeFevre.[4]

There appears initially to be a good deal of common ground between LeFevre and George. Both championed freedom, a market economy, and free trade. Both opposed income taxes, excise taxes, and taxes on wealth in general. LeFevre had some understanding of George's program:

> He [the Georgist] favors a tax to be levied exclusively upon the value of land. And it is his contention that if such a tax could be relied upon, economic justice and prosperity would eventuate; no other taxes would be required; . . . and conceivably at this point the "war on poverty" would cease for want of an enemy to fight.[5]

And LeFevre was at least remotely aware of contemporaneous Georgist activity, for he quoted the stated principle of the Henry George School of New York:

> The community, by its presence and activity, gives rental values to land, therefore the rent of land belongs to the community and not to the landowners. Labor and capital, by their combined efforts, produce the goods of the community—known as wealth. This wealth belongs to the producers. Justice requires that the government, representing the community, collect the rent of land for community purposes and abolish the taxation of wealth.[6]

Yet LeFevre would have none of this. He stated:

> It is the purpose of this paper to challenge this principle and to demonstrate as clearly as possible that (1) the Henry George single-tax concept will not produce the benefits claimed; (2) no feasible method can be devised wherein the value of land can be determined by land rents; and

(3) instability followed by gross invasion of human rights would tread upon the heels of any general adherence to the Georgist panaceas.[7]

The scope of this chapter is limited to an examination of those arguments that LeFevre contributed to the criticism of Henry George that were new with LeFevre, or to which LeFevre contributed some novel feature. We will also confine ourselves to what LeFevre wrote in the two articles mentioned above.

### LeFevre's Interpretation

LeFevre was not entirely univocal in the way he understood George's single-tax proposal. He derived his main interpretation primarily from the following passage from *Progress and Poverty*, which he quoted in a footnote:

> I do not propose either to purchase or to confiscate private property in land. The first would be unjust; the second, needless. Let the individuals who now hold it still retain, if they want to, possession of what they are pleased to call *their* land. Let them continue to call it *their* land. Let them buy and sell, and bequeath and devise it. We may safely leave them the shell, if we take the kernel. It is not necessary to confiscate land; it is only necessary to confiscate rent. . . . We already take some rent in taxation. We have only to make some changes in our modes of taxation to take it all. . . . In this way the state may become the universal landlord without calling herself so, and without assuming a single new function. The form, the ownership of land would remain just as now. No owner of land need be dispossessed, and no restriction need be placed upon the amount of land anyone could hold. For, rent being taken by the state in taxes, land, no matter in whose name it stood, or in what parcels it was held, would be really common property, and every member of the community would participate in the advantages of ownership.[8]

Ignoring George's metaphor of the kernel and the shell, and George's insistence that the state would not assume a single new function, LeFevre fixed his attention on the single clause "the state may become the universal landlord." LeFevre developed what he thought this implied: "They [Georgists] see a society in which land is never to be privately owned."[9] "The land remains in the ownership of the state, or of that committee, group, or agency empowered to own the land and presumably endowed with the ability to assess the land on the basis of its value."[10] "The individual who today owns rental property would be prevented by law from collecting rents."[11] "The device which is presumed to maximize distribution for use only, and to prevent land speculation, is the device of central ownership of land. The state becomes the landlord, entering into contractual agreements with individuals or groups of individuals (firms) who will agree to put the land into use."[12]

This misinterpretation was not new with LeFevre. Its pedigree goes back at least to Laveleye. (See the chapters on Laveleye; Walker; and Ingalls, Hanson, and Tucker in this book.) But LeFevre did draw two consequences from it that are worth remarking.

First, LeFevre reasoned that if the state is to be the universal landlord, then uses of land that involve subleasing, which would include "hotels, rooming houses, guest houses, motels, apartment houses, tenant farms, and so on (wherever rent could be collected) would all either become the monopolies of the state, owned and controlled by the state, or any such type of business venture would be eliminated."[13] Thus either the role of the state would increase dramatically or the types of commerce allowed would be severely curtailed.

Clancy responded to this argument appropriately:

> As for those businesses which depend on subleasing, Mr. LeFevre is here confusing precisely the two things that the single tax separates—the land, and the improvements on land. Apartment houses, hotels, and motels are improvements, and they can certainly be built and leased by private enterprise with our blessings. The returns for capital investment (economic interest, not rent) and for services (wages) will go as they should, to the persons making available the capital and service—completely untaxed. That part which represents the rent of land is to be turned over in taxes to the community.[14]

Second, LeFevre claimed "that the system advocated by George would invariably follow conquest. The conqueror of a territory would, by conquest, have gained control of all land. It would be to his advantage to distribute the land to producers and at the same time retain control of it. This would result in something similar to the feudal system of land distribution."[15] Of course the historical record supplies ample refutation of this claim. Nonetheless, LeFevre concluded that "there is a kind of harmony between conquest and the Georgist system of land management."[16] This imagined harmony would become important to LeFevre later.

LeFevre's misinterpretation pervades almost his entire analysis of George, but at times he seemed to back off from this misinterpretation. For example, in his rebuttal to Clancy he said:

> Mr. Clancy contends that George did not propose that the state would dictate the use of land or fix the value of land. I did not quote him as so stating. Rather, I pointed out that if the state can set the land rental values, by means of taxation, this alone *will*, in practice, determine land use and will fix the value of land.[17]

Clearly the question of what *effect* land-value taxation will have is not a matter of interpretation; it is a question of economics. And LeFevre did go on to give a number of economic arguments regarding the effect of land-value taxation that either do not depend on his misinterpretation of George, or can be abstracted from it. We turn now to an examination of LeFevre's economic arguments.

### The Transitional Problem

LeFevre correctly observed that land-value taxation would reduce the price of land and remarked that "if land values fall to zero, those who have invested in land lose their investment."[18] "This would induce wide-scale poverty among the thrifty who have invested their savings in land."[19]

But what this argument indicates is at most a transitional problem. After the single tax has been fully implemented, the purchase price of land would be negligible so there would be little or no investment in land to lose. Prior critics, notably Alfred Marshall, had noticed the transitional problem, and it has been fully examined elsewhere in the present work.

Still following Marshall in spirit, LeFevre amplified his treatment of the transitional problem by imagining the example of a retired couple who have invested their life savings in "land." They are too feeble to work at physical chores, but they can manage their "rental properties." But LeFevre added a new twist by pointing out that such an investment would typically yield them a higher return than they could obtain "were the same sums to be invested in stocks, bonds, or other securities."[20] LeFevre concluded that a rather numerous class of people would be thus devastated by the implementation of the single tax.

But this example, particularly with LeFevre's new twist, does not help his argument. The higher rate of return that the elderly couple realize is not a return on their investment at all. It is wages of management. Additionally, one cannot help but get the impression that these "rental properties" are not bare land, but also include significant amounts of capital. This is because bare land hardly needs "management." It is the dwelling units, not the land, that need management in the case of rental property like apartment houses, for example. Even in the case of farmland, what needs to be managed is what and when to plant, maintenance of fences, tiling and terracing, and barns and sheds, whether and what fertilizers and pesticides to apply, etc. and these are all improvements—capital, not land. But George argued that wages and interest would rise under the single-tax system,[21] a contention that LeFevre never disputed. So the new twist that LeFevre put on the old argument does not help his case.

Although LeFevre never directly addressed the issues of wages and interest in his critique, he did challenge the Georgist view on land speculation and use. The Georgist argument that wages and interest would rise under the single-tax system depends partly on the contention that the single tax would discourage land speculation and encourage better land use. We therefore turn to what LeFevre had to say about land use and speculation.

### Concentration of Land

LeFevre thought that the single tax would lead to a concentration of land in the hands of a few and would not discourage land speculation. He argued:

> It should be seen at once that if land use is to be absolutely at the discretion of the contracting party, then the Georgist theory will have only this result. The taxes (land value rents) paid to the state would enormously increase, thus impairing the willingness of many people to try to become original contractors for land. But speculation would continue, and, indeed, on the basis of the newly invoked land scarcity, it could be expected to increase. The long-range result could be expected to produce a new class

of land holders who, while not actually owning the land, would in all respects be a privileged land-holding aristocracy. Since only the very affluent could attempt such holdings, it is reasonable to assume that land holdings would become consolidated into huge estates, each reserved for its own special kind of use. The very evils which George presumed to wipe out with his theory would be extended.[22]

LeFevre did not indicate why he thought that if fewer people tried to acquire land it would become more scarce and speculation would increase, but his argument for greater concentration seems to be: (1) Under the Georgist system the tax on land would be "enormously" higher than it is now. (2) Consequently only the very affluent could afford to acquire land. (3) Therefore land will become concentrated in the hands of a few holders, "a privileged land-holding aristocracy." LeFevre was concerned in the previous argument that the price of land would drop to zero. But here he claims that the single tax would make land so expensive that only the super rich could afford it. So what effect would land-value taxation really have on the affordability of land?

It would have three effects. (1) It would eliminate any speculative premium: that portion of its present price that is based on the expectation that its price will go higher in the future. The elimination of this speculative premium would make land more affordable. (2) Land-value taxation is capitalized (negatively of course because it is a tax) rather than shifted. Hence when land-value taxation is fully implemented the price of land goes to zero and stays at zero. This is the cause of the first effect but should not be confused with it. Furthermore, this second effect in itself neither increases nor decreases the affordability of land. Paying the tax would be the economic equivalent of paying the interest on what, without land-value taxation, one would need to borrow to buy the land. If everyone had sufficient credit the affordability would be the same. Because not everyone has sufficient credit, land-value taxation would actually remove an obstacle to the acquisition of land. (3) With better use of the most valuable land, the margin of production would contract, raising wages and reducing rent. But some of the relocations of economic activity to more advantageous sites could result in a more efficient clustering of businesses in some of the best locations, raising rent there. In any case, these shifts in usage should have no effect on the affordability of land for those who use it optimally, because any rise in taxes would only absorb increases in rental value and leave wages and interest at their new, higher, level. So land-value taxation does not make land less affordable.

LeFevre apparently did not make up his mind on whether a tax on land is shifted or capitalized. There are two other passages in which he seemed to indicate that he thought it would be shifted. "The man who owns land and rents it to another includes, in the rent he charges, the amount of the taxes he expects to pay. Thus, the user of the land actually pays the taxes in any case."[23] "It should also be remembered that the Georgist theory does not suppose that existing rentals would be eliminated and the present tenant simply required to pay existing taxes. On the contrary, existing rentals, plus the taxes, plus whatever increase the state deemed feasible and correct (on the basis of rental bidding) would be assessed against each user of the land."[24] LeFevre correctly observed that the tenant would ultimately pay the land-value tax in the sense that the tax comes out of rent and the tenant pays the rent. But from this fact he apparently inferred that the tenant would pay *more* than he now pays: what he now pays in rent *plus* the land-value tax. This inference assumes that the owner, against whom the land-value tax is assessed, could raise the rent to cover the new tax and still leave himself with the same net revenue as before. But he could not raise the rent at all, because the imposition of a land-value tax would neither decrease the amount of land available nor increase the demand for it.

### Land-Value Taxation and Development

LeFevre gave three economic arguments that purported to show that land-value taxation would inhibit development. First, LeFevre argued that land-value taxation would discourage development because it would increase the risk of the developer losing his investment.

> With the state as landlord, the profit motive respecting the development of land, while not eliminated, would be thwarted and twisted. It is implicit in the Georgist proposal that the more the land is developed, and the

larger the populations depending on its output, the larger the value it has. The larger the value is presumed to be, the larger the land rent will become. Assuming that the state would abide by its contract and not increase rents during an existing contract, the fact would emerge that with each passing month and year the leasehold decreases in value.[25]

Here LeFevre anticipated a phenomenon that could occur, but he did not understand it. Removing the remnants of LeFevre's misinterpretation, consider land-value taxation in a region where land values are rising and reassessment is done infrequently but at predictable intervals. In such a case it is likely that land-value taxation would not capture all the rent all of the time, so the land would have a non-negligible selling price at all times. But the rent that is left to the landholder would not be at a constant level. It would be near zero just after each reassessment and then rise to a peak just before the next assessment. The price of the land would also not be constant, because, with a cyclically fluctuating income stream, it matters whether one can expect a valley first and then a peak, or a peak first and then a valley. And the price would begin to decline *before* each reassessment, in anticipation of the next valley. LeFevre saw this minor temporary downward adjustment in the price of land, due to the anticipation of a sudden predictable but temporary drop in an income stream, and thought someone was at risk of losing an investment.

But he went on: "This would be especially true were the land to be improved. If the contracting party enhances the value of his land holdings by investing money in improvements, he finds that each additional dollar invested increases the likelihood of an increased rent at the time his contract expires."[26] Here he was just mixed up. Either he thought that George was proposing a tax on both land and improvements, or that the improvements on each parcel significantly increased the value of that particular parcel. But neither is the case. At any particular time, the land-value tax on an improved parcel would be equal to the tax levied on a similarly situated parcel that is unimproved, so it cannot discourage development in the way LeFevre thought.

LeFevre went on in this fashion for two paragraphs and then concluded his argument with the following remarkable passage:

In the event of an eviction occasioned either by the expiration of the lease or the increase in land rent, or both, the occupant would be able to take with him only those things which are portable. Certain types of land improvement would thus become highly risky and extravagant; for example, sewer systems, underground wiring, underground development of water resources. Additionally, structures built on the land would tend to become flimsy and portable rather than solid and fixed. Dwellings would tend toward prefabrication, toward a maximization of sheet material and the elimination of brick and masonry work. Landscaping, the planting of trees and flowers, the installation of walks and driveways, and other appurtenances which become a part of the land itself, would become risky investments.[27]

So according to LeFevre, under a full implementation of the Georgist system we would face the distressing prospect that all future development would be wigwams and port-a-potties.

But taking one's improvements with one is not the only alternative to staying put and paying higher taxes as the value of one's location rises. One could sell one's property without losing the cost of one's investment in improvements if the improvements were appropriate to the location and of the sort for which there is demand. A tax on land values would not interfere with the incentive, which already exists, to build what there will be a demand for in the future, nor would it interfere with the risk that the improvements one builds might not be in demand in the future. And an advocate of the market, as LeFevre claimed to be, could hardly object to this prospect of risk/reward.

Second, LeFevre pointed out that the use of planning and zoning and eminent domain undermine "the supposed 'security' of the individual occupant of land."[28] In doing so, they introduce an element of uncertainty that discourages full development of land. He claimed further that the prospect of an increase in land value taxation, which would of course occur if rent increased, would similarly deter development.[29] While LeFevre is certainly correct that the prospect of eminent domain deters development, the prospect of an increase in land-value taxation should not have such an effect, because the increase would occur equally on undeveloped, under developed, and fully developed sites.

Finally, LeFevre sought to prove that the elimination of existing taxes on land would tend "to put land into its most fruitful and profitable use."[30] His premises are, first, that "the person seeking profits and willing to expend capital in order to ultimately obtain profits is in the best position to know and to develop land to its highest utility," and, second, that "he cannot afford to do otherwise."[31] LeFevre has given a good reason why the possession and development of land should be left to private entrepreneurs, not that the rent should also be left to them. Without land-value taxation it is sometimes more profitable to hold land for a future rise in its price than it is to develop it optimally.

### Speculation

LeFevre attacked George's concern about land speculation in three stages. First, he claimed that "every commercial enterprise is speculative in character."[32] Second, he tried to show that speculation in land is just like speculation in anything else. Third, he contended that the land speculator "prevents prices [of land] from falling to zero."[33] We will consider his arguments for these positions in that order.

His favorite example of a commercial enterprise seemed to be the retailing of refrigerators. He gave three reasons why the retailing of refrigerators is speculative in character. Retailers depend on selling at a higher price than they pay. Retailers maintain inventories. Retailers assume some risk that their stock may not in fact sell at a higher price than they have paid. Let us examine the retailing of refrigerators to see if these three features actually make it speculative in character.

Retailers do indeed buy refrigerators wholesale and sell them at a higher retail price. They also maintain stores at visible and accessible locations where there is sufficient parking for their customers. They have showrooms where they keep floor models of refrigerators and employ sales people so that their customers can choose the refrigerators with the size and features that will best meet their needs. They employ delivery men who install the refrigerator and put it into service in the buyer's home. All of this is the application of labor and capital to land. It is production, not speculation.[34] The difference between the wholesale price at which the dealer buys refrigerators and the retail price at which he sells them is not a speculative premium. It is his and his employees' wages, interest on his capital, and rent on the location of his store.

But what of the retailer's inventory? Is he speculating on that? Generally speaking, no. The difference is in the way the retailer manages his inventory. A speculator buys in quantity when demand for the commodity he is speculating on is low, withholds it from the market, and brings it back onto the market when it is scarce and the demand for it is high. Those refrigerator retailers who stay in business manage their inventories very differently. They constantly monitor sales, and such indicators as housing starts, so as to have just enough refrigerators on hand to serve their customers. They buy fewer refrigerators, not more, when demand is low, and more, not fewer, when demand is high. When their estimates miss their target, and demand is slower than expected, they most emphatically do not withhold their excess inventory from sale as a speculator would. Even if the price of refrigerators in general goes up in the future, the price of those refrigerators that the retailer has on hand now is not likely to go up. New features and materials will be introduced and consumer tastes in color and style will change. The refrigerators the retailer has on hand now will be obsolete in the future. Far from speculating on a price rise when demand picks up in the future, our retailer will put his overstock on sale when demand is weak. Indeed, one of the best indicators of whether a retail enterprise will be successful is "inventory turns per year," which is sales revenue during the year divided by the average cost of inventory on hand during that period. Clearly any withholding of merchandise off the market, unavailable for immediate sale, would reduce inventory turns.

What of the risk involved in retailing refrigerators? Does that mean the retailer is a speculator? No. Risk is a fact of life. One assumes a risk every time one crosses the street. Risk alone is not an indication of speculation. Not every commercial enterprise is speculative in character.

Stage two of LeFevre's argument is to try to show that speculation in land is just like speculation in anything else. He pointed out that all speculators seek to buy when prices are low and sell when prices are high. In doing so they prevent prices from going lower still or from going higher still. This has the beneficial effect of moderating swings in the market.[35]

This is, of course, true. However, because land is fixed in quantity and is not humanly produced, withholding land from the market speculatively can only create an artificial shortage. Purchasing it when it is cheap and keeping it out of use does not mean that there will be more of it at some later time than there otherwise would have been. The amount of land that exists is constant.

LeFevre admitted that this point has "some validity."[36] But he countered with examples such as the Dutch reclamation of land from the sea, the building of Mexico City over a lake, and the fanciful possibility of constructing large floating earthen islands.[37] But the land the Dutch have reclaimed from the sea is not newly created land but just pre-existing land improved for further development, just as the swampy field that the farmer has made arable by tiling is not newly created land. Should floating earthen islands be constructed, they would not be land at all in the economic sense because they are humanly produced. The fact that they are made partly of dirt is irrelevant. Adobe houses are not land either.

The third and final stage in LeFevre's attack on George's strictures concerning land speculation was to contend that the land speculator "prevents prices [of land] from falling to zero."[38] This is just false. Without any land-value tax, even if there were no speculative premium on the price of land, the difference in productivity between the best land and marginal land would be capitalized into a nonzero price. And if there were a tax of 100 percent of the rental value on land, the price of land would drop to zero even if someone were so foolish as to buy some and speculatively withhold it from its best use.

### Land Assessment

LeFevre claimed that land cannot be assessed fairly. To support this contention he sought to undermine the idea that there is an objective basis for the value of land. First he claimed that "the value attributed to any item relates to individual desire for that item and not to the labor that has been expended in producing it."[39] But this is irrelevant because no one, no matter what his theory of value were, would suggest that land should be assessed by measuring the labor expended in producing it. Land is not produced by human labor.

LeFevre then distinguished between value and price in the following way:

> In actual fact, value is an abstract, subjective, terminal supposition, whereas the prices by means of which land privately owned is conveyed are determined by the conflicting forces of supply and demand working between freely bargaining agents. Thus, the value (or the tax) attached to any piece of land is invariably an arbitrary and subjective finding, whereas the pricing by means of which conveyances occur results from an objective finding in which competing forces reach, at a given moment, a point of voluntary agreement.
>
> Understanding of this point reveals that value and price are not only not a part of the same process, one being subjective, the other objective, they are not even related.[40]

But a paragraph later, value and price are part of the same process, and they are related in the following way: "The seller would value the money or goods he receives for his property at a level higher than the property he conveys. Contrariwise, the buyer would value the property he obtains at a level higher than the money or goods he exchanges for the property."[41] This distinction is also irrelevant because what most economists are referring to when they speak of value is not the subjective gleam in eye of the beholder, which Lefevre calls "value," but market value, what Lefevre calls "price." True, economists of the Austrian School maintain that value is subjective, but subjective valuations are reflected objectively in market prices, and this applies to land just as it does to everything else.

Lefevre then gave two reasons why price could not be assessed fairly. One, such assessment "requires an arbitrary decision, provided . . . on the basis of past pricing (which will probably never again hold true)."[42] Two, assessment depends on "the subjective judgment of the assessor, who knows less of the utility of the property and its presumed market pricing potential than either the last seller, the present owner, or any future buyer."[43]

But these objections are entirely superficial. To base assessment on observation of actual market transactions is neither arbitrary nor subjective. The fact that prices change merely means that re-appraisal should be done frequently. The fact that the appraiser is not a seller, owner, or buyer does not prevent him from objectively observing the relevant prices in the market place. Prospective buyers and sellers also base their offers and counter-offers at least in part by comparison with other market transactions.

Furthermore, if LeFevre's objections to assessment were cogent then they would apply to every class of objects. But in fact all manner of things from diamonds to vintage baseball cards are appraised with sufficient connection and objectivity for practical purposes, such as insurance. Of course LeFevre might have welcomed the implication that nothing can be appraised fairly, because he claimed "all taxation, however it is levied, is an exaction taken by force from the rightful owner of property, real or otherwise."[44] So for LeFevre, if nothing can be appraised fairly, so much the better!

### Land and Wealth

Because LeFevre opposed all taxes, he was heartened by George's insistence that wealth should not be taxed. But of course he was disappointed that George would exclude land from the category of wealth and therefore leave it open to taxation. LeFevre therefore gave two arguments that purport to show that land really is wealth and therefore, to be consistent, George should not have advocated taxing it.

LeFevre's first argument must be quoted:

> If land is the "source of wealth," a Georgist contention, then wealth derives from land. If wealth derives from land, it must be that land has some relationship to wealth. George assumes that it is man's labor applied to land that provides wealth and creates value. If man's labor occurred (in some fanciful manner) removed from the land, then he might be forgiven for contending that land is not wealth, nor in that case could it be the source of wealth, IF labor created wealth. Wealth does not come out of nothing. It certainly does not emerge from labor removed from land. Wealth emerges from land because wealth must come out of something and not out of nothing. Land is wealth and wealth is land.[45]

The mind boggles.

LeFevre's second argument is more revealing. He observed that George sought a more equal (or equitable) distribution of wealth.

"But the only point wherein his theory is to be applied relates to the unequal distribution of land."[46] Yet, LeFevre reasoned, if one is to achieve a more equal distribution of wealth by removing only the inequality in the distribution of land, then land must itself be wealth. So LeFevre concluded that George's "entire theory is predicated upon the assumption that land is wealth. His theory speaks louder than his definition."[47] But for LeFevre to convict George of tacitly admitting that land is wealth on these grounds, is to assume that the only way to achieve a more equal or equitable distribution of wealth is to redistribute wealth, an assumption that socialists often make. To the contrary, George sought to remove special privileges, private appropriation of rent being the chief one, and then let the market take care of equity in the distribution of wealth. "I do not mean that each individual would get the same amount of wealth. That would not be equal distribution, so long as different individuals have different powers and different desires. But I mean that wealth would be distributed in accordance with the degree in which the industry, skill, knowledge, or prudence of each contributed to the common stock."[48] Had LeFevre noticed this passage he might have taken a very different view of George.

### LeFevre's Theory of Ownership

LeFevre preceded his statement of his own theory of ownership with a confused passage ostensibly concerning "the labor theory of ownership."[49] He started this section with the accusation that "perhaps the most fundamental fallacy of the Georgist theory relates to the supposition that the value of anything derives from the element of human labor which is 'mixed' with the product."[50] But this is the labor theory of value, which George did not hold,[51] not the labor theory of ownership. Moreover, the metaphor of mixing one's labor "with the raw materials nature has provided"[52] comes from John Locke, as LeFevre knew. In fact LeFevre quoted a passage in which Locke argued that every person owns himself; therefore every person owns his labor; therefore every person owns whatever he has mixed his labor with, subject to the proviso that there be "enough, and as good left in common for others." George also derived property rights from self-ownership, but without relying on the metaphor of mixing one's labor with nature, which LeFevre seemed to find objectionable. George observed that wealth is produced by labor and otherwise not produced at all. "Hence, as nature gives only to labor, the exertion of labor in production is the only title to exclusive possession."[53]

LeFevre stated his own theory of ownership, which he called "the rule of first claimant," by means of a long, elaborate narrative. The gist of it is this. "Historically, all property, including the property of land, comes into ownership through the establishment of claim."[54] Claims can be established in a variety of ways, some of which involve conquest, others not. The most practical way to establish a claim without conquest is "the establishment of visible or easily identifiable boundaries and public notification."[55] "When an item to be owned is unclaimed, the first person to establish a claim becomes the justifiable owner."[56] LeFevre called this the rule of first claimant. He contrasted it with his misinterpretation of George. "If we were to rely on conquest exclusively, then government could seize the land and, instead of deeding it to private persons, could hold it as the universal landlord; thus, both the theory of conquest and of Henry George would be satisfied."[57]

The rule of first claimant is very similar to the theory of first occupancy, which George refuted in *Progress and Poverty*,[58] and that other critics had previously tried to resuscitate against George. (In particular, see the chapters in this book on Cathrein, Carver, and Ryan.) Three points need to be made.

First, the rule of first claimant appears to be more general than the theory of first occupancy because many of the products that we seem to own are things that could be claimed but not occupied. In fact these items that might be claimed, but not occupied, would generally be a subset of labor products, so this increase in generality could be important. LeFevre applied his view to labor products.

> Many a man will labor to produce something. His labor may entail long hours and much devotion. But when the item for which he labored stands ready before him, he may find it wholly unworthy of his esteem and affection. He will, in this case, DISCLAIM it. He may have created it. But he does not own it because he DISOWNS it. Thus, possessive desire may lead to labor and to ownership. But it is the emotional tie the man retains

with what he owns that causes him to continue as the owner. His labor is of less duration than this emotion, in most cases.[59]

The labor theorist can grant all of this. The question is what would justify a claim of ownership, should someone make one. Even disowning something suggests that the person disowning it had some prior justification to own it, or his disowning would be an empty gesture. To say that the claim justifies ownership would suggest that if I were to tour the Ford assembly plant in Dearborn, MI, and claim a brand new Focus just before Ford claimed it, then it would be rightly mine. But this is ludicrous. So LeFevre achieves greater generality only by sacrificing plausibility.

Second, being first to claim something, rather than to occupy it, does not escape the objections to the first occupancy theory that George had already given in *Progress and Poverty*. The rule of first claimant and the theory of first occupancy both derive whatever plausibility they might have from the fact that unowned land, which one could be *first* to claim or occupy, is generally at or beyond the margin, and is no-rent land. The rule of first claimant is as incapable as the theory of first occupancy to justify any entitlement on the part of the first claimant (or occupant) to future rent, as a community grows around the site that was claimed (or occupied). Unfortunately, LeFevre took no notice of George's objections to the theory of first occupancy and refused to consider the issue of rent apart from use and control of land.

Finally, it is worth pointing out that the rule of first claimant is subject to an objection to which the theory of first occupancy is immune. This is because people really have claimed other people, as in the practice of slavery, whereas a person is not the kind of thing that can be occupied by another person in the way land or buildings can be occupied. LeFevre was sensitive to the fact that one might attempt to use the rule of first claimant to justify slavery, and he defended his rule against this charge in the following way:

> It appears at once that man's ownership of slaves, spouses, and children is, in each case, an act of conquest. No man may justifiably own any other human being, although he may have a contractual interest in the services of human beings. To seek to own another human being is to seek

to super-impose a claim over the primary claim each individual has over himself.[60]

But to salvage the rule of first claimant in this fashion is implicitly to give it up in favor of the labor theory of ownership, as Clancy pointed out:

> What about the reduction of slaves to ownership? Mr. LeFevre says (p. 52): "To seek to own another human being is to seek to superimpose a claim over *the primary claim each individual has over himself*" (italics mine). He here gives away the case. It is on this principle that a man belongs to himself that the produce of his labor belongs to him—the same principle of John Locke's that Mr. LeFevre had set out to refute! What is the essence of slavery but taking away the produce of the slave?[61]

So LeFevre's rule of first claimant has no plausible advantage over the theory of first occupancy, it is subject to the same fundamental weakness, and it has a further drawback from which to defend it is to give it up in favor of the labor theory of ownership.

### Conclusion

There are two things that struck this writer about LeFevre's critique of George. One of them is how far astray a critic can be led by making just a few simple mistakes. The misinterpretation whereby the single tax is taken to imply state control of land, the vacillation over whether a land-value tax is capitalized or shifted, and the repeated blindness to the role of production in the economy are the chief mistakes. Had he taken the time to discuss his concerns informally with a knowledgeable and congenial Georgist, we might have seen a very different critique. This should not have been difficult for him to do, since Frank Chodorov, once director of the Henry George School, and a committed Georgist until the day he died, was a frequent lecturer at the Freedom School.

The second thing that struck this writer is that LeFevre never explicitly argued against the Georgist view that the rental value of land is a by-product of the presence and activity of the community, and not attributable to any contribution that landholders make in their capacity as landholders. Therefore rent can be collected by the community without "predation." LeFevre clearly did not believe this, and obviously assumed the contrary throughout his critique, but he never offered a direct argument against it. Perhaps in his heart he knew he did not have one.

### Notes

1. See LeFevre's posthumously published two-volume autobiography, *A Way to be Free* (Culver City, CA: Pulpless.Com. Inc., 1999). I thank the editor of the present book for writing the first two paragraphs of this chapter, and for his counsel on the remainder.

2. Robert LeFevre, "A Challenge to the Georgists," *Rampart Journal of Individualist Thought* Vol. I, No. 2 (Summer 1965): 25–58.

3. Robert Clancy, "A Challenge to Libertarians," *Rampart Journal of Individualist Thought* Vol. I, No. 3 (Fall, 1965): 9–15.

4. Robert LeFevre, "On the Other Hand," *Rampart Journal of Individualist Thought* Vol. I, No. 3 (Fall, 1965): 95–99.

5. LeFevre, "A Challenge," p. 27.

6. Ibid., p. 30.

7. Ibid.

8. Ibid., pp. 28–29. I quote from LeFevre's footnote 5. *Progress and Poverty* is actually slightly misquoted in it but the differences are of no consequence. See Henry George, *Progress and Poverty* (centenary ed.; New York: Robert Schalkenbach Foundation, 1979), pp. 405–06.

9. LeFevre, "A Challenge," p. 27.

10. Ibid., p. 28.

11. Ibid., pp. 28–29.

12. Ibid., pp. 32–33.

13. Ibid., p. 33.

14. Clancy, "A Challenge to Libertarians," p. 11.

15. LeFevre, "A Challenge," p. 31.

16. Ibid., p. 32.

17. LeFevre, "On the Other Hand," p. 96.

18. Ibid., p. 97.

19. LeFevre, "A Challenge," p. 29.

20. Ibid., p. 43.

21. The argument that wages would rise runs throughout *Progress and Poverty* and is summarized nicely on page 442. The argument that interest would rise or fall with wages is on pages 198–99.

22. LeFevre, "A Challenge," p. 34.

23. Ibid., p. 39.

24. Ibid., p. 43.

25. Ibid., pp. 39–40.

26. Ibid., p. 40.
27. Ibid.
28. Ibid., pp. 41–42.
29. Ibid., p. 44.
30. Ibid., p. 47.
31. Ibid.
32. Ibid., p. 35.
33. Ibid., p. 37.
34. See George on this subject. George, *Progress and Poverty*, p. 66.
35. LeFevre, "A Challenge," pp. 36–37.
36. Ibid., p. 36.
37. Ibid.
38. Ibid., p. 37.
39. Ibid., p. 57.
40. Ibid., p. 38.
41. Ibid.
42. Ibid.
43. Ibid., pp. 38–39.
44. Ibid., p. 41.
45. Ibid., p. 56.
46. Ibid.
47. Ibid.
48. George, *Progress and Poverty*, pp. 452–53.
49. LeFevre, "A Challenge," p. 49.
50. Ibid.
51. Henry George, *The Science of Political Economy* (New York: Double-day & McClure Co., 1898), p. 261.
52. LeFevre, "A Challenge," p. 49.
53. George, *Progress and Poverty*, p. 336.
54. LeFevre, "A Challenge," p. 50.
55. Ibid., p. 51.
56. Ibid., p. 52.
57. Ibid., p. 51.
58. George, *Progress and Poverty*, pp. 344–46.
59. LeFevre, "A Challenge," p. 51.
60. Ibid., p. 52.
61. Clancy, "A Challenge to Libertarians," p. 14.

# 33
# Oser: Reservations of a Friendly Commentator

By Oscar B. Johannsen

In 1974 Twayne Publishers, which six years before had brought out Edward J. Rose's biography of Henry George, issued, as part of its "Great Thinkers Series," a study of George by Jacob Oser, professor of economics at Utica College of Syracuse University and author of several well-known books on the history of economic thought. While also largely biographical, this work contains a chapter devoted to the critical analysis of the arguments in *Progress and Poverty*, George's magnum opus.

Oser's approach is generally sympathetic, and the chapter in question begins with a section endorsing George's rejection of the wages-fund theory, his development of Ricardo's Law of Rent, his contention that the landowner as landowner does nothing to earn his income, and his insistence that to tax away all economic rent would stimulate rather than retard production. However, Oser then goes on to find George's thinking defective in the following ways: (1) he was wrong in believing that the landlord's share of national income would rise and that of labor would fall with industrial progress; (2) he confused the law of diminishing returns, increasing returns to scale, and growing efficiency; (3) he was naively optimistic as to the fiscal adequacy of a single tax on land rent; (4) he misconceived the nature of capitalism, failing to realize that the private ownership of capital is a more powerful cause than is the private ownership of land in explaining the uneven distribution of income in industrial societies.

There is merit in some of Oser's criticism. Quite properly, he observes that George's generalization that wages and interest tend to rise and fall together is a dubious one. But issue must be taken with much of his analysis.

American Journal of Economics and Sociology, Vol. 63, No. 2 (April, 2004).
© 2004 American Journal of Economics and Sociology, Inc.

### Does Industrial Progress Raise Rent at the Expense of Wages?

Oser contends that "George was wrong in believing that wages probably would fall as society progresses, and the percentage of the nation's income that goes to labor certainly would fall; he was just as wrong in believing that the share going to landowners would increase."[1] As proof he quotes data supplied by the U.S. Department of Commerce that list the value of privately held land in the United States to have been $27 billion in 1900, and indicate that its value as a percentage of Gross National Product decreased from 159 percent in 1900 to 66 percent in 1968, when its value was said to have been $571 billion. Although popular today in economic circles, the use of statistics to prove or disprove economic principles is a questionable technique. Ludwig von Mises, the celebrated economist of the Austrian School, in his attack on the substitution of "quantitative economics" for "qualitative economics," pointed out that "statistical figures referring to economic events are historical data. They tell us what happened in a non-repeatable historical case."[2] No doubt statistics may be useful in developing some corroborative evidence in analyzing a particular problem, but even in such an instance they must be treated with great circumspection. Controlled economic experiments being seldom possible, the statistics in use are rarely of the type that induce great confidence. Men, in their activities, do not bother to set down all the precise factors influencing their actions, hence the statistics that economists are forced to utilize, particularly if they are in terms of money, often are little better than proxies for what actually may have occurred.

In the ideal society, however, the real point at issue is not whether labor's share tends to decrease and the landlord's share to increase as society progresses. After all, if George's remedy were to be put into operation, the rent would all accrue to the people either indirectly through the provision of a multiplicity of services or directly through a per capita division. Under those conditions the division of income between labor and landlord (since the landlord, in effect, would be the people themselves) would probably not be nearly so important as it is today.

Now, however, since for all practical purposes the land, particularly in the Western world, is all enclosed, the real issue is that of the point at which a tendency to stabilization comes to exist, for this will determine how impoverished the mass of the people will be. That point tends to be where labor's share is at its subsistence level. Above this point it cannot remain, for competition among laborers for access to land will bring it down. Below this it cannot fall, for labor will starve or revolt.

Although Oser does not think it is possible, the absolute impoverishment of workers can occur if their subsistence point is low enough. In nations such as India the subsistence level is so low that many people actually starve. But the subsistence level in other nations, such as the United States, is far from being at that point. Long before starvation is reached, labor revolts. It may take the actual form of revolution, but often, instead of a bloody convulsion, the revolt is a demand for governmental interference to mitigate the effects of labor's decreasing share of the production pie. But this does not mean that George's analysis was in error, any more than the erection of a dam disproves the principle that water tends to flow downward.

Of course, the fact that there may be millions of landlords in a country does not mean that they do not act like monopolists, any more than the fact that there may be millions of patent holders prevents them from acting as monopolists. Just as each inventor holding a patent has a monopoly on the particular product involved, so the millions of landowners have a monopoly on the particular pieces of land they own. Ask any entrepreneur wishing to erect an office building on Wall Street in New York City if the owner of the land on which he wishes to construct the building acts as a monopolist when the entrepreneur approaches him with a request for the terms of sale.

### Returns to Scale and Growing Efficiency, or Diminishing Returns?

Oser rebuts George's refutation of Malthus's theory on the grounds that George "was confusing increasing returns to scale and growing efficiency with the law of diminishing returns."[3] But he weakens his own charge subsequently, for toward the end of his book, in commenting on *The Science of Political Economy*, he notes that George

was ahead of the orthodox economic thinking of his time in empha-
sizing that the law of diminishing returns applied to industry as well
as to agriculture. And if book 3, chapter 7 of the cited work is read,
one of the clearest and best explanations of the law of diminishing
returns ever written will be found. As for the principle that has now
come to be known as "increasing returns to scale," Oser himself
points out that George noted that one hundred men will produce
more than one hundred times what one man can produce. In view
of all this, it is a mystery why Oser asserts that George confused these
laws.

Oser appears to make a practice of vitiating his own criticisms,
for after scorning "George's preposterous statement that the earth
could support a thousand billion people as easily as one billion," he
immediately goes on to say: "Only phenomenal, and as yet unseen,
improvements in technology could make this possible."[4] Apparently,
then, while the notion of the existence of a trillion people on the
earth is an absurdity, it is still possible if technology develops sufficiently. No one, of course, knows whether a trillion people could
be supported or not. But we do know that in America, under the impetus of the partially free economy existing, highly sophisticated
machinery was invented in the nineteenth century (for example, the
McCormick reaper) that enabled the United States to produce phenomenal amounts of food products. Just as no one in the seventeenth
or eighteenth centuries could have foreseen such technological
improvements, so we cannot foresee what new improvements may
be made if needed and desired.

But the burden of George's attack on the Malthusian doctrine had
nothing really to do with the maximum number of people who could
possibly exist on our finite globe. The principal reason for attacking
this theory was that it beclouded the whole issue of man's relationship to the land. It implied that an imbalance existed between man's
sexual proclivities and his ability to produce. This imbalance was the
cause of poverty amidst plenty and, because it was Mother Nature
who was responsible, there was little man could do to remedy the
situation.

Such an assumption was eminently satisfying to those possessing
special privileges, such as landlords, particularly at the time that

Malthus wrote, when people were beginning to question the absurdity of poverty amidst plenty. It is doubtful that George was particularly concerned with how many people could exist on the earth. What
he wanted was to upset the theory, so comforting to privileged interests, that nature was to blame for the growing poverty with increasing productivity and to redirect men's attention to attempting to
discover what institutional arrangements might be the cause of this
enigma.

### Would Economic Rent Provide Enough Public Revenue?

Oser questions George's contention that a 100 percent collection of
economic rent would be sufficient to defray the expenses of government without the imposition of other taxes, claiming that while it
was true in George's day, it is not so today. Again he resorts to statistics to prove his point, noting the fantastic increase in governmental expenditures within the past generation. But after doing so he
undermines his own argument by noting that George believed that
his fundamental reform would not only unleash productivity and
growth, but would also result in a decrease in governmental functions. For example, in a peaceful world military expenditures would
be unnecessary.

If an argument is to be leveled against the adequacy of the so-
called single tax as a resource for governmental revenues, it would
appear that logically one should first specify what the true functions
of government are. If government is expected to supply every possible need or want of the people, then no amount of revenue, not
even total confiscation of all income generated, would be sufficient.
If the socialists are correct in holding that all revenue, and not merely
land rent, belongs rightfully to the state, then the question of the suf-
ficiency or insufficiency of a tax on land values becomes meaningless. On the other hand, if the anarchists are correct in holding that
no government is necessary, then whatever revenues are garnered
would be actually superfluous.

But the question of the adequacy or inadequacy of the single
tax for the raising of governmental revenues is not germane to
what George was attempting to do. George was not interested in

proposing a tax reform by means of which government might indulge itself in every form of do-goodism. Rather, he wished to establish those conditions predicated on the principles of justice wherein involuntary poverty would not exist and wherein the individual would attain his maximum potential. He wished people to be free to tread whatever paths they wished in order to give expression to the capacities with which they were born.

Man comes into this world with nothing but the ability to expend his physical and mental energy. But on what? Initially, in economic terms, the only thing in existence outside of man is land. If man is denied access to land, he is denied the opportunity to utilize his inborn talents to the utmost. Above all else, *Progress and Poverty* is a paean to justice and freedom, that even after a century, still has the power to quicken the hearts and kindle the souls of those who hold these values dear.

### Misconceptions about Capitalism?

Oser believes that George suffered from misconceptions about the nature of capitalism. Regrettably, because Oser does not explicitly state what he himself means by capitalism, much less capital, a comparison between his and George's views cannot be made directly. He does state that to George "capital includes those things that are not either land or labor . . . capital covers such things as buildings, cattle, tools, machinery—man-made goods used for further production."[5]

Although he derides George's assertion that labor is the actual employer of capital, the definition of capital that he attributes to George clearly implies that labor is the employer. If the above quotation is reduced to its simplest terms, does it not state that capital is but a synonym for tools? And who uses tools but labor? Oser scorns the idea of a workman's telling the chairman of General Motors that he, the laborer, is the employer of capital. But such is unnecessary. The chairman has learned from sad experience that the workers are the actual employers, for when they go out on strike the capital lies idle awaiting their return.

In contending that George had mistaken notions about the nature of capitalism, Oser asserts that George was looking backward to a

Jeffersonian agrarian democracy and not ahead to the problems of an industrial society. This presumption that George's view of the ideal society revolved around small-scale producers and craftsmen is an error that has been repeated over and over again and, no doubt, will be time and again in the future. It may be that this is because of the simple examples George used to explain his points; because he was writing for general consumption, naturally he kept his illustrations as elementary as possible. But to imply, as Oser does, that George was blind to the startling growth of business and industry and what effect it might have, is to assume that George was not only insensible to his surroundings but was lacking in a grasp of the fundamentals involved. Oser himself states that in the introductory chapter of *Progress and Poverty* George noted the prodigious increase in wealth-producing power. This monumental increase in man's ability to produce wealth was part of the perplexing paradox he had determined to elucidate. Presumably, not only the necessities of life but luxuries undreamed of in previous times should be at the disposal of all with but a modicum of effort. Instead, horrendous poverty existed and was growing rather than decreasing as the mountains of wealth spewed forth from the gigantic industrial machine that man was building. It was this enigma that led George to focus his attention on economic phenomena.

That business and industry were increasing in complexity, requiring greater time and distances to accomplish their aims, did not becloud George's comprehension of the fundamentals in operation. Such growth did not affect the principles at work in the least any more than a twentieth-century jet liner is, in principle, different from the primitive plane of the Wright brothers, which for the first time enabled man to realize his centuries-old dream of emulating the birds in flight. Oser believes that the great distances and time involved in modern production have made a difference—the difference being the importance of accumulating capital in advance. Implied in this assertion is that capital is money. It may well be that because this appears to be the major ingredient in his conception of capital, he attacks George's contention that wages are drawn from the product of labor and not capital. Parenthetically, it should be remarked that Oser's attack seems strange coming from one who earlier lauded George's perception in denying the wages-fund theory.[6]

Yet George does not restrict his definition of capital to the one attributed to him by Oser. George also included goods in the process of production and exchange. Thus he claims that in building a ship capital is being produced, and wages represent the purchase by the entrepreneur of the additional capital that the laborers had created. Since Oser apparently equates capital with money, he takes the position that, on the contrary, it is necessary first to have accumulated capital in order to finance the vessel's construction.

But it is clear that such is not the case when it is appreciated that, theoretically, laborers could cooperate with one another to build a ship without the necessity of any previous financing whatever. They could spend part of their time constructing the ship and the rest producing the necessities and luxuries they desired. When completed, the ship would be their property, which they could offer for whatever they thought it was worth. Even the materials and tools employed by them could be produced on the same basis by other laborers. Thus if one were to trace the production of all the materials and tools back to the land, from which all wealth comes, it is patent that it is not necessary for money first to have been accumulated. This is the method the Indians used in building their war canoes, for they did not bother first to accumulate the wampum they used as money before they commenced construction.

What modern business does is to eliminate the need for such cumbersome arrangements, thus permitting laborers to concentrate all their working time and effort on such a project as a ship. Instead of selling it upon its completion, they sell the part they have produced bit by bit as it is being constructed and use the funds obtained to purchase the necessities and luxuries they desire. This is precisely the point George expounded in his discussion of the building of the ship. If one assumes that only tools constitute capital, then George's error was in assuming that the laborers were producing more capital as they built the vessel, when all they were doing was producing wealth in the form of a ship.*

---

*That the article as a ship may subsequently be used as a tool and thus constitutes capital when so employed does not negate the fact that while it is being built it is merely an article of wealth that is being produced.

Of course, even under modern business conditions, if a project is of long duration—say five years—while financial arrangements may all be completed in advance, the actual finances need not be in existence. Instead, those financing the project will gear their investments so that the finances will be available as required.

Oser believes that George's view that labor is independent of capital sprang from his ignoring the fact that a certain amount of capital is necessary to establish even a small farm. Thus the Homestead Act, which granted settlers in the West 160 acres free except for some filing fees, was of little use to urban laborers. This was because, typically, $1,000 was required to obtain the equipment and livestock needed to get started and to feed their families until the first crop came in. Because apparently capital is money to Oser, he assumes that George could not admit that labor was dependent on capital's first being accumulated, for to do so would weaken the remedy George suggested.

But as for the necessity to have an accumulation of capital first, ask the American pioneers who landed on the forbidding shores of this continent what capital they had. It was practically nothing. Yet out of the forest they hewed their farms with only the minutest amount of capital—the few tools they had brought with them such as axes, shovels, and hoes. To the degree that they had even these simple tools they were at a great advantage. But had they waded ashore with nothing but their bare hands, it would have been only a question of time before they made whatever capital they needed, using the raw materials they found in the land. Naturally, however, because Europe with its huge quantity of capital existed, they exchanged their produce for the tools they needed from the Old World.

Surprisingly, without offering proof, Oser states that "the ownership of capital gives more wealth and power to a small group of people than the ownership of land."[7] One would assume that after having made such a sweeping statement he would give at least some arguments in support, but he neglects to do so.

To many it would appear that George, purely on the basis of logic, had proved quite conclusively that it is control over land that gives wealth and power to small groups of people. But even if his reasoning had made little impact, certainly the actions of the OPEC states, which own the land from which much of the world's oil comes, gave dramatic pragmatic proof of where power lies. As is well known, some years ago they instituted a boycott, refusing to sell more than a trickle of their crude oil. If the ownership of capital gives more power than the ownership of land, why was it that the most powerful nation in the world, the United States, as well as Japan and all the nations of Western Europe, had almost to beg the OPEC states to end their boycott? As long as these nations did not wish to use military might, the fact that they owned most of the capital, that is, the refineries necessary to process the crude oil, meant nothing. Even if one considers money to be capital, they were helpless. The Western world no doubt has most of the world's money, but as long as the OPEC states refused to sell their oil, what power could money exert?

While Oser may thus be faulted for many of his criticisms, his evaluation of George is both objective and provocative.

## Notes

1. Jacob Oser, *Henry George* (New York: Twayne Publishers, Inc., 1974), p. 54.

2. Ludwig von Mises, *Human Action* (New Haven, Conn.: Yale University Press, 1949), p. 56. [The statistics in this case are themselves questionable. See Mary M. Cleveland's chapter in the present volume (ed.)].

3. Oser, *Henry George*, p. 56.

4. Ibid., p. 62.

5. Ibid., p. 34.

6. Ibid., p. 51.

7. Ibid., p. 67.

# 34

# Blaug: Edging Toward Full Appreciation

## By MARY M. CLEVELAND

I owe the decision to study economics to the influence of the writings of
Henry George and Karl Marx. In 1944 I was 17 years old and attending
Peter Stuyvesant High School in New York City. I enrolled for a course in
Commerce, and in the last week of the term the teacher took some of the
better students, which included me, to a special lecture at a nearby Henry
George School. The lecture was an explanation of why the unrestrained
growth of land rentals had produced poverty, wars, and all the other ills
of modern civilization. Henry George had long ago provided both the
diagnosis of the evil and the treatment that would cure it: a single confiscatory tax on ground rent! At the end of the lecture, we were all
presented with free copies of Henry George's *Progress and Poverty*, which
I duly read without understanding much of it. But years later when I finally
studied the Ricardian theory of differential rent, I did have a moment of
excitement at discovering the true source of George's theory.[1]

Thus begins the intellectual autobiography of noted economic historian Mark Blaug. Over the years, Blaug has retained what he calls
a "soft spot" for George. In the November 1980 issue of *Economica*,
he reviewed the first edition of *Critics of Henry George*, not unfavor-
ably.[2] In 1992, he edited a collection of 26 articles on Henry George.[3]
In May 1996 he reviewed—rather less favorably—the three Georgist
Paradigm books published by Shepheard-Walwyn.[4] In June 1999, he
gave an invited lecture on Henry George at Macquarie University,
Sydney, Australia, part of a series funded by the F. J. Walsh bequest.
He published this lecture in 2000 as "Henry George: Rebel with a
Cause."[5] On June 29, 2002, I interviewed Blaug at his home in the
Dutch university town of Leiden.

Blaug was born into an Orthodox Jewish family in the Netherlands,
where his father was a successful raincoat manufacturer, "the Raincoat King of the Netherlands." In 1940, when the Nazis invaded
Holland, the family fled to New York City. "I was brought up as an
orthodox Jew, achieved pantheism by the age of 12, agnosticism by

American Journal of Economics and Sociology, Vol. 63, No. 2 (April, 2004).
© 2004 American Journal of Economics and Sociology, Inc.

the age of 15, and militant atheism by the age of 17, from which I have never wavered."[6]

Following high school, Blaug attended New York University, where he quickly became an avowed Marxist. "I was always a bit of a smart alec when I was young and Marxism was made to order for me: it allowed me to pontificate on every subject with a cocksureness that suited me perfectly."[7] He also joined the Communist Party, and was quickly expelled for signing a petition in support of the Party president, who had himself been expelled for disagreeing with an item of doctrine. "To those who have never been a member of a conspiratorial or quasi-conspiratorial group, the speed with which party members will ostracize a heretic is hard to believe."[8]

The Marxist theory that "economic interests and economic forces are the foundations of all social and political conflicts" led Blaug to the study of economics, and to a rapid abandonment of his Marxist view. He graduated from Queens College of the City University of New York in 1950 and began Ph.D. work at Columbia. In 1952, while he was an instructor at Queens, three senior professors at Queens refused to cooperate with U.S. Senator Joseph McCarthy's communist-hunting committee—and were summarily fired. Blaug signed a petition in their support, and was immediately forced to resign, leaving him broke and depressed. But from out of nowhere a grant materialized to send him abroad to write his Ph.D. thesis. He spent the "best two years" of his life in London, where he discovered that "scholarly research was my true métier."[9] His dissertation on the rise and fall of the school of David Ricardo, supervised by George Stigler, was published in 1958 as *Ricardian Economics*.[10]

In 1954, Blaug became an assistant professor at Yale. Assigned to teach history of economic thought—a required subject in those days!—he created a massive set of notes that became the basis of his best-known publication, *Economic Theory in Retrospect*,[11] now in its fifth edition.

In 1962, still considering himself a European, Blaug joined the London Institute of Education as a professor in the new field of economics of education, a position he held for twenty-three years. He began as an enthusiastic proponent of human capital theory, but ended up disillusioned, concluding, "not that human capital theory is wrong, but that it is thin and unproductive despite its early promise, and unable to vanquish its principal competitor, the screening hypothesis, credentialism, the diploma disease, call it what you will."[12] During this period he also spent much time in Africa and Asia as an educational consultant for various UN agencies and the World Bank. He became equally disillusioned, concluding that, "The whole business of UN aid missions and advice to Third World governments on what to do or not to do in economic policy was a gigantic charade,"[13] designed to justify aid, much of which would end up lining the pockets of local politicians.

After the Institute of Education, Blaug held positions at the University of Buckingham and the University of Exeter. Since 1998, he has chaired the Research Group in the History and Methodology of Economics at the University of Amsterdam and, more recently, has co-directed the Center for the History of Management and Economic Thought at Erasmus University, Rotterdam. He and his wife live part of the year in the Netherlands, and part in Great Britain.

### Economics, Philosophy, and Politics

Blaug's passion is the history of economic thought. "In the final analysis, I find nothing as intellectually satisfying as the history of ideas. I have never been able to grasp how one can understand any idea without knowing where it came from, how it evolved out of previous ideas . . . [W]ithout the history of economics, economic theories just drop from the sky; you have to take them on faith."[14] He is distressed, but not surprised, by the disappearance of history of economic thought as a required subject in graduate schools, a matter he elaborates in a 2001 article entitled "No History of Ideas, Please, We're Economists."[15]

Besides history of economic thought, Blaug also studies economic methodology. In 1980 he published *The Methodology of Economics, or How Economists Explain*.[16] In his autobiography, he describes himself as "an unregenerate Popperian,"[17] an adherent of Karl Popper's concept of "predictionism, that is, the idea that theories must ultimately be judged by the accuracy of their prediction."[18] To put it another way, theories cannot be considered valid unless they are falsifiable, that is, unless tests can be designed that would corroborate them.

His concern for history and methodology make Blaug very critical of economics as practiced today. In a 1997 article in the Canadian journal, *Policy Options*, he writes:

> Modern economics is sick. Economics has increasingly become an intellectual game played for its own sake and not for its practical consequences for understanding the economic world. Economists have converted the subject into a sort of social mathematics in which analytical rigour is everything and practical relevance is nothing. To pick up a copy of *The American Economic Review* or *The Economic Journal* these days is to wonder whether one has landed on a strange planet in which tedium is the deliberate objective of professional publication. Economics was once condemned as "the dismal science" but the dismal science of yesterday was a lot less dismal than the soporific scholasticism of today.[19]

As to what economists *should* be doing, he writes:

> Economic hypotheses can be judged by their coherence, their explanatory power, their plausibility and, ultimately, their ability to predict. Why are economists, like all scientists, concerned with predictability? Because it is the ultimate test of whether our theories are true and really capture the workings of the economic system independently of our wishes and intellectual preferences. That is not to say that we should always discard hypotheses that have not yet yielded falsifiable implications but simply that theories such as general equilibrium theory, which are untestable even in principle, should be regarded with deep suspicion. At the same time, economists have been unduly narrow in testing the falsifiable implications of theories in the sense that this is invariably taken to mean some statistical or econometric test. But history is just as much a test of patterns and trends in economic events as is regression analysis . . . It is high time economists re-examined their long-standing antipathy to induction, to fact-grubbing, to the gathering of data before and not after we sit down to theorise.[20]

Politically, Blaug describes himself as "schizophrenic: rather right-wing on questions of economic policy, such as privatization, deregulation, trade union legislation and the like, but fiercely left-wing on questions of social policy such as welfare payments, unemployment compensation, positive discrimination in favour of women, blacks and gays, the right to abortion, legalization of soft drugs and so forth."[21]

On some topics, Blaug's opinions can show all the consistency of a patchwork quilt. He freely admits in his autobiography that he has changed his mind many times on many subjects. He has even grown skeptical of his beloved David Ricardo, subject of his dissertation, and after whom he named his son: "Over the years I came to identify Ricardo's 'telescopic' tendency to collapse the long run into the short run as if there was no transition period as the abiding vice of ortho-dox economics."[22] Yet he still remains prone to making dogmatic pro-nouncements—perhaps a relic of his "smart alec" youth—and then qualifying or even outright contradicting them. His ambivalence is nowhere more apparent than in his treatment of Henry George.

### Blaug on Henry George in *Economic Theory in Retrospect*

Writers of textbooks on the history of economic thought approach George in two ways: They omit him altogether, as does Jürg Niehans in *A History of Economic Theory*,[23] or William Barber in *A History of Economic Thought*.[24] Or they grant him a few dismissive paragraphs, as does Robert Heilbroner in *The Worldly Philosophers*.[25] In *Economic Theory in Retrospect*, Blaug takes the second approach, according George and related ideas approximately two and a half pages.[26]

Even though Blaug has subsequently somewhat softened his view, these pages deserve examination. Most students of economics, if they encounter George at all, will encounter him here.

Blaug begins with a section on "Land as a factor of production." He cautiously circles his subject poking at it here and there. He equiv-ocates on whether land can be separated from capital, and draws no clear line between the average opinions of the economics profession and his own. In certain passages, he almost seems to accept the old anti-George canard that "land" refers only to agricultural land.[27] In George's scheme, land included water, mining, fishing, and timber rights, road and rail rights-of way, and some patents. George described at length the benefits of urban synergy, reflected in high urban land values. Land today also includes taxi medallions, cable franchises, bank and insurance charters, pollution "rights," and—very important—licenses to use portions of the electromagnetic spectrum in specified territories. Blaug cautiously mentions "spectrum rent" at the end of "Rebel with a Cause," but does not clearly include the spectrum in "land."[28] Blaug altogether misses another key difference between capital and land: society creates and maintains title to land—without which there can be no rent. Capital needs no recorded "metes and bounds." But land title can be created by the stroke of a pen thousands of miles away, as happened when James I chartered the Virginia Company to found the first British North American colony in 1606. Land title can be destroyed at a distance too, as Robert Mugabe has done to the white farmers of Zimbabwe.

Blaug then moves on to a section on "Site Value Taxation."

> Ricardian theory showed that ground rent, being a return to a nonre-producible natural agent, was eminently suitable for taxation. His mentor and disciple, James Mill, was the first to draw the obvious corollary that all future increments in rent from some current base year could be taxed away without serious harm. Ricardo himself was not happy with the pro-posal but it remained an academic question in his lifetime. But with the publication of John Stuart Mill's *Principles* in 1848, a section of which reproduced his father's arguments, and the subsequent formation of the Land Tenure Reform Association under Mill's aegis, the idea caught on. John Stuart Mill proposed totally to exempt present rents and to tax "the future increment of unearned rent" by taxing the capital gains of increases in the price of land. Henry George in *Progress and Poverty* (1879) went a little further and proposed to confiscate all rents in the manner of the physiocrats, a measure that he claimed would abolish poverty and eco-nomic crises, the latter being simply the result of speculation in land values. This would be a "single tax" because he thought that its proceeds would be sufficient to defray the entire expenses of the state. His proposal was widely misunderstood, partly because of his own clumsy exposition, as advocating nationalisation of land. In point of fact, he only proposed to tax pure ground rent, exempting the returns from site improvements. In short, "the single tax" was designed to reduce the price of land as mere space to zero, leaving untouched the rentals of property located on the land; it was intended to put all property on the same basis irrespective of its location.[29]

So far so good. Maybe as a matter of strategy, George should not have written "we must make land common property,"—even though he immediately explained what he meant.

Blaug continues:

> The Marshallian objection to the "single tax" is obvious: all economic agents, not simply land, may earn "rents" in the short run; and even Ricar-

dian differential rents are incentive payments in the long run; encouraging the economical use of fertile and therefore scarcer land. George might have replied that no quasi-rent has either the persistence or the generality of ground rent and Marshall would probably have agreed with that. Furthermore, if it were administratively feasible to distinguish pure economic rent for land as a distance-input from rent for site improvements of all kinds, the Marshallian argument would lose some of its force: the elasticity of supply of space is indeed very low (notice, however, it is not zero because land has depth as well as length and width). What George was after was to destroy land speculation and he should have devoted all his energies to clarifying the distinction between a tax on "site values" and a tax on "betterment." But this aspect of his argument was little developed in *Progress and Poverty*. Instead, George directed all his fire at the suggestion that landlords should be compensated once and for all for the rents that the state would tax away; he realised that this would reduce his proposal to that of taxing merely future increments of the rental values.[30]

George and Marshall held a heated debate before an unruly crowd at Oxford in 1884.[31] Nonetheless, Alfred Marshall still saw land as a distinct factor of production, and still favored taxing land, as Blaug admits elsewhere. And George surely sought more than destroying land speculation. Unfortunately, "land speculation" has become an ill-defined, confusing Georgist buzzword. George focused on the withholding of large tracts of valuable land from its best uses, forcing development and population onto more marginal land. Some holders of such land have indeed bought it in expectation of a large rise— rendered more likely by good political connections.* Other landholders are too rich, or distant, or ignorant, or incapacitated by age or legal tangles to manage properly. George observed what we today would call "land market failure."[32] Once we start to notice it, we find it everywhere: downtown parking lots and crumbling lofts belonging

*President George W. Bush made his fortune as a land speculator. As reported in Nicholas Kristof's column in the *New York Times*, Mr. Bush was able to transform a $600,000 stake into $14 million as part of a consortium that built a stadium for the Texas Rangers in Arlington Texas. "Essentially, Mr. Bush and the owners' group he led bullied and misled the city into raising taxes to build a $200 million stadium that in effect would be handed over to the Rangers. As part of the deal, the city would even confiscate land from private owners so that the Rangers owners could engage in real estate speculation" (7/16/02, op-ed page).

to estates and trusts; abandoned railyards on the shores of the East River in New York City and the shore of San Francisco Bay; or weedy absentee-owned tracts in the middle of prime farmland. As to whether George should have concentrated on distinguishing site value from betterment taxes—again Blaug seems to struggle with the feasibility of separating land from improvements.

Then Blaug turns the blender on high and whirls a virtual gazpacho of objections onto site-value taxation, without justifying or even really explaining them:

> The administrative difficulties of putting a Georgian tax scheme into action are no greater than those involved in distinguishing income and capital under the progressive income tax. Provided there is no deception that such a tax would raise much revenue except in rapidly growing cities, there would seem to be nothing wrong with the principle of site value taxation, that is, the taxation of land values with full or partial exemption of the improvements made on the land. Ultimately, of course, the issue rests on the violability of property rights: the property rights of landowners must be weighed against the stimulus which a Georgian tax would give to improvements of existing sites. Still, if we want to stimulate investment in slum property, there are many easier ways of doing it than that of taxing site values. On the other hand, if it is land speculation and "unearned income" from land that we dislike, a change in the treatment of capital gains under the income tax and a surtax on absentee landlords might be the answer. If all this should be deemed to raise too many administrative difficulties, we might advocate nationalisation of land. We must realise, however, that land speculation performs an economic function: people differ in their expectations of the future economic development of particular locations and the profits of those who have forecast correctly are, of course, matched by the losses of those who have not. If we nationalise land, the community will have to bear the costs of mistaken forecasts; the existence of ghost towns and declining neighbourhoods shows that such mistakes are not uncommon: land values do not always rise everywhere.[33]

If it is no more difficult to distinguish land from capital than to distinguish income from (changes in) capital for income tax purposes, why criticize George for not making the distinction clearer? Next Blaug gets to what will remain his principal objection to site value taxation: it won't raise much revenue—an issue to be addressed at length later. Then he says the real issue is the "violability of property rights," which must be weighed against the economic stimulus of a site value tax. But *any* tax (or subsidy) affects the value of property rights, and imposes either marginal and/or wealth effects on an owner's incentives. Then he says there are many easier ways than site-value taxation to stimulate investment in slum property. What easier ways? Then he leaps to nationalization of land, as an alternative if we want to get rid of speculation. Then he justifies speculation as a means of allocating risks to those more willing to bear them—a function that would be lost if land were nationalized.

Blaug concludes with a condescending sweep:

> Be that as it may, *Progress and Poverty*, a wonderful example of old-style classical economics, was thirty years out of date the day it was published and the idea of confiscating the income of a leading social class was deeply shocking to a generation bred on Victorian pieties. In consequence, the concept of site value taxation was never seriously discussed, and to this day the only examples of it are to be found among local governments in the United States, Australia and New Zealand.[34]

Thirty years out of date! Elsewhere in the same book Blaug himself dates the beginning of the marginal revolution to the 1870s with the publications of Jevons, Walras, and Menger, incorporating the concept of diminishing marginal utility. In 1879, when George published *Progress and Poverty*, John Stuart Mill's *Principles of Political Economy* was the leading economics text, which it remained until supplanted by Alfred Marshall's *Principles of Economics* in the 1890s. Blaug admires Mill, and gives a lengthy and generous treatment to his more radical ideas, the same ideas that George carried to their logical conclusion. Moreover, elsewhere in the same textbook Blaug sharply criticizes the neoclassical revolution. As he tartly sums up: "An unkind critic might say that neoclassical economics indeed achieved greater generality, but only by asking easier questions."[35] With his remark about "confiscating the income," Blaug indicates that after all, he does understand that George was about redistributing wealth, not just curbing speculation. Finally, as to the allegation that "site value taxation was never seriously discussed" —to the contrary, site-value taxation was a central theme during the Progressive Era, a fact Blaug later acknowledges in "Rebel with a Cause."

One hopes that if he publishes a sixth edition of *Economic Theory in Retrospect*, Blaug will treat Henry George more carefully and fairly.

## Blaug on Henry George in "Rebel with a Cause"

In "Henry George: Rebel with a Cause," his 1999 Australian lecture, Blaug at least implicitly retracts many of the objections he lobbed at George in his textbook—except for the killer objection that land makes an inadequate tax base. When I interviewed Blaug in June 2002, I asked him what had changed his views. He replied quite simply that he had read and thought more about George in preparing the lecture.

### 1. Introduction

Blaug acknowledges the historical importance of George: that *Progress and Poverty* was "the greatest economics best-seller of all times," that it was "sufficiently subversive to call forth refutations from all the leading economists of the day," and it was nonetheless influential at least with local governments in the United States, Canada, Australia, New Zealand, and Britain. (Blaug misses a few, like South Africa and Denmark.[36])

### 2. A Little History of Ideas

Blaug reviews Ricardian rent theory and its adoption by James and John Stuart Mill to argue for taxing future increments in land value. He concludes that while Alfred Marshall thought that Ricardian analysis was essentially correct, "increasingly into the twentieth century, mainstream economists followed John Bates Clark and Frank Fetter in abandoning the notion that land is a unique factor of production and hence that there is any need for a special theory of ground rent. . . . this is in fact the basis of all the attacks on Henry George by contemporary economists and certainly the fundamental reason why professional economists increasingly ignored him."[37]

### 3. The Content of Progress and Poverty

Blaug offers overall a reasonably fair and accurate description. He still hesitates over the separation of land from improvements. In characteristic Blaugean overstatement, George "virtually concedes that there are improvements in landed property which in time become indistinguishable from the land itself, a fatal concession for the Georgean programme." (Yet as Blaug told me in 2002, "just because there are hermaphrodites doesn't mean we can't distinguish the sexes.") He comments that George's "all-devouring rent thesis" "is never convincingly demonstrated." Here he seems to conflate two issues: the increase and the absolute importance of rent share in national income. George predicted that, all else being equal, economic growth *increases the share* of rent in national income. So many factors have been so far from equal—including the influence of reformers like George—as to preclude a convincing test of this prediction. However, Blaug also minimizes the absolute *importance* of rent in national income, which is a different issue, about which more below.[38]

### 4. *Criticisms of George*

"Henry George was attacked during his lifetime by just about every leading economist in the USA and by many minor, now forgotten economists and political commentators in both the USA and Britain. . . . At the bottom of much of the criticism was irritation with an amateur who had never studied economics or even attended a university at a time when economics was becoming increasingly professionalized."[39] Blaug reviews five major contemporary objections to George:

1. The Anti-Landlord Thesis: Since unearned surpluses are ubiquitous in a capitalist economy, why single out land and landowners?
2. The Inseparability Thesis: It is impossible to separate the value of land from the value of improvements to it.
3. The Adverse Incidence Thesis: Land taxes would simply be shifted forward in terms of higher prices and higher rents.
4. The Inelasticity Thesis: An exclusive tax on land would be unresponsive to the changing requirements of public revenue.
5. The Moral Hazard Thesis: A land tax would nullify the individual ownership of land and have negative incentive effects.

Blaug demolishes 1: "Land as pure territory is non-reproducible and almost perfectly inelastic in supply; hence the income of landowners resulting from the relative scarcity of land is an unearned income par excellence. This is pure Ricardo and if wrong makes nonsense of not just George's single tax, but also the Ricardian theory of rent."[40] He also demolishes 5 as "grossly unfair to George . . . *Progress and Poverty* comes back time and time again to the adverse efficiency effects of excise duties sales taxes and income taxes . . . and the entire weight of his case for a tax on pure ground rents is that it would cause no dead-weight loss."[41]

Blaug equivocates on 2, the Inseparability Thesis, "probably the most popular of all objections against LVT and a particular hobby-horse of Richard Ely, America's leading land economist . . . George spent pages rebutting this thesis in *Progress and Poverty*, noting that it must at least be possible in practice to tax land values independently of taxing betterment because it was done habitually in the property taxes of many American States . . . The fact that a tax has been levied does not demonstrate that a valuation problem has been solved and so, despite the history of LVT around the world, the Inseparability Thesis remains troublesome."[42] Ely's student and colleague, statistician Willford I. King, wrote his Ph.D. dissertation in 1914 on *The Valuation of Urban Realty for Purposes of Taxation*, an excellent how-to manual for assessors, providing separate statistical techniques for valuing buildings and land.[43] Yet in 1924, in a long sarcastic attack on a leading Georgist economist, Harry Gunnison Brown, King claims the impossibility of separating land from improvements.[44]

Blaug regards 3, the Adverse Incidence Thesis, as a "corollary of the Inseparability Thesis: if ground rent is indistinguishable from rent for betterment, then of course a tax on total contractual rent does not fall on landlords but is passed on to consumers. But the idea that a tax on an input in inelastic supply cannot be shifted forward is an elementary theorem in public finance, found in every modern textbook, which only brings us back to the basic question whether unimproved land is such an input and indeed whether there is such a thing as unimproved land—the Inseparability Thesis all over again. Another way of stating the Inseparability Thesis is to deny that land is a factor of production distinct from capital. As we shall see, the melding together of land and capital that came increasingly to characterize American mainstream economics at the turn of the century was perhaps the central cause of the declining attraction of the Georgist programme."[45]

It is 4, the Inelasticity Thesis, "the claim that an exclusive tax on land would be unresponsive to the changing requirements of public revenue, sometimes raising too much and sometimes too little to finance government expenditures," that gives Blaug the most difficulty. He does defend George from E. R. A. Seligman's charge that a land tax, by reducing land values, would destroy its own base. But then he concludes, as elsewhere, that land is an inadequate tax base (see below).

### 5. A Final Appraisal

Blaug repeats his assertion that land is not an adequate tax base, lists some endorsements of LVT by major economists, and then concludes:

> Henry George triumphed in the end despite himself: the growth of land rentals in a capitalist economy never was a convincing explanation of the persistence of poverty despite growing affluence and it became an even less convincing explanation as manufacturing expanded and agriculture shrank. Land speculation never was the root cause of business fluctuations and LVT would dampen but never eliminate periodic booms and slumps; the revenue that LVT, fully and properly applied, was capable of raising may at one time have been sufficient for the expenses of government but ever since 1930 the very notion of LVT as a single tax has seemed almost laughable. But none of this in any way detracts from LVT as one tax among many whose yield ought to be maximized because of its unique features. Perhaps for us in 1999, the perfect Georgist rent is "spectrum rent," the imputed scarcity value of a broadcast license. Since the electromagnetic spectrum exists in the state of nature and is of course non reproducible and fixed in supply, the spectrum space leased to a licensee earns a spectrum rent, which surely ought to be taxed away to subsidize public broadcasting. This is an argument which comes naturally to anyone brought up on Georgist doctrines.[46]

### The Inadequacy of Land as a Tax Base: A Challenge to Blaug

Throughout his writings, Blaug maintains one consistent criticism of George: rent forms an ever declining part of national income, making land ever less adequate as a tax base.

*Arguments from Willford I. King*

In his 1996 review of the three Georgist Paradigm books, Blaug claims that "the Georgist assertion that the yield of a single tax on land rentals would suffice to defray all the expenses of government, which was absolutely true for its day and age, was no longer even half-true by 1920."[47]

In the section on criticism of Henry George in "Rebel with a Cause," he writes:

> In any case, Wilford [sic] King's National Bureau study of *The Wealth and Income of the People of the United States* (1915) showed that a confiscatory tax on ground rent would have been insufficient to defray the expenses of government as early as 1910 and after the growth of government expenditure in World War I it was clear to everyone that the LVT could not be the only tax (ibid: 122, 234). Then and there, the idea of a truly "single tax" died a sudden death.[48]

When I interviewed him in June 2002, I asked Blaug why he rested his primary argument on the 1915 work of Willford I. King?[49] As noted above, King (1880–1962) was a student of Richard T. Ely at Wisconsin and, like Ely, a venomous critic of George's ideas. Like some other American economists of his era, perhaps he let his opinion of George color his work. Blaug replied that in the early twentieth century, King was *the* authority on national income. Everyone cited him. Afterward, the matter appeared settled.

Although its publication actually predated the 1920 founding of the National Bureau of Economic Research (NBER), King's *The Wealth and Income of the People of the United States* did indeed set the pattern for national income accounting. King joined the staff of the New York City-based NBER at the founding, leaving in 1929 to become professor at New York University. Politically and economically arch-conservative, an ardent Malthusian and opponent of immigration, King stood poles apart from George.[50] Nonetheless, King's *Wealth and Income* offers but weak support to Blaug's assertions. To begin with, King's data is sketchy and his methods questionable. Using Census data from 1850 through 1910 and other sources, King assembled *Wealth and Income* in only a year and a half. It is a small book, 278 pages; King's preface states it is "intended to give an impressionistic picture of the subject."[51] Three reviewers praised the book's ambition, while criticizing inconsistencies, failure to explain methods or sources of numbers, implausible assumptions in indexing, and King's anti-immigrant diatribes.[52]

King's chapter on "The Distribution of the National Income Among the Factors of Production" is especially problematic. He starts with *four* factors of production: land, capital, labor, and the entrepreneur, which earn rent, interest, wages, and profits.[53] He calculates rent crudely by taking 4 percent of his estimated land value, for which he gives no source.[54] Since profits are a mixture of rent, wages, and interest, by including profits he necessarily underestimates rent. He puts his land rent estimate into a table with numbers for wages, interest, and profits, all three of which dwarf rent. Below are figures from King's Tables XXX and XXV, Columns A–G. I have added column H, Rent minus Government Expenditures.

| A | B | C | D | E | F | G | H |
|---|---|---|---|---|---|---|---|
| Census | | | | | | | Rent – |
| Year | Total | Wages | Interest | Rent | Profits | Government | Gov't |
| 1850 | 2213.8 | 792.8 | 276.5 | 170.6 | 973.9 | 100.3 | 70.3 |
| 1860 | 3635.6 | 1351.1 | 532.6 | 321.2 | 1430.7 | 161.7 | 159.5 |
| 1870 | 6720.1 | 3269.5 | 864.5 | 463.2 | 2122.9 | 436.6 | 26.6 |
| 1880 | 7390.7 | 3803.6 | 1373.2 | 642.3 | 1571.6 | 458.3 | 184.0 |
| 1890 | 12081.6 | 6461.8 | 1738.9 | 913.8 | 2967.1 | 784.9 | 128.9 |
| 1900 | 17964.5 | 8490.7 | 2695.7 | 1396.0 | 5382.1 | 1469.0 | −73.0 |
| 1910 | 30529.5 | 14303.6 | 5143.9 | 2673.9 | 8408.1 | 2591.8 | 82.1 |

Amounts in Millions of Dollars
Columns A–F are copied from Table XXX[55]
Column G, Government Expenditures, comes from Table XV[56]
Column H is Column E, Rent, minus Column G, Government

Here is Blaug's evidence that land rent was "insufficient to defray the expenses of government as early as 1910." Note that the table shows insufficient land rent only in 1900. King interprets his statistics more cautiously than Blaug:

> The single taxer has told us that all the improvements of industry result only in the enrichment of the landlord. A glance at Table XXX shows us how absurd this statement is. The value of our products has increased since 1850 to the extent of some twenty eight billions of dollars while rent has gained less than three billions. Evidently it has captured but a very meager part of the new production. In fact, it has only tended to keep its constant share of the output, the percentage being the same in 1860 as in 1910. As a matter of fact, the indications are that rent plays a much less important role in distribution than the followers of Henry George would have us believe. It is interesting, in this connection, to note the relative size of the rent item and the expenses of government. Reference to Tables XXV and XXX shows us that, before the Civil War, the rent bill was large enough to pay all governmental charges nearly twice over. In 1910, however, the rent would have been barely sufficient to pay off the various governmental budgets as at present constituted and, with the growing concentration of activities in the hands of government, it appears that rent will soon be a quantity far too small to meet the required charges. With increasing pressure on our natural resources, however, it is probable that the percentage of the total income paid for rent will gradually increase and, since this is true, the lag behind the growing governmental expenses will be considerably less than would otherwise be the case.[57]

King's urge to discredit Henry George seems to collide with his fear that the population bomb threatens an explosion of Ricardian rents! And ten years later, when King hurls his armload of grenades at Harry Gunnison Brown, he fails to claim that land is an inadequate tax base! Did King not quite believe his own arguments?

### Arguments from Modern Georgists

Blaug also cites modern Georgists in support of his position. In his "Rebel with a Cause" article he writes:

> Georgism was effectively killed off by the dramatic fall in rental shares in both the USA and the UK from something like 15 per cent in the 1870s to 6 per cent in the 1960s (Andelson 1979: 88). Even when we include the imputed rent of owner-occupiers and allow for the stimulating effect of the withdrawal of non-land taxes, we still get no higher than 20 per cent of national income in modern times (Tideman 1994: 18, Hudson et al 1995: 150–51). In short, whatever the other merits of LVT, the "all-devouring rent thesis" is now dead as a doornail.[58]

Unfortunately, Blaug's sources do not support these assertions. The source in Andelson is a table in a chapter by Fred Harrison, refuting some British critics of George. As Harrison carefully notes, the table shows shares of ordinary rent, that is payments by tenants to landlords, not economic rent.[59] The source in Tideman is another article by Harrison, which in turn cites research by Gaffney estimating national income rent share at around 40 percent, not 20 percent.[60] The source in Hudson et al. is a section of a chapter by Feder explaining why the national income accounts greatly understate rent. As she points out, the accounts are constructed from Census and tax data, that is, data on individuals and corporations. Allocation of this estimated income to factors of production is necessarily somewhat arbitrary. In practice, imputed rents are omitted, and actual rents are counted as business profits or capital gains, if they are counted at all. Rents from other forms of "land" like the broadcast spectrum do not enter the picture.[61]

Andelson, the editor of this volume, did assume a limited tax potential of land at the time of the first edition in 1979 (when the Cold War was still going on). He wrote: "While the demands of national security make it today utopian to suppose that land rent could meet the total revenue requirements of government, let alone beget a surplus, its appropriation in taxes would substantially lessen the necessity for revenue from other sources . . ."[62] Some Libertarian-leaning Georgists consider limited tax potential a virtue, as a check on the size of government. However other modern Georgists, including Gaffney, Harrison, Tideman, Feder, and Hudson, argue that land, broadly conceived of course, offers an ample tax base—one that would in fact grow if all taxes were shifted to it!

### *Evidence on the Adequacy of Land as a Tax Base*

Blaug's Popperian methodology considers a theory valid only when it can be stated in a form subject to corroboration. Blaug also repeatedly emphasizes the importance of getting the data rather than building abstract models. So, how strong are the arguments or the data that seem to disprove the adequacy of land as a tax base? And how strong are the arguments and data on the other side?

Corrected for biases and omissions, land values loom large. In a 1970 article on "The Adequacy of Land as a Tax Base"[63] Mason Gaffney reviews at length the many reasons why assessed or reported land values vastly understate actual values. Due to lack of resources, incompetence, or political considerations, assessors typically lag many years or decades behind the market. Moreover, they tend to assign too large a portion of combined value to improvements—which are depreciable for income tax purposes. Often they omit underground mineral resources altogether, such as coal in Appalachia. Meanwhile, resource-holding corporations such as oil or steel companies carry reserves at acquisition costs generations ago. Broadcast corporations may have paid next to nothing for licenses now worth billions. And so forth. Gaffney suggests corrections based on market data. He concludes that, "Land values today equal or exceed building values in the United States."[64]

Moreover, there is what Gaffney has called the "ATCOR concept . . . 'All Taxes Come Out of Rent.' "[65] Assuming that buyers and sellers of land use discounted cash flow—as taught in every business school around the world—then at the micro level, market values of land are already *net* of existing taxes and subsidies. For example, consider the would-be purchaser of a broadcast license. She subtracts from projected operating revenues her estimated corporate income tax, payroll taxes, and other taxes and fees, runs a discounted cash flow analysis, and decides how much she can afford to pay for the license. The seller makes the same sort of computation. If they reach a deal, that is the market value of the license. Ditto for the builder of a shopping center, who must decide how much he is willing to pay for the land. Now suppose a business school professor approaches the broadcaster or builder and says, "Assume you could pay the exact amount of your projected taxes as a fixed lump sum each year. How much would you be willing to pay for the broadcast license or the land parcel?" The broadcaster and builder would quickly compute their increased business with a lump-sum instead of variable tax, and realize they would pay more for the license or land. How much more? The capitalized value of the dead-weight loss. (This is presumably what Blaug means in the quotation above by "the stimulating effect of the withdrawal of non-land taxes.")

Considering only the micro level, how can we claim that a land tax couldn't support modern government—when it apparently already does so—leaving plenty of land value to spare? Of course, the fact that something seems to happen in practice doesn't necessarily make it right in theory. Blaug cannot quite accept the theoretical possibility of separating land from improvements, even recognizing that appraisers do it every day. Landowners may behave as if taxes were already capitalized, but that doesn't make it so.

If we switch taxes to land at the micro or local level, all else remains equal. At the macro, regional, or national level, all else does not remain equal. Suppose that we shift all existing taxes in a large economy to land, keeping collections the same for each jurisdiction. What will happen? Will land remain an adequate tax base?

1. Marginal effects. At the macro level, untaxing labor and capital will raise wages and interest rates, cutting into rents. As a double whammy, land value being capitalized rent, the increase in interest rates will lower land values. At the micro level a shift of taxes to land unambiguously increases land values; at the macro level, the shift may raise or lower land values, and will surely affect different locations differently. Note that rent may still increase, due to elimination of dead weight loss, while land value decreases due to higher interest rates.

2. Land market effects. Georgists emphasize that land taxes counteract land market failure, pressuring owners to put land to its "highest and best use." That should encourage more development of centrally-located urban land, and more frequent cutting of flat, accessible timber land—drawing development away from the urban fringe, and lumbering off steep mountain slopes. This land market effect suggests that central land values will increase and peripheral values will decrease—increasing the tax base of central jurisdictions at the expense of the base of peripheral jurisdictions. Complicating the picture, demand for services will rise in more central areas and fall in more peripheral areas. But as Georgists emphasize, denser areas can be served at lower per capita costs, adding to the benefits of taxing land only.

3. Distributive effects. Ownership of wealth including land—direct and indirect through corporate shares—is highly concentrated, orders

of magnitude more concentrated than receipt of income. For example according to the *Current Population Reports* of the U.S. Census, in 1997 the top 1 percent of income receivers took in 16.6 percent of income; while in 1998 the top 1 percent of wealth holders owned 38.1 percent of net worth and 47.3 percent of financial wealth. The top 20 percent received 56.2 percent of income, and held 83.4 percent of net worth, and 90.9 percent of financial wealth.[66] Ownership of land is even more concentrated than ownership of wealth.[67] Consequently, if existing taxes all shift to land, assuming good administration, the resulting system of taxes becomes both highly progressive and very difficult to evade—more progressive overall than the present mix of sales, income, corporate, and general property taxes. The system will collect the same taxes from on average deeper pockets. That in itself suggests, but does not prove, that the base will remain adequate.

Georgist economists must build models incorporating these effects. They should test the models to see if under any reasonable assumptions a shift of current taxes to land could absorb all rents, collapsing land values and paralyzing the economy. The obverse challenge falls to economists who assume land cannot support even current levels of taxation: try to build a bullet-proof testable model in which land rents cannot support current levels of taxation.

## Conclusion

When I interviewed Mark Blaug in Leiden, I told him that a group of economists on the board of the Robert Schalkenbach Foundation were seeking ways to revive Georgist scholarship. What could he advise? "Throw money at it!" he replied, observing how admirers of Austrian economics had successfully raised large sums for the Ludwig von Mises Institute.* More seriously, he observed that "George is threatening to the powers that be," making it "extremely tempting to put him down." He added, "Economists don't want to waste time looking at threatening ideas."

But then what about Marx? Economists still study Marx. Blaug's textbook, *Economic Theory in Retrospect*, includes a whole chapter, some

*Coincidentally, the Mises Institute includes a Willford I. King Collection.

seventy pages, on Marxian economics. "George is not of Marx's intellectual stature," he replied, "even though Marx is fundamentally wrong." George, like Marx (despite the latter's Ph.D.) was essentially self-taught—an omnivorous reader in every field. Like Marx, he developed not only a theory of economics, but a theory of history, philosophy, and ethics. To judge from his textbook, Blaug admires the grandeur of Marx's vision, while faulting errors, inconsistencies, and internal contradictions in Marx's work. If Blaug were more familiar with George he might recognize a similar grandeur of vision, within a much more consistent system.

Eventually, Blaug brought up a final obstacle to reviving Georgist scholarship: "There's an aura of quackiness about George. It is a reputation that is extremely difficult to reverse." Of course George's opponents worked overtime to create that aura of quackiness. Willford King pronounces "that the single taxers are not merely advocates of an economic policy but that they are a religious cult and that their intense devotion to their creed has little connection with logic or reasoning."[68]

And who is quackier, Marx or George? In his autobiography Blaug writes, "Of course, the more economics I learned, the less Marxian economics I believed in. I could soon see that Marx's grasp of the economic problems of running a socialist society was ludicrous: he really thought it would present no more than an accounting problem rather like a corner grocery store writ large."[69] George on the other hand developed a simple, eminently practical solution: Increase the rates on one familiar, widely-used tax; eliminate all other taxes. In the late nineteenth and early twentieth centuries, democratic societies around the world implemented this solution to varying degrees, not by violence but by popular vote.

Clearly, while he is friendly to Henry George, and has abandoned many of his earlier criticisms, Blaug still does not take him very seriously. He does not bother to practice the method he preaches, that is, to express George's theories clearly in a form that can be tested, and to muster the evidence carefully.

Will Blaug reconsider? He has changed his mind many times in the past, and has had the courage to admit it. He has stood up to petty tyrants, from dogmatic Communists, through McCarthyites to

*American Journal of Economics and Sociology*

third-world dictators. His political views—a belief in markets combined with a conviction that society must support its less fortunate members—coincide with the views of the more liberal end of the Georgist spectrum. He rejects the dead ends and mathematical games that characterize much of neoclassical economics today. He combines a vast knowledge of history of economic thought with years of practical experience in development and educational economics. He could provide a tremendous resource to new scholarship exploring George's ideas.

## Notes

1. Mark Blaug, "Not Only an Economist: Autobiographical Reflections of a Historian of Economic Thought," *Recent Essays by Mark Blaug* (Cheltenham, UK; Brookfield, US: Edward Elgar, 1997), p. 3.

2. Mark Blaug, "Review of Robert V. Andelson, ed., *Critics of Henry George, A Centenary Appraisal of Their Strictures on Progress and Poverty*, *Economica*, 47, (Nov. 1980): 471–91.

3. Mark Blaug, ed., *Henry George* (Cheltenham, UK; Brookfield, VT: Edward Elgar, 1992).

4. Mark Blaug, "Review of the Georgist Paradigm Series: *The Corruption of Economics* by Mason Gaffney and Fred Harrison; *A Philosophy for a Fair Society*, by Michael Hudson, G. J. Miller and Kris Feder; and *Land and Taxation*, by Nicolaus Tideman, ed." *Economic Journal*, Vol. 106, Issue 436 (May, 1995): 745–46.

5. Mark Blaug, "Henry George: Rebel with a Cause" *European Journal of the History of Economic Thought*, Vol. 7, No. 2 (Summer 2000): 270–88. This article will be referred to as "Rebel."

6. Blaug "Not Only an Economist," p. 19.

7. Ibid., p. 4.

8. Ibid., p. 5.

9. Ibid., p. 8.

10. Mark Blaug, *Ricardian Economics: A Historical Study* (New Haven: Yale University Press, 1958, 1964).

11. Mark Blaug, *Economic Theory in Retrospect* (1st ed., 1962, 5th ed., 1996; Cambridge, UK: Cambridge University Press, 1996). The fifth edition of this book will be referred to as *Retrospect*.

12. Blaug "Not Only an Economist," p. 14.

13. Ibid., p. 16.

14. Ibid., p. 12.

15. Mark Blaug, "No History of Ideas, Please, We're Economists," *Journal of Economic Perspectives*, Vol. 15, No. 1 (Winter 2001): 145–65.

16. Mark Blaug, *The Methodology of Economics, or How Economists Explain* (New York: Cambridge University Press, 1980).

17. Blaug "Not Only an Economist," p. 19.

18. Ibid., p. 18.

19. Mark Blaug, "Ugly Currents in Modern Economics," *Policy Options* (Montreal, Canada, Institute for Research on Public Policy, http://www.irpp.org, September 1997), p. 3.

20. Ibid., pp. 7–8.

21. Blaug "Not Only an Economist," p. 9.

22. Ibid., p. 24.

23. Jürg Niehans, *A History of Economic Theory* (Baltimore and London: The Johns Hopkins University Press, 1990).

24. William Barber, *A History of Economic Thought* (London and New York: Penguin Books, 1967, 1991). Barber does however accord George an endnote to a discussion of John Bates Clark: "his dissatisfaction with a popular view that wage levels (and the distribution of income generally) were determined primarily by the real income available to labourers on rent-free land stimulated him to produce an alternative analysis of income distribution" (p. 205). The endnote adds: "The view against which Clark was reacting had many notable classical features, though he was responding specifically to doctrines propagated by Henry George, the advocate of a single-tax on land" (p. 214).

25. Robert Heilbroner, *The Worldly Philosophers* (New York, Simon & Schuster, Inc, 6th ed., 1986).

26. Blaug, *Retrospect*, pp. 81–83.

27. Ibid., pp. 81–82.

28. Blaug, "Rebel," p. 285.

29. Blaug, *Retrospect*, p. 82.

30. Ibid., pp. 82–83.

31. George J. Stigler, "Alfred Marshall's Lectures on Progress and Poverty," *Journal of Law and Economics*, XII (1), (April 1969): 181–226.

32. Mason Gaffney, *Land Speculation as an Obstacle to Ideal Allocation of Land*, 1956. Ph.D. dissertation (Berkeley, CA, University of California). Gaffney gives a full-length treatment of the confusion of land speculation with land market failure.

33. Blaug, *Retrospect*, p. 83.

34. Ibid., p. 83.

35. Ibid., p. 282.

36. Blaug, "Rebel," p. 270.

37. Ibid., p. 274.

38. Ibid., pp. 277–79.

39. Ibid., p. 279.

40. Ibid., p. 280.

41. Ibid., p. 282.

42. Ibid., p. 280.

43. Willford I. King, *The Valuation of Urban Realty for Purposes of Taxation* (Madison, WI: Bulletin of the University of Wisconsin, No. 689, 1914).

44. Willford I. King, "The Single-Tax Complex Analyzed," *Journal of Political Economy* (Vol. 32, Issue 5, Oct., 1924): 604–12.

45. Blaug, "Rebel," p. 281.

46. Ibid., pp. 284–85.

47. Blaug, "Review of Georgist Paradigm," p. 746.

48. Blaug, "Rebel," p. 281.

49. Willford I. King, *The Wealth and Income of the People of the United States* (New York and London: The Macmillan Company, 1915). Henceforth referred to as *Wealth and Income*.

50. Willford I. King, *The Keys to Prosperity* (New York: Constitution and Free Enterprise Foundation, 1948). See Martin Bronfenbrenner's hilarious review in *Journal of Political Economy*, 56:6 (December 1948): 539–40.

51. King, *Wealth and Income*, p. ix.

52. C. K. Hobson, "Review of *Wealth and Income*," *Economic Journal*, Vol. 26, Issue 102 (Jun., 1916): 252–54. Hobson quotes with evident distaste one of King's anti-immigrant passages to the effect that immigrants' parents were "incompetent, ignorant, or unwilling to restrain their animal passions" (p. 254). G. P. Watkins, "Review of *Wealth and Income*," *American Economic Review*, Vol. 6, Issue 2 (June, 1916): 441–43. After pointing out a number of errors and contradictions, Watkins concludes, "the author of the book under review is evidently fair minded and he has done important work in bringing together a large and varied mass of statistics. But his faculty of statistical analysis does not meet the requirements of his task, or else he did not take time enough for the necessary critical reconsideration of his data and results." Allyn A. Young, review of *Wealth and Income* and a parallel book by Scott Nearing, *Quarterly Journal of Economics*, Vol. 30, Issue 3 (May, 1916): 575–87. Young, who would later be on King's Board of Directors at the NBER, is a little kinder to King. He complains about various errors, as well as "a philippic against unrestricted immigration," but nonetheless concludes "Dr. King is somewhat uncritical of the quality of his sources, and he sometimes pushes his statistical adventures a little too far into the wilderness. But he has made a large and important contribution to economic statistics."

53. King, *Wealth and Income*, pp. 154–55.

54. Ibid., pp. 156–57.

55. Ibid., p. 158.

56. Ibid., p. 143.

57. Ibid., pp. 161–62.

58. Blaug, "Rebel," p. 283.

59. Fred Harrison, "Long and Wrightson: Conservative Critics of George's

Wage Theory," 72–94 in Robert V. Andelson, ed., *Critics of Henry George: A Centenary Appraisal of Their Strictures on Progress and Poverty* (Rutherford, Madison, Teaneck, New Jersey, Fairleigh Dickinson University Press, 1979).

60. Fred Harrison, "Rent-ability" in *Land and Taxation*, Nicolaus Tideman, ed. (London: Shepheard-Walwyn, 1994), p. 18.

61. Kris Feder, "Public Finance and the Co-operative Society" in *A Philosophy for a Fair Society*, by Michael Hudson, G. J. Miller, and Kris Feder, (London: Shepheard-Walwyn, 1994), pp. 150–51.

62. Robert V. Andelson, "Neo-Georgism" in Robert V. Andelson, ed., *Critics of Henry George*, p. 383. Andelson cites Willford King correctly at pages 160–62, to the effect that land rent was clearly quite adequate for government in George's day. Blaug's page citations to King, 122 and 234, seem to be erroneous.

63. Mason Gaffney, "Adequacy of Land as a Tax Base," in *The Assessment of Land Value*, Daniel M. Holland, ed. (Madison, WI: Committee on Taxation Resources and Economic Development, University of Wisconsin Press, 1970), pp. 157–212.

64. Ibid., p. 207.

65. Mason Gaffney, "The Philosophy of Public Finance," in *The Losses of Nations: Deadweight Politics versus Public Rent Dividends*, Fred Harrison, ed. (London: Othila Press, 1998), p. 188.

66. Edward N. Wolff, "Recent Trends in Wealth Ownership, 1983–1998," Working Paper No. 300 (Annandale-on-Hudson, New York, Jerome Levy Economics Institute, http://www.levy.org, April 2000), Table 2.

67. I deal at length with concentration of land ownership as a consequence of capital market failure in my dissertation, *Consequences and Causes of Unequal Distribution of Wealth* (Ann Arbor, MI, and London: University Microfilms International, 1984). Essentially, larger corporations and richer individuals experience a lower internal discount rate, giving them a comparative advantage in holding more durable assets—land, which appreciates, as opposed to capital improvements, which depreciate.

68. Willford I. King, "The Single-Tax Complex Analyzed," *Journal of Political Economy* (Vol. 32, Issue 5, Oct., 1924): 612.

69. Blaug "Not Only an Economist," p. 6.

# PART V

# Conclusions

# 35
# Neo-Georgism

## By ROBERT V. ANDELSON

In order to reflect developments in my thinking since the first version of this chapter twenty five years ago, I have taken the liberty of incorporating into it substantial passages from my introduction to the third edition of *Land-Value Taxation Around the World* (2000), as well as some completely new material prepared expressly for this new edition.

### Henry George and His Critics: Where Do They Stand Today?

If Henry George had created a system capable of withstanding a century of criticism in all its details, he would have been *sui generis* among social scientists and philosophers alike—not a mortal theorist but a veritable god. Contrary to what some people mistakenly believe, Georgism is not a cult. It may inspire deep loyalty and fervor, yet it maintains no establishment for the determination or preservation of orthodoxy, and many of its most ardent adherents are quick to point out their disagreements with the master. To be a Georgist in the larger sense does not mean subscribing to the notion that everything Henry George penned must be accepted as holy writ, or that no aspect of his system is open to question. To be a Georgist in this sense is just to believe that, in the main, on the most vital points, more than any other single social ethicist or political economist, George had it right. To recognize that some of his ideas are flawed does not destroy his stature as a thinker of the first magnitude whose economic methodology was, in fact, far more informed and sophisticated than is generally appreciated, and whose prescription for reform contains basic features that have enduring relevance.

Possibly George misconceived the problem, and was mistaken in assuming that, absent his prescription, poverty necessarily increases

American Journal of Economics and Sociology, Vol. 63, No. 2 (April, 2004).
© 2004 American Journal of Economics and Sociology, Inc.

with industrial advance.* At least, so it might appear. Yet when we look behind appearances, we may discover that the expedients whereby this grim outcome has been forestalled give rise to ultimate consequences still more grim, consequences now presaged by inflation and ever-mounting public debt. We may discover, in other words, that we have been living in a fool's paradise, that George was a better prophet than we realized, and that welfare spending, monetary tinkering, and union pressure have purchased temporary respite from the process he descried at the eventual price of a total and possibly irreversible collapse. This is, of course, a long-run augury; those who live only for the immediate present will dismiss it with Lord Keynes's flippant quip that "in the long run we are all dead."

Which is not to say that George's "all-devouring rent thesis" (to use Professor Cord's apt phrase) should be accepted unreservedly. One may nevertheless contend that land rent is a highly important economic factor and that George performed a real service in calling attention to this truth, however extreme his inferences from it may have been. The role of land rent in the United States, even if overemphasized by George, is yet far from inconsiderable; in most other countries (where land monopoly is more acute) it must be still greater by no small degree.

For the most part, George's errors are, as in the case of his "all-devouring rent thesis," errors merely of exaggeration. For example, descanting upon the growth of morality to be anticipated from the adoption of his proposal, he is not content merely to predict a marked diminution in crime and vice that stem from the brutalizing effects of poverty, but pictures a veritable Peaceable Kingdom in which greed has virtually disappeared along with the need for judges, police, and lawyers, and in which liberated human energies are spurred by pure and noble promptings to ever more exalted heights of creativity.[1] Alas!

---

*The reader should bear in mind that this assumption had to do with the proportion received by labor as its share of the product. In certain of his less flamboyant passages, George was careful to disclaim the notion that wages are universally diminished as an absolute quantity by industrial progress. (*Progress and Poverty*, 75th Anniversary Ed. [New York: Robert Schalkenbach Foundation, 1954], pp. 216, 233 f.). Because of his many paragraphs that fail to specify the distinction between proportion and amount, this disclaimer is apt to be overlooked.

There is in human nature an intractable perverseness, which George's evangelical parents called "original sin" and that no social rearrangement can dispel. Material security and equality of opportunity, however desirable, will not usher in a moral paradise. Well-fed, well-housed, well-educated Sweden, with its disturbing incidence of alcoholism, suicide, and juvenile delinquency, may be cited as a case in point.

In keeping with the classical tradition, George insisted upon interpreting land rent as a monopoly price. For this he has been reproved by various critics from Marshall to Oser, who correctly observe (in Hébert's paraphrase) that "as long as land has alternative uses and many owners it comes to be supplied under conditions approaching competition." Again, however, George's error was essentially one merely of exaggeration. In the first place, land ownership in much of the world, including many parts of the United States (e.g., Orange County, California, where the Irvine Estate holds approximately 20 percent of the land, and is a major factor in keeping up prices in the small areas it develops and sells), is sufficiently concentrated that monopoly, or, at any rate, oligarchy, actually does obtain. In the second place, the fact that the supply of land is inelastic as respects location means that even where land ownership is diffuse, land rent still involves a *monopolistic element* not characteristic of the price of capital goods (except for such economically insignificant items as antiques and works by famous artists). For although land may have alternative uses, and in that regard not be perfectly inelastic as to supply, its inherent inelasticity of location gives the owner a built-in advantage.

> It is not the intention to suggest that the buyer or renter of land space has no alternative. He may use a smaller piece of land more intensively instead of a larger piece less intensively. Thus, he may put a twenty-story building on a small area instead of putting a ten-story building on a larger area. He may choose a poorer site instead of a better one. But the buyer or renter of capital has alternatives of these kinds and has *in addition* the alternative of becoming himself a producer of the sort of capital wanted.[2]

On this account, and for other reasons more ethical than economic, I am satisfied that there is a broad sense in which it is legitimate to speak of land rent as a monopoly price, even though, from a narrow, technical standpoint the phrase may be inaccurate.

It could, in addition, be charged that George exaggerated the revenue-generating adequacy of his proposal. But this would hardly be fair. Even Willford I. King, who otherwise denigrated land rent as a significant share of national income, demonstrated that the land-rent fund would have been large enough before the Civil War to pay for all government expenses nearly twice over, and that it continued to be at least sufficient until 1915.[3] Steven Cord thinks that it could probably have been adequate until the 1930s.[4] During George's lifetime there would doubtless have been an ample surplus available for communal amenities or for distribution on a per capita basis, especially when one considers the savings to be looked for from his reform in reduced need for public assistance and government bureaucracy. This is one reason why his expectation that his remedy would "extirpate" involuntary poverty should be regarded as only mildly extravagant. Other reasons are, of course, the stimulus to productivity and the tendency toward equalization of opportunity that his reform might reasonably be anticipated—on the basis of both theoretical deduction and partial experiment—to engender. While environmental considerations and the demands of national security make it today perhaps utopian to suppose that land rent could meet the total revenue requirements of government, let alone beget a surplus, its appropriation in taxes would substantially lessen the necessity for revenue from other sources, and would materially help to ameliorate involuntary poverty even if it did not wholly justify George's faith by extirpating it.

Closely related to the inadequacy argument is the objection that a single tax on land values (or on anything else if the full amount were taken) would be inflexible, incapable of adjusting to changing conditions. But Charles F. Collier points out that this objection is valid only with respect to the *percentage* of the tax rate. The *amount* of the yield would vary in response to the business cycle.[5] Collier's rejoinder would not be employed by a strict Georgist, for George held that under the single tax the primary cause of the business cycle would be dispelled. Instead, the strict disciple would rely upon the claim, cited by George Raymond Geiger,[6] that in a fundamental sense a sole tax on land is highly flexible since it correlates directly with the progress and demands of any taxpaying and tax-requiring community—a point made by George in *Progress and Poverty*[7] and more particularly in his *Open Letter to Pope Leo XIII*[8] and in "Thy Kingdom Come," his Glasgow speech of 1889.[9] Whether it would be sufficient to satisfy extraordinary demands such as those of national defense in today's world is, of course, quite another story.

The inflexibility, such as it is, of a sole land-value tax, has been accounted a merit by some Georgists (and even some non-Georgists[10]), as constituting a check upon the aggrandizement of government. Private individuals are expected to live within their proper means; why should not governments do the same? When George envisaged public baths, dancing halls, shooting galleries, and the like,[11] he was merely speculating as to the ways in which a surplus rightfully belonging to the public might be spent, not advocating that such indulgences be funded through coercive exaction. Although present conditions make the question of the use of a surplus academic, per capita apportionment in the form of dividends to be used according to private choice would seem to be more consonant with his essential individualism.

Collier asserts that the benefits from a single tax on land values could be only temporary, since with the rise of population, settlement would extend to (and probably beyond) the point that had been the margin of production prior to the adoption of the tax. "Quite simply, the remedy would work once and only once in any society because it relied in a special way on ending speculation in land. That speculation can be ended once and only once."[12] Granting continuous population growth (or growth in productive activity and hence land use), his point about the extension of the margin is well taken, and is one that George, to my knowledge, did not anticipate. But his analysis disregards four important considerations. To begin with, there is nothing inevitable about population increase; the population of France has been stable ever since the Great Revolution, long before the advent of modern birth control techniques. Second, given the population increase assumed by Collier (or enhanced productive exploitation), the margin would be pushed *much further* downward and outward were it not for the halting by the tax of speculation.

Third, in a Georgist economy the extension of the margin is likely to be postponed by the reduction, stemming from heightened productive efficiency, of the actual acreage used. Finally, Collier overlooks a formidable advantage that would continue to accrue regardless of the location of the margin—namely, the diversion of land rent to the public with the accompanying lifting of the burden of taxation from wages and interest.

George's arguments on the population question suffer from such excesses as his astonishing assertion that "the earth could maintain a thousand billions of people as easily as a thousand millions"[13]—a conceit that stems from his refusal in *Progress and Poverty* to apply the law of diminishing returns to the employment of labor and capital on land.* Also, his inveterate environmentalism kept him from perceiving that even if increased numbers should, as he maintained, enhance productivity infinitely, there still might be a population problem of a genetically qualitative nature. (It is worthy of remark that Harry Gunnison Brown, the academic champion of George, was also a professed Malthusian.[14]) Genetically qualitative considerations aside, however, George's inordinate optimism with respect to population seems no more unwarranted than do the dire predictions of the latter-day disciples of Malthus. In our preoccupation with such horror-spots as Bangladesh, we tend to overlook the facts that Taiwan, with a population density matching that of Holland, has a net export of food, and that one hydroponic acre in Arizona produces 240,000 pounds of tomatoes annually. (This should not, of course, be taken as an argument against family planning or the conservation of natural resources.)

George has sometimes been faulted for inconsistency in relying on Ricardian rent theory while rejecting Malthusian population theory. That Malthusianism was assumed by Ricardo is a historical fact, and George accepts his view that rents are raised by "the increasing pres-

*In the *Science of Political Economy*, his treatment of this matter is unclear. There, instead of refusing to apply the law of diminishing returns to agriculture and the extractive industries, he criticizes Mill and others for their failure to extend it to all modes of production, evidently thinking that he has thus weakened rather than strengthened the Malthusian position (bk. 3, chap. 4). Had he lived to complete the book, he might have revised and clarified his treatment.

sure of population which compels a resort to inferior points of production."[15] But he claims that this view really gives no countenance to Malthusianism, and has been enlisted in its support only because of the misapprehension "that the recourse to lower points of production involves a smaller aggregate produce in proportion to the labor expended."[16] And he holds that rent is also raised by other causes—the technological and social improvements that increase productive power. Now, his treatment of Malthusianism suffers (as I have already remarked) from his refusal to apply the law of diminishing returns to the division of labor. And his "all-devouring rent thesis" is weakened by his failure adequately to recognize that technological and social improvements are reflected in cheaper and better goods and hence in higher real wages. Yet, however unsatisfactory his analysis in these respects, he stands absolved of the charge of inconsistency to which I have alluded, for the pressure of population upon resources is not only offset, as he sees it, by the greater yield per person made possible by greater population, but is, in any case, merely one (and perhaps to him the least important) element in his version of the law of rent. Moreover, as Teilhac observes, "while George shows . . . that social evil is only the consequence of economic progress, contrary to Ricardo, he demonstrates that it is, nevertheless, only the artificial consequence of a natural law."[17] In other words, for George, unlike Ricardo, the law of rent *need not* culminate in an "iron law of wages"; poverty is not attributable to inexorable forces built into the order of nature, but to corrigible features of human economic arrangements.

At least two of the contributors to this volume agree with certain of George's critics that landowners and speculators (even when they are not themselves developers) sometimes perform entrepreneurial services that give them a legitimate, if perhaps qualified, claim on land values. George doubtless failed to recognize that part of the rise in land prices may at times reflect owners' constructive allocation efforts. (In terms of his classificatory system, that part would fall under wages rather than under rent.) Against this, however, must be placed the fact that constructive allocation has (to put it conservatively) not infrequently been thwarted by withholding on the part of owners. At any rate, by permitting owners to retain a percentage of the value of their land large enough to induce them to retain title even when not developers or users, George's plan would provide a market premium for entrepreneurship, since the size of the owner's "brokerage fee" would depend upon his success in finding the most profitable use for his site. But even if all private titles were to be extinguished, I see no reason why there should be any diminution of incentive for skillful allocation, or why decisions as to allocation need become other than a private function (except perhaps where dictated by ecological or other public considerations). Not ownership but security of tenure is the decisive factor in encouraging optimum use—witness the phenomenon that so much intensive development occurs on leased land. The entrepreneur would have the same incentive as at present to find the most appropriate locations for development and use, but would simply lease them from the public rather than from a private owner.

One may freely grant that George omitted to give sufficient weight to the subjective element in value—a consequence of his failure to appreciate the considerable contributions of the Austrian school of economic theory. Also, one may recognize that government intervention in the marketplace, particularly federal manipulation of the supply of money and credit, has created aberrations and distortions not addressed by his analysis. His assumption that characteristically land held for speculation is kept absolutely idle is scarcely tenable. And it is patent that, for all its seductive neatness, his idea that wages and interest rise and fall in unison is not supported by the empirical data, although the situation might be different if the figures available represented only *real* wages instead of including transfer payments, and only *real* interest instead of including various extraneous elements that tend to be lumped with it. As for the "reproductive modes" aspect of George's theory of interest, it has been accepted only by his most doctrinaire followers. I confess that for me the concept holds a certain fascination, providing, as it does, an almost metaphysical basis for an explanation of why abstinence brings return, and I know of at least one person who was weaned away by it from Marxism because he considered that it definitively undercuts the theory of surplus value. Collier shows that some of the attacks upon it are invalid;[18] whether the reproductive modes concept is itself invalid is of little moment here, since it is in no sense vital to George's system.

James Haldane Smith, in fact, argues that it actually contradicts the remainder of the system[19]—a view that I believe could be refuted if doing so were worth the effort. In any case, a powerful justification of interest, wholly independent of that concept, may be readily inferred from George's general theory of capital.

There is a critic of Henry George to whom no chapter in this book has been devoted—none other than his most distinguished and assiduous academic champion, Harry Gunnison Brown, mentioned in passing above. Brown rejected George's "all-devouring rent thesis," his population and interest theories, and his theory of business depression.[20] Yet he gave unstinting support to George's distinctive policy proposal. The fact is that the proposal does not really depend upon the deductive structure that George developed in *Progress and Poverty* to support it. That structure is magnificent, and (as the present book has shown) many of the criticisms of it are ill-considered and fallacious. Reading *Progress and Poverty* can be an exhilarating experience. But the structure is not flawless. Once the lay student has mastered it (usually with little interest in examining other systems), he is likely to have acquired an emotional investment in it that makes him reluctant to perceive or acknowledge that any of its parts are less than perfect. Thus comes "the popular picture of the single-taxer" as "the aged crank whose ideas have been refuted, who has outlived his usefulness, and who need not be taken seriously."[21]

Conversely and ironically, in many instances the structure as set forth in *Progress and Poverty* may actually have thwarted the embrace of George's policy proposal, since not everyone has the patience to follow 328 pages of close reasoning before arriving at a statement of that proposal. At any rate, all that is actually required is the acceptance of the following three theses:

1. Land rent absorbs a disproportionate share of wealth.
2. Rent is a social product.
3. The social appropriation of rent has no adverse effect upon production, but rather encourages it.

While I am certainly not suggesting that these propositions are self-evident, they can be individually supported far more readily than can the total deductive structure George advanced.

The doctrines of natural law and natural rights undergird the entire framework of George's thought. There was a time when they were, in sophisticated circles, supposed to be hopelessly outmoded; more recently, they have undergone something of a revival.[22] These doctrines are not subject to empirical proof or disproof, since they are, in the last analysis, metaphysical, or at least axiological. The present writer, who subscribes to them wholeheartedly (without, however, regarding them as self-evident or self-contained), believes that they lead inestimable strength to George's teaching. Still, there have been those who, like Thomas G. Shearman, have embraced George's proposal solely on fiscal grounds; and those who, like Geiger, have endorsed all the main elements of his system while recasting his view of natural rights in terms of John Dewey's instrumentalism. I am persuaded that the system, in its economic essentials, can stand without the doctrines of natural law and natural rights. I am equally persuaded that, for those who can accept them, they not only give it added logical support but also provide a motive, not otherwise entirely intelligible, for personal commitment to its furtherance.

On the tactical ingenuousness of certain of George's terminological idiosyncrasies we need not dwell. "We must make land common property"[23] has hung from the beginning like a millstone around the neck of the movement he created, notwithstanding that even as he used the phrase he took pains to explain that by "common property" he meant something very different from what it is ordinarily understood to mean. Similarly, "association in equality"[24] is a locution not altogether felicitous: it conjures up images of Dostoevski's "unanimous and harmonious ant-heap," which are dispelled only if one happens to note George's passing statement that he is using *equality* as a synonym for *freedom*.[25] And libertarians, reading his allusion to "the noble dreams of socialism,"[26] will deem the reference offensive unless they apprehend that in this context the word *socialism* signifies not leveling collectivism but merely a cooperative order devoid of privilege.

It is worth observing at this point that a preponderance of George's more recent critics, as evidenced in this book, write from a libertarian perspective. I shall now venture an explanation for this: Socialists and other collectivists seldom seek to refute the Georgist outlook. They either ignore it altogether or view it condescendingly as a quaint relic that is marginally useful insofar as it embraces arguments for taxing land values, if nothing else. Libertarians, on the other hand, sense a natural affinity with Georgists but see them as having gone astray in this one area and want to "straighten them out."

Yet, ironic though it may appear, it is my contention that (if one excludes anarchism, which, advocating no government at all, need offer no theory on how to fund one) Georgism is the most consistently libertarian of all systems of political economy. Even a minimal state must be supported.* So the question arises: Shall government, however limited, be supported by true taxes, even if light ones, which are imposed upon all forms of wealth, no matter how produced? Or shall it be supported by something that is not actually a true tax at all, but rather a charge for the use of a natural good in limited supply, the value of which is socially, not individually, produced? If society supports itself through a fund of its own creation (now largely siphoned off into the hands of privilege), the wealth created by individuals may be left to that extent in their own hands. What could be more libertarian than this?

### Georgism in the Larger Sense: Equal Demands, Equal Sacrifices

The view articulated here might be called *Georgism in the larger sense*. This phrase signifies an attitude or outlook—one that may concede that George's original position was vulnerable here and there, but maintains that when all is said and done, George was right on the essentials. I shall use the term *Neo-Georgism* to refer to a specific policy program reflective of this outlook. The modern friend of George's thought who views the "Prophet of San Francisco" as a profound and perceptive guide rather than as an infallible oracle, will find the majestic symmetry of his system vitiated somewhat by the qualifications and adjustments dictated by candid analysis in the light of changed circumstances and refinements in economic methodology. Georgism in the larger sense will be less satisfying than the original

---

*True, there have been theories advocating voluntary, fee-supported protective associations, but insofar as they lack territorial inclusiveness one wonders if such arrangements really qualify as "government" as the term is used politically. In any case, the "free rider" problem renders them impractical except in a supplemental sense.

article from an aesthetic standpoint. But aesthetic satisfaction must yield to intellectual honesty, and the basic truth of George's central thrust remains, in any event, intact. What is this central thrust? It is the insight that natural opportunity should be open on the same terms to all, and socially created values socially appropriated, while the fruits of private effort should be left inviolate to their producers or to the designees thereof. Here we find the authentic verities respectively inherent in socialism and individualism organically combined without detriment to the integrity of either. Here we see, not a confusing welter of compromises and half-measures, but a clear and logical relationship in which each pole is balanced and complemented by the other.

The moral case for land-value taxation is clear enough. It represents an indemnity to the rest of society for the privilege of monopolizing something the owner did nothing to create, and the market worth of which is a social, not an individual, product. Such a levy is, as George put it, "the taking by the community, for the use of the community, of that value which is the creation of the community."[27]

Under a Neo-Georgist regime, everybody would pay society for the use of land, according to its market value. Those who own land would pay directly. Those who do not would pay indirectly via their landlords, who would keep a small percentage of the payment as an agency or collection fee. The proceeds would be used for the purpose of general benefit in lieu of taxes on labor and capital. This contrasts with most present systems, in which people who don't own land pay twice—first to the landlord, for the privilege of using the land, and second to the government, for public services. (Of course, I am using the term *landlord* in the literal sense; if the same individual happens to own the building in which one lives or conducts a business, one's payment for the use of it, as distinguished from the land under it, is actually interest on capital, and would not be subject to social appropriation under Neo-Georgism.)

Heavy imposts upon land, even if offset by reductions in improvement, income, and other taxes, will be decried as confiscatory by some parties on the excuse that the land was purchased in good faith under the protection of the laws extant at the time. But this assertion (which could apply equally to almost any change in the tax structure that might have an adverse effect upon anyone) rests upon the assumption that every transaction is entitled in perpetuity to the same legal protections as those under which it was entered into—an assumption that, if valid, would render all reform, or, for that matter, any kind of legislated change, impossible. Whenever public authority does *anything* that constitutes a policy departure, someone's expectations are bound to be negatively affected, yet nobody contends that all present policies should therefore be carved in stone. Why, then, should policies that affect landowners be any different? People have the right to speculate in land just as in pork bellies or Picassos, but regardless of what they put their money into, society is under no obligation to ensure that their speculation is risk-free. Practical wisdom, of course, dictates that changes insofar as possible be phased in gradually enough to enable people to make necessary adjustments, and this applies to the taxation of land values as it does to other matters.

Without neglecting the traditional emphasis on ground rent, Neo-Georgism will also focus on nonground forms of rent that have risen in prominence since the days of Henry George—rent for the electromagnetic spectrum, aircraft landing slots, patent protection (in the latter case collection being waived in the public interest in favor of time and other restrictions), etc. While such things do not fall within the category of "ground," they are subsumed under the broad Georgist definition of land as consisting of "all natural materials, forces, and opportunities" apart from "man himself."[28]

Whereas the availability of such amenities as water, sewerage, gas, and electricity certainly enhances the value of sites and ought to be reflected in their assessments, there is no reason why separate charges should not be made for their actual use. The same may be said of libraries, parks, recreation, and even some educational opportunities.

To the extent that the rent of land is *not* appropriated for social purposes, the fruits of private effort, initiative, and productive savings are almost certain to be so appropriated. The burden of proof lies with one who would contend for the moral superiority of the latter.

According to the standard wisdom, a *sine qua non* for a system of public revenue is that it be broadly based. It is argued that if revenue is drawn from many and varied sources, it is less likely to be seriously affected should any of them dwindle. It is argued, moreover, that the more widely the burden is spread among the various interests, the more lightly it will weigh upon any one of them.

This is all very well as far as it goes, but other considerations are also relevant. The more numerous and varied the sources, the more complex the system must be, and hence the more elaborate, expensive, and inquisitorial its collection apparatus and process. Sometimes the argument that public revenue must be broadly based is couched in terms of equity. Thus the sales tax is defended because "it spreads the burden more evenly to all consumers of public services."[29] But equity does not necessarily call for a widespread distribution of the burden where the distribution of benefits is not similarly widespread; in fact, many would maintain the contrary. At best, one might concede it to be desirable that public revenue be broadly based, *all other things being equal.* Yet I trust that I have shown that, in the case of the land-value tax, all other things are *not* equal.

An argument that is probably the most uncompromising as well as the most theoretically elegant assertion of the adequacy of land value as a tax base was advanced by Shearman. It was his contention that it is logically impossible for the average annual cost of necessary government ever to be greater than the average annual value of its land:

> How can any government be necessary, which costs more than the privilege of living under it is worth? And what is the cost of the privilege of living in any particular place, except the ground rent of that place? . . . Any pretended taxation that takes more from the people than this is extortion, not genuine taxation.[30]

The less local the jurisdiction, the more attenuated Shearman's argument becomes, so that the case for financing national defense, for instance, out of rent is not so clear and unequivocal as is the case for thereby financing services such as local law enforcement. Yet the advantage of being located in a free country with secure borders might conceivably confer some rent even upon a site that had little else to recommend it. Let us grant for the sake of argument that Shearman is mistaken—that land rent would be insufficient to meet the necessary and legitimate expenses of government. The obvious riposte is: Why should this prevent us from using it as far as it can go? To be a Georgist in the larger sense, one need not be a single taxer. All that is necessary is that one favor land rent as the primary and preferred source of public revenue.

Instrumental to the application of the central thrust of the Neo-Georgist program is the idea that public fiscal burdens be distributed according to the criterion of benefits received from society. This idea has long been out of vogue, having been supplanted by the now-dominant position that taxes should be levied on the basis of ability to pay. In less polite words, they should "soak the rich." The ostensible justification for this position is that ability to pay is a gauge of equal sacrifice. Yet it is by no means clear why persons who do not make equal demands upon society should, in fairness, be expected to make equal sacrifices in its support. Furthermore, specialists in public revenue theory are not agreed as to what is really meant by equal sacrifice, or that it is actually best measured by progressive rates determined by ability to pay.[31] A free market can measure the marginal utility of relative satisfactions and therefore sacrifices as among its participants, but since taxes, being compulsory, do not reflect a market situation, it is difficult to see how they can be apportioned in terms of equal sacrifice. In view of these complications, some thinkers would assess the desirability of a tax system solely in terms of the system's efficacy in meeting broad social needs, without reference to its relative burden upon individual taxpayers except as that burden may have public consequences. (It was, in fact, upon just such grounds that Carver endorsed land-value taxation.) But social utility is, unless balanced by other considerations, a dangerous criterion for a tax or any other kind of compulsory system. Everything depends upon who defines society's needs, and the rights of the individual are all too likely to be swallowed by Leviathan.

The best surety for the protection of these rights, so far as the question of public revenue is concerned, is the restoration of the benefit principle. (Taxes based upon this principle are, technically speaking, not true taxes at all, but rather public fees; thus the term *single tax* is really a misnomer, and the proposal of Henry George has sometimes been spoken of by its adherents as a program for the abolition of taxation. George, however, reluctantly called it a tax as a concession to popular usage,[32] and I follow him in this.) Since the privilege of exclusive use and disposition of a site is a benefit received by the owner at the expense of the rest of society, the Neo-Georgist, like the Georgist, will insist that it be paid for in full, as measured by the value of the site. But he will not be a single taxer, except in the sense of maintaining that (apart from genuine emergencies, such as war) payment for benefits should be the single criterion for taxation. Recognizing that, of all special benefits, land ownership is by far the most important, he will accord the land-value tax (which further commends itself because of its nonshiftability and benign effect upon production) a premier place in his table of priorities.* Second place will go to use taxes, of which the gasoline tax (assuming it be spent on highways or related functions) is a salient example. If taxes for special benefits prove insufficient to meet the cost of necessary services of a general nature, the Neo-Georgist will admit the legitimacy of general levies to take up the slack. But he will insist that the services in question be truly necessary and truly general (e.g., police and fire protection, national defense, the control of communicable diseases, etc.). And he will demand that the obligation for their support be divided in terms of a formula that involves at least some approach to objectively equal payment—possibly a nongraduated percentage of incomes. Finally, he will concede that really desperate exigencies, where the very survival of the community is at stake (and where, for instance, as Brown reminds us, millions of men might be "required to risk their lives at the fighting front"[33]) may temporarily justify whatever measures are capable of quickly raising the needed revenues, regardless of whether the burden be distributed with the same equity that normal conditions would enjoin.**

---

*Where, in the case of certain exhaustible natural resources, conservation is a prime desideratum, the benefit principle could be implemented through a severance tax in lieu of at least part of the land-value tax.

**A libertarian refinement of the program described above might be to distribute the revenue from land rent on a per capita basis, giving each individual the option of using

To recapitulate, the Neo-Georgist will neither claim that land-value taxation should always be the sole source of public revenue, on the one hand, nor see it, like the Fabians on the other, as merely a highly desirable source to be employed as one tax among many without discrimination as to their ranking. He will have a definite order of priorities, governed by the regulating principle of benefit, which commands reliance, first, upon payment for special benefits by their recipients (the preference within this category being given to payments that cannot be shifted and that do not deter production); and second, upon general payments for general benefits,[34] with payments not geared to benefits exacted only as a temporary last resort in extraordinary crises. He will advocate the restriction of government spending to necessary protective functions apart from the first category, and also within the first subdivision of that category except for the hypothetical eventuality of a surplus.

Like George, and in contrast to the "single tax limited" of Shearman and Charles B. Fillebrown, Neo-Georgism will stand for the public appropriation of the full land rent, less a percentage just large enough to induce owners to retain private title. In will do so not only on the ground of public right, but also because legitimate government expenditure today would probably leave no excess in the land-rent fund, as might have been the case in Shearman's day. Yet, unlike George, it could accede to a policy of providing some form of temporary and limited compensation where the full public appropriation would cause extreme hardship to the owner; not, however, as a matter of justice but simply as a pragmatic gesture to smooth the way of implementation. Better, as Brown remarks, that special provision be made for the ubiquitous land-owning "widows and orphans" whose anticipated distressful state has been made the basis for opposition to reform, than that a bad system be retained forever.[35]

his share to purchase domestic public services, or of doing without them. As a practical matter, this option could not very well extend to the support of national defense, since there would be no way of denying defense against foreign aggression to freeloaders. But the rent fund might not in any event suffice to support national defense in addition to legitimate domestic public services in today's world.

## The Beckoning Vision

The year 2002 witnessed the passing of John Rawls and Robert Nozick, two Harvard political philosophers who together may be said to have rescued their discipline from triviality. Both began with individualistic premises in the classical liberal tradition, but for Rawls, these premises were thoroughly undermined by considerations that led him to advance the model of a thoroughgoing welfare state. Nozick's critique not only exposed the self-defeating character of Rawls's approach, but also pointed to a way in which essential welfare concerns may be satisfied without sacrifice of individual freedom. ("You must have been reading Henry George!" I remarked to him at a meeting of the American Philosophical Association in 1978, four years after the appearance of his *Anarchy, State, and Utopia.* He replied that others had told him the same thing, and that reading George was high on his agenda.)

It is in the thought of George that key ideas of these two thinkers find their synthesis anticipated: a basic social income that enables production instead of hindering it by cutting into its rewards. Personal freedom and social security here find common ground, for the latter does not impinge upon the former, nor does the former trench upon the latter. Both exist by right and not by compromise, yet form the basis for a social compact that is truly organic because it is geared to the statics of human nature as well as the tested canons of wealth production.

Thus wherever land-value taxation has a foothold, it is essential that the officials charged with its administration be educated as to its advantages, both technical and moral, that this education be ongoing, and, insofar as possible, that it be extended to the general population. The absence or inadequacy of such education may be one reason why the system has been brought to the verge of extinction in Denmark, and weakened in Taiwan despite its being mandated in the Taiwanese Constitution and having played a major role in moving that nation from penury to prosperity in the third quarter of the twentieth century.

Even limited experiments in land-value taxation are cumulatively helpful in establishing an empirical record. The record thus far established has consistently been quite positive, even where the experiments have, for various extraneous reasons, been abandoned. I recognize that political realities frequently preclude bolder action, that opportunities must be taken advantage of when they present themselves, and that they are normally of such a nature as to be linked with other issues and to admit only of partial legislative attainment. For those reasons, I do not disparage the modest approaches recounted in the pages of *Land-Value Taxation Around the World.*[36]

Yet I cannot but venture to suggest that their very modesty may be one reason for the fact that land-value taxation now seems to be in retreat in so many places where it was established. Too mild an application of a beneficial program will produce benefits too mild to stimulate strong and enduring general support. Almost invariably in these instances, not enough land rent was socially appropriated to ensure that the system's good effects were clearly attributable to it, and could not be ascribed to other factors. A closely associated reason could be that the approaches were too mixed—even including other taxes that watered down its impact by penalizing production, so structured that their explicit aim was not the capture of land value more than of any other type of economic value. Such circumstances blur the moral imperative of land-value taxation, making it seem but one fiscal tool among many. Indeed, it has proponents who view it in that way.

Only homeopathy maintains that remedies are very effective in minute doses. If the record of land-value taxation has been one of consistent but only moderate success, that is most likely because it has been administered only in greatly diluted form. Even the best medicine, if too diluted, may readily be overwhelmed by stronger counteragents. A stout enough course of the unadulterated Georgist "remedy" might demonstrate that the claims made on its behalf are not really so extravagant, after all.

In recent years, the Georgist camp has sustained something of a rift between those who would direct its limited resources toward local (usually two-rate) property tax reform, and those who would focus on ambitious nationwide agendas. While the power and drama of George's moral vision are unquestionably compromised by what opponents of the more modest approach are pleased to call "the

724 *American Journal of Economics and Sociology*

municipal trivialization," there are two good reasons for not wholly abandoning that approach.

The first is a matter of "doability." The American and Australian federal systems afford opportunities for experimentation at the state and local levels that rarely arise at any national level. Examples are the Alaska Permanent Trust, the California Irrigation District Act, and nearly a score of two-rate local jurisdictions in Pennsylvania. "Putting all its eggs into a national basket"—whether that of Russia, Scotland, or wherever, could swamp the movement's resources very quickly, leaving nothing to show for the effort and expenditures.

The second is the need for empirical examples. The very fact that those that now exist are all partial and tentative is all the more reason why they need to be multiplied: with increasing numbers, an inescapable pattern will emerge, so that claimed advantages cannot be dismissed as attributable to extraneous factors.

Having said all this, it is necessary to insist that the local approach never replace the greater goal of national Georgism. In New Zealand and South Africa, the former became so ingrained as to be taken for granted—a complacency that left it virtually without defenders when jettisoned in major cities by the central governments. In addition to the danger of losing sight of George's vision, the local approach, if broadly implemented, has the probable disadvantage pinpointed by Cannan—that of causing demographic distortions. He intended this as a hostile criticism; let it be taken, rather, as a cautionary admonition.

Of course, the full-scale implementation of the ultimate ideal would be *international*—involving the distribution among nations of what Nicolas Tideman has termed "world territorial rent"[37]—rent attributable to natural rather than to population factors. Some progress has been made along related lines in treaties concerning Antarctica, the deep-sea beds, etc., but the prospect of such distribution on a major scale is too remote to warrant more than a mention here.

A distinguished contributor to the first edition of this volume rightly stated that "George did not suggest any specific timetable for the implementation of [his] proposal, but no present-day Georgists of stature urge that it be done except in gradual stages. Large, sudden, arbitrary changes in established rules do not belong in 'the good society.' But gradual changes to achieve large results constitute the responsible way to progress."[38] Michael Hudson explains why, under current circumstances, the role of mortgage interest makes gradualism especially imperative:

> In today's world the land has become so heavily mortgaged that nearly all the growth in land-rent over the past half-century has been taken by mortgage lenders as interest. Taxation of the land and other real estate has shrunk proportionately. Indeed, to raise the land tax too sharply (to say nothing of suddenly collecting the entire land rent for the public sector) would create a financial crisis because the rental income cannot be paid both to the government and to creditors. Higher taxes would "crowd out" the creditor's mortgage claim, wiping out the savings that are the counterpart to these debts. This would injure the economy's financial viability. . . .
>
> If public capture of economic rent were phased in gradually, interest on real estate debt would be replaced by tax payments. And as fewer savings were invested in mortgages, they would be lent to other sectors, establishing similar debt-claims there.
>
> Restoring the land tax to its historic role as the major source of fiscal revenue would reduce the rental income free to be pledged to creditors. This would shift the flow of credit away from mortgage lending to either more directly productive uses (such as the financing of industry or other direct investment), or to consumer debt, the funding of corporate takeovers and so forth. To the extent that these loans found their counterpart in new direct investment and employment, the economy would benefit.[39]

No doubt, fanatical enthusiasts for the "single tax," who see it not as a regimen to build up the social body in increasing degrees to a state of health but as a magical elixir to be swallowed in one gulp, have alienated potential sympathizers of more sober temperament. But the Georgist vision is not, as some of its adherents' rhetoric might lead one to conclude, inherently simplistic. Their veritably evangelical fervor, although it might superficially appear almost ludicrous in the context of advocating a tax, ought not be viewed with condescension or disdain. For the tax they advocate is a tax in name only, and its significance as a fiscal measure pales beside its significance as an engine of social justice.

Assuming careful and knowledgeable implementation, it commends itself to common sense much more than do competing approaches.

By now, the bankruptcy of socialism should be evident to all. The market economics of the New Right, however, while a welcome enough corrective to collectivist schemes in many nations throughout the world, has largely proven a disappointment, as evidenced by the return to power of center-left parties, however chastened, in the United Kingdom, Germany, New Zealand, and elsewhere. Yet such parties' programs, if they may be called that, exhibit no clear, coherent structure. They are mere patch-works of compromise, stitched together without design apart from that of appealing to powerful voting blocs and other interest groups. Why should it be too much to hope for, that, after enduring failure upon failure and disillusionment upon disillusionment from Left and Right alike, the world will awaken to the realization that if it socializes that which is inherently social because it has been produced by society—namely, the rent of land and natural resources—it may safely leave in private hands the wealth that individuals in their private capacity produce? If such a regime cannot be fully instituted overnight without too great a shock, that is scarcely a conclusive point against it. Let it be instituted, if need be, in stages that allow for adaptation and adjustment. Let it be instituted with due consideration for circumstances of time and place. Let it even be instituted with temporary modifications for special cases such as the ubiquitous "poor widow" whose conjectured plight is the subject of lachrymose ritual invocation by the adversaries of reform. But let it be instituted!

Although words attributed to Helen Keller laud Henry George's "splendid faith in the essential nobility of human nature,"[40] it is to his credit that his system of political economy rests on no such faith but rather on the mundane observation that "men seek to gratify their desires with the least exertion."[41] While his language might at times ascend to rhapsody, his approach was uncommonly practical—radical in the sense of attacking the preeminent social problem at its root, but basically conservative as to method.[42] It might be characterized as being, both literally and figuratively, "down to earth." This is by no means to depreciate the powerful moral, even spiritual, appeal of his position. But it is precisely the seamless union of that moral and spiritual appeal with an eminently reasonable plan of reform that doubtless accounts for the remarkable persistence of the movement that bears his name. When Henry George died, that name was a household word. But so was the name of Edward Bellamy, and so was the name of William Jennings Bryan. Bellamy's Nationalist Clubs, which once spanned the continent from coast to coast, disappeared without a trace in less than a decade. Bryan's banner of free silver was furled for good after the campaign of 1896. In due course, later panaceas were proclaimed. Multitudes hailed the Townsend plan and sang the praises of Technocracy. Where are they now? Yet followers of Henry George are active still. Their political advances may be rather few in number and of relatively slight degree. Yet they soldier on.

Like Plato's ideal city, the full Georgist paradigm has been realized nowhere on earth. Only in pale and evanescent glimmerings here and there may faint terrestrial traces of its lineaments be glimpsed. But it remains a steady vision in the heavens. It is not, as in the *Republic*, too sublime for human nature, necessitating a "second best" substitute like the city of Plato's *Laws*, better adapted to man's frailty; rather, it is eminently applicable to the problematic human situation. It awaits only the day, be it soon or in the far distant future, when thoughtful citizens, finally recognizing the hollowness of the Left and the obtuseness of the Right, and the futility of all the unstable mixtures in between, their gaze directed by the Remnant to that supernal vision, are kindled by it to affirm with one mighty and united voice: "Let it be instituted! Let it be instituted *starting now!* To that end we dedicate ourselves." When that day shall come, no one can say. But meanwhile, the vision beckons.

**Notes**

1. Henry George, *Progress and Poverty*, 75th Anniversary Ed. (New York: Robert Schalkenbach Foundation, 1954), p. 456.

2. Harry Garrison Brown, *Economic Science and the Common Welfare*, 6th Ed. (Columbia, Mo.: Lucas Bros., 1936), p. 246 n.

3. Willford I. King, *The Wealth and Income of the People of the United States* (New York: Macmillan, 1915), pp. 160–62.

4. Steven B. Cord, *Henry George: Dreamer or Realist?* (Philadelphia: University of Pennsylvania Press, 1965), p. 234.

5. Charles F. Collier, "Henry George's System of Economics: Analysis and Criticism," Ph.D. dissertation, Duke University, 1976, p. 220.

6. George Raymond Geiger, *The Philosophy of Henry George* (New York: Macmillan, 1933), p. 157, n. 90.

7. George, *Progress and Poverty*, p. 456.

8. Henry George, "The Condition of Labor: An Open Letter to Pope Leo XIII," in *The Land Question [and Other Essays]* (New York: Robert Schalkenbach Foundation, 1953), p. 10.

9. Henry George, *Thy Kingdom Come* (New York: Robert Schalkenbach Foundation, n.d.), p. 13.

10. E.g., E. Benjamin Andrews, "Economic Reform Short of Socialism," *International Journal of Ethics* 2 (April 1892): 281–82.

11. George, *Progress and Poverty*, p. 456.

12. Collier, "Henry George's System," p. 261.

13. George, *Progress and Poverty*, p. 133.

14. See Harry Gunnison Brown, *Basic Principles of Economics*, 3rd Ed. (Columbia, Mo.: Lucas Brothers, 1955), pp. 403 ff., 416. The present writer vividly recalls hearing Brown make the flat announcement, "I am a Malthusian," to an audience of Georgists in 1960 or thereabouts.

15. George, *Progress and Poverty*, p. 228.

16. Ibid., p. 231.

17. Ernest Teilhac, *Pioneers of American Economic Thought in the Nineteenth Century*, trans. E. A. J. Johnson (New York: Macmillan, 1936), p. 141.

18. Collier, "Henry George's System," pp. 154–55, 158–60.

19. James Haldane Smith, *Economic Moralism: An Essay in Constructive Economics* (London: George Allen & Unwin, 1916), p. 73.

20. Christopher K. Ryan, *Harry Gunnison Brown: An Orthodox Economist and His Contribution* (Malden, MA and Oxford, U.K.: Blackwell Publishers, 2002), p. 215. His criticisms appeared exclusively in Georgist publications and in correspondence.

21. Martin Bronfenbrenner, "Early American Leaders—Institutional and Critical Traditions," *American Economic Review* (Dec., 1985), quoted in ibid., p. 218.

22. See Charles Grove Haines, *The Revival of Natural Law Concepts*, Harvard Studies in Jurisprudence, vol. 4 (Cambridge, MA: Harvard University Press, 1958).

23. George, *Progress and Poverty*, p. 328.

24. Ibid., p. 508.

25. Ibid., p. 525.

26. Ibid., pp. xvi, 456.

27. Ibid., p. 421.

28. Ibid., p. 38.

29. Jon Kidwell, guest columnist in the *Birmingham News*, Birmingham, AL, March 12, 2000, p. 3C.

30. Thomas G. Shearman, *Natural Taxation*, 3rd Ed. (New York: Doubleday & McClure, 1898), pp. 132–34.

31. See Walter J. Blum and Harry Kalven Jr., *The Uneasy Case for Progressive Taxation* (Chicago: University of Chicago Press, 1953).

32. See Charles Albro Barker, *Henry George* (New York: Oxford University Press, 1955), pp. 519 f.

33. Harry Gunnison Brown, *Fiscal Policy, Taxation and Free Enterprise* (New York: Robert Schalkenbach Foundation, n.d.), p. 14.

34. Although very minor, another source of public revenue, also second to the land-value tax in priority, might be escheatment to the community of all estates to which there are no immediate heirs in the direct line, unless the decedent has provided otherwise by will. I do not classify this, even non-technically, as a tax, but simply as the public appropriation of property to which the title has become from any standpoint of rational justice, vacant.

35. Harry Gunnison Brown, *Economic Science and the Common Welfare*, 2nd Ed. (Columbia, MO: Lucas Brothers, 1925), pp. 251 f.

36. R. V. Andelson, ed., *Land-Value Taxation Around the World*, 3rd Ed. (Malden, Mass. and Oxford, U.K.: Blackwell Publishers, 2000).

37. Nicolaus Tideman, "Commons and Commonwealths: A New Justification for Territorial Claims," in R. V. Andelson, ed., *Commons Without Tragedy* (London, U.K. and Savage, MD: Shepheard-Walwyn Ltd. and Barnes and Noble, 1991), pp. 117–21 and *passim*.

38. C. Lowell Harriss, in R. V. Andelson, ed., *Critics of Henry George*, 1st ed. (Rutherford, NJ: Fairleigh Dickinson University Press, 1979), p. 365.

39. Michael Hudson, in R. V. Andelson, ed., *Land-Value Taxation Around the World*, pp. 23–24.

40. This quotation was cited for many years in the annual brochure of the Henry George School of Social Science. Its source is a letter written around 1930 by Miss Keller to the Robert Schalkenbach Foundation.

41. George, *Progress and Poverty*, p. 12.

42. See Joseph A. Schumpeter, *History of Economic Analysis*, ed. Elizabeth Boody Schumpeter (New York: Oxford University Press, 1954), p. 865.

# Notes on Contributors

*(Views expressed in this work are not necessarily those of any organizations or institutions with which their authors are associated.)*

ROBERT V. ANDELSON (Ph.D., University of Southern California) is professor emeritus of philosophy, Auburn University, and distinguished research fellow, American Institute for Economic Research. His books include *Imputed Rights: An Essay in Christian Social Theory* (University of Georgia Press), *Commons Without Tragedy* (Barnes & Noble), *From Wasteland to Promised Land* (with James M. Dawsey) (Orbis Books), the second and third editions of *Land-Value Taxation Around the World* (Blackwell), and the first edition of the present work (Fairleigh Dickinson University Press). He is past president of the International Union for Land-Value Taxation and Free Trade, and of the Alabama Philosophical Society, and serves on the boards of the Robert Schalkenbach Foundation and the *American Journal of Economics and Sociology*. Early in his career, he spent three years as executive director of the Henry George School of Social Science, San Diego.

GEORGE BABILOT (Ph.D., University of Oregon), professor emeritus of economics, San Diego State University, was director of the Center for Public Economics at that institution. He is author of monographs, essays, and articles on taxation, public finance, and welfare economics. He serves on the board of directors of the Foundation for Economic Justice.

JAMES L. BUSEY (Ph.D., Ohio State University) is professor emeritus of political science at the Cragmore campus of the University of Colorado, where he served as department chairman for many years. He has many books and articles to his credit, including *Latin American Political Institutions and Processes* (Random House), *Notes on Costa Rican Democracy* (University of Colorado Press), and *Political Aspects of the Panama Canal* (University of Arizona Press).

MARY M. CLEVELAND (Ph.D., University of California, Berkeley) has taught accounting and computer systems at Rutgers University. Since 1994, she has been director of research at the Partnership for

Responsible Drug Information. She has published articles in periodicals sponsored by such bodies as Friends of the Earth and the Urban Land Institute, and produced chapters in books and numerous working papers and reports on topics ranging from property taxes to pollution hazards. She serves on the board of the Robert Schalkenbach Foundation, and is a former president of the Henry George School of San Francisco.

CHARLES F. COLLIER (Ph.D., Duke University) wrote the original versions of his chapters in this volume while he was an assistant professor of economics at Hamilton College, Clinton, NY. He is now an analyst for the U.S. government, and revised his piece on Simon N. Patten on his own time while serving as such.

STEVEN B. CORD (Ed.D., Columbia University) is professor emeritus of history at Indiana University of Pennsylvania, and served as president of the Henry George Foundation of America for twenty-three years. He is author of *Henry George: Dreamer or Realist?* (University of Pennsylvania Press), as well as of other books and articles. He is currently the editor of two newsletters.

ROY DOUGLAS (Ph.D., University of Edinburgh) served as reader in the general studies department of the University of Surrey prior to his retirement. His books have made him a recognized authority on modern political history. They include *The History of the British Liberal Party, 1895–1970* (Fairleigh Dickinson University Press), *Land, People and Politics* (St. Martin's Press), *In the Year of Munich* (Macmillan), and *The Advent of War, 1939–40* (Macmillan). He is also a barrister.

KRIS FEDER (Ph.D., Temple University) is associate professor of economics and chair of the environmental studies program at Bard College. She has contributed chapters to three books, including two in the Georgist Paradigm Series. She serves on the board of the Robert Schalkenbach Foundation and of the *American Journal of Economics and Sociology.*

FRED E. FOLDVARY (Ph.D., George Mason University), teaches economics at Santa Clara University. He is the author of four books, *The*

*Soul of Liberty* (Gutenburg), *Public Goods and Private Communities* (Edward Elgar), *Beyond Neoclassical Economics* (Edward Elgar), and *Dictionary of Free-Market Economics* (Edward Elgar).

AARON B. FULLER (Ph.D., University of Virginia) serves as an economist on the staff of a government-related think tank He is the author of various articles and papers on the history of economic thought, and of monographs related to the economics of national defense.

MASON GAFFNEY (Ph.D., University of California at Berkeley) is professor of economics at the University of California at Riverside. His previous positions include founder and executive director, British Columbia Institute for Economic Policy Analysis; professor and chair, department of economics, University of Wisconsin, Milwaukee; and professor of agricultural economics, University of Missouri. He is the author of many monographs, chapters, and articles on taxation, land use, and intergovernmental relations, including a complete issue of *House and Home* magazine, co-auther of *The Corruption of Economics* (Shepheard-Walwyn), and serves on the board of the *American Journal of Economics and Sociology.*

DAMON J. GROSS (Ph.D., University of Iowa) is a businessman who has taught philosophy on a temporary or part-time basis at various colleges and universities. He has published in *Reason Papers* and other journals, and contributed chapters to two other books on George. He serves on the boards of directors of Common Ground-USA and the Robert Schalkenbach Foundation.

FRED HARRISON (A.B., Oxford University, M.Sc., University of London) is executive director of the Centre for Land Policy Studies, London, and editor of *Geophilos,* journal of the Land Research Trust, London. Among his books is *The Power in the Land* (Shepheard-Walwyn).

ROBERT F. HÉBERT (Ph.D., Louisiana State University) is Russell Foundation professor emeritus of economics, Auburn University, and visiting professor of economics and finance, University of Louisiana at Lafayette. He is a former Fulbright senior research scholar (France), and visiting professor at the Sorbonne. Dr. Hébert has authored, co-authored, or edited six books, including *A History of Economic Thought and Method* (McGraw-Hill), which has been translated into three languages and is now in its fourth edition. He is a past president of the History of Economics Society.

OSCAR B. JOHANNSEN (Ph.D., New York University) earned his doctorate in economics after retiring as secretary to the president of the United States Steel Corporation. He then served for many years as executive director of the Robert Schalkenbach Foundation, on the board of which he now sits, and then as president of the Henry George School of Social Science. A longtime board member of the *American Journal of Economics and Sociology*, he is the author of several articles and pamphlets in economic and social theory. In 1975, he was awarded the Grand Prize by the National Association of Manufacturers for the best essay on the free enterprise system.

HAROLD KYRIAZI (Ph.D., University of Pittsburgh) is a full-time research associate in the University of Pittsburgh School of Medicine. He has held various offices in the Libertarian Party in Pennsylvania, and for four and a half years produced a local, bi-monthly LP newsletter. He was the invited contributor of "The Ethics of Organ Selling: A Libertarian Perspective" (*Issues in Medical Ethics*, India), has co-authored a dozen scientific articles, and is the author of *Libertarian Party at Sea on Land* (Schalkenbach), which has been praised by John Hospers, the party's first presidential candidate.

FLORENZ PLASSMANN (Ph.D., Virginia Polytechnic Institute and State University) is assistant professor of economics at Binghamton University (SUNY). Parts of his research have been published in the *Journal of Urban Economics* and the *Journal of Law and Economics*.

JACK SCHWARTZMAN (J.S.D., St. Lawrence University; Ph.D, New York University), a native of Russia, practiced law in this country for more than sixty years. In addition, he was professor of English at Nassau Community College (SUNY). In 1974, he won the New York State Chancellor's Award for Excellence in Teaching. He is author of *Rebels of Individualism* (Exposition Press) and of some 300 articles, and was chairman of the editorial board of the occasional journal, *Fragments*, which ceased publication after his death.

NICOLAUS TIDEMAN (Ph.D., University of Chicago) is professor of economics at Virginia Polytechnic Institute and State University. From 1969 to 1973, he was an assistant professor at Harvard, and in 1970–71 served as a senior staff economist for the President's Council of Economic Advisors. He has published numerous articles, primarily in the areas of public finance and efficient public decision-making, and is editor of *Land and Taxation* (Shepheard-Walwyn). He serves on the board of the Robert Schalkenbach Foundation and of the *American Journal of Economics and Sociology.*

WILLIAM B. TRUEHART (Ph.D., Claremont Graduate School) was director of the Henry George School of Social Science, Los Angeles, a lecturer in economics for the San Diego Community College District, a staff executive with the Lincoln Institute of Land Policy, and a member of the San Diego County Board of Assessment Appeals. He was author of several articles and study guides in economics.

LOUIS WASSERMAN (Ph.D., University of California at Berkeley) was professor of philosophy and government at San Francisco State University, author of *Modern Political Philosophies* (Doubleday, New Home Library) and of many articles in political theory, joint-author and editor of *American Institutions and Ideals* (Gutenberg), and co-author of *Self-Help Cooperatives in Los Angeles County* (University of California Press).

# Index of Names

American Journal of Economics and Sociology, Vol. 63, No. 2 (April, 2004).
© 2004 American Journal of Economics and Sociology, Inc.

Nozick, Robert, 722
Nulty, Thomas (Bishop), 514

Oppenheimer, Franz, 630
Oser, Jacob, 17, 667–76, 707

Parnell, Charles Stewart, 56, 58
Patten, Simon Nelson, xi, 358,
   395–405
Pentecost, Hugh O. (Rev.), 615
Petridis, Anastasios, 78
Phelps Brown, E. H., 111
Pigou, Arthur, 541, 548–49
Pinchot, Gifford, 527
Plato, 139, 727
Plehn, Carl C., 535
Polak, Edward, 441
Popper, Karl, 679
Post, Louis F., 355, 407, 529
Proudhon, Pierre Joseph, 11, 275–76

Quesnay, Francois, 5n

Rae, John (author), 199–210
Rae, John (economist), 209n1
Ralston, Jackson H., 419, 440
Rawls, John, 722
Reader, John, 604
Redfearn, David, 603
Ricardo, David, 3, 5n, 31, 68,
   97–102 *passim*, 137, 154, 162,
   205, 237, 289n, 307, 319, 324,
   353, 359–61, 455, 577–78, 625,
   632, 667–82, 688, 710–11
Rima, Ingrid Hahne, 390
Rogers, Thorold, 525
Roosevelt, Theodore, 521
Rose, Edward J., 667
Rothbard, Murray Newton, xi, xii, 9,
   573, 611–44
Rousseau, Jean Jacques, 177–82
Russell, Bertrand, 279n
Rutherford, Reuben C., 13, 297–314
Ryan, John A. (Msgr.), 479–95, 521,
   661

Samuels, Warren J., 395
Sanford, Hugh Wheeler, 17
Satolli, Francesco (Archbishop), 514
Schmoller, Gustav, 6

Schoenberg, G., 163
Schumpeter, Joseph, 4, 200n
Schwarz, Gerhard, 593n
Seager, Henry Rogers, 17
Seligman, Edwin R. A., 19, 407–32,
   689
Senior, Nassau, 353
Shaw, George Bernard, 259
Shearman, Thomas G., 5, 346, 532,
   714, 716, 721
Shell, Karl, 253
Shields, Charles H., 15, 424
Sidgwick, Henry, 3, 208
Silvers, E. B., 15
Simons, Algie M., 13, 14, 261n
Sinclair, Upton, 440
Singer-Kérel, Jeanne, 266
Smart, William, 14
Smith, Adam, 3, 4n, 68, 106, 139,
   199–202, 209, 321, 353, 365, 435,
   441–42, 455, 502, 534–35, 552,
   563, 625, 632, 708, 714
Smith, Al, 441–42
Smith, James Haldane, 713
Smith, Samuel, 11
Snowden (Lord), 440
Sorge, F. A., 259
Spahr, Charles B., 420
Spence, J. C., 5
Spence, Thomas, 286
Spencer, Herbert, 5, 12, 178
Starke, Viggo, 597
Stebbins, Giles Badger, 11
Stigler, George, 448, 541, 678
Stirner, Max, 336
Sullivan, James L., 20n5
Sumner, William Graham, 7
Sun Yat-sen, 4, 526

Taft, William Howard, 443
Taussig, Frank, 17, 65, 79, 208, 304
Taylor, A. J. P., 282
Taylor, Helen, 260
Teilhac, Ernest, 711
Temple, (Archbishop), 603
Tezanos Pinto, Mario de, 16
Thorburn, S. S., 287
Thornton, William T., 207–08, 372n
Tideman, Nicolaus, 593, 615, 617,
   631, 692–93, 724

# Index of Subjects

Ability to pay theory of taxation: Seligman on, 413; advocated by Ely, 531–34; George on, 534; defects of, 719

Agriculture: oppressive levies on production, improvements of farmers, 38; role of in rent, 99; effect of Green Revolution on, 107–08; Gronlund's disingenuous tactics on, 273; cost of land a hindrance to development of, to Marx, 274; on need to reorganize, Marx on, 279; Rutherford's focus on economy of, 298; Ricardo criticized by George for not extending margin beyond, 307; Atkinson on, 347–48; George on effect of land-value tax on, 347, 500; Walras on, 425; land, actually used for recreation, taxed too low, 438; absentee owners and soil depletion, 470; Ryan on, 492; collective syndicates of, advocated by Alcázar, 499, 501; land burdened by land-value tax, other confusions of Alcázar, 500, 502; Knight on, 558; land, decrease in as population rises, 609n8; accelerating concentration of land values in, 624n; George accused of focus on agrarian, rather than industrial, society, 673

Alaska: land-value tax dividend in, 436

Alcázar: on George's ideas, including separability of land from improvements, 500–02; mistaken beliefs that George opposed private property, advocated nationalization or equal division of land, emphasized society over individual, would focus tax on agriculture, 500–05; contends that labor on land creates its value, 500–05; on labor theory of ownership, 502; extreme conservatism of his Roman Catholic views, 507–08; expects religion to solace ills of poverty, 511–13. See also Agriculture

Altruism: a marginal motive, to Hardin, 603

American Economic Association: 3, 231, 353–54, 395, 465, 521, 541

American Social Science Association: conferences (1886, 1890) debate single tax, 245, 402, 407

Aimes, H. H.: on study of Cuban slave economy, 89–91

Anarchists: Haymarket Affair, George attacked by Tucker on, 317; on profit, 318, 320; views of compared with George's, 337–38 (table); semantics among chief differences with George, 329. See also Hanson, Ingalls, Tucker

Anarcho-capitalism. See Heath, Rothbard

Andelson, Robert V.: supports George on territorial sovereignty, 195; on effect on land ownership of George's proposal, 501–02, 509–10; on land-value tax as best system of environmental utilization, 609; on Neo-Georgism, 705–29; on summary of criticisms of George, 705–29

American Journal of Economics and Sociology, Vol. 63, No. 2 (April, 2004).
© 2004 American Journal of Economics and Sociology, Inc.

outdated, later retracts some objections, 685; questions merits of neoclassical ideas, 683, 685; on George, Mill, Ricardo, Marshall, 683–86, Seligman, 689; contends abandonment of land as unique factor, by Clark, Fetter, inhibited advances in land rent theory, 686; on criticisms of George by current economists, 687–89; need for land-value tax models, 693–96; Marx, George compared, 696–98

Blum, Walter: his tax book cited, 729n31

Böhm-Bawerk, Eugen von: of Austrian school, xii, 677–701; George misunderstands ideas of, 4n, 358

Bolivia: example of less developed nation unready for land-value tax, 505

Bramwell, George William Wilshere (Lord): misinterprets George, answered by Hirsch, 5, 7

Britain: 1970s depression in, 268–69; advantages of free trade to, 426

Broadcasting, public: subsidization of by spectrum rent [land-value tax] logical, 689

Brown, Harry Gunnison: on interest, 330; on land monopoly, 326–29; against Ely's conflation of land and capital, 536; on multiple contributors to land value rises, 615; a Malthusian, 710; questions George's "all-devouring rent thesis," 713

Brown, J. Bruce, on assessment of land value, 349

Brunner, Emil: theologian, calls Cathrein important Roman Catholic representative, 161

Buchanan, James: property rights theorist influenced by Knight, 541–42

Bureau of Statistics, 231

Butler, Nicholas Murray (Columbia U. president): praises George, 4

Byington, Stephen: his correspondence with Tucker, 335–36

California: *See* U.S.

Callaghan, James: Social Contract policy of in British government, 269

Canada: western, claim of development surge in with land-value tax, 16; land-value tax in, 25 424, 529

Cannan, Edwin: editor of *Wealth of Nations*, critic of Marshall, Keynes, 435; negative effects of his law of locational decisions, based on services provided, 435–36; advocates national land-value tax (site rating), as do Marshall, 436–37, Colin Clark, 447–48, who, with Gaffney, see it more distributively just than local, which has demographic distortions, 437–42

Capital: justification of return to above that due labor, 10; as economic category, 24; defined by George, 27, 121–22; liberation of through land-value tax, 36; rise in as important as rise in rent on inequality, to Laveleye, 48–54; primacy of over land in production, to Longe, 95; increasing use of as substitute for land, 107–08; as stored up labor, 153–54; no inherent conflict with labor, 166; conflated with land by Huxley, 187, Gronlund, 272, Ely, 535, leads to decline in influence of classical political economy, George, 535–36, 686; rights to as well as to land, in Gronlund, 261–62; employment of by labor disputed by Dixwell, 224–25, Oser, 672–74; monopoly of based on land monopoly, according to Marx, 281; George inconsistent on definitions of, and Rutherford's criticism of, 304–06; enemy of labor, to Ingalls, 315;

Capital: *(cont.)*
and interest, George's views of
attacked by anarchists, 324–28;
includes land, to Clark, 357–60;
and labor, distinctions between
blurred by Clark, 364; real
aggregate of, Clark's attempt to
measure, 391n26; Geiger on
social determination of, 431n32;
Davenport major opponent of
George on, criticized inaccurately
by Geiger, 451–52; defined by
Davenport, 454–58, Hirshleifer,
455, George, 674–75; Davenport's
concern with budgeting problem
of, 455–56; goods, land included
in, according to Davenport,
without denying uniqueness,
456–58; ownership of, compared
to land ownership, creates more
wealth and power, according to
Oser, 672–75; human, theory of,
678–89
Capital failure: land ownership and,
701n67
Capital gains: tax, changed, could
be alternative to land-value tax,
to Blaug, 684
Capital goods: Clark's definition of
equivalent to George's wealth,
373–74, Clark's confusion of,
in exchange with production,
373–74; Davenport on, 456–58
Capitalism: *Progress and Poverty*
its last ditch, to Marx, 259, his
opposition to, contradictions on,
278–84; monopoly oppressor of
labor, according to anarchists,
324–28
Capitalist: George labeled
antagonistic to, 8; multiple
functions of, 52
Carey, Henry C.: influenced Harris,
245; arguments against Ricardian
rent theory already refuted by
Mill, 246, later by Marshall,
Walker, 247
Carrying capacity. *See* Environment
Carver, Thomas Nixon: Social
Darwinist, 465–66; economic

views of dictated by his moral
and religious beliefs, 466–67; on
state's role, his three wealth
categories, and social utility, 468,
472–73; on land, and landowner
as steward of earth, 469–70;
distinguishes between land and
capital, 475; on prior occupancy
as basis of ownership, 471–72;
on inheritance, on merits of land-
value tax, 474–76
Catholic Church: *See* Roman
Catholic
Cathrein, Victor (Fr.): disputes
George on progress bringing
proportionately greater gains to
landowners than to labor or
capital, 162, on Ricardo, 162–63,
on labor theory of ownership,
163–66; reliability of statistics of
questioned, 162; views of on
distribution, 162; on urban land,
labor, 163, 166; flaws of on
interest, 163–65; confuses amount
with proportion, 164; contrasted
with George on natural rights,
165; accepts first-occupancy
view of ownership, 166–69; his
landownership views echoed by
Pope, and George's retort,
169–70; confuses George's ideas
with Marx's, 172; his theological
justification of economic
inequality, 173
Chalmers, Thomas: classical
political economist, questions
competitive industrial system, 3,
137
Chamberlain, Austen: U.K.
politician, opposes proposed
national land tax, 440, 444
Chamberlain, John: wrote foreword
to Heath book, assisted in other
ways, 573, 581
Chamberlain, Neville (Prime Min.):
half-brother of Austen C., 440
Chicago: *See* U.S.
China: effect of Marxism on, 291;
heavily taxed, 510; taxes land
values in Kiao-chau, 534

Chodorov: individualist Georgist, influenced Rothbard: 573, 611; criticized by Rothbard for proposing local, not national, land-value tax, 630, 636; lectures at LeFevre's school, 663

*Christian Socialist*: recognizes growing gulf between George, socialism, 57

Churchill, Winston: on land monopoly as greatest of monopolies, 418, 420; on huge costs of land monopoly to government, production, and wealth distribution, 528

Clancy, Robert: refutes article by libertarian, 646–49

Clark, Colin: on advantages of a national land-value tax, 447

Clark, Colin W.: on maximizing gains as possibly destructive ecologically, 608

Clark, John Bates: admits George's insights helped him develop marginalism theory, xi–xii, 200n, 303, 328–29, 354–57; influenced by study in Germany, sees society more important than individual, 354; attacks George in debates, books, for years, 355, 402; asserts absolute private property in land essential to market functioning, exchange, state 355, 368, 379–84; on rent not as differential surplus but marginal product of land, 355–56; on capital, 357–58, 378, productivity, time, 363, 367, wages, 382; on law of diminishing returns, on equilibrium, competitive, static, 356–57, 364; capital theory his greatest contribution, two-factor economics eliminates land rent as income category, deliberately undermining George, classical political economy's three factors, 357–58, 535, 686; combines marginal productivity theory, microeconomic model of

competitive static equilibrium for new analysis of production, distribution, 357; on land, not as original or distinct factor, but mere type of capital good, 357–60, 362–63, 366–67, 372, 374, 380, 382–86, 390; assumed homogeneity of inputs major flaw in marginalism theory, 361–64; his static analysis of economy vs. George's real, dynamic, 365, 371–72; on land speculation, 366–67; on wealth, value from production, 373; two-factor theory of arbitrary, misleading, 375, compared with George's three-factor, 388–92; on natural justice, 382–87; ideals of like George's, but denies community creation of, entitlement to, rent, 384; rent-seeking encouraged by ideas, errors, omissions of, summarized in three versions today, 368–69, 387–90

Clarke, Samuel B.: on natural rights, 183

Cleveland, Mary M.: questions Blaug's use of statistics, 690–96

Cleveland, Ohio: *See* U.S.

Coase, Ronald: influenced by Knight on property rights analyses, 542

Colins, de, J. G. C. A. H. (Baron): land reform plan cited by Gide, 7

Collier, Charles: summarizes Ely's conflation of land, capital, 187; supports Walker's criticism of George on land held for speculation not necessarily totally idle, 234; criticizes Walker on wages and rent, 236; on land-value tax adequacy as revenue, 708–09; on invalidity of some attacks on George's theory of interest, 712

Commons: tragedy of, in Cannan, 435. *See also* Hardin

Commons, John: participant in ongoing wages-fund debate, 208; student of Ely, 521; on land monopoly as creator of fortunes, 420

Communist: Alcázar's description of George as, on misconception George would collectivize, divide, or nationalize, land, 501; Heath on land-value tax as "land communism, 573. *See also* Grunland, Marx, Socialism

Community: right of to social increment from land rent, 30, 43n11; disincentives to better services in, 436; right of to land or rent denied or questioned by Tucker, 317, Ryan, 488–90, Rothbard, 614; and proprietary governance, Heath's theory of, 572, 580–87; existence of provides developer opportunity, to Day, 599n4

Compensation of landowners: rejected by George, 39, 509; differences on between Marshall, George, 75; insisted on by Walker, 239–41; Ryan on, 486–87, 509; possibility of limited, temporary in Neo-Georgism, 721

Competition: Marshall on, 67; ability of to avoid damage of recurrent overproduction questioned by Moffat, 137, 148–49; Clark on, 354–55. *See also* Markets

Confiscation: of improved as well as unimproved land values, 11; of rent condemned, 15; of rent, not of land, proposed by George, 34, 509; Ryan on, 485–87, Knight on, 542, 557; Heath's explanation of, 581; of land rent, criticized by LeFevre, 647–48; arguments for, 717

Conservation: possible negative effects of land-value tax on, to Walker, 241–42, to Carver, 469–70; and benefit tax theory, 719–20. *See also* Environment

Considérant, Victor: George accused by Miller of plagiarizing ideas from, 11

Consumption: final aim of economic activity, to Davenport, Fisher, 455; opportunity costs, land, and maximization of, 456; taxes hit rich without harming poor, according to Ely, 529–30

Copyrights and patents: George's differences from anarchists on, 330–31

Cooke, Isaac B.: opposes labor theory of ownership, 8, 17

Cord, Steven B.: on views of American economists, historians on, and revived appreciation of George. 5, 410; on labor theory of ownership, 416–17; fails to combine labor and utility theories of ownership, 418; on rent, compensation, 487; coins phrase "all-devouring rent thesis," 706–08

Corn Laws: use of monopoly power under to boost profits artificially, 267

Corrigan, Michael (Archbishop): author of preface in Holaind's book attacking George, Spencer, 12; influential in McGlynn's excommunication, 513–14

Crump, Arthur: attack of on George, 8

Cuba: wage structure in, from slavery to Marxism, 291

Daily, Gretchen: environmentally concerned economist uses term "natural capital" to adjust for two-factor economics' omission of "land,", 390

Darwin, Charles: role of with fellow biologists Huxley, Marshall, 177

Darwinism, social: of Huxley, 177–78, 183; defined, 190; Carver endorses, 465–66; Alcázar praises George for rejecting, 507

Davenport, Herbert J.: on wages-fund theory 19, 208, 451–54;

critique of George on capital,
and Geiger's mistaken rebuttals
of, 451–57; sympathies with
"single taxers" in principle, not
method, opposing retroactive
collection of accrued rent, 452;
similarity of his major ideas
(opportunity costs, optimal
investment decisions) to George's
(law of least exertion, theory of
production and distribution),
reinforcing latter's standing as
economist, 453, 459–62;
definition of capital, capital
goods influenced by Fisher,
455–59; on economic
methodology, 460–62; critical of
George's normative (ethical), not
theoretical, ideas, 462–63
Davies, H. Llewelyn: on Toynbee's
critique of George, 8
Davitt, Michael: on land reform,
56–57
Dawson, Thomas (Fr.): fully
supports George, 514
Debs, Eugene V.: Gronlund's
influence on, 260
Dead-weight loss: in land value,
capitalized, 694
Decentralization: and individualism,
opposed by Marx, Gronlund,
278, 636, 638n18
Deduction: use of by classical
economists criticized by Harris,
Carey, 245
Denmark: land-value tax in, 25,
529
Depressions: caused by land
speculation, to George, 71, 152;
and economic cycles, Dixwell on,
221, 225–26; Gronlund, Marx,
George on, 263–65; British, mid-
1970s, 268–69; Flamant and Kérel
on, 266
Dewey, John: on George as
America's greatest social
philosopher, 20n4;
instrumentalism of seen in
George's natural rights theory by
Geiger, 4, 24, 714

Diminishing returns: Ricardo on,
68; George on, 148, 400, 579;
George, Dixwell compared,
223–24; and Clark, law of
variable proportions, 356; law of
confused with increasing returns
to scale by George, according to
Oser, 669–70; George's failure
to apply to division of labor,
710–11; in George's *Science of
Political Economy*, criticism of
Mill, others for failing to extend
to all production modes, 710n.
*See also* Distribution, Returns
Distribution: laws of, on income,
George on, 27–28, 67, 128–32,
163–64: Marshall on, 65, 67;
Moffat's rejection of George on,
150–58; compared with
Cathrein's, 168–69; theories of
Marx on, 262–63; influence of
George's ideas on Clark's on
diminishing returns, marginal
productivity, 328–29; of rent,
wages, interest ignored by
Atkinson, 345; Rutherford, Patten
on, 400–01
Dividend, citizen: in Alaska, 436;
contemporary reform proposal,
advocated by Gaffney, others,
446; as possible use of
economic surplus, 709; libertarian
proposal for use of land-value
tax, 720n
Dixwell, George Basil: heterodoxy
of, 214; appreciations, critiques
of George, 214–226 *passim*; on
free trade, 215–18; misinterprets
cause of land values, 220–22,
227–28, and George's concept
of justice, 225–27; Malthusian
views of, denies labor theory
of ownership while opposing
wages-fund theory, 222–26; on
overproduction as cause of
economic cycles, 225–26; on
private ownership, 227–28
Douglas, Paul (Sen.): on U.S.
census of governments, tax
equalization, 447

application in Denmark, Taiwan, 722–23

German Historical School: stresses evidence over theories, state over individuals, influences U.S. economists trained abroad, transforms classic political economy to neoclassic economics, rejected by George, 353–354

German Social Democratic Party, 200. *See* Lassalle

Gide, Charles: reviews *Progress and Poverty*, urges landowner compensation for land-value decrements, 7

Glasgow Land Value Assessment Bill, 14

Goldman, Eric: on Ryan's early enthusiasm for George, 479

Goods and services: untaxing of, under land-value tax, would mean lower prices, 38

Gordon, Scott: on production, continuous, 303

Government: contractual: alternative forms of, 581; Rothbard's views on, 612; functions of and whether land-value tax would reduce them, 671; intervention's effect on marketplace, 712. *See also* Anarchists, Heath, LeFevre, State

Gronlund, Laurence: most serious Marxist critic of George, including two tracts against, 260–73; denies land monopoly as chief cause of poverty, 261; on interest, 262; sees capitalism, not land speculation, as chief cause of depressions, 263–64; on inadequacy of land as revenue base, 269–71; equivocates on taxing farm land, 271n; sees no difference between capital, land, 271–72; opposes decentralism, individualism, 277–78; Marx disagrees with, 262–63, 272, 274

Growth: national, local constraints on, 442–44

Gwartney, Ted: on ease of assessing land, improvements separately, 596

Hadley, Arthur: on wages-fund theory, 208

Hanson, William: anarchist, calls land-value tax "state landlordism," 316; criticizes idea of unearned increment, 316, 321–22; argues against George on ownership, 316–20; land monopoly, 334–35; on rent, land value, profit, interest, 322–24; on equilibrium, 328–29

Hardin, Garrett: neo-Malthusian views of, 601; regards inheritance as injust, 601–610; on tendency of individuals, pursuing own interests, to overgraze, abuse commons (equated by Andelson with utility or profit maximizers who value their individual goods more than social goods), 603; on land's carrying capacity, degraded if exceeded, 604; uses term, *commons* not as municipal enclosure but as "ideal type," one of four politico-economic systems of environmental utilization, 605; sees morality relative, to a specific system at a specific time, requiring periodic re-examination of property rights, social justice, 608; Andelson suggests land-value tax as a fifth system, with least flaws, 609

Harris, William Torrey: influenced by Carey, Hegel, 245; attacks George at 1886 American Social Science Association conference, 245; claims single tax would be shifted to poor, 245–58; uses imprecise data, flaws in his critique noted, 248–51; on poverty, 252–53; property rights, 253–55; confuses land-value tax with land tax, 254–55; misunderstands, objects to George's methodology, statistics,

Ingalls, Joshua K.: *(cont.)*
318–20, land value, 323–24;
identifies capitalism with
monopoly, 315; on copyrights,
patents, 330; condemns land-
value tax as socialist, 331; on
shifting land-value tax to
consumer, 333
Inheritance: Carver's argument for
taxation on, 474, 476; unjust, to
Hardin, 609
Innovations: effect of, especially
transportation, on demand for
land, to Walker, 236. *See also*
Progress
Input-output production concept: of
Leontief, 364n
Institute for Research in Land
Economics and Public Utilities
(later Institute for Economic
Research). *See* Ely
Instrumentalism: and George's
views on natural rights, 24. *See
also* Dewey
Interest: George's theory of, 12; as
economic category, 24;
determined also by market,
contrary to George's theory, 67;
rate of; Marx vs. Gronlund on,
263; George, Rutherford's
differences on, 305–06;
anarchists on, 325–29; as
marginal return from use of
capital, 378; George's static
theory of weakest component
of his system, 399; Patten on,
401; rate of affected by time,
457–58; as return to all
production factors, to Knight,
Fisher, 566n10; whether wages
rise or fall in unison with,
664n21; critics of George's
theories of, 705–15 *passim*. *See
also* Equilibrium
Internalities. *See* Externalities
Ireland: land question in, 172–73,
193, 227; George, Moffat on
causes of poverty in, 142–43
Is-Ought Fallacy: of Davenport, 454,
Carver, 466

Jalladeau, Joel: book on Clark by,
391
Jamaica: example of feasibility of
separating land from
improvement values, 534
Jefferson: elements of Rousseau in,
182
Jevons, William Stanley: and
marginal utility, 685
Johnson, Alvin S.: claims unearned
increment necessary lure for
development, 15
Johnson, Edgar H.: condemns
George but acknowledges truth
of his most important principles,
14–15
Johnson, Tom: U.S. Congressman,
reform mayor of Cleveland, close
George friend, 516
Jorgensen, Emil O.: attacks Ely,
Institute for Economic Research,
on land, rent, speculation, and
taxation, with enumerated
reasons, 523–31
Joslyn, R. W.: on Kitson's critique of
George, 13
Justice: in economic systems,
according to George, 24; in land
rights, George vs. Ryan, 
484–87; natural, views of Clark,
George contrasted, 386–87;
compared with charity, 493n12;
defined by Carver, 473; Ryan on,
484–87; Alcázar on, 503; seen by
Hardin as relative, needing
constant redefinition, 508;
land-value tax as engine of
social, 725

Kalven, Harry, Jr.: tax book by
cited, 729n31
*Kapital, Das. See* Marx
Keller, Helen: praises George's
faith in human nature, 422,
726
Kendrick, M. Slade: on George,
17
Keynes, John Maynard: some ideas
of fail as land speculation
overlooked, 269n; cited, 706

Land: *(cont.)*
Europe's peasants, tenants,
55–56; Laveleye's historical
analysis of issues of, 53–58;
historical laws on, 192;
interdependence of with other
forms of property, 63;
competitive nature of supply of,
according to Marshall, 63;
alternate uses for as opportunity
costs, 68; location versus use of,
70; role of entrepreneur in,
71–72; annual income of,
including of owner-occupiers'
imputed, not fully reflected in
statistics, 108; equal right of all to
opportunity to use, 196, 672; as
inelastic factor, 233; agricultural,
Walker's focus on, 234;
distinction between tax on and
tax on land value, misunderstood
by many, 255; no different from
capital, to Gronlund, 271–74,
Alcazar, 503, Ely, 535, Marx
disagreeing, 271–74; to Blaug,
whether distinct from capital,
681, as unique factor of
production, theory of abandoned
when conflated with capital,
686, 688–89; not a factor of
production, to Clark, 355–90
*passim*; defined by Knight,
547–48; as common property,
words often held against George,
601–02, 714; Rothbard on,
including misunderstandings,
612–15; four major aspects of,
according to Kyriazi, 613;
markets, and management,
government vs. private, 629–31;
leased from government vs.
private sale of, 629; 642n52;
separated from improvements,
misunderstood by LeFevre, 648;
Hayek on special problems of
propinquity of residents of urban,
639n23; reclaimed or built, 657;
privately held in United States,
alleged decline in value of, 668;
ownership of more concentrated

than ownership of wealth, 696;
inelasticity of reduced by
dimension of depth as well as
length and width, 683; Blaug on
inelasticity of, 688; non-ground
forms of, 717. *See also*
Assessment, Land values, Land-
value tax, Monopoly
Land Acts and Land Purchase Acts,
56
Land assessment. *See* Assessment
Land economics: scarce attention to,
23; and fiscal policy, George's
contribution to, 26; Ely's views
on criticized by Jorgensen,
523–31
Landlords. *See* Landowners
Land market: failure, Rothbard
on, 628–31; better description
of some varieties of land
speculation, 683, 695
Land monopoly. *See* Monopoly
Land nationalization: wrongly
attributed to George, 4–5n, 11,
500–05; varying and misleading
uses of term, confusion of with
land-value tax, 54–55; Wallace's
definition of includes state
control as well as ownership,
57; Walker's two objections to,
241–42
Landowners: non-contributors to,
but controllers of access to,
physical basis of, production, 28;
role of in land value creation,
30; inadequate tax on, 33; large,
effect of land-value tax on,
38–39; Anglo-Irish, effect on
struggle for economic justice due
to rise in number of, 56; wealth
to at expense of labor, capital,
disputed by Cathrein, 162;
beneficent role of, to Dixwell,
227–228; unfair power of, to
Marx, 274; role of in capitalist
production mode, 280; rights
of absolute, to Clark, 385–86;
cannot shift land tax to tenant,
431n16; when sole or few
occupants of municipality,

marginal revolution credited, 89, 200n, 329; associated with Marshall, 89; rejected by Longe, 91; principle of misrepresented by Clark's use of capital, 363; led to dominance by neoclassic economics, decline of classic political economy, 354. *See also* Clark

Marginal utility theory: Patten on, 397; elucidated by Davenport, 451; diminishing, concept of, 685

Market economics: LeFevre and, 645; failure of, 726

Market, free: distorted by monopoly of natural opportunity, to George, 172; private property essential to, in Clark, 355; libertarian exponents of and Ramparts College, 645

Markets: competitive, explain wage changes, according to Marshall, exposing George's alleged fallacies, 67; anarchic, to Gronlund, 278; Knight on, 542, 549–50; in land, including distortions in where state, large entities are landlords, Rothbard on, 628–33

Marlo, Carl: socialist criticized by Rae, 200

Marshall: lectures of on *Progress and Poverty*, 61–79 *passim*; oral exchange with George at Oxford, 62–63; his criticism of four basic propositions of George, 64–73; on income distribution theory, 65–68; on competitive markets, 68–72; sees rent only partly monopolistic, 68, 74; attacks George on, 71–72; favors land-value tax, supports Britain's 1909 land-value tax budget, views of reexamined, 76–77, 437, 447–48; motives behind his hostility to George, 78; on continuous production, 303; on monopoly, 564

Marx, Karl: ideas confused with George's by Cathrein, 172; Rae

on, 200; misunderstood by Harris, 258n40; his estimate of *Progress and Poverty*, George's estimate of him, George's unintentional role in promoting *Das Kapital*, 259; opposes decentralism, 278; on capitalist's role in production, 262, 280; growing shares of unearned increment appropriated by landowners, 262–63, interest, 263, 283, rent in aggregate, 263, surplus value going to capitalist, 265, land, 272–76, monopoly, 278–82, 285; some ideas of like George's, 261, 273–75; on disagreements of with Gronlund, 262–63, 272–73; sees overproduction, underconsumption, income maldistribution as causes of economic crises, 264; contradictions of on landownership's role in capital, 278–284; contrasted with George, 259–63 *passim*, 272–91 *passim*, 696–98; and labor theory of value, 502

Marxism: critiques of George, 259–81 *passim*; contemporary evaluation of, 291–92; theory of economics as source of social, political conflicts influences Blaug, 678

Maximization: utility or profit: 603

McCarthy, Joseph (Sen.): loyalty oath required during his hunt for communists, 678

McGlynn, Edward (Fr.): excommunication of for supporting George reversed, 12, 513; Heath criticizes his support of George's "land communism," 582

Meagher, M. W.: founder of National Debating Association, attacks on George, 12

Menger, Carl: of marginal utility, 358, 685

Mulhall, Michael: imprecise data of used by Harris, 249–52

Munro, Thomas: formulator of Ryotwari land settlement, India, 289

Murphy, Liam: on taxes and justice, 389, 393n79

Murray, J. F. N.: on assessments, separability of land values, improvements, 349

Nagel, Thomas. *See* Murphy

National Bureau of Economic Research: on national income accounting, King on staff of, 700n52

Nationalization: *See* Land nationalization

Natural law: Hanson advocate of, 316; on justice of income distribution, of Clark, 382–83; related to economic rent, 479; concept of valuable, not essential to George's policy, 713

Natural rights: differences on between George, Cathrein, 163–72 *passim*; Huxley on, 177–87; Tucker on, 336; George on, 410–11, 641n33, attacked by Seligman, 412; Ryan on, 489–92; Knight on, 561–62

Natural resources. *See* Environment, Resources, natural

Neoclassical economics: George's criticism of, 358–60; supplants term political economy, 396; differences from classical criticized by Blaug, 685

Neo-Georgism: described, modifying George's proposals, retaining essentials; examples, 715–21

New York City: George twice candidate for mayor of, 11, 441–42: pioneers separation of values of land from improvements, 442, 529. *See also* U. S.

New Zealand: assessments, land-value tax in, 25, 485, 529

Nichols, James Hastings: considered Ryan U.S.'s chief theorist of social Catholicism, 479

Niebuhr, Reinhold: on impossibility of perfect justice, 599

Niehans, Jurg: omits George in his history of economics, 681

Nock, Albert Jay: influences Rothbard, 612

Nozick, Robert: moral philosophy of, stressing individualism, similar to George's, 722

Nulty, Thomas (Bishop): strongly supports George, 514

Occupancy and use theories of land ownership or tenure: first occupant source of ownership, to Cathrein, 166, 168; vaguely defined by anarchists, 315–16; developed by Evans, 335; proposed by Ryan, 480–84; Knight on, and Tideman's responses, 556–57; first user as first owner, to Rothbard, 612, 625; and LeFevre's idea of first claimant as owner, 661–63

Organization of Petroleum Exporting Countries (OPEC): 268; effect on non-OPEC nations of oil production halt shows power of land over capital, 675–76

Oppenheimer, Franz: on taxation, feudal rent in his *The State*, 630

Opportunity: equality of enabled by land-value tax, 37; as condition of democracy, 417; advocated by George, 716. *See also* Distribution, Justice

Opportunity-cost: Marshall on, 447; theory, Davenport's, 451, 456; similar to George's law of least exertion, 453, 460–61

Oser, Jacob: biographer of George, on huge circulation of *Progress and Poverty*, 667; disagrees with George on parallel movements of wages, interest, 667–69, adequacy of single tax as revenue source, 671–72, employment of capital

Slavery: *(cont.)*
compared with land ownership
by LeFevre, 662–63
Smart, William, 14
Smith, Adam: influence on George,
4n; sees land rent as monopoly
price, 68; defines farmer's
circulating capital as wages fund,
87–88; his canons of taxation
satisfied by land-value tax, 34,
534; Rae's biography of ignores
most theoretical ideas of, 199,
201–02; on passion's dominance
over reason in decisions,
advocates natural liberty of
human action over planning, 202;
holds labor theory of ownership,
502; on effect of progress on
land values, 525; on monopoly,
563–64
Smith, Al: example of political
interests coinciding with good tax
reform, 441–42
Smith, James Haldane: rejects
George on reproductive interest,
713
Smith, Samuel: condemns what he
mistakenly considers George's
program, 11
Snowden (Lord): and British
budget, 440
Social contract: of Callaghan in
British Labor government, 181
Social Darwinism. *See* Darwinism,
social
Social democracy: Rae's two types,
Centralist and Anarchist, 199
Social philosophy. *See* Ethics,
George, Philosophy
Social utility theory of ownership:
Marshall, 74, 78, Carver, 468, on;
attempts by Cord, Geiger to
combine with labor theory of
ownership, 418; priority of over
labor, 482–84, and natural rights,
Ryan on, 489–92; and income
tax, 534; dangerous criterion as
basis of taxation, 719
Socialism: George accused of
advocating, 12; analysis of on

role of capital versus land on
poverty, 51; gulf between George
and, 57; ambiguous appeal of to
Marshall, Mill, 61; Fabian, claims
George as catalyst, 79, 259;
Gronlund on superior logic of,
272; evaluation of, 291–92, 726;
and laissez-faire, 293n14; as used
in a passage by George, 332; and
collectivism, contradiction
inherent in, 518n27; Ely accused
of by Board of Regents,
exonerated, 522; Ely on, 530;
Knight on, 542; greater appeal of,
compared with George's theories,
696–98; interpreted as
cooperation without privilege by
George, 714; 79, 259; considers
land-value tax merely one of
many levies, 721. *See also*
Communism, Gronlund, Marx
Society: needs of versus individual,
188–89; responsible nature of
questioned by Rutherford, 310; as
organic whole to Clark, Spencer,
354; in Seligman's organismic
state, 421–22
Somers system of land valuation:
successfully used in U.S.,
elsewhere, cited by Jorgensen,
529
Sorge, F. A.: Marx's evaluation of
George in letter to, 259
South Africa: land-value tax in, 25,
529
Sovereignty, territorial: justification
of on George's premises denied
by Huxley, Lecky, 194; affirmed
by Andelson, 194–96; Hirsch on,
195
Spahr, Charles B.: argues not all
individuals equally responsible
for creating land values, 420
Species: cooperation, competition
within, 184–86
Spectrum rent: cited by Blaug as
non-ground form of rent, 689
Speculation. *See* Land speculation
Spence, J. C.: criticism of George
answered by Hirsch, 5

Tiltman, H. Hessel: on George's unintentional promotion of *Das Kapital*, 259

Time: importance of in George's theories, regarding wages as a flow, not a stock, 302; role of in production, 363–64; time-preference theory of interest, Patten's, 401; critical element in capital budgeting, 455; George's, Rothbard's recognition of in capital formation, Rothbard's errors on, 635

Tolstoy, Leo N. (Count): on public's lack of familiarity with George's ideas, 3, 581

Toynbee, Arnold (1851–1883): his two lectures critical of George, 8; asserts poverty has not risen with progress, disputes George, Ricardo, on dismal prospects for masses unless existing property system reformed, 204–05

Toynbee, Arnold J. (1889–1975): develops challenge-and-response theory of history, 119

Trade, free: views of Bastiat, George, criticized by, contrasted with Dixwell, 215–18; George on inadequacy of as main poverty solution, 218; advantages of, to Britain, 426; Alcázar on, 499; Heath's agreement with George on, 571–72. *See also* Protectionism

Transition: from traditional to proprietary communities, 586–87; other proposals, 587–88

Two-factor: theory of production and distribution, hypothetical, 102; Clark's, 357–58, 360; interpretation of productivity, Clark's, arbitrary and misleading, 375; theory of economics, Clark's, contrasted with George's classical three-factor, 358–67; as neoclassical economics, responsible for decline of interest in classical economics, land-value tax, George, 357–58, 535, 686

Tucker, Benjamin R.: identifies capitalism with monopoly, 316, 325; asserts occupancy and use theory of ownership, 317; attacks George for Haymarket stand, 317; replies to Marxists on state, society, taxation, 317; his dual concept of rent, 321; on interest, 327; condemns single tax, 335; ultimately rejects natural rights, embraces Stirner's philosophy, 336

Tulberg, Rita: her interpretation of Marshall's motives for hostility to George, 78

Turgot, A. R.: mistakenly said by Atkinson to have introduced single tax in France, 351

Turner, Frederick Jackson: Ely's student and theorist of frontier, 521

Turner, Ted: as large landlord, 623

Unearned increment of land: confiscation of, 8; garnered by suburban landowners, 11; lure of essential to development, 15; 321–34; George on, 40–41; identified with rent, as a monopoly price, by Smith, 68; misunderstood by Harris, 254; appropriated by landowner, according to Marx, 262–63; criticized by Hanson, 316, anarchists on, 321–22; defined by Mill, 321; Seligman on, 419; not in land rent but in wages, interest, to Ely, 526; not limited to land values, according to Rothbard, 612–14, Knight, 621. *See also* Rent

Unemployment: George on, 33, 36, 265–66. *See also* Wages

Unions: necessary when government become sole manager, 100; restrictive practices of, 110

United Labor Party: George expels socialists from, 260

Wagner, Adolf: his review of
*Progress and Poverty*, 6
Wakefield, E. G.: Marx on his
theory of colonization, 281
Walker, Francis Amana: attacks
wages-fund theory, 231–32; his
statistics challenged by George,
232; criticizes George on effects
of progress, relationship of rent
rises to wages, on poverty, land
speculation, 235–39, 241–42;
claims land-value tax would
harm conservation, 241–42; calls
George's proposal "infamy,"
confusing it with land
nationalization, 239, 241–42;
refutes Carey against Ricardian
rent theory; lessens hostility to
George, 239; would compensate
landowners, 239–41
Wallace, Alfred Russel: favors land
nationalization, 57, other land
reforms, 61; differed from George
in application rather than
principle, 177
Walras, Léon: on assessment of
agricultural land value, 425;
marginal revolutionist, 685
Warren, Josiah: develops occupancy
and use theory of land tenure,
335
Wasserman, Louis: Andelson credits
book by for stimulating his
interest in George, xiii
Wealth: and poverty, Cooke on, 9;
landed, 23; as economic
category, 24; Moffat's unusual
theory of, 139–141;
maldistribution of denied by
Cathrein, 162–63; George on,
218–19; distribution of proportion
vs. amount of, 262; defined
differently by business and
political economy, by Clark,
George, 373; Knight on, 544;
Carver's three categories of, 468;
and poverty, gap between, 696.
*See also* Poverty

Webb, Sidney J.: on wages-fund
theory, 208; on impact of
*Progress and Poverty* on socialist
movement, 259
Weber, B. *See* Phelps Brown
Wehrein, George S.: an Ely co-
author, 523
Welfare state: individual freedom
and, 707, 722
Wicksteed, Philip: on Toynbee's
lectures on George, 8
Weimar Republic: role of land
speculation in its collapse,
Hitler's rise, 267
Wieser, Friedrich von: marginalist of
Austrian school, 358
Woodhull, Victoria: feminist,
Tucker's lover, 316
Work ethic: Carver on, 466–67
Wrightson, Francis: critique of
George, 97–104; denies law of
rent, 97–98; misrepresents George
on wages, rent, 98; ignores urban
land, failing to note references by
Ricardo, Mill to location value,
98; admits some urban land held
speculatively, 99; denies margin
of production affects wages,
101–04; misreads Ricardo, Mill on
income distribution, 102; on
national income, 103–04
Wunderlich, Gene: on concentration
of farm real estate value growing
faster than that of farm acreage,
624n
Wyndham Land Purchase Act:
peasant proprietorship in, 56

Young, Allyn A.: an Ely co-author,
531
Young, Arthur Nichols: on James
Mill's pioneer advocacy of
taxing land value increments,
321

Zangerle, John A.: his book on
separability of land from
improvement values, 529

# References

Space does not permit inclusion of more titles, many cited in Chapter 1, or any except the most relevant works of each critic analyzed. As for Henry George, there are many editions of his books, by publishers here and abroad. All were issued in centennial editions by the Robert Schalkenbach Foundation, New York, between 1979 and 1988. Most authors refer to the 1954 or 1979 edition of *Progress and Poverty*; pagination is the same in both.

Aimes, H. H. S., *A History of Slavery in Cuba 1511 to 1868*. NY: Knickerbocker Press, 1907.

Alcázar Alvarez, Juan (Fr.), *Estudio filosófico crítico del libro "Progreso y miseria," de Henry George en sus cuestiones fundamentales y el alivio social*. Madrid: Perlado, Paez y Compania, 1917.

Andelson, Robert V., *Imputed Rights*. Athens GA: University of Georgia Press, 1971.

Andelson, R. V., ed, *Critics of Henry George*, 1st ed. Rutherford NJ: Fairleigh Dickinson University Press and London: Associated University Presses, 1979.

———. *Land-Value Taxation Around the World*, 3rd ed. Malden MA and Oxford UK: Blackwell Publishers, 2000.

———. "Where Society's Claim Stops: An Evaluation of Seligman's Ethical Critique of Henry George," *American Journal of Economics and Sociology* 27 (January 1968).

Andrews, E. Benjamin, "Economic Reform Short of Socialism," *International Journal of Ethics* 2 (April 1892).

Arnott, Richard J., and Joseph E. Stiglitz, "Aggregate Land Rents, Expenditure on Public Goods, and Optimal City Size," *The Quarterly Journal of Economics* 93 (1979).

Atkinson, Edward, "Mr. Atkinson's Correction," *Century Magazine* 41 (November 1890).

———. "A Single Tax Upon Land," *Century Magazine* 40 (July 1890).

Back, Kenneth, "Land Value Taxation in Light of Current Assessment Theory and Practice," *The Assessment of Land Value*, D. M. Holland, ed. Madison: University of Wisconsin Press, 1970.

American Journal of Economics and Sociology, Vol. 63, No. 2 (April, 2004).
© 2004 American Journal of Economics and Sociology, Inc.

782    *American Journal of Economics and Sociology*

Backhaus, Jurgen G., "Reading Henry George in 1997," paper from conference, Henry George Re-Considered. Maastricht University, 28 October 1997.
Barber, William, *A History of Economic Thought.* London; NY: Penguin Books, 1967; 1991.
Barker, Charles Albro, *Henry George.* NY: Oxford University Press, 1955.
Barrett, William, "This Land is Their Land," *Worth* (Feb. 1997).
Bastiat, Frederic, *Economic Harmonies,* George B. de Huszar, ed.; W. Hayden Boyers, tr. Princeton NJ: D. Van Nostrand Company, 1964 [1851].
Beard, Charles, *An Economic Interpretation of the Constitution.* NY: The Macmillan Co., 1935.
Beedy, Mary E., "Dr. William T. Harris and His Reply to Henry George," *Education* 8 (Oct. 1887).
Bellamy, Edward, *Equality.* NY: Appleton & Co., 1897.
Blaug, Mark, *Economic Theory in Retrospect.* Cambridge UK: Cambridge University Press, 5th ed., 1996 [1962].
——. ed., *Henry George.* Cheltenham UK/Brookfield VT: Edward Elgar, 1992.
——. "Henry George: Rebel with a Cause," *European Journal of the History of Economic Thought* 7, No. 2 (Summer 2000).
——. "No History of Ideas, Please, We're Economists," *Journal of Economic Perspectives* 15, No. 1 (Winter 2001).
——. *The Methodology of Economics, or How Economists Explain.* NY: Cambridge University Press, 1980.
——. *Recent Essays by Mark Blaug.* Cheltenham UK/Brookfield VT: Edward Elgar, 1997.
——. "Review of the Georgist Paradigm Series: *The Corruption of Economics,* Mason Gaffney and Fred Harrison; *A Philosophy for a Fair Society,* Michael Hudson, G. J. Miller and Kris Feder; and *Land and Taxation,* Nicolaus Tideman, ed., *Economic Journal,* Vol. 106, Issue 436 (May 1995).
——. "Review of Robert V. Andelson, ed., *Critics of Henry George,*" *Economica* 47 (Nov. 1980).
——. *Ricardian Economics: A Historical Study.* New Haven: Yale University Press, 1958.
——. "Ugly Currents in Modern Economics," *Policy Options.* Montreal: Institute for Research on Public Policy, http:/www.irpp.org (September 1997).
Blum, Walter J., and Harry Kalven, Jr., *The Uneasy Case for Progressive Taxation.* Chicago: University of Chicago Press, 1953.
Bose, Atindranath, *A History of Anarchism.* Calcutta: The World Press Private Ltd., 1967.
Boswell, James L., *The Economics of Simon Nelson Patten.* Philadelphia: Winston, 1934.

Breit, William, "The Wages Fund Controversy Revisited," *Canadian Journal of Economics* 33 (4) (1967).

Bronfenbrenner, Martin, "Early American Leaders–Institutional and Critical Traditions, *American Economic Review* (Dec. 1985).

——. "Review of King's Keys to Prosperity," *Journal of Political Economy.* 56:6 (Dec. 1948).

Brown, Harry Gunnison, "Anticipation of an Increment and the 'Unearned Decrement' in Land Values," *The American Journal of Economics and Sociology.* 1943. Reprinted in Brown, H. G., *Selected Articles by Harry Gunnison Brown.* NY: Robert Schalkenbach Foundation, 1981.

——. *Basic Principles of Economics.* Columbia MO: Lucas Bros., 1955.

——. *The Economic Basis of Tax Reform.* Columbia MO: Lucas Bros., 1932.

——. *Economic Science and the Common Welfare.* 6th ed. Columbia MO: Lucas Brothers, 1936.

——. *Fiscal Policy, Taxation and Free Enterprise.* NY: Robert Schalkenbach Foundation, n.d.

Brown, Harry Gunnison and Harold S. Buttenheim et al., eds, *Land-Value Taxation Around the World*, 1st ed. NY: Robert Schalkenbach Foundation, 1955.

Brown, J. Bruce, "The Incidence of Property Taxes under Three Alternative Systems in Urban Areas in New Zealand," *National Tax Journal* 21 (September 1968).

Brown, James R., *The Farmer and the Single Tax*, 4th ed. NY: Manhattan Single Tax Club, n.d.

Brownlee, W. Elliot, "Wilson and Financing the Modern State: the Revenue Act of 1916," *Proceedings of the Am. Philosophical Society* 129 (2). 1985.

Calabresi, Guido and Douglas Melamed, "Property, Liability and Inalienability: One view of the Cathedral," *Harvard Law Review* 85 (1972).

Cannan, Edwin, *The History of Local Rates in England.* London: P. S. King & Son, 2nd ed. 1912 [1896].

——. "The Proposed Relief of Buildings from Local Rates," *The Economic Journal* 17 (1907).

Carey, Henry C., *Principles of Social Science.* Philadelphia: Lippincott, 1858.

Carver, Thomas Nixon, *The Distribution of Wealth.* NY: Macmillan, 1904.

——. *Essays in Social Justice.* Cambridge MA: Harvard University Press, 1915.

——. *The Religion Worth Having.* Boston: Houghton, 1912.

Cathrein, Victor, *The Champions of Agrarian Socialism: A Refutation of Émile de Laveleye and Henry George* (tr., revised, enlarged by Rev. J. U. Heinzle, S. J. Buffalo: Peter Paul & Bros., 1889.

Churchill, *Liberalism and the Social Problem.* London: Hodder & Stoughton, 1939.

——. *The People's Rights.* NY: Taplinger Publishing Company, 1971 [1909].

Clancy, Robert, "A Challenge to Libertarians," *Rampart Journal of Individualist Thought* I (3): (Fall 1965).

Clark, Colin, "Land Taxation: Lessons from International Experience," *Land Values*, Peter Hall, ed. London: Sweet and Maxwell, Ltd., 1950.

Clark, Douglas H., "Canadian Experience with the Representative Tax System," *Intergovernmental Perspective* (Winter/Spring 1986).

Clark, John Bates, *The Distribution of Wealth: A Theory of Wages, Interest and Profits*. NY: Augustus M. Kelley, 1965 [1899].

——. "The Ethics of Land Tenure," *International Journal of Ethics* 1 (October 1890).

——. *The Philosophy of Wealth*. Boston: Ginn & Co., 1886.

Clarke, Samuel B., "Criticisms upon Henry George, Reviewed from the Stand-Point of Justice," *Harvard Law Review* 1, no. 6 (1887–1888).

Cleveland, Mary M., *Consequences and Causes of Unequal Distribution of Wealth*. Berkeley CA: University of California, Ph.D. dissertation, Ann Arbor MI; London: University Microfilms International, 1984.

Coase, J. Ronald, "Three Lectures on Progress and Poverty by Alfred Marshall," *Journal of Law and Economics* 12 (April 1969).

Collier, Charles F.,"Henry George's System of Economics: Analysis and Criticism." Durham NC: Duke University, PhD dissertation, 1976.

Collins, W. G., and L. D. Stamp, *The Common Lands of England and Wales*. London: Collins, 1963.

Commons, John R., *The Distribution of Wealth*. NY: Macmillan, 1893.

Cord, Steven B., *Henry George, Dreamer or Realist?* Philadelphia: University of Pennsylvania Press, 1965.

Crump, Arthur, *An Exposure to the Pretentions of Mr. Henry George*. London: Effingham Wilson, 1884.

Daily, Gretchen C., and Katherine Ellison, *The New Economy of Nature*. Washington DC: Island Press/Shearwater Books, 2002.

Davenport, Herbert J., *The Economics of Enterprise*. NY: Macmillan, 1913.

——. "The Single Tax in the English Budget," *Quarterly Journal of Economics* 24 (1910).

——. "Theoretical Issues in the Single Tax," *American Economic Review* 7 (1917).

——. *Value and Distribution*. Chicago: University of Chicago Press, 1908.

Day, Philip, *Land: The Elusive Quest for Social Justice, Taxation Reform & a Sustainable Planetary Environment*. Brisbane: Academic Press, 1995.

DeMille, Anna George, *Henry George: Citizen of the World*, Don Shoemaker, ed. Chapel Hill NC: University of North Carolina Press, 1950.

Dixwell, George Basil, *"Progress and Poverty." A Review of the Doctrines of Henry George*. Cambridge: John Wilson and Son. University Press, 1882.

——. "Review of Bastiat's Sophisms of Protection," *Bulletin of the National*

*Association of Wool Manufacturers* II (1881). Relevant articles by Dixwell in other issues of *BNAWM.*

Dorfman, Joseph, *The Economic Mind in American Civilization, 1865–1918.* NY: Viking, 1949; Augustus M. Kelley, 1969.

Douglas, Roy, *Land, People, and Politics.* London: Allison and Busby, 1976.

Dunkley, Godfrey, *That All May Live.* Cape Town: Godfrey Dunkley, 1990.

Dutt, Romesh, *Economic History of India,* 2nd ed. London: Routledge & Kegan Paul, 1906.

Echols, James, "Jackson Ralston and the California Single Tax Campaign, 1933–38." Fresno State College, California, unpublished M.A. thesis, 1967.

Ekelund, R. B., Jr., "A Short-Run Classical Model of Capital and Wages: Mill's Recantation of the Wages-Fund," *Oxford Economic Papers* 28 (March 1976) [1898].

Ellison, Katherine. *See* Daily.

Ely, Richard T., *Ground Under Our Feet.* NY: Macmillan, 1938.

——. and Edward W. Morehouse, *Elements of Land Economics.* NY: Macmillan, 1924.

——. *The Labor Movement in America.* NY: Macmillan, 1886.

—— and George S. Wehrwein, *Land Economics.* Madison: University of Wisconsin Press, 1964 [1940].

——. *Outlines of Economics.* NY: Macmillan, 1905 [1893].

——. Thomas S. Adams, Max O. Lorenz, and Allyn A. Young, *Outlines of Economics,* 5th rev. ed. NY: Macmillan, 1930.

—— and Ralph H. Hess, *Outlines of Economics,* 6th ed. NY: Macmillan, 1937.

—— and Mary L. Shine and George S. Wehrwein, assistants, *Outlines of Land Economics.* Ann Arbor MI: Edwards Bros., 1922.

——. *Property and Contract in their Relations to the Distribution of Wealth.* Port Washington NY: Kennikat Press, 1971 [1914].

——. *Recent American Socialism.* Baltimore: Johns Hopkins University Press, 1884.

——. "The Single Tax," *Christian Advocate* 25 (December 1890).

——. *Taxation of Farm Lands.* St. Paul: Webb Publishing Company, 1924.

Engels, Frederick, *The Condition of the Working-Class in England* in Marx and Engels, *On Britain,* 2nd ed. Moscow: Foreign Languages Publishing House, 1962.

Feder, Kris, "Henry George on Property Rights: Reply to John Pullen," *American Journal of Economics and Sociology* 60 (April 2001).

Fetter, Frank A., "Clark's Reformulation of the Capital Concept," *Economic Essays Contributed in Honor of John Bates Clark,* Jacob Hollander, ed. NY: Macmillan, 1927. Reprinted in Fetter's *Capital, Interest and Rent: Essays in the Theory of Distribution,* Murray Rothbard, ed. Kansas City: Sheed, Andrews and McMeel, 1977.

———. "The Relations Between Rent and Interest," *Publications of the American Economic Association.* 3rd ser., 5, no. 1, pt.1.

Fillebrown, Charles B., *The Principles of Natural Taxation.* Chicago: A. C. McClurg, 1917.

`Fisher, Franklin and Karl Shell, *The Economic Theory of Price Indices: Two Essays on the Effects of Taste, Quality and Technological Change.* NY: Academic, 1972.

Fisher, Irving, *The Rate of Interest: Its Nature, Determination and Relation to Economic Phenomena.* NY: Macmillan, 1907.

———. Irving, *The Theory of Interest.* NY: Macmillan, 1930.

Fiske, John, *The Critical Period of American History.* Cambridge: The Riverside Press, 1888.

Flamant, Maurice and Jeanne Singer-Kérel, *Modern Economic Crises.* London: Barrie & Jenkins, 1970.

Flürscheim, Michael, "Professor Huxley's Attacks," *Nineteenth Century* 27 (1890).

Foldvary, Fred, *Public Goods and Private Communities.* Aldershot UK: Edward Elgar, 1994.

Foldvary, Fred, ed., *Beyond Neoclassical Economics: Heterodox Approaches to Economic Theory.* Cheltenham UK/Brookfield VT: Edward Elgar, 1996.

Friedman, David, *Hidden Order.* NY: HarperCollins, 1996.

Friedman, Milton, *Essays in Positive Economics.* Chicago: University of Chicago, 1953.

Fuller, Aaron B., "Henry George and the Wages Fund," History of Economics Society Conference Paper, 1974.

Fuller, Aaron B., "The Passions of Adam Smith." Chicago: *History of Economics Society* Conference Paper, 1976.

Gaffney, Mason, "Adequacy of Land as a Tax Base," *The Assessment of Land Values,* Daniel M. Holland, ed. Madison: University of Wisconsin Press, 1970.

———. "Changes in Land Policy: How Fundamental are They?" *Real Estate Issues* (Fall 1976); *Western Journal of Agricultural Economics* (June 1977).

———. *Henry George, Dr. Edward McGlynn, and Pope Leo XIII.* NY: Robert Schalkenbach Foundation, 2000.

———. "Land as a Distinctive Factor of Production," *Land and Taxation,* Nicolaus Tideman, ed. London: Shepheard-Walwyn, 1994.

———. "Land Speculation as an Obstacle to Ideal Allocation of Land," Berkeley CA: University of California, Ph.D. dissertation, 1956.

———. "Land Value Gains and the Capital Gains Tax," unpublished paper. Riverside CA:1991.

———. "Neoclassical Economics as a Stratagem against Henry George," *The Corruption of Economics,* Mason Gaffney and Fred Harrison, eds. London: Shepheard-Walwyn, 1994.

——. "The Philosophy of Public Finance," *The Losses of Nations: Deadweight Politics versus Public Rent Dividends*, Fred Harrison, ed. London: Othila Press, 1998.

——. "The Regeneration of New York City after 1920," ms. available from author, 2001.

——. "Revenue Sharing," *Good Government* 867 (December 1986).

——. "Soil Depletion and Land Rent," *Natural Resources Journal* 4, no. 3 (January 1965).

——. "Tax Reform to Release Land," *Modernizing Urban Land Policy*, Marion Clawson, ed. Baltimore: Johns Hopkins University Press, 1973. Republished in *Compact Cities: a Neglected Way of Conserving Energy*. Washington DC: U. S. Government Printing Office, 1980. Republished in *Land-Value Taxation*, Kenneth Wenzer, ed. Armonk NY: M. E. Sharpe, 1999.

——. "Tax Treatment of Land Income," *Economic Analysis and the Efficiency of Government*, U. S. Congress Joint Economic Committee hearings. Washington DC: U. S. Government Printing Office, 1970.

——. "Vituperation Well Answered," *Land and Liberty* (December 1952).

Galbraith, J. K., *The Great Crash 1929*. Hammondsworth: Penguin, 1975.

Geiger, George Raymond, *The Philosophy of Henry George*. NY: Macmillan, 1933.

——. *The Theory of the Land Question*. NY: Macmillan, 1936.

George, Henry, "The Condition of Labor," *The Land Question [And Other Essays]*. NY: Robert Schalkenbach Foundation, 1965 [1881, as *The Irish Land Question*].

——. *Our Land and Land Policy*, National and State. San Francisco: White & Hauer, 1871.

——. *A Perplexed Philosopher*. NY: Robert Schalkenbach Foundation, 1940 [1892].

——. *Progress and Poverty*. NY: Robert Schalkenbach Foundation, 1954 [1879].

——. *Progresso e pobreza (Progress and Poverty)*, tr. Americo Werneck Junior, 2$^{nd}$ ed. Rio de Janeiro: Grafica Editora Aurora Ltda., 1946.

——. *Protection or Free Trade*. NY: Robert Schalkenbach Foundation, 1992 [1886].

——. *The Science of Political Economy*. NY: Robert Schalkenbach Foundation, 1962 [1898].

——. "A Single Tax on Land Values–Reply to Mr. Atkinson," *Century Magazine* 40 (July 1890).

——. *Social Problems*. NY: Robert Schalkenbach Foundation, 1996 [1883].

——. "The Study of Political Economy," *Popular Science Monthly* (March 1880).

——. *Thy Kingdom Come*. NY: Robert Schalkenbach Foundation, n.d.

——. *Why the Landowner Cannot Shift the Tax on Land Values.* NY: Robert Schalkenbach Foundation, n.d.

George, Henry and H. M. Hyndman, *The Single Tax versus Social-Democracy* (debate). London: Twentieth Century Press, 1906.

George, Henry, Jr., *The Life of Henry George.* NY: Robert Schalkenbach Foundation, 1960 [1900].

Gihring, Thomas A., Incentive Property Taxation: A Potential Tool for Urban Growth Management, *Journal of the American Planning Association* 65 (1) (1999).

Goldman, Eric F., *Rendezvous with Destiny.* NY: Vintage Books, 1956.

Gordon, Scott, "The Wage-Fund Controversy: The Second Round," *History of Political Economy* 5 (Spring 1973).

Gronlund, Laurence, *Cooperative Commonwealth.* Cambridge MA: Harvard University Press, 1965 [1884].

——. *Insufficiency of Henry George's Theory.* NY: New York Labor News, 1887.

——. *The New Economy: A Peaceable Solution of the Social Problem.* Chicago: H. S. Stone & Co., 1898.

——. *Socialism vs. Tax Reform: An Answer to Henry George.* NY: New York Labor News Co., 1887.

Hacker, Louis, *Triumph of American Capitalism.* NY: Columbia University Press, 1947.

Haig, Robert Murray, *The Exemption of Improvements from Taxation in Canada and the United States.* NY: The Committee on Taxation, 1915.

Haines, Charles Grove, The Revival of Natural Law Concepts, *Harvard Studies in Jurisprudence*, vol. 4. Cambridge MA: Harvard University Press, 1958.

Hamilton, Alexander. *The Federalist* #12.

Hanson, William, *The Fallacies in "Progress and Poverty" in Henry Dunning Macleod's Economics and "Social Problems," with the Ethics of Protection and Free Trade and the Industrial Problem Considered a-Priori.* NY: Fowler and Wells Co., 1884.

Hardin, Garrett, "Ethical Implications of Carrying Capacity," *Managing the Commons*, G. Hardin and John Baden, eds. San Francisco: W. H. Freeman and Co., 1977.

——. *Exploring New Ethics for Survival.* NY: Viking, 1972.

——. "The Feast of Malthus: *The Social Contract*," Journal Archives. Spring 1988.

——. "An Operational Analysis of Responsibility," *Managing the Commons.*

——. *Stalking the Wild Taboo.* Los Altos CA: William Kaufman, Inc., 1973.

——. "The Tragedy of the Commons," *Science* 162 (Dec. 13, 1968).

Harris, William T., "Henry George's Mistake about Land," *The Forum* 3 (July 1887).

——. "The Right of Property and the Ownership of Land," *Journal of Social Science* 22 (June 1887).

——. "Statistics versus Socialism," *The Forum* 24 (October 1897).

——. "To the Reader," *Journal of Speculative Philosophy* (January 1867).

Harrison, Fred, ed., *The Losses of Nations: Deadweight Politics versus Public Rent Dividends*. London: Othila Press, 1998.

Harriss, C. Lowell, "Rothbard's Anarcho-Capitalist Critique," *Critics of Henry George*, Robert V. Andelson, ed., [1st ed]. London: Associated University Presses and Rutherford NJ: Fairleigh Dickinson University Press, 1979.

Haxo, Gaston, *The Philosophy of Freedom*. NY: Land and Freedom, 1941.

Hayek, Friedrich A. von, *The Constitution of Liberty*. Chicago: University of Chicago Press, 1960.

——. *Hayek on Hayek: An Autobiographical Dialogue*, Stephen Kresge and Leif Wenar, eds. Chicago: University of Chicago Press, 1994.

——. *Register of the Hayek Papers*, 1906–1992. Stanford CA: HooverInstitute Archives.

Heath, Spencer, *Citadel, Market and Altar*. Baltimore: Science of Society Foundation, 1957.

——. "Outline of the Economic, Political, and Proprietary Departments of Society," in "Politics Versus Proprietorship." Manuscript, 1935.

——. *Progress and Poverty Reviewed and its Fallacies Exposed*. NY: The Freeman, 1952.

——. *The Trojan Horse of "Land Reform": A Critique of Land Communism or 'Single Tax' as advocated in the Doctrinal Statement prepared by the Rev. Dr. Edward McGlynn*. N.p., n.d.

Heilbroner, Robert, *The Worldly Philosophers*. NY: Simon & Schuster, Inc., 6th ed., 1986. Heilig, Bruno, "Why the German Republic Fell," *Why the German Republic Fell and Other Studies of the Causes and Consequences of Economic Inequality*, A. W. Madsen, ed. London: Hogarth Press, 1941.

Hirsch, Max, *Democracy versus Socialism*, 4th ed. NY: Robert Schalkenbach Foundation, 1966 [1901].

Hirshleifer, Jack, "On the Theory of the Optimal Investment Decision," *Journal of Political Economy* (August 1958).

——. *Investment, Interest and Capital*. Englewood Cliffs NJ: Prentice-Hall, 1970.

Hobson, C. K., "Review of *Wealth and Income*," *Economic Journal* 26.

Holland, Daniel M., ed., *The Assessment of Land Value*. Madison: University of Wisconsin Press, 1970.

Holland, Stuart, *The Socialist Challenge*. London: Quartet Books, 1975.

Hooper, Charles, "Henry George," *The Fortune Encyclopedia of Economics*, David K. Henderson, ed. NY: Warner Books, 1993.

Hudson, Michael, G. J. Miller, and Kris Feder, *A Philosophy for a Fair Society*. London: Shepheard-Walwyn, 1994.

Hunter, L. C., and D. J. Robertson, *Economics of Wages and Labour.* NY: Augustus M. Kelley, 1969.

Hutchinson, A. R., *Public Charges Upon Land Values.* Melbourne, Australia: Land Values Research Group, 1963.

Hutchison, T. W., "Economists and Economic Policy in Britain after 1870," *History of Political Economy* 1. Fall 1969.

——. *A Review of Economic Doctrines, 1870–1929.* Oxford: Clarendon Press, 1953.

Huxley, T. H., *Collected Essays.* London: Macmillan, 1894.

Hyndman, Henry M., *Record of an Adventurous Life.* NY: Macmillan, 1911.

Ingalls, Joshua K., *Reminiscences of an Octogenarian in the Fields of Industrial and Social Reform.* NY: M. L. Holbrook, 1897.

——. *Social Wealth: The Sole Factors and Exact Ratios in Its Acquirement and Apportionment.* NY: Social Science Publishing Co., 1885.

Jacker, Corinne, *The Black Flag of Anarchy: Antistatism in the United States.* NY: Charles Scribner's Sons, 1968.

Jalladeau, Joel, "The Methodological Conversion of John Bates Clark," *History of Political Economy* 7 (Summer 1975).

Jansdon, Annmari I., ed., et al., *Investing in Natural Capital: The Ecological Economics Approach to Sustainability.* Washington DC: Island Press, 1994.

Jorgensen, Emil O., *False Education in Our Colleges and Universities: An Expose of Prof. Richard T. Ely and His "Institute for Research in Land Economics and Public Utilities."* Chicago: Manufacturers and Merchants Federal Tax League, 1925.

Keynes, John Maynard, *The General Theory of Employment, Interest and Money.* London: Macmillan, 1967.

Keynes, John Neville, *The Scope and Method of Political Economy.* London: Macmillan, 1890.

King, Willford I., *The Keys to Prosperity.* NY: Constitution and Free Enterprise Foundation, 1948.

——. "The Single-Tax Complex Analyzed," *Journal of Political Economy* 32, N. 5 (Oct. 1924).

——. *The Valuation of Urban Realty for Purposes of Taxation.* Madison: University of Wisconsin Bulletin No. 689, 1914.

——. *The Wealth and Income of the People of the United States.* NY and London: The Macmillan Company, 1915.

Knight, Frank, "Capital and Interest," *Readings in the Theory of Income Distribution,* American Economic Association, ed. Philadelphia: The Blackiston Company, 1947.

——. "Ethics and the Economic Interpretation," *The Quarterly Journal of Economics* 36 (1922).

——. "The Ethics of Competition," *The Quarterly Journal of Economics* 37 (1923).

——. "Fallacies in the Interpretation of Social Cost," *The Quarterly Journal of Economics* 38.

——. "The Fallacies in the Single Tax," *The Freeman* (August 10, 1953).

——. "The Planful Act: The Possibilities and Limitations of Collective Rationality," *Freedom and Reform*, Frank Knight, ed. NY and London: Harper and Brothers, 1947.

——. Review of George R. Geiger, *The Philosophy of Henry George*, *Journal of Political Economy* 41 (1933).

——. "The Ricardian Theory of Taxation and Distribution," *Canadian Journal of Economics and Political Science* 1 (1935).

——. *Risk, Uncertainty and Profit*. London: Lund Humphries, 1948.

——. "Socialism: The Nature of the Problem," *Ethics* 50 (1940).

Kravis, Irving B., "Income Distribution: Functional Shares," *International Encyclopedia of the Social Sciences* 8, D. L. Sills, ed.

Kyriazi, Harold, *Libertarian Party at Sea on Land*. NY: Robert Schalkenbach Foundation, 2000.

Laveleye, Émile de, "La Propriété terrienne et le pauperisme," *Revue scientifique de la France et de l'étranger*, no. 30, 24 (January. 1880).

——. "'Progress and Poverty,' A Criticism," *Contemporary Review* (November 1882).

——. Primitive Property, tr. G. R. L. Mariott. London: Macmillan, 1878.

Lawrence, E. P., *Henry George in the British Isles*. East Lansing: Michigan State University Press, 1957.

Lecky, W. E. H., *Democracy and Liberty*. London: Longmans, 1896.

LeFevre, Robert, "A Challenge to the Georgists," *Rampart Journal of Individualist Thought* I (2) (Summer 1965).

——. "On the Other Hand," *Rampart Journal of Individualist Thought* I (3) (Fall 1965).

——. *A Way to be Free*, 2 vols. Culver City CA: Pulpless Com. Inc, 1999.

Leidecker, Kurt F., *Yankee Teacher: The Life of William Torrey Harris*. NY: Philosophical Library, 1946.

Leo XIII, *Rerum Novarum* (Encyclical letter). Vatican: May 15, 1891.

Lewis, Arthur M., *Ten Blind Leaders of the Blind*. Chicago: Chas. H. Kerr & Co., 1919.

Locke, John, *An Essay Concerning the True Original Extent and End of Civil Government*, in *Social Contract*. NY and London: Oxford University Press, 1948 [1690].

Locke, John, *The Second Treatise of Government*. [1690].

Longe, Francis D., *A Critical Examination of Mr. George's 'Progress & Poverty' and Mr. Mill's Theory of Wages*. London: Simpkin & Marshall, 1883.

Lucke, Robert B., "Rich States–Poor States: Inequalities in our Federal System," *Intergovernmental Perspective* (Spring 1982).

MacCallum, Spencer H., *The Art of Community.* Menlo Park CA: Institute for Humane Studies, 1970.

MacCallum, Spencer H., ed., "Spencer Heath on Henry George and Land Administration: Correspondence & Private Notes, Published & Unpublished, from the Spencer Heath Archives," assembled for this study at Tonopah NV. The Heather Foundation: 2002.

MacCallum, Spencer Heath, "The Entrepreneurial Community Concept in Light of Advancing Business Practice and Technology," *The Half-Life of Policy Rationales: How New Technology Affects Old Policy Issues*, Fred Foldvary and Daniel Klein, eds. NY: New York University Press, 2003.

Madison, Charles A., *Critics & Crusaders: A Century of American Protest.* NY: Henry Holt and Co., 1947.

Madison, James. *The Federalist* #10.

Mallock, W. H., *The Landlords and the National Income.* London: W. H. Allen & Co., 1884.

——. *Property and Progress.* London: John Murray, 1884.

——. *Social Reform.* London: John Murray, 1914.

Mandel, Ernest, *Marxist Economic Theory.* London: Merlin Press, 1968.

Marshall, Alfred, Letter to Henry Foxwell, *The Early Economic Writings of Alfred Marshall*, J. K. Whitaker, ed. NY: The Free Press, 1975.

——. *Industry and Trade.* London: Macmillan, 1919.

——. "Some Aspects of Competition," [1890] and "The Old Generation of Economists and the New," [1897], *Memorials of Alfred Marshall*, A. C. Pigou, ed. London: Macmillan, 1956.

——. *Principles of Economics*, 8th ed. London: Macmillan, 1964.

Martin, James J., *Men Against the State: The Expositors of Individualist Anarchism in America, 1827–1908.* DeKalb IL, 1953.

Marx, Karl, *Capital.* Moscow: Foreign Languages Publishing House, 1962 [1889].

——. *Grundrisse*, tr. Martin Nicolus. Hammondsworth: Pelican Books, 1973.

——. *The Nationalization of the Land* in *Selected Works.* Moscow: Progress Publishers, 1973.

——. *The Poverty of Philosophy.* Moscow: Progress Publishers, 1966.

Marx, Karl, and Friedrich Engels, *Communist Manifesto*, tr. Samuel Moore, 1888. Hammondsworth: Pengun Books, 1968.

——. *Selected Correspondence*, tr. I. Lasker, 1955. Moscow: Progress Publishers, 3rd revised ed., 1975.

——. *Selected Works.* Moscow: Foreign Languages Publishing House, 1951.

McLure, Charles E., Jr., "Fiscal Federalism and the Taxation of Economic Rents," *State and Local Finance*, George Break, ed. Madison: University of Wisconsin Press, 1984.

———. "The Taxation of Natural Resources and the Future of the Russian Federation," *Whither Russia: Fiscal Decentralization in the Russian Federation*, Christine Wallich, ed. Washington DC: The World Bank, forthcoming.

McLure, Charles E., Jr., and Peter Mieszkowski, eds., *Fiscal Federalism and the Taxation of Natural Resources*. Lexington MA: Lexington Books, 1983.

McWilliams-Tulberg. *See* Tulberg.

Milgrom, Paul and Robert J. Weber, "A Theory of Auctions and Competitive Bidding," *Econometrica* 50. 1982.

Mill, James, *Elements of Political Economy*. London, 1826.

Mill, John Stuart, "The Claims of Labour," *Edinburgh Review* 81 (April 1845).

———. *Dissertations and Discussions*. London: Longmans Green, Reader and Dyer, 1875.

———. *Principles of Political Economy: With Some Applications to Social Philosophy*, 3$^{rd}$, 7$^{th}$ eds. 9$^{th}$ ed., W. J. Ashley, ed. NY: Kelley, 1965 [1848].

———. "Thornton on Labour and Its Claims," *Fortnightly Review* 29 (1 May 1869).

Milliken, Samuel, "Forerunners of Henry George," *Single Tax Year Book*, Joseph Dana Miller, ed. NY: Single Tax Review Publishing Co., 1917 [1901].

Mises, Ludwig von, *Human Action*. New Haven: Yale University Press, 1949.

———. *Socialism*. New Haven: Yale University Press, 1951.

Moffatt, Robert Scott, *Mr. Henry George the "Orthodox": An Examination of Mr. George's Position as a Systematic Economist; and a Review of the Competitive and Socialistic Schools of Economy*. London: Remington & Co., 1885.

Moss, Laurence S., ed., *City and Country*. Malden MA/Oxford: Blackwell Publishers, 2001.

Mulhall, Michael, *History of Prices Since the Year 1850*. London: Longmans, Green, 1885.

Murphy, Liam and Thomas Nagel, *The Myth of Ownership: Taxes and Justice*. NY: Oxford University Press, 2002.

Nagel, Thomas. *See* Murphy.

Nelson, Robert, "Privatizing the Neighborhood: A Proposal to Replace Zoning with Private Collective Property Rights to Existing Neighborhoods," *The Voluntary City*, David Beito, Peter Gordon, and Alexander Tabarrok, eds. Ann Arbor: University of Michigan Press, 2002 [1999].

Newman, Philip Charles, *The Development of Economic Thought*. NY: Prentice-Hall, 1952.

Nichols, James Hastings, *Democracy and the Churches*. Philadelphia: Westminster Press, 1951. Niebuhr, Reinhold, *An Interpretation of Christian Ethics*. NY and London: Harper & Brothers, 1935.

Niehans, Jurg, *A History of Economic Theory*. Baltimore and London: Johns Hopkins University Press, 1990.

Nock, Albert Jay, *Our Enemy, The State*. San Francisco: Fox & Wilkes, 1992 [1973; copyright 1935].

Oppenheimer, Franz, *The State*. New Brunswick NJ: Transaction Publishers, 1999 [1908].

Oser, Jacob, *Henry George*. NY: Twayne Publishers, Inc., 1974.

Patten, Simon Nelson, "The Conflict Theory of Distribution," *Yale Review* (August 1908). Reprinted in *Essays in Economic Theory*, Rexford G. Tugwell, ed. NY: A. A. Knopf, 1924.

———. *The Consumption of Wealth*. Philadelphia, Ginn, 1901.

Petridis, Anastasios, "Alfred Marshall's Attitudes to the Economic Analysis of Trade Unions: A Case of Anomalies in a Competitive System," *History of Political Economy* 5 (Spring 1973).

Phelps Brown, E. H., and B. Weber, "Accumulation, Productivity and Distribution in the British Economy, 1870–1938," *Economic Journal* (1953).

Polak, Edward, "Reduction of Tax on Buildings in the City of New York," *AAAPSS* 58 (1915).

Post, Louis F., *The Prophet of San Francisco*. NY: Vanguard Press, 1930.

Proudhon, P. J., *What is Property?* NY: Dover Publications, 1970.

Rae, John, *Contemporary Socialism*. London: S. Sonnenschein & Co., Ltd., 1908.

———. *Life of Adam Smith*. NY: Augustus P. Kelley, 1965 [1895].

Raico, Ralph, "Murray Rothbard on His Semicentennial," *Libertarian Review* V (2) (March–April, 1976).

Raimondo, Justin, *An Enemy of the State: The Life of Murray N. Rothbard*. Amherst NY: Prometheus Books, 2000.

Ralston, Jackson H., "Adventures in the Life of a Washington Lawyer." University of California, Bancroft Library, ms. in Ralston Papers, n.d.

———. *What's Wrong with Taxation?* San Diego: Ingram Institute, 1932.

Reader, John, "Human Ecology: How Land Shapes Society," *New Scientist* 1629 (Sept. 8, 1988).

Ricardo, David, *Principles of Political Economy and Taxation*. NY: Dutton, 1965.

———. *Principles of Political Economy and Taxation* in *The Works of David Ricardo*, J. R. McCulloch, ed. London: John Murray, 1888.

Rima, Ingrid Hahne, *Development of Economic Analysis*, 5th ed. NY: Routledge, 1996.

Rose, Edward J., *Henry George*. NY: Twayne Publishers, Inc., 1968.

Rothbard, Murray, *Economic Thought Before Adam Smith: An Austrian Perspective on the History of Economic Thought*, Vol. I and *Classical Economics: An Austrian Perspective on the History of Economic Thought*, Vol. II. Northampton MA: Edward Elgar, 1995.

———. *The Ethics of Liberty*. Atlantic Highlands NJ: Humanities Press International, 1982.

———. *Man, Economy, and State*. Princeton: Van Nostrand, 1962.

———. *For a New Liberty: The Libertarian Manifesto*. NY: Collier Books, rev. ed, 1978 [NY: Macmillan, 1973].

———. "Frank Chodorov, R. I. P.," *Left and Right* 3 (1) (Winter 1967).

———. *The Logic of Action I: Applications and Criticisms from the Austrian School*. London: Edward Elgar, 1997.

———. *Power and Market: Government and the Economy*. Kansas City: Sheed, Andrews and McMeel, Inc., 1970.

———. *A Reply to Georgist Criticisms*. Irving/On-the-Hudson, NY: Foundation for Economic Education, July 1957.

Rutherford, Reuben C., *Henry George versus Henry George*. NY: D. Appleton and Co., 1887.

Ryan, John A., *Declining Liberty and Other Papers*. Freeport NY: Books for Libraries Press, 1927.

———. *Distributive Justice*. NY: Macmillan, 1927, rev. ed. [1916].

———. *Social Doctrine in Action*. NY: Harper, 1941.

Ryan, Christopher K., *Harry Gunnison Brown: An Orthodox Economist and His Contribution*. Malden MA and Oxford UK: Blackwell Publishers, 2002.

Sabine, George H., *A History of Political Theory*, 3$^{rd}$ ed. NY: Holt, Rinehart and Winston, 1961. Sakolski, Aaron M., *The Great American Land Bubble: The Amazing Story of Land-Grabbing, Speculations, and Booms From Colonial Days to the Present Time*. NY and London: Harper & Brothers, 1932.

Samuels, Warren J., "George's Challenge to the Economics Profession," *American Journal of Economics and Sociology* 42, n.1 (January 1983).

Schumpeter, Joseph A., *History of Economic Analysis*, Elizabeth Boody Schumpeter, ed. NY: Oxford University Press, 1954.

Scott, Anthony, *Natural Resource Revenues: A Test of Federalism*. Vancouver: University of British Columbia Press, 1975.

Seligman, Edwin R. A., *Essays in Taxation*, 9$^{th}$ ed. NY: Macmillan, 1923.

———. "Halving the Tax Rate on Buildings," *Survey* 31 (17 March 1914). Reprinted in *Selected Articles on the Single Tax*, 2$^{nd}$ ed., Edna Bullock, compiler. NY: H. W. Wilson Co., 1917.

———. *The Shifting and Incidence of Taxation*, 4$^{th}$ ed. NY: Columbia University Press, 1921.

Seligman, Edwin R. A., Henry George, et al., "The Single Tax Debate," *Journal of Social Science: Containing the Transactions of the American Association* 27 (October 1890).

Senior, Nassau, *Outline of the Science of Political Economy*, 6$^{th}$ ed. London: Allen & Unwin, 1872 [1836].

Shearman, Thomas, *Natural Taxation*. NY: Doubleday and McClure, 1888.
——. "Henry George's Mistakes," *The Forum* 8 (Sept 1889–Feb 1890).
Shell, Karl. *See* Fisher, F.
Shields, Charles H., *Single Tax Exposed*, 7th ed. Seattle: Trade Register, Inc., 1914.
Sinclair, Upton, *I, Candidate for Governor: And How I Got Licked*. Pasadena: U. Sinclair, 1934.
Smith, Adam, *An Inquiry into the Nature and Causes of the Wealth of Nations*. NY: Modern Library, 1957 [1776].
——. *The Theory of Moral Sentiments*. New Rochelle NY: Arlington House, E. G. West, ed. [1759].
Smith, James Haldane, *Economic Moralism: An Essay in Constructive Economics*. London: George Allen and Unwin, 1916.
Spahr, Charles B., "Single Tax," *Political Science Quarterly* (December 1891).
Spence, Thomas, *The Nationalization of the Land*, H. M. Hyndman, ed. London: E. W. Allen, 1882 [1775].
Spencer, Herbert, *Social Statics*. NY: Robert Schalkenbach Foundation, 1970, 1995 [1850].
Starcke, Viggo, "Our Daily Bread," *Proceedings of the Eighth International Confererence on Land-Value Taxation and Free Trade*. London: International Union for Land-Value Taxation and Free Trade/Danish Georgist Union, 1952.
Stigler, George, "Ricardo and the 93% Labor Theory of Value," *American Economic Review* 48 (June 1958).
——. *The Theory of Price*, 3rd ed. NY: Macmillan, 1966.
——. "Three Lectures on *Progress and Poverty*," *Journal of Law and Economics* 12 (1969).
Taussig, Frank W., *Wages and Capital: An Examination of the Wages Fund Doctrine*. NY: Augustus M. Kelley, 1968 [1896].
Teilhac, Ernest, *Pioneers of American Economic Thought in the Nineteenth Century*, tr. E. A. J. Johnson. NY: Macmillan, 1936.
Temple, William, *Christianity and Social Order*. London: Shepheard-Walwyn Ltd., 1976.
Tideman, Nicolaus, "Commons and Commonwealths: A New Justification for Territorial Claims," *Commons Without Tragedy*, R. V. Andelson, ed. London UK and Savage MD: Shepheard-Walwyn Ltd. and Barnes and Noble, 1991.
——. "Creating Global Economic Justice," *Geophilos* (Spring 2001).
——. "The Economics of Efficient Taxes on Land," *Land and Taxation*, Nicolaus Tideman, ed. London: Shepheard-Walwyn Ltd., 1994.
——. "Global Economic Justice," *Geophilos* (Autumn 2000).
——. "Integrating Land-Value Taxation with the Internalization of Spatial Externalities," *Land Economics* 66 (1990).

——. "Integrating Rent and Demand Revelation in the Evaluation and Financing of Services," *Does Economic Space Matter?*, Hiroshi Ohta and Jacques-Francois Thisse, eds. London: Macmillan, 1993.

——. "Peace, Justice, and Economic Reform," *The Path to Justice: Following in the Footsteps of Henry George*, Joseph A. Giacalone and Clifford Cobb, eds. Malden MA/Oxford: Blackwell Publishers, 2001.

——. "Property Rights and the Social Contract: The Constitutional Challenge in the U. S. A., *Now the Synthesis: Capitalism, Socialism and the New Social Contract*, Richard Noyes, ed. NY: Holmes and Meier, 1991.

Tolstoy, Leo, "A Great Iniquity," *The Public* 19 (August 1905).

Toynbee, Arnold, *Lectures on the Industrial Revolution in England.* London: Rivingtons, 1884.

Truehart, William B., "The Impact of Real Property Versus Land Value Taxation in Los Angeles County." Claremont CA Graduate School, Ph.D. dissertation, unpublished, 1973.

Tucker, Benjamin R., *Henry George, Traitor.* NY: Benjamin R. Tucker, 1896.

——. *Individual Liberty.* NY: Vanguard Press, 1926.

——. *Instead of a Book By a Man Too Busy to Write One.* NY: Gordon Press, 1972 [1897].

Tulberg, Rita McWilliams-, "Marshall's Tendency to Socialism," *History of Political Economy* 7 (Spring 1975).

Vickrey, William, "A Modern Theory of Land-Value Taxation," *Land-Value Taxation: The Equitable and Efficient Source of Public Finance*, Kenneth C. Wenzer, ed. Armonk NY/London: M. E. Sharpe/Shepheard-Walwyn, 1999.

Walker, Francis Amana, *First Lessons in Political Economy.* NY: Henry Holt and Company, 1893.

——. *Land and Its Rent.* Boston: Little, Brown, 1883.

——. *Political Economy.* NY: Henry Holt and Company, 1888.

——. "The Tide of Economic Thought," *Reports of the Proceedings of the American Economic Association.* 1890.

Wallace, A. R., *Land Nationalization: Its Necessity and Its Aims.* London: Land Nationalization Society, 1882.

Wasserman, Louis, *Modern Political Philosophies and What They Mean.* 1941.

Watner, Carl, "Benjamin Tucker and His Periodical, Liberty," *Journal of Libertarian Studies* (Fall, 1977).

Webb, Sidney, *Socialism in England.* London: Swan Sonnenschein & Co., 1890.

Wenzer, Kenneth C., ed., *An Anthology of Henry George's Thought*, Vol. I, Henry George Centennial Trilogy. Rochester NY: University of Rochester Press, 1997.

Whittaker, Edmund, *A History of Economic Ideas.* NY: Longmans, Green, 1940.

Williamson, Harold Francis, *Edward Atkinson: The Biography of an American Liberal.* Cambridge MA: Riverside Press, 1934.

Woodcock, George, *Anarchism: A History of Libertarian Ideas and Movements.* NY: The World Publishing Co., 1962.

Woodruff, A. M., and L. L. Ecker-Racz, "Property Taxes and Land Use Patterns in Australia and New Zealand," *Tax Executive* 8. October 1965.

Wolff, Edward N., "Trends in Wealth Ownership, 1983–1998," *Working Paper No. 300.* Annandale-on-Hudson: Jerome Levy Economics Institute, April 2000.

Woolsey, Theodore D., *Political Science, or the State.* NY: Charles Scribner's Sons, 1877.

Wrightson, Francis, *Henry George's "Progress and Poverty": The Cause–The Remedy. An Analysis and a Refutation.* Birmingham: Cornish Brothers, 1885.

Young, Allyn A., Review of *Wealth and Income, Quarterly Journal of Economics* 30 (3) (May 1916).

Young, Arthur Nichols, *The Single Tax Movement in the United States.* Princeton NJ: Princeton University Press, 1916.